THE NEW WORLD ORDER EXPOSED

VICTOR THORN

Sisyphus

Press

SISYPHUS PRESS
P. O. Box 10495
State College, Pa. 16805-0495

First Edition 2003

Cover Design by Peter Currenti

Manufactured in the United States of America

ISBN 0-9701950-2-8

<u>DEDICATED TO:</u>

Peter Currenti

For leading me along the proper path

and

Lisa Guliani

For spreading the word

"The great enemy of truth is very often not the lie – deliberate, contrived and dishonest – but the myth – persistent, persuasive and unrealistic"

President John F. Kennedy
Yale University
June 11, 1962

TABLE OF CONTENTS

Introduction

Section One: 9-11

Section Two: Banks, Oil, Drugs & War

Section Three: Control Systems

Section Four: The Federal Reserve System

Section Five: Technology & Intelligence

Section Six: History

Section Seven: The American Presidency

Section Eight: The Media & Society

Section Nine: The Man Who Runs Happy Valley

Section Ten: Finale

INTRODUCTION

Whenever the truth starts to surface about what is really going on in the world, the corporate-run mass media always marginalizes this information by calling it conspiracy theory. But as you read this book, please remember: something does not remain a theory once it's proven to be true. The information contained within this book is factual, and what makes it even more damning is that most of it comes from the very mouths of those who most want to conceal it from the public. The New World Exposed will not only bring to light the high-crimes of those who rule the world by pulling strings behind the scenes, but it also shows a psychological element of the way they think. By continually setting one segment of society against another – their tried-and-true divide and conquer tactics – the Controllers want us to continually fight against one another instead of focusing our attention on the real enemy – them!

I realize that this book may be daunting due to its size, but all I can ask of you is this: read one chapter a day, and in less than three months I guarantee your outlook on life will be dramatically different. In fact, I promise that it will be. What you'll come to realize is that we are systematically being lied to on a daily basis, and that certain forces lurking behind the scenes are making decisions that are not in the American people's best interests.

If we fail to not only expose these nefarious individuals, but to also eradicate them from our government, our lives will be substantially different in the near future. It's time to take action and to take back our country. Hopefully this book will be a first step.

Victor Thorn – Happy Valley, Pa.   January 13, 2003

SECTION ONE:

9-11

CHAPTER ONE

FORTY REASONS THAT SUGGEST THE CONTROLLERS KNEW ABOUT THE 9-11 TERRORIST ATTACKS BUT DID NOTHING TO STOP THEM

I am deeply indebted to two individuals for the following article: Russ Kick, who wrote "September 11, 2001: No Surprise" in the 2002 edition of the *Loompanics* main catalog, and Christopher Bollyn, who wrote "Former Top German Spy Says U.S. Wrong About September 11" in the January 28, 2002 edition of the *American Free Press*. Both articles are incredibly eye-opening, and are used as the basis of what follows.

In the opening paragraph of his article, Russ Kick says: "The US has the Central Intelligence Agency, the Federal Bureau of Investigation, the National Security Agency, the Defense Intelligence Agency, the National Reconnaissance Office, the Secret Service, and a host of other intelligence and security agencies. These agencies employ Echelon, which monitors the majority of electronic communication in the world; Carnivore, which intercepts email; Tempest, a technology that can read a computer monitor's display from over a block away; Keyhole satellites that have a resolution of four inches; and other spy technologies, probably most of which we don't know about. In 2001, the US spent $30 billion on intelligence gathering and an additional $12 billion on counter-terrorism. With all these resources, and more, we're supposed to believe that the government didn't have the slightest inkling that terrorists were planning to attack the United States, much less hijack planes and send them careening into major landmarks."

After you read the following list of examples, you'll KNOW that the Controllers not only KNEW about the 9-11 attacks, but also allowed them to happen.

1) In its second annual report issued on September 12, 2000, the Advisory Panel to Assess Domestic Response Capabilities for Terrorism Involving Weapons of Mass Destruction said, "We are impelled by the stark realization that a terrorist attack on some level inside our borders is inevitable."

2) There were similar reports released by the Congressional Research Service (September 10, 2001), and the National Security Commission, which was sponsored by the Department of Defense (on both September 15, 1999 and March 15, 2001).

3) After the attacks, CIA Director George Tenet acted surprised, yet on February 2, 2000, he gave a speech warning that "Osama bin Laden is still foremost among terrorists because of the immediacy and seriousness of the threat he poses."

4) Andreas Von Bulow, former Head of the Parliamentary Commission that watches the German Secret Service, stated: "The planning of the attacks was technically and organizationally a master achievement -- to hijack four huge airplanes within a few minutes, and within one hour drive them into their targets with complicated flight maneuvers ... is unthinkable without years of support from state intelligence services."

5) Less than two hours after the attack, London's *al-Quds-al-Arabi* newspaper reported: "Osama bin Laden warned three weeks ago that he would attack American interests in an unprecedented attack." One must conclude that if the writers at a British newspaper knew about these attacks, why didn't the Secret Service?

6) After the four planes were hijacked, why were our military fighter planes kept on the ground for over an hour -- for over 60 whole minutes -- when this time was so crucial?

7) The State Department issued a strict warning for worldwide caution on September 7, 2001 (four days before the attacks), specifically saying, "Americans may be the target of a terrorist threat from extremist groups with links to Osama bin Laden's al Qaeda organization."

8) The Airjet Airline World News reported on June 23, 2001, "US Airlines May Be a Terror Risk over Next 3 Days." They were two-and-a-half months off, but they knew something was awry.

9) San Francisco Mayor Willie Brown was supposed to fly from his San Francisco home to New York City on the morning of September 11, 2001. The night before, at 10 o'clock PM (PST) which would be 1:00

AM (EST), he received a phone call from his "security people at the airport." Mayor Brown subsequently canceled his flight. And guess what? He lived. Over 3,000 other people without "insider information" weren't so lucky.

10) During the week before the attacks, stock traffic for American Airlines, United, plus an assortment of associated insurance companies rose 1,200 % to the tune of over $15 billion!!!

11) *The London Times*, September 27, 2001 reported: "The author Salman Rushdie believes that U.S. authorities knew of an imminent terrorist strike when they banned him from taking internal flights in Canada and the United States only a week before the attacks. The FAA told the author's publisher that U.S. intelligence had given a warning of "something out there," but failed to give any further details."

12) The FBI knew about certain terrorists learning to fly planes within the U.S. On two occasions they asked the Aiman Flight School vice president about these terrorists at his school -- once in 1999, and the other time in August, 2001!!!!! They learned that one specific terrorist, Zacarias Moussaoui, only wanted to learn how to steer the plane while it was flying, and didn't care about taking off or landing it.

13) The supposed terrorist ringleader, Mohammed Atta, reported his passport stolen many months before the attacks. Miraculously, all of a sudden it appeared atop the burning rubble of the World Trade Center Towers ... and guess what? It was in pristine condition!

14) Seven of the 19 hijackers listed by the FBI are actually still alive -- they were misidentified.

15) Our Secret Service supposedly knew NOTHING about these attacks, but less than two days after they occurred they had a complete list of the suicide flyers.

16) Ten days before the attacks, French Intelligence warned the FBI about Muslim pilot connections to potential terrorist attacks.

17) In June, 2001, three Middle Easterners were arrested by Federal Protective Officers in New York City after photographing federal

buildings. They took pictures of surveillance cameras, security checkpoints and police posts. Surprisingly, these men were let go even though the *New York Post* reported on September 16, 2001 that "anxious authorities expressed concern that plans for terror attacks were under way."

18) A few suspicions: Here is an excruciatingly complex plan to hijack planes and run them into symbolic American landmarks. It obviously took years of dedication and planning. So what do the terrorists do? They make all their transactions via credit card under their OWN NAMES! Also, they gave their flight instructors their real names and conveniently "forgot" flight manuals written in Aramaic in their Rent-A-Car. With this in mind, Andreas Von Bulow (mentioned earlier) says, "95% of the work of intelligence agencies around the world is deception and disinformation."

But our Secret Service says that they had NO IDEA this group of terrorists was going to strike, yet the leads they left (see the above listed examples) were similar to the tracks left by "a herd of stampeding elephants." Rather convenient, huh?

19) Mohammed Atta, the brains behind the operation, was under CIA watch from January to May, 2000 while he lived in Frankfurt, Germany. Yet the CIA said they had no inkling he was involved with terrorism, even after he started taking flight lessons!

20) The CIA claimed they caught a jubilant phone call from Osama bin Laden AFTER the attacks, yet they also said they couldn't monitor him BEFOREHAND. Why not? Was it a miracle that they were suddenly able to tune into him?

21) *The Washington Times* reports that a Senior Administration Official told them that on September 10, 2001, U.S. Intelligence intercepted a call from an Osama bin Laden follower to the al Qaeda discussing an imminent "big attack." Earlier in the year they also heard a call referring to "Hiroshima."

22) German Intelligence was also listening to the terrorists. CNN reported on October, 2, 2001: "German Intelligence Services intercepted a phone call on September 11 after the terrorist attacks on the U.S. in which

the followers of Osama bin Laden applauded the deadly assaults." So they were miraculously able to suddenly tune into that frequency, also?

23) The British Government noted, "In two interviews broadcast on U.S. Television in 1997 & 1998, Osama bin Laden referred to the terrorists who carried out the earlier attacks on the WTC in 1993 as 'role models.'"

24) A British Government Report (October 4, 2001) entitled "Responsibility for the Terrorist Atrocities in the U.S." said, "In August and early September close associates of bin Laden were warned to return to Afghanistan from other parts of the world by September 10."

25) In *Counterpunch Magazine*, September 12, 2001, Alexander Cockburn and Jeffrey St. Clair reported that security at the WTC was considerably heightened three weeks prior to 9-11. For the first time ever, sniffer dogs were used and all trucks admitted into the WTC were thoroughly searched.

26) The BBC reported on September 18, 2001 - "Niaz Naikia, former Pakistani Foreign Secretary, was told by senior American officials in mid-July, 2001 that military action against Afghanistan would go ahead by the middle of October."

27) Florida Governor Jeb Bush (George W's brother) called up the State National Guard on September 7, 2001 -- four days before the attacks -- for no specific reason except "the potential massive damage to life and property that may result from an act of terrorism at a Florida port, and the necessity to protect life and property from such acts of terrorism" (under section 3). Hmmm, do you think he knew something we didn't know?

28) The FBI embarked upon a massive interrogation of people in New York City who had foreknowledge of a terrorist attack on 9-11, especially Arab Americans. The Journal News of Westchester, NY reported on October 11, 2001 that a long-standing New York policeman said so many people in the city spoke about an upcoming catastrophe that "the number of leads turning up was so overwhelming that it was difficult to tell who had heard about the attacks from second-hand sources and who had heard it from someone who had been a participant."

29) Children in three different parts of the country spoke specifically and with startling accuracy about an impending attack on the World Trade Center in New York City. Each of them proved to be correct.

30) Saddam Hussein instructed his army to be on its highest state of alert two weeks before the attacks, something Iraq hadn't done since the Gulf War. Hussein went into hiding in his underground bunkers at the same time, for NO APPARENT REASON. Think about it -- why should he do this? There weren't any wars going on, and no one was attacking Iraq. Do you mean to tell me that HE, yet not ONE person in the U.S. Secret Service – KNEW beforehand about the WTC attack?

31) The Russian media clamored with reports about an attack that would take place in America, and prompted citizens to trade dollars for Russian currency. Dr. Alexander Nemets writes about this phenomenon for *NewsMax* on September 17, 2001 in an article entitled, "Expert: Russian Knew in Advance, Encouraged Citizens to Cash Out Dollars."

32) Dr. Tatyana Koryagina, who is employed by the Russian Ministry of Economic Development, told *Pravda* on July 12, 2001, "The US has been chosen as the object of financial attack because the financial center of the planet is located there. The effect will be maximal. The strike waves of economic crisis will spread over the planet instantly, and will remind us of the blast of a huge nuclear bomb."

33) David Shippers, a lawyer who led impeachment hearings against President Clinton, repeatedly tried to warn John Ashcroft, members of Congress, Speaker of the House Dennis Hastert, and the Senate Intelligence Committee that Islamic madmen were planning to attack the United States. No one listened. Why not?

34) On September 14, 2001, three days after the attacks, the German newspaper *Neue Presse* told of an Iranian man who was being held in Hanover, Germany. He said that he told the United States Secret Service of an impending terrorist act that would happen the week of September 10th. Then, only hours prior to the attack, he tried to fax President Bush with this news, but was forbidden the opportunity.

35) London's *Daily Telegraph* reported that two senior Mossad experts (Israel's version of the CIA), were dispatched to Washington, D.C.

in August, 2001 to tell the CIA and FBI of "the existence of a cell of as many as 200 terrorists said to be preparing a big operation."

36) According to the *Washington Times*, September 16, 2001, the Russian Secret Service urged American authorities on numerous occasions that an attack was in the making. Nikolai Patrushev (head of the FSB, an updated version of the KGB), told the Times: "We had clearly warned them," but those in positions of power "did not pay the necessary attention."

37) A direct quote from Russ Kick: "According to the highly respected German newspaper Frankfurter Allgemeine Zeitung, members of German Intelligence confirmed that U.S., UK, and Israeli Intelligence agencies had indeed picked up on the plot by Muslim terrorists to hijack jetliners and crash them into U.S. landmarks." The author continues, "Using the global snooping system of Echelon, these countries knew six months in advance about the 9-11 attacks."

38) *Washington Times* headline, 9-13-2001: "Echelon Gave Authorities Warning of Attacks."

39) A direct quote from Russ Kick about PROJECT BOJINKA: "Authorities in the Philippines uncovered Project Bojinka, the radical Muslim plot to ram hijacked jets into American landmarks and to blow up eleven U.S. airliners in two days. They turned over this information to the FBI." *The Washington Post* adds on September 23, 2001 in an article entitled "Borderless Network of Terror": "Watching the attacks in New York and Washington unfold on television earlier this month, an investigator gasped, 'It's Bojinka. We told the Americans everything about Bojinka. Why didn't they pay attention?'"

40) The CIA knew! David Wellna of National Public Radio's *Morning Edition Show* on the DAY OF THE ATTACKS as the Capitol Building was being cleared, reported, "I spoke with Congressman Ike Skelton -- a Democrat from Missouri and a member of the Armed Services Committee -- who said that just recently the Director of the CIA warned there could be an attack -- an IMMINENT attack -- on the United States of this nature. So this is not entirely unexpected."

The World Trade Center attacks were a precursor to the war in Afghanistan for four primary reasons:

- Huge oil reserves in Russia's Caspian Territory
- Illegal drug trafficking
- A loss of rights under the guise of "Homeland Security"
- Profits for those who benefit from the "war machine"

I'd like to augment this brief explanation with a quote from Christopher Bollyn's above-mentioned article:

"The image of the new enemy comes from Zbgniew Brzezinksi and Samuel Huntington, two policy-makers of American intelligence and foreign policy. Already in the 1990s, Huntington believed people in Europe and the U.S. needed someone they could hate -- this would strengthen their identification with their own society. And Brzezinski, the mad dog, as advisor to President Jimmy Carter, campaigned for the exclusive right of the U.S. to seize all the raw materials of the world, especially the oil and gas.

"In his analysis of political processes, von Bulow said a global map of civil wars and conflicts coincides with the locations of strategic minerals. The same is the case with the third map: nodal points of the drug trade. The huge raw material reserves of the former Soviet Union, as well as the pipeline routes, are now at the disposal of the United States and Britain."

In the end, we have to ask ourselves this question: Why did it take Christopher Bollyn and Russ Kick to compile this information, and not Dan Rather, Rush Limbaugh, *The New York Times*, or Peter Jennings? We have to start seriously asking ourselves, what kind of information are we being fed?

CHAPTER TWO

25 MORE REASONS THAT SUGGEST THE CONTROLLERS NOT ONLY KNEW ABOUT THE 9-11 TERRORIST ATTACKS, BUT ALSO ALLOWED THEM TO HAPPEN (WHILE FAILING TO DISCLOSE THE FULL STORY TO US)

----

1) Colonel Donn de Grand Pre: formerly employed as a top Pentagon official and author of *Barbarians Inside the Gates*, said in a quote from 2-11-02 edition of the *American Free Press*: "Especially revealing is a Fox 5 News tape depicting the sudden implosion of the two towers, the first of which took place at 10 AM. The crucial segment is from 9:58 AM to 10:03 AM. At 10:00 AM, the screen goes blank and, a few seconds later, a great white cloud of smoke rises from the base of the tower. The news anchor exclaims, "There is an explosion at the base of the building … white smoke from the bottom … something has happened at the base of the building … then another explosion. Another building in the World Trade Center Complex has blown up ..."

2) A CNN still photo with the caption "Breaking News: American Under Attack -- Voice of Tom Clancy, Author," clearly shows a significant column of smoke rising from one of the other buildings at the World Trade Center Complex WHILE the towers are still standing.

3) The following information was compiled from articles written by Christopher Bollyn, the staff of the *American Free Press* (2-25-02), and a transcript from a talk show called *Radio Free America* between writer Steve Martin and host Tom Valentine.

4) CNN reported that on January 29, 2002, President George Bush directly requested a private meeting with Senator Majority Leader Tom Daschle and other Congressmen, then requested that they "limit the Congressional investigation into the events of September 11." The only thing he wanted them to look into was the security breakdown as opposed to a full-scale inquiry.

5) Four days earlier, on January 25, 2002, Tom Daschle said, "The Vice President (Dick Cheney) expressed the concern that a review of what happened on September 11 would take resources and personnel away from the effort in the war on terrorism." Tom Daschle agreed, and the scope of what occurred on 9-11 was greatly reduced.

6) Extremely important evidence, like the WTC's steel girders, were promptly taken away to a scrap yard rather than being dispatched to a metallurgical lab and inspected.

7) *Fire Engineering* magazine, which has been in existence for 125 years, wrote a commentary on FEMA's handling of 9-11, saying that it "has good reason to believe that the 'official investigation' blessed by FEMA and run by the American Society of Civil Engineers is a half-baked farce, commandeered by political forces whose primary interests lie far afield of full disclosure."

8) An array of different factors point out that forces other than fuel fires made the towers collapse, such as the short duration and low temperature of jet fuel fires in relation to the fact that the rubble stayed on fire for more than 90 days while being doused with water on a continual basis.

9) Many of the deceased had been "vaporized" as opposed to being simply crushed.

10) There has been no information forthcoming from the hijacked airplanes' "black boxes."

11) High-tech weapons may have been involved in this attack, as was reported by an East German physicist and research scientist who was associated with the GPU (Russia's version of the CIA). "I have enough experience to judge that the WTC Towers have been burning too quickly, too hot, and too completely to have been caused by the kerosene [jet fuel] fires that resulted from the crashes."

12) We need to re-examine one of the most glaring absurdities of this event. How could Muhammed Atta's passport drift out of the North Tower as fires raged, girders melted, dust swirled, and chaos ensued, then

land pristinely atop the rubble to -- coincidentally -- be found by investigators?

Even more ridiculous: If the passport was so conveniently found, why weren't the jet parts, which would be crucial to an investigation, able to emerge intact?

13) Digital surveillance photos were taken at the Portland, Maine Airport that would positively identify Muhammed Atta before he caught a "prop plane" to Logan International in Boston, but all the public was shown were hazy video clips.

14) Jane Eisenberg, who purportedly identified Atta and his associate, Abdul Aziz Alomari from FBI photographs, later reneged when asked directly if she could positively ID them. Eisenberg said she could not identify them.

15) A group of terrorists that were in no way associated with Osama bin Laden took responsibility for the attacks. Calling themselves the Japanese Red Army, they called Al-Jazeera Television and said they were the ones who did it. Of course it's unlikely that they were actually responsible. But we need to ask ourselves, if our Intelligence services knew NOTHING of these attacks, how could they come to such conclusive results almost immediately, ruling out ANY other alternative? In addition, why didn't the mainstream media report on this story, or any other alternatives?

16) Of the four hijacked planes (two at the World Trade Center, one at the Pentagon, and one shot down near Pittsburgh), two were 767's capable of holding 375 people each, while the other two were 757's, with a maximum capacity of 289 each. If you add these numbers, they would total 1,328 potential passengers. In addition, the routes they were flying that day were quite popular, and more often than not were OVERBOOKED. Yet on the day of the attacks (a Tuesday morning), there was only a total of 266 people on all four planes combined! That means planes that were usually overbooked and had to turn people away were only 20% full -- or 80% UNDER filled -- with 1,062 EMPTY seats.

In my line of work where I'm quite frequently at airports, I know that not only are pilots extremely cognizant of such matters, but those who run the airlines also are. In other words, if a flight is under-booked by

80%, they either cancel it, or come up with an excuse like "mechanical difficulties."

Think about it. Planes that hold 375 passengers and are usually overbooked now only have 75 people on it with 300 EMPTY SEATS. Wouldn't that raise some eyebrows? Well, all FOUR planes had the same extremely low number of passengers and were taking off within an hour of each other.

The big questions are: Why wasn't anyone on these flights, why isn't the media reporting this aspect of the story, and why weren't the flights grounded? Maybe it's because with less people on each plane, the terrorists would have fewer outraged passengers to ward off after they hijacked it.

17) The CIA, according to a *Washington Post* report on December 23, 2001, financed a group of Afghani's to track Osama bin Laden for four years. Then, mysteriously, "just before or after September 11, the team members lost track of bin Laden."

Hmmm, the CIA has no problem following bin Laden for four years, then right before he's ready to strike, he "vanishes." Worse, following the attacks, they can't find him either. Here's a 6'4" guy with a big turban, an ugly beard and a bed sheet for clothes, but he can't be found?

Go out and rack up a few parking tickets and see how long you can remain anonymous without getting caught.

18) *Newsweek* ran a story on September 24, 2001 stating that on September 10, 2001, a group of Pentagon officials unexpectedly canceled their flights due to "security concerns." Since certain segments of our Military and Intelligence communities knew, why didn't they tell the rest of us? Over 3,000 lives could have been spared.

19) A German Public Television station, ARD, ran a report on November 23, 2001, which said the FBI traced mastermind Muhammed Atta's whereabouts for quite some time during 2000 when he bought explosives and journeyed between Frankfurt and Hamburg, Germany.

20) A direct quote from the BBC on Muhammed Atta: "The evidence reinforces concerns that the international intelligence community may have known more about Atta before September 11 than was previously thought, BUT IT FAILED TO ACT. Atta came to the attention

of U.S. authorities in the course of several occasions in 2001. In January he was allowed to reenter the United States after a trip to Germany despite the fact that he was in violation of his visa status. He landed in Miami on a flight from Geneva on January 10 on a tourist visa, although he told immigrant inspectors that he was taking flying lessons in the U.S., for which an M-1 student visa is required."

21) According to Dean Butterfield, who works for the American Immigration Lawyers Association, the *Washington Post* reported that "nine times out of ten" anyone without the proper immigration papers would not be granted entry into the United States, especially if they had been under FBI surveillance!!

22) A big question: why didn't the Air Force dispatch planes to alleviate this disaster when it was clear that the planes had been hijacked and weren't flying according to flight schedules? Steve Martin refers to a summation of this situation that appeared on *Rense.com*: "Dozens of Air Force and Air National Guard bases are within ten to thirty minutes intercept time of both the Pentagon and the World Trade Center. Most of these installations have fighter jets such as F16s ready on a moment's notice to intercept troubled aircraft.

"It is a fact that air defense units DID receive notice from air traffic controllers and Federal Aviation Administration officials that a number of aircraft on the East Coast had broken communications and had deviated radically on the morning of September 11. It is a fact that standard intercept procedures for dealing with these kinds of situations are in force 365 days a year."

23) *The New York Daily News* reported that at 9:06 AM on the morning of 9-11, the New York Police Department dispatched a message declaring, "This was a terrorist attack -- notify the Pentagon."

24) Almost 60 minutes after two airliners crashed into the World Trade Centers, another terrorist plane zoomed into the Pentagon. At Andrews Air Force Base -- only ten miles from the White House -- military planes sat idling on the runway despite the fact that they had reports from air traffic controllers, news broadcasts, and the New York City Police Department. Yet they still didn't do ANYTHING but sit there while another plane lambasted the Pentagon. What was going on?

25) *Newsday*, located in New York City, reported that a Pentagon spokesman by the name of Vic Warzinski, an Air Force Lieutenant Colonel, stated, "The Pentagon was simply not aware that this aircraft was coming our way." This example seemed to be another "conflicting statement," for the *London Sunday Telegraph* reported on September 14, 2001: "Within minutes of the attack, American forces around the world were put on one of their highest states of alert -- Defcon 3, just two notches short of all-out war."

Again, why didn't our armed forces protect us on 9-11? We spend over $300 billion a year on the Military. For what? To have the Controllers hold them back while terrorists kill our people? The San Diego Tribune reported a day after the attacks: "Air defense around Washington is provided mainly by fighter planes from Andrews Air Force Base in Maryland near the District of Columbia border. The D.C. Air National Guard is also based there and equipped with F-16 fighter planes ... But the fighters took to the skies over Washington only after the devastating attack on our Pentagon."

This view is corroborated by *NBC News*, which reported on 9-11: "It was AFTER the attack on the Pentagon that the Air Force then decided to scramble F-16s out of the D.C. National Guard Andrews Air Force Base to fly protective cover over Washington."

Well, hey, thanks for the "protective cover!" With friends like you, who needs enemies?

The total number of reasons I've come up with that suggest the Controllers knew about the 9-11 attacks (and didn't do anything to stop them) is 65. Sixty-five reasons! Listen! Can you hear me? Watch the videos of 9-11 again and relive the horrors. Then let these 65 reasons burrow into your brain.

Do you get it? The Controllers KNEW ABOUT IT! They KNEW!!!!! And not only didn't they stop the attacks; they WANTED them to happen to further promote their War Machine Big Brother agenda.

How does this settle with you? Does it sicken you? And more importantly: what are we going to do about it? Are we going to roll over and play dead, or are we going to make them pay? It's time for action!

CHAPTER THREE

MILITARY SMOKESCREEN: WHO COMMANDED OUR AIR FORCE TO 'STAND DOWN'?

Of all the peculiarities, unanswered questions, and things that simply don't add up about the 9-11 terrorist attacks, the one aspect that keeps nagging at me revolves around our military's incredible lack of response to the hijacking of four airliners. Anyone who investigates this matter will soon find that the United States Air Force and the FAA both have established procedures that have been in place for at least 25 years regarding planes that veer abnormally off course. Specifically, federal law MANDATES that the Air Force must dispatch a plane to investigate why a certain craft has strayed from its predestined route. These interceptors are only allowed to shoot an airliner from the sky under orders from the President, but that doesn't negate that they are still required to investigate the situation in a timely manner. Yet, on 9-11, NO ONE FOLLOWED ORDERS! Why? Who gave these orders? Plus, Washington, D.C. has the most restricted air space in the country, yet from 9:03 a.m., when the second tower was hit, to 9:47 a.m. when the Pentagon came under attack … when the Air Force KNEW that a jet was headed toward the Capitol, no planes were dispatched to intercept it. Who gave the orders for these planes to 'stand down,' and, God forbid, were some even called back after they had taken off?

To begin understanding how appalling this situation is, we first need to know that there are at least twelve National Guard and Air Force installations in close proximity to the World Trade Center and Pentagon. Plus, Andrews Air Force Base is only ten miles from the heart of Washington, D.C. Why wasn't something done to avert this catastrophe, and why isn't the mainstream media asking some very hard questions regarding this deliberately ordered "crime"?

Yes, I said crime, and once you get a load of the following timeline, you'll concur with this strong terminology. Between 7:59 a.m. – 8:10 a.m., the airliners that would ultimately crash into the WTC and Pentagon were hijacked. By 8:15 a.m., air traffic controllers knew that these planes were in trouble. At this point, the Air Force should have dispatched, per standard operating procedures, fighters that would determine why these jets veered from their normal route. By 8:15 a.m.!

At 8:45 a.m. – a half-hour later – American Airlines flight 11 struck the WTC's North Tower. (This flight took off at exactly 7:59 a.m., thus controllers knew it was in trouble for at least 35 minutes, if not more.)

At 9:03 a.m., United Airlines flight 175 crashed into the South Tower. (It took off at exactly 8:10 a.m.)

At 9:05 a.m. (supposedly), Andrew Card told President Bush of the unfolding catastrophe. At the same time, American Airlines Flight 77 veered off course near Chicago and headed toward D.C. for an impending attack.

At 9:06 a.m., the New York Daily News reported that on the morning of the attack, the NYPD dispatched a message declaring, "This was a terrorist attack – notify the Pentagon."

Still, NO Air Force jets had yet been scrambled! None! Why?

At 9:35 a.m., American Airlines flight 77, which had been tracked by radar all the way from Chicago, circled the Pentagon, yet this military installation was not evacuated! Plus, the Air Force had still not sent out any jets! How completely incredible is this scenario?

A few minutes later, with the utmost precision, American Airlines flight 77 drops 7,000 feet in 2 ½ minutes. Do you realize what a truly difficult maneuver this is? It is flying so low at this point that the plane is taking out utility poles and clipping trees en route to its target. The jumbo jet finally zeroes in EXACTLY on the Pentagon while traveling at 460 knots (approx 529 mph). Are we really to believe that this precision "Top Gun" style flying was executed by a group of desert-trained Afghani's who had only flown Cessna and Piper prop-planes at a flight school in Florida for six months, many of them reportedly unable to even take off or land them adequately? Come on! This is the most inept cock-n-bull story since the 'surprise attack' on Pearl Harbor.

Finally, at 9:40 a.m., a full hour and 31 minutes after the FAA knew that the first airliner had been hijacked ... guess what happened. The Air Force dispatched their jets!

The Pentagon was aware of these hijackings since at least 8:45 a.m. when the first tower was struck (and more likely before then), yet it took them 55 minutes to take action. 55 minutes! By 8:15 a.m., when the FAA learned of the hijackings, federal law required that the military dispatch planes to either divert the plane's course, or determine the need to shoot them down. This is normal procedure! But the Pentagon waited until 9:40 a.m. after all the damage was already done.

Who commanded the Air Force to stand down, and why is the media still feeding us the "incompetence" line? The Wright Brothers at Kitty Hawk could have had a plane up in the air in that much time!

Barry Zwicker, a Canadian media analyst, wrote on January 21, 2002: "That morning no interceptors responded in a timely fashion to the highest alert situation. That includes the Andrews squadron that is 12 miles from the White House. Whatever the explanation for the huge failure, there have been no reports, to my knowledge, of reprimands. This further weakens the incompetence theory! Incompetence usually earns reprimands. This causes me to ask whether there were 'stand down' orders."

To add more weight to the peculiarity of this situation, consider the flight capacity of the four hijacked airliners. These routes were extremely popular ones, most of them filled to 100% capacity during weekdays. In fact, oftentimes, fliers were asked if they wanted to give up their seats to another traveler. Yet on 9-11, the four flights in question were uncharacteristically empty.

American Airlines 11 – filled to only 39% of capacity
American Airlines 77 – filled to only 27% of capacity
United Airlines 175 – filled to only 26% of capacity
United Airlines 93 – filled to only 16% of capacity

In an industry that pays extremely close attention to such matters, why didn't anyone see the red flags that were being waved? Did someone tell them to neglect these glaring inconsistencies to lessen the collateral damage (or the insurance payouts)?

Since I mentioned United Airlines flight 93, consider this odd bit of information. The Reuters news agency reported on 9-13-2001 in an article entitled, "Troubling Questions in Troubling Times": "Pennsylvania State Police officials said on Thursday debris from the plan had been found up to EIGHT MILES AWAY from the crash site." Do you realize how immense an eight-mile stretch of land is? Do you also realize that when a plane drops from the sky, the impact does not cause the wreckage to scatter for eight miles? Think about it. Eight miles is the length of 140 football fields laid end-to-end! Obviously, something else happened to bring Flight 93 out of the sky. Strong evidence points to the Air Force shooting it down, then the plane disintegrated during its eight-mile descent into a rural Pennsylvania field. Yet the powers-that-be lied once again to the American people. Now do you know why President Bush personally asked Tom Daschle to limit their Congressional inquiry?

Another aspect of this case that makes me scratch my head is this: why won't the FAA release the entire records of the pilot conversations with their air-traffic controllers?

Another pertinent question revolves around the pilot's curious reactions during these hijackings. Once they got the first inkling that they were being overtaken, why didn't they simply perform a "rollover" to incapacitate or disable the hijackers? The "barrel roll" is an easily-performed procedure for veteran pilots, especially when one considers the backgrounds of the four men who manned these flights. As Colonel Donn de Grand Pre reports:

> John Ogonowski – Vietnam Air Force fighter pilot
> Leroy Homer – Former Air Force pilot
> Victor Saracini – Former fighter pilot
> Chic Burlingame – Naval Academy graduate who flew F-4's in Vietnam

All of these pilots were described as being strong, agile, healthy, in excellent physical condition, and certainly capable of performing a simple rollover. Now I'm not blaming these men by any means … it just seems like, if given the opportunity, these pilots would have disoriented the "hijackers" enough to gain control of the situation and avert disaster. Rather, we're being led to believe that these three jumbo jets were flown into buildings by Middle Eastern hijackers brandishing nothing more than box cutters, and all of them had only six months flying experience. I don't know about you, but if everything were on the up-and-up, I'd put my faith in these pilots being able to nullify the hijackers any day of the week. But again, we're not being given the entire story because something doesn't add up.

I could continue with dozens of other inconsistencies, but instead I'll close on this note:
- Who in the mainstream media is asking these, and other, pertinent questions? No one!
- Who in the Pentagon is answering these questions? No one!
- Finally, who in the Pentagon has been made accountable for the Air Force stand-down? Again, no one!

Do you think it's time our government and the media started addressing these issues? I do.

CHAPTER FOUR

NOTES AND QUOTES: THE WAR ON TERRORISM – MONEY, FEAR AND RIGHTS

War = Profits: it's that simple. Here's how the equation works. Banks lend money to countries to fight their battles; then extend further loans after the war is over to help rebuild the nation that was defeated. By utilizing this strategy, the banks always win because the victor is deeply indebted to them via loans, while the loser is controlled through the extended political influence associated with their indebtedness.

Those in the know also make a killing during war by manipulating the stock market; utilizing inside information and knowing the markets will be volatile. They short-sell while the stocks are high (making a huge profit), then wait for the market to drop (as it inevitably does), and re-buy at rock bottom prices, knowing full well they'll rise again after everything settles down (thus, more financial gains).

War is hell for some, and big bucks for others. Which category do you think the Controllers fit into?

Three days after the World Trade Center attack, Congress approved a $40 billion spending bill, with half of the money being used on increased military spending. Congress has also earmarked $15 billion to bail out the airline industry, and $100 million for the New York City clean up.

Here's another thing to think about. Collectively, the World Trade Center generated 74 million dollars a year in taxes that went to New York City. That revenue has now been eliminated. The Federal Reserve is also getting in on the game, pumping out over $100 billion in new loans. The insurance companies are taking a royal bath during this catastrophe.

What point am I trying to make? I'm not taking a judgmental stance by saying these expenditures are good or bad. All I'm trying to point out is that an enormous amount of money is currently being spent, and at some point we're going to have to pony up for it. When we do; who's going to make the brunt of these payments and take it on the chin – us, or the Controllers? Whose pocket do you think the money is going to come out of -- Those who control most of the money (the Controllers) or those who have little (ours)? It's something to consider.

Our Government does not control the Federal Reserve. It is a privately owned company. Five banks account for almost 60% of the Federal Reserve's ownership. Think about it. Five banks literally rule the world. Also, when we make payments on our national debt (the interest payments alone equal $359 billion a year), who does the money go to? Answer: the international bankers! Who do the international bankers answer to? No one except the utmost tier of the power pyramid -- the Controllers themselves.

Despite the capitalist credo of competition, the multinational companies that comprise the New World Order despise competition. John D. Rockefeller said it best: "Competition is a sin." They love monopolies. Why doesn't the media point out any of these disturbing facts to us? Isn't it their job to be society's watchdog? The reason they don't is because ABC is beholden to Texaco, NBC is affiliated with British Petroleum, and Time-Warner is associated with Mobil.

Remember, the four largest industries in the world are: 1) usury, 2) energy, 3) drugs, and 4) war. When the oil industry barks orders, the media falls in line. Instead of being this country's watchdog, the corporate media is nothing more than a pacified lap dog.

Network USA stated: "The biggest threat to Americans' freedom is not going to come from terrorists; it is going to come from politicians guided by the manipulated fears of the public."

If you look back over the last sixty years, the Theater of Terror has played a prominent role in putting this country in its current predicament. What do I mean by the "Theater of Terror?" It is a single act that is so dramatic and terrifying it leaves a permanent mark, or indentation, on the collective national psyche. The most striking examples of this phenomenon would be: Pearl Harbor, the atomic bombs of Nagasaki and Hiroshima, the Cuban Missile Crisis, JFK's assassination, the Manson murders, the Challenger explosion, the Oklahoma City Bombing, and the World Trade Center terrorist attacks.

Other countries, for example Australia with its Port Arthur Massacre, have also experienced these traumas. This Theater of Terror is so intense and foreign to what we're accustomed to, at first glance it almost seems like a Hollywood production -- except it's real. The fear factor paralyzes us, temporarily curbing progress.

Imagine what would happen if someone had the ability to manipulate this Theater of Terror to their own advantage. On a small scale, how many children have been severely impaired in their development due to a parent or institution's use of terror?

The results are all around us. Now, think of this phenomenon on a larger scale. How can a world-shattering event be used to manipulate people in a certain direction?

A perfect example is Hitler's invasion of Europe. After the atrocities of World War I, America wanted nothing to do with another monumental war. The Controllers were aware of our collective aversion to entering another protracted battle, so they needed a catastrophic event to motivate us. Thus, Pearl Harbor. Do you see how it works? Manipulate the Theater of Terror to derive a desired outcome. If we examine this concept in regard to trauma-based mind control, we'd realize the more fearful a person becomes, the more susceptible they are to control.

How easy is it to control a lion out on the range? Extremely difficult. Yet if this lion is caged and turned into a cowering shell of its former self, how easy would it be to control? Here's the formula: Trauma = Susceptibility = Manipulation

Ever since 9-11, think about how much fear has been laid upon us. We're afraid of certain types of people, white powder (anthrax), the mail, airplanes, smallpox, etc. Through fear and insecurity, the Controllers are destroying our confidence, chipping away at the invincibility of our country, and eroding the belief in ourselves.

What if this reign of terror continues and we begin to see the loss of our national sovereignty, a military defeat, and a full-scale economic collapse? Then, how would deliberately-induced fear relate to our confidence?

Controlled Chaos is one of the oldest fear-inducing tactics the Controllers have used throughout the years. If this situation is viewed in terms of Hegelian Dialectics, you can see how controlled conflict is used to weaken a citizenry:

Thesis: Freedom
Antithesis: Real or simulated threats
Predetermined synthesis: The loss of our rights

I started thinking about how much fear currently exists in this country, and it struck me that it's the first time people my age have had to live under this cloak of paranoia. I wasn't even alive when the atrocities of World War II befell us, or while children were told to hide under their school desks during the 1950s (a byproduct of the Cold War). Nor was I forced to endure the Cuban Missile Crisis or the Vietnam War draft.

In this sense, my generation has never had to live under an umbrella of fear. And even though I'm not personally afraid of what the Controllers are doing (because I understand their tactics), I see the seeds being planted for a new type of society -- increased intelligence operations, the National Guard at airports carrying M-16's, and chemical and biological attacks.

What it all boils down to is that the Controllers go to GREAT lengths to prevent actual, REAL threats to society; but they have no problem creating situations that inspire fear in people so they can be more easily manipulated to toe the line.

THE LOSS OF RIGHTS (NOTES AND QUOTES)

Associated Press article by Jesse J. Holland - October 24, 2001: "Police would be able to conduct secret searches of suspects' homes, tap all their cell & home phones and track their use of the Internet under anti-terrorism legislation moving toward final approval in the House."

Justice Ralph Forbes, Arkansas Congressional Candidate: "In 1984 there is a chilling passage where the Interrogator is describing the future to the character Winston Smith, and he says, 'Imagine the heel of a boot grinding in a human face throughout all eternity. That's our view of the future.'

William Safire, in an article for The New York Times on November 14, 2002 entitled, "You Are a Suspect": "If the Homeland Security Act is not amended before passage, here is what will happen to you: Every purchase you make with a credit card, every magazine subscription you buy and medical prescription you fill, every Website you visit and e-mail you send or receive, every academic grade you receive, every bank deposit you make, every trip you book and every event you attend – all these transactions and communications will go into what the Defense Department describes as 'a virtual, centralized grand database.' To this computerized dossier on your private file from commercial sources, add every piece of information that the government has about you – passport application, driver's license and bridge toll records, judicial and divorce records, complaints from nosy neighbors to the FBI, your lifetime paper trail plus the latest hidden camera surveillance – and you have the super snoop's dream: a "Total Information Awareness" about every U.S. citizen."

HOMELAND SECURITY FORCE = BIG BROTHER

How about the use of technology to diminish our rights and bolster surveillance? Video cameras are now being installed all over America on every downtown street corner in the guise of "catching red-light runners." How do you feel about instant DNA tests if you're pulled over for a routine traffic violation? What would happen if satellites were able to actually shut off your automobile if it was producing too much pollution? What if you were forced to carry a national I.D. card that had your fingerprints on it?

To better monitor what you're looking at on the Internet, what if you had to undergo a retinal scan prior to logging on? Do you know that right now the FBI has a file on EVERY U.S. citizen -- even those who have never broken a law or been arrested? Did you know that when you walk through an airport, the authorities have equipment that can tell EXACTLY how much money you're carrying (via the metallic strips imbedded inside the bills), and if you have over $1,000 in cash, they're allowed to stop and search you?

This is part of the increased search, seizure, detention, and wiretapping laws that are currently being passed with alarming speed. Technology exists right now where a CCTV camera can zoom in on you at a stadium filled with people, transfer the information to a computer with face-recognition programs and identify you as someone who's a "threat."

What if Congress passes a bill stating every person in the United States must submit to mandatory fingerprinting? To insure that everyone adheres to this policy, what if they create fingerprint scanners at every check-out counter, and the only way you'll be able to buy something is if it scans your fingerprint ID card?

Here's the deal with National ID cards that certain members of the media are trying to push on us. At some point a National ID card WILL be issued, but only as a stepping stone to "bigger and badder" things. Why? Because this card is going to be created to deliberately FAIL! Yes, because of its propensity to be counterfeited (which will be built into the card in the first place), we'll then be "SEDUCED" into accepting an actual IMPLANT.

What will these implants entail? Basically, they'll be set into your palm, be powered by lithium batteries, and they'll carry at least 400,000 bytes of information. They will let the Watchers know your family relationships, criminal background, travel activities, health information, purchasing and financial history, what you read, what you look at on the Internet, and a slew of other data. They will be updated on a daily basis every time you go to the store, log onto your computer, go to the doctor, withdraw money, etc. Sounds like the perfect vehicle for Big Brother, huh?

The Controllers are already experimenting with these implants in actual human beings AS WE SPEAK! The New World Order isn't something that's coming in the future -- it's already here.

The other day, after listening to me deliver all this information, a woman asked, "So what if they do all that stuff? They can look in my bank account, or where I've been on the computer. I'm not a terrorist. I don't have anything to hide."

I told her that by only looking at the small picture, she's right. She's not a terrorist. But what if Big Brother says: "Victor Thorn is a dangerous character. He's a THREAT, and he's letting the cat out of the bag. So, what we're going to start doing is targeting everyone who reads *Babel Magazine* or the writings of Victor Thorn.

Guess what, folks? Big Brother just put you on his list! Now do you care?

CHAPTER FIVE

9-11 SMOKESCREEN

"How could there be a conspiracy of silence in regard to the 9-11 terrorist attacks?" some people may ask. "Look at the news every day with endless reports about what President Bush did or didn't know. The mainstream media is really on this story. There's no denying it! They'll get to the bottom of it."

On the surface, most people would be satisfied with this analysis. The 9-11 'foreknowledge story' is on the cover of *Newsweek* and the *Washington Post*, while Rush Limbaugh and the CBS Evening News give updates daily. Also, the media is supposedly sniffing out new clues and looking at every angle: ignored FBI reports, terrorist visas, flight schools, "who knew what" in the Bush cabinet, and the lack of shared knowledge between the various intelligence agencies.

The Sunday morning pundits argue endlessly about it and Dick Cheney makes his rounds while Congressmen grandstand and rattle off sound-bytes.

With all this information coming our way, the mainstream media must be giving us the whole story, right?

I hate to break it to you, but if you rely solely on all of the above sources for your information, no, you're not getting the whole story. Why? The answer lies in the scope of what is being presented to you. Stated differently, the media is continuing a long-standing practice of conditioning the masses by only giving them half-truths, and half the picture.

More specifically, through the use of "psychic driving" (a certain message repeated over and over again), they constantly refer to George Bush (or any other President) as the head of the decision-making process in this country, with no one above or beyond them.

Nothing could be further from the truth.

Here's why. I hear plenty of well-intentioned people talking about what's wrong with America. Some even provide ways to make things better. But first we must make one fundamental change. It's imperative that we alter the way we view the world's control system.

Let me clarify. If Americans don't break free of the multi-faceted conditioning that begins as soon as we make contact with the external world (school, news, prevailing myths, etc.), then *nothing* will ever improve. Nothing!

Most of us have believed from an early age that the President of the United States is the Commander-in-Chief and he has the ultimate authority to lead our country. This notion is continually reinforced by our public education (indoctrination) system, the media, and a type of cultural mythology.

This is an illusion. Hidden powers, specifically international bankers, heads of multinational corporations, secret societies and elite families actually call all the shots.

By controlling the world's purse strings through the Federal Reserve, World Bank, IMF and socialistic taxation, these veiled figures lurk in the shadows out of public view, yet determine virtually every vital decision made in our world.

This concept is the key to understanding not only our political system. It is also the first step necessary for changing our destiny. As things stand now in relation to the 9-11 terrorist attacks, every major media source has reinforced the lie that George Bush is at the top of the American decision-making pyramid.

Before we continue, let's examine what happened on 9-11, and what we know for sure.

First, the World Trade Center Towers in New York City were destroyed, while the Pentagon was also severely damaged in a similar fashion. Second, the airliners that caused this destruction were hijacked, although we can't be certain by whom, as FBI Director Robert Mueller admitted in a speech to the Commonwealth Club in San Francisco on April 19, 2002: "In our investigation, we have not uncovered a single piece of paper -- either here in the United States or in the treasure trove of information that has turned up in Afghanistan and elsewhere -- that mentioned any suspect of the September 11 plot."

Third, there is a preponderance of evidence pointing out that numerous individuals knew exactly when, how and where these attacks were going to take place.

With the above information laying a foundation, we have to next make a few well-conceived assumptions. First of all, America spends billions of dollars on intelligence, and it's not stepping too far out on a ledge to say that considering the advanced nature of our computer systems, black budget technology, tracking devices and infiltration of foreign governments, we have a pretty good idea of what's going on in the world.

The second assumption (well-founded in documented fact) is that certain groups on this planet have an immense hatred of America. Let's assume one of those is the Osama bin Laden/Al Quaeda/Taliban connection.

Without delving into the mountains of evidence that have been compiled since 9-11 suggesting that scores of people in a variety of different of walks of life had foreknowledge of these attacks, and considering how our Intelligence agencies pride themselves on being aware of this data, we need to start drawing some conclusions.

The men who rule this planet are able to protect their positions of power for one important reason: they have an obsessive hunger or demand for knowledge and information. In other words, when one studies the world control pyramid, they'll notice that directly below the ultimate Controllers are the intelligence agencies. Secret, beyond the law and largely unaccountable to Congress or anyone else, these agencies are an integral part of the very framework that allows the Controllers to survive.

To perpetuate themselves, the ultra-elite are heavily dependant upon their spies and spooks to keep them abreast of what's going on in this complicated world. Without these aides, their house of cards would crumble.

Considering how vital information gathering is, and in light of the volumes of evidence that a variety of people had at least an inkling of foreknowledge that an attack was going to occur on September 11 -- and that's just what *we* know -- I assure you the NSA and CIA know *much* more than we do. Thus, I propose this question: why are the media and Congress so fixated on whether George Bush knew about the attacks beforehand?

The answers may surprise you. First of all, considering how divisive the 2000 Presidential election was, there are still huge chasms in the American populace between the Bush lovers and Bush haters. Thus, if the media can further exploit this rift, then the Controllers can yet again use their favorite tactic: Divide and Conquer. By keeping everyone fighting among themselves, we won't focus our attention on who the real enemy is!

Can't you see? It's the oldest trick in the book. By directing our attention away from the source of this conflict, we'll never get to the bottom of it. The Controllers are masters of this Wizard of Oz type misdirection ("There's nobody behind the curtain!"); they'd rather we worry about symptoms and not the *real cause*!

But there's more to the story. Every entity I mentioned in the first paragraph -- network news, influential daily papers, Congress, national magazines and syndicated talk show hosts -- refuse to recognize or acknowledge that the hidden power-elite Controllers even exist.

To them -- and this point is crucial -- the American President, currently George Bush -- is at the head of the decision-making process. The buck stops with him and that's it! But as we know, nothing could be more ludicrous.

In fact, Bush, Clinton, Reagan, Carter, etc., were and are nothing more than implementers. Decisions are made for them which they implement. The same can be said for Congress. This is the reality of our worldwide political control system.

So, what does it really matter if George Bush had foreknowledge of the 9-11 terrorist attacks (except for ethical reasons; of course)? By the time anyone has "risen" to that level, ethics have almost entirely been thrown away anyway. Can you see where I'm coming from?

Let's cut through all the rhetoric and lay it on the line. George Bush, Bill Clinton and Tom Daschle don't make decisions. They carry them out for others who prefer to remain hidden.

Thus, the important question we should be asking, considering the wealth of evidence, is: who DID have foreknowledge of the 9-11 attacks?

I'll answer this question by asking a few more questions:

1)   Who was in a better position than anyone to gain access to not only United States Intelligence, but also intelligence information from around the world, especially the Mossad? Answer: the Controllers.

2)   Who had the resources to obtain this information via surveillance, Carnivore (e-mail spying), wiretaps, undercover spies, and a wealth of other cloak and dagger techniques? Answer: the Controllers.

3)   Who, more than anyone else, could have known about a sect of America-haters who wanted to enact a form of revenge on us? Answer: the Controllers.

4)   Who needed a dramatic excuse (similar to sinking the Lusitania, Pearl Harbor, or the Gulf of Tonkin) to draw America into another war so they could extract oil and resume opium exportation from Afghanistan, punish those who didn't fall in line with their New World Order goals, and set into action a Big Brother dismissal of our civil rights? Answer: the Controllers.

5)   Who was most able to enact a cover-up in the media – the same media that they own? Answer: the Controllers.

6)   Finally, who NEEDED to know this information more than anyone else, and who benefited from it more than anyone else? The victims? No, they're all dead. The American people? No. War is going to plunge us so much further into debt, we'll never crawl back out. The country of Afghanistan? No – they're getting bombed to smithereens. The terrorists themselves? No -- they're all dead. How about the Controllers? Yes!

Yes, THEY knew, but all the while, what is everyone obsessing over? Whether George Bush knew! Well, maybe he did, and maybe he didn't. But personally, if for nothing other than ethical reasons, it doesn't really impact our situation because he's not calling the shots.

Bush, similar to his predecessors, is a figurehead -- furniture -- window-dressing. I want to know the names of those people who *really* make the decisions and intentionally allowed this disaster to occur.

There is no longer any question that powerful people had foreknowledge of the terrorist attacks. Look at the stock market irregularities, the Fortune 500 CEO's being whisked away before tragedy struck, or the military and political figures being told not to board planes that fateful morning.

The Controllers allowed a group of dirtballs to hijack our airliners and crash them into the WTC, killing nearly 3,000 people. Can't you see what happened? They INVADED America, traumatized us horribly, and to top it off, they're getting away with it by having their State-run media fiddle around with whether George Bush knew or not.

But the picture is so much bigger and more serious. We're setting the stage for World War III, and the 9-11 crime was step one. But Dan Rather continues to snow us, as do the *New York Times* and *Newsweek*.

Here's the way the news should be reported:

Dan Rather: "Today the Rothschild banking family decided that steps will be taken to implement a U.N. sanctioned World Tax. Here's John Roberts with the details."

John Roberts: "That's right, Dan. Upon orders from N. M. Rothschild in London, David Rockefeller telephoned President Bush and let him know that at some point next year, he'll agree to start a smokescreen in unison with Congress to vote in favor of the U.N.'s World Tax.

"Zbigniew Brzezinski and Henry Kissinger also entered the picture, with Kissinger writing your script for you, Dan, while Brzezinski briefed Bush on everything he would tell the American people at his next State of the Union Address. Back to you, Dan."

Dan Rather: "In other news, Frankfurt's Warburg financial family sent an edict to American's Alan Greenspan, director of the privately-owned monopolistic Federal Reserve Corporation, telling him to raise the prime lending rate, thus creating billions of dollars in profits for all the leading stockholders."

Instead, we still keep getting the same old tried-and-true psychic driving conditioning.

The Controllers, those with no ties or allegiance to any nation, are getting ready to start having people killed again on a large scale in their next WAR. It's death-time in the theater of destruction. The same people who allowed the WTC to be destroyed are the ones calling the shots to send our boys into battle. American lives and American blood are going to be sacrificed at the altar of the greedy, evil, globalist money interests.

Every major war and revolution of the 20th century did not originate from the people. They were planned, orchestrated, financed and dictated from the top of the Control Pyramid. As Black Sabbath sang many years ago: "Generals gathered in their masses, just like witches at black masses." It's that simple: the evil-doers are plotting to eliminate more American lives – and those from other countries, too.

What is it going to take to propel us into action? Why don't we force the Controllers out of the shadows? Rather than letting them call the shots like rats under the cloak of darkness, let's shine a light on them and expose their motives. Then we'll actually see what's going on instead of being bamboozled by this ludicrous media game they keep playing on us.

Folks, before we can change our circumstances, we need to change the way we view the world. Our lifetime of conditioning needs to be erased; then replaced with a world-view that is more accurate. We can no longer tolerate media deceit. Instead, we need to make everyone aware of who really calls the shots and run them out of their elitist towers of control. If we don't, then get ready because the blood is going to start flowing in rivers across the land.

Do we have the guts to stand up to these greedy monsters, or are we going to allow them to roll over us and kill our sons? We'd better act now before it's too late (and God forbid if that time arrives).

CHAPTER SIX

FEAR, PSYCHIC DRIVING, AND PAVLOV'S DOGS

Terrorist hijackers steer their planes into the World Trade Centers on a sunny Tuesday morning -- flames, smoke, people leaping 90 stories to their death, screaming, sirens, pandemonium, then the Towers come crashing to the ground in Battery Park. And, oh yeah, television cameras ... many, many television cameras, then the major networks and news channels re-broadcasting the horrifying event over and over again -- every scene, every angle, every snippet of the jets, flames, impact, and both Towers falling to the earth.

Over and over, over and over ... the hijacked jet, the Towers, the moment that forever changed American life. September 11, 2001 -- TV, TV, TV, bleary eyes fixated on CNN, Fox, CBS, NBC & ABC. Television – TV -- video images drawing viewers to it like a morbid magnet.

Shortly thereafter, anthrax scares send the country reeling with more panic. Don't open your mail, white powder, respiratory damage, biological terrorism, Senators evacuated, postmen falling dead -- and every day on the radio, on TV, in newspapers and magazines -- more hysteria, more coverage, more fear.

During the same time, air travelers are filled with anxiety -- everyone suspected of being a terrorist -- long waiting lines, the National Guard holding M16's, evacuations, more long lines, inspections, X-rays, no toenail clippers, bomb threats, and rumors of more terrorists lurking behind every pillar.

Now we have pipe bombs in mailboxes, the new weekly computer virus that makes us tremble with fear over e-mails and attachments, plus color-coded terror alerts and reports about banks, malls and train stations being targeted for destruction. And all the while there's CNN, the *New York Times* and *Newsweek* continuing their psychic driving hour after hour, day after day.

Psychic driving? What's that? Psychic driving is the repeated exposure to a specific message over and over and over again -- a continued, systematic replay of the same theme until the subject is thoroughly indoctrinated into accepting a certain belief. In this day and age, it's fear ... pure, oozing, strip-away-the-veneer Total Fear.

The Heartland trembles and leaves their mailboxes open ... tomorrow it might be Floridians and psychotic drive-by bazooka shootings perpetrated by ... you guessed it ... faceless, nameless "terrorists" who can't be seen or heard or located.

But I'm tellin' ya, folks, the whole thing is a ruse! Sure, a few people had their mailboxes blown up by a mind-controlled punk rock zombie, and a few citizens died from anthrax (not high-ranking public officials, if you noticed). But in all, those who are setting this entire theater of fear into motion are the REAL terrorists -- the international Controller cabal that's ready to raise another level on their pyramid of power. A few events in the recent past set the stage for this onslaught -- Waco, the first WTC bombing, and the government set-up at Oklahoma City where explosives inside the Murrah Building did more damage than little ol' mind-controlled Timothy McVeigh.

Of course, when you sprinkle in some remote-controlled high school shooters (especially at Colombine), the stage is set to seize control.

And that happened on September 11, 2001 with the World Trade Center terrorist attacks. Y'see, the Controllers usually do things in small steps, patiently boiling us like frogs in a pot. But every once in awhile they need to kick it up a notch, a la the WTC attacks. That way, similar to the Charles Manson murders, a huge, indelible emotional scar is permanently imbedded on the human psyche. These are the events that rip us to shreds, give our children nightmares, and leave most of us trembling in the relative safety of our homes.

In September 2001 this country was essentially chopped off at the knees. We reeled day in and day out from the psychological impact. I know one lady who sat in front of her TV for eighteen hours a day and became such a debilitated wreck, she said even her dog got sick from all the terror-filled vibes she was emitting.

But don't get fooled into thinking its over. Just last week we received an e-mail from a woman giving us firsthand chemtrail accounts. When we asked her if we could reprint her e-mails anonymously in *Babel Magazine*, she instantly shrieked and retreated with fear. God forbid someone from the "big bad government" might find out who sent us this information.

Our society is being crippled by a faceless, nameless form of fear that is being crammed down our throats by every media source available. Radio talk show hosts, television images, newspaper editorials and op-ed letters, gory magazine photographs, plus Internet rumors and half-truths are all contributing to this fear. And America is falling prey to it.

Where did our fighting spirit go? With overwhelming evidence that the Controllers not only knew about the 9-11 attacks, but allowed them to happen; with this evidence now openly reported in the mainstream press, why aren't we gathering in the streets to bring these monsters to their knees?

These same Controllers are setting America up for a great Fall, only to replace us with China as the next world super-power. But we sit idly by without taking action. Why?

We are numb with fear. The entire planet is "kept in its proper place" because of fear. Religions use it, as do governments, police, parents, social groups, schools, and faceless bureaucratic institutions such as the IRS. Soon this fear will be all-encompassing in the image of Big Brother, just as George Orwell predicted in his novel, *1984.*

The saddest part is, we know how the Controllers use fear, yet we still allow them to manipulate us. It's similar to a scrawny, 150-pound lion tamer keeping ten Bengal Tigers at bay inside a cage at the circus. Not only that, but he also has them perform emasculating tricks, jump through hoops, and bow to him simply because he cracks his whip. These gorgeous, regal, powerful animals are completely slavish to his desires, demeaned to the point that it fills me with rage.

But then again, are we any different? Think of how great humanity could be, and how much potential we possess. But we allow the Controllers to rule us.

It wouldn't even be so bad if they made our world idyllic and utopian. But they don't. Look around. We have wars and upcoming wars everywhere, starvation on a massive scale, homelessness, and a man-made AIDS virus running rampant in Africa and the Orient. These people are ADULTS, but they sure don't act like it.

The finger can't always be pointed at them, and our problems shouldn't all be externalized. We're the ones allowing them to control us. Why? Aren't we any smarter than the Bengal Tigers in that cage? Why don't we all pull together (instead of letting THEM tear us apart) and rip the Controllers to shreds? There are only a few of them, and MILLIONS of us.

We can do it!

Fear … the concept that levels and reduces us to lowly animals rather than beings who could transform this world into something great. But Pavlov realized this concept years ago. In fact, he learned that if a well-trained dog were suddenly traumatized by incredible doses of fear, everything it learned could be erased; then replaced with an entirely new form of programming. Yes, re-programmed right from scratch.

Well, folks, guess what? We're the dogs, Pavlov is the Controllers, and the 9-11 terror attacks are the traumatic events (or at least the start of them ... and be certain, there will be more). And yes, all the things we've learned until this point -- concepts such as civil liberties and freedom of expression -- are going to be erased, then replaced with a new form of programming (one that better suits THEM).

Get ready for the New World Order and Big Brother because they're on their way.

But we can derail this juggernaut if we want to. There's only one thing stopping us: FEAR! So, I'll officially go on the record and say, like John Hancock signing his name in large, powerful letters on the Declaration of Independence, that I am not afraid! Are you?

SECTION

TWO:

BANKS, OIL,

DRUGS & WAR

CHAPTER SEVEN

DRUG TRAFFICKING: A BRIEF HISTORICAL OVERVIEW

Of all the pieces I've written for *Babel Magazine* -- AIDS as a man-made disease, mind-control projects, assassinations, and the motives behind war -- none are as murky, dirty, and downright sleazy as this one about drug trafficking.

As someone who in the past did every type of drug known to man, I'm well aware of what these substances can do to a person. I've also been keeping an eye on the supposed "War on Drugs" that's been a ruse for the last three decades. Why is it a sham? Because factions of our own government, specifically the CIA, have been running drugs into this country since at least the 1960s on a wide-scale basis. Not only is the CIA the prime moving factor behind bringing drugs to America, but many high-level government officials know full well what is going on and have decided to blatantly ignore the problem.

A BRIEF HISTORY

The imperative word in the above heading is "brief," for there have been countless books written about the drug trade. For me to do an exhaustive study would fill hundreds of pages, so I'll simply begin by saying that in the Middle Ages, drugs were used as currency and those who possessed them wielded a great deal of economic leverage.

These individuals who cornered the opium market eventually became some of the wealthiest and most influential people on the planet. They reached this state by monopolizing the shipping lanes (sea-lanes were the primary mode of transportation at that time), and thus went on to become the world's rulers.

By the 15th century, nearly every war revolved around gold, diamonds, or the opium trade. Drugs became such a prevalent aspect of civilization, when history books refer to the "spice trade" it is actually a thinly veiled reference to opium. In fact, when Christopher Columbus set sail, he was trying to find a quicker route to the Far East in order to make it easier to score opium. Along the way he happened to stumble upon America.

Speaking of our country, the Pilgrims not only moved to America in order to practice religious freedom, but also to escape Europe's cycle of drugs and ongoing wars. Across the ocean, the British East India Company was the wealthiest organization on earth at that time, and the mighty British Empire was founded on monopolizing the opium market.

By the 19th century, morphine was invented by a German scientist named F.W.A. Seturner between 1805-1817, and the syringe was developed during the Civil War.

American drug running started in 1823 with a man named Samuel Russell who began Russell & Company. This man bought opium in Turkey, then smuggled it through China. In 1830, he purchased the Perkins Opium Syndicate of Boston and established a base of operations in Connecticut. One of his primary wheeler-dealers was Warren Delano, Jr., who was the grandfather of FDR!

By 1832, along with William Huntington, Russell formed the Skull & Bones secret society at Yale. Over the years its members included family names such as Bush, Rockefeller, Taft, Whitney, Harriman, Pillsbury, Kellogg, Goodyear, Perkins, and Weyerhauser.

At the same time, these people formed the nation's first intelligence operation -- the Culper Ring. So, what we see is a trend that will continue throughout the future -- the intermingling of secret societies, drugs, and the intelligence community.

While the Skull & Bones were building their drug empire on the East Coast, two other events were also occurring on the West Coast. These events, the California Gold Rush in 1849 and the building of the Transcontinental Railroad, were instrumental in bringing drugs to America.

Chinese Coolies were used as mules to import drugs into our country. Here is the pattern once again: two of the key components that make the world go 'round: gold and drugs.

By 1889, heroin was developed by the I. G. Farben Company -- the same folks that 40 years later produced the Zyklon B used to gas the Jews during World War II. Thus, the first true "drug wave" to hit our country occurred between 1870-1920.

Another factor that influenced this phenomenon was World War I, which served to "expand" the world by moving people into areas they never would have encountered if it weren't for battle.

Heroin and morphine are pain killers. Since large numbers of people were wounded and maimed during the war and were given these drugs to alleviate the pain, they became addicted. Thus, drug addition became widespread throughout the world.

By the time World War I ended, two more important factors entered the equation. First, drugs were made illegal in America during the early 1920s, and also internationally by the League of Nations, thus making its distribution extremely profitable. Second, cocaine was introduced to the general public.

People in the jungles had always gotten a buzz off of chewing the coca leaves, but now the sensation was heightened by delivering it in concentrated powder form.

In the early 1930s, consumers could no longer walk into a store and buy cocaine-laced soft drinks or over-the-counter hard drugs. Now they had to buy them on the streets. This was also the same time that the Mob entered the picture.

The United States could have entirely eradicated its drug problem during World War II because our attention was focused on defeating the Axis Forces.

But we had already dug a hole for ourselves by entering into an agreement with the Mafia. Y'see, during World War II, to secure Italy, the United States Government formed an alliance with the Mob -- specifically Lucky Luciano -- who was imprisoned in New York. Since Mussolini didn't hold the La Cosa Nostra in high esteem and tried to break them, Luciano turned to the American authorities and enabled us to ultimately dock and take over Italy during the war. As payment for his services, Luciano was released from prison and deported back to Italy after the war, where he revived the Mafia and established links in the United States.

This fact is very important, for after Prohibition was abolished, the Mob began trafficking drugs, which had a much higher profit margin than alcohol.

Also, another window of opportunity opened up after World War II because up until that point, Japan had dominated the manufacture and distribution of heroin. They used this money to finance their war efforts and also flooded China with it to undermine that country.

So, between 1936-1946, there was virtually no drug abuse in this country. But then in 1948, as an offshoot of the OSS, the CIA was formed to "stop communism." In the process, they also became major league players in the trafficking of drugs.

By interacting with other intelligence communities, mobsters, international dealers and guerillas, they soon began running drugs from the Middle East through Europe, and eventually into the United States.

THE CIA

The REAL war on drugs is this: The CIA is eliminating all unwanted competition so they can have total control of running the world's drug business. It's that simple. Fletcher Prouty, the "Mr. X" in Oliver Stone's film, *JFK*, called this rogue element "The Secret Team."

This parallel government doesn't use its resources to stop the production, transport, and sale of drugs, but instead, uses the drugs themselves to finance its own covert operations. Called "Black Budgets," this money is utilized above-and-beyond what Congress appropriates to the CIA in their yearly budget.

In other words, since this Secret Team has a clandestine, self-appointed mission that isn't authorized by any branch of the government, it needs to have a variety of ways to finance itself.

Where does this funding come from? In addition to drug dealing, the CIA runs guns and launders money (to name just a few of their "covert arts"). Not only did the CIA formerly "occupy" their own private airline (Air America), but they also joined forces with the World Finance Corporation in Florida, which is a money laundering bank, and the Nugan Hand Bank in Florida.

If times got rough, they could also fall back on the Vatican to run their money (no traces).

While we're on the topic of front companies, there's always the Far East Trading Company that the CIA used to run opium and clean their money.

And why does the Secret Team need all this dough? Well, there's always a need for someone to run the world's illegal operations. You know what I mean -- assassinations, financing puppet governments, laying the groundwork for wars in third world countries, quieting people who get out of line, inciting riots (and then quelling them), grabbing control of states or countries that we could better operate; or hell, just creating entirely new governments.

And who carries out these missions? Of course you have intelligence forces, those from academia, politicians, spies, bankers, and businessmen who are working on the sly. But to really get the job done, the CIA gets those people who know how to get down n' dirty -- outlaws, warlords, and fanatical religious leaders ... anyone who is completely amoral and beyond the law.

If you really want to read an interesting story, look into the airport at Mena, Arkansas that was a huge drug drop-off point while Bill Clinton was Governor of that state. This airport was the prime stopping area (known as "A-12") from South America to the United States. Or, if you're really interested in what these folks are capable of, track down a series of articles written by Gary Webb that appeared in the San Jose *Mercury News* during 1996. These stories chronicle how the CIA flooded the Los Angeles streets with crack cocaine during the 1980s. Yeah, they're a real nice bunch of guys.

VIETNAM AND THE GOLDEN TRIANGLE

One of the primary reasons that America was involved in the Vietnam War (apart from the obvious profit motive) was to control and monopolize the opium trade in the Golden Triangle. We were so militarily superior that we could have won that war in a matter of months. But winning the war wasn't our objective. We had another one: to gain control of the area's opium fields and the ultimate production of the drug (heroin) trade.

Before America ever entered Korea or Vietnam, the Golden Triangle was run by French Intelligence and the Corsican Mobsters. Our interest in this area began in about 1950 when we realized how important the Golden Triangle (the Southeastern Asian countries of Laos, Burma, and Thailand) and the Golden Crescent (Middle East) were in terms of opium production.

Burma was by far the Golden Triangle's focal point, and the CIA began infiltrating it until 1961, when our mercenaries were driven from the area by warlords in power who recognized their country was now a major player in the international drug scene. By the late 1960's, the Golden Triangle accounted for 70% of the world's opium production. With output sky high, entire villages became totally dependent upon opium.

As the Vietnam War raged out of control, 57,000+ American soldiers were killed in those jungles and the CIA became the largest mover of drugs in the world. While our troops were fighting, at least 15-30% of them became addicted to smack ("China White").

The CIA went in with their small planes and helicopters and re-opened the transport routes that had been destroyed or made unsafe. They then moved heroin from one of the largest drug labs in the world (in

Northern Laos) via three different routes into Nam (through the S. Vietnamese government), then eventually to our troops.

If you doubt that factions of our government were (and still are) involved in the drug trade, keep reading. In a *Wall Street Journal* article, Jonathan Kwitny reveals how heroin was shipped to the United States in the corpses of killed American soldiers. Their bodies were slit open, their innards removed, then crammed full of heroin -- sometimes up to 50 pounds per body. They were then flown to America (with "Priority Status") via the CIA's own personalized airline (Air America), where they landed at Norton Air Force Base in California.

What's more intriguing about this situation is that opium stinks. It has a very distinct aroma … one that is inescapable. Thus, all the pilots, loaders and everyone at the bases who unloaded these "shipments" definitely knew what was going on. The CIA became so brazen in their efforts they even set up a brand name soft drink company in Laos as a front operation for processing heroin.

After the United States "officially" pulled out of Vietnam in 1973, fighting continued in this area -- Cambodia, Laos, and Thailand -- right up through the 1980s. But after we left, guess what we left behind -- Prisoners of War.

Our government made a half-assed attempt, via Operation Grand Eagle, to rescue these men, but they didn't really want them to come home. Why? Because these guys knew too many of our dirty drug dealing secrets.

Years later, Ross Perot, an ardent supporter of POW's and their families, started snooping around. He discovered a troubling situation. In a conversation with George Bush, Sr., Perot said: "Well, George, I go in looking for prisoners, but I spend all my time discovering the government has been moving drugs around the world and is involved in illegal arms deals. I can't get at the prisoners because of the corruption among our own people!"

In 1986, the infamous Burmese Warlord Khun Sa stated on videotape that his country's entire supply of opium -- 900 tons per year -- was purchased by the United States Government. Numerous individuals involved in the POW recovery movement tried notifying our government and the national media of this debacle, but their attempts rained on deaf ears.

THE CONTRA WAR

Prior to ever becoming involved with the countries that we now associate with the "Contra War," the first area of major drug trafficking occurred in Cuba while Battista was still in power. During that time, Santo Trafficante, Jr. ran the show, and Cuba was a major pipeline for heroin coming into the States. It also harbored scores of gangsters who kept their enterprises going with gambling, booze, arms, and prostitution.

When Fidel Castro came into power in the late 1950s, the Mob's entire operation was shut down. Since the CIA had their fingers in the same pie for years, both of them were affected by this turn of events. After seven or eight unsuccessful attempts to knock off Castro between 1959-1965 (under code names ZR/RIFLE, Operation Mongoose, and JM/WAVE in which they used poisoned cigars, hallucinogens, etc., to kill and discredit Castro), the CIA turned their attention to new horizons -- Panama, Nicaragua, and beyond.

In the late 1970s, some of the same folks who tried to snuff Castro and were used in the Kennedy Assassination and Watergate burglary traveled to Central America. Headed by Ted Shackley, Thomas Clines, Felix Rodriguez, Frank Sturgis and Edwin Wilson, the program had over 12,000 operatives at its height. If you do any research, you'll keep finding the same names popping up over and over again.

The most recognizable personality from this era was Manuel Noriega. While head of the CIA in 1976, George Bush, Sr. would routinely have lunch with the Panamanian strongman and authorize hundreds of thousands of dollars in CIA payments to him each year in exchange for his assistance in transporting contraband into America.

Noriega's name also appeared on at least 50 CIA files as a drug dealer. There is even an infamous photograph of Bush and Noriega standing side-by-side with shit-eating grins plastered across their faces.

Everything was rolling along smoothly until Noriega bucked the system and tried to become "independent." Here's the scenario:

1)   Noriega would receive CIA payments for his involvement in the flow of drugs through Panama.
2)   He then used this money to build a national, independent network in his country.
3)   He eventually tried to go solo and keep all the drug money for himself instead of transferring it to the CIA.

Realizing that Noriega was out of line and unable to be controlled any longer, our government marked him as a drug lord, vilified him in the media, invaded his country, wiped away his operations, arrested him and then put a new man in his place – someone who'd better mind his P's and Q's.

Pretty simple. We even sent one of our notorious Golden Triangle high-rollers, Richard Armitage, to tell Noriega that he'd better get back in line, or else. Since he wouldn't see things "our way," Noriega was captured and imprisoned. What a lovely business!

LSD AND DRUG COMPANIES

Reams of material have been published that document our government's experimentation with drugs on both witting and unwitting subjects. Administered under the CIA's nefarious "MK-ULTRA" program and also by the Department of Defense, one thing needs to be very clear: segments of our government were intensively involved in experimentation with drugs and many of the agents became big-time trippers and users themselves.

Below are a few random notes that expose the tip of this disturbing iceberg:

- LSD was discovered in 1948 by Dr. Albert Hoffman, who worked for Sandoz Pharmaceuticals in Switzerland.
- At the National Institute for Mental Health in Lexington, Kentucky, under the supervision of Dr. Harris Isabell, seven different drug addicts were administered LSD so that they continuously tripped for 77 days straight.
- Operation Midnight Climax was an MK-ULTRA program in which hallucinogens were used on unsuspecting subjects to see if a Manchurian Candidate could be created to become an assassin, all the while testing LSD's effectiveness in regard to brainwashing.
- "Heroin" is a trade name created by Bayer.
- Eli Lilly was the first company to produce synthetic LSD for the CIA.
- Eli Lilly is the largest drug company that produces the precursor chemicals needed to manufacture cocaine and heroin. When you think about it, you have cocoa plants and poppy bulbs, but without the necessary ingredients needed to transform them into their final state, their use would never be so widespread.

•   Eli Lilly sends materials directly to Columbia to process their coca leaves into cocaine, and our government does nothing to stop these shipments, although they know full well what they're being used for. Two recognizable political names of the 1990s own huge shares in this company -- George Bush and the Quayle family.

CONCLUSION – GOVERNMENT KNOWLEDGE

Drugs are used as a tool by the Controllers to quell what they see as problems.

To reiterate a few things: First, there are mind-boggling amounts of money to be made from trafficking drugs. (The world's four largest industries are: (1) Usury, (2) Energy, (3) Drugs, and (4) War).

Political takeovers, business empires and personal fortunes have been built on the above four premises. Some people even say the CIA is the biggest drug dealer in the world, and it's no secret that their Black Budgets are largely financed via the transport of drugs, arms, and money laundering. The "Secret Team's" practices are also well-known by all branches of the government, including the FBI, National Security Council, State Department and DEA, and every potential investigation into it is quickly thwarted.

Finally, if all illegal drugs were completely eliminated at one time, it would send the world's economy into such a tailspin, it would make the Great Depression look like a day at the circus.

With this information in mind, we need to look at the recent figureheads who have "run" this country: George Bush, Sr. and Bill Clinton. Elder Bush was the head of the CIA from 1975-76 and his link with this organization dates back to the late 1950s or early 1960s. His Zapata offshore oil rigs have also been linked to the transfer of narcotics shipments from South America to the States.

When the biggest drug smuggler in American history (Barry Seal) was killed by a volley of gunfire, guess whose private phone number was found in his wallet? George Bush, Sr.'s! As head of the CIA, do you really think he didn't know what was going on? C'mon!

As for Bill Clinton, his link to the Mena Airport in Arkansas is so strong it would be easy to graduate from turning a blind eye at the state level to a national scale. Now we need to look at our current President -- George W. Bush. Considering who his father is and his own cocaine/party past, do you think there's any possibility that he's ignorant of what the Secret Team is doing?

Some people may say, "Since everyone knows the CIA is the biggest drug dealer in the world, why not just legalize drugs?" The answer is this: We can't legalize drugs because there is too much of a MACHINE associated with it. Think about how many people LEGITIMATELY make their living off of drugs -- drug companies, pharmacists, the court system, police officers, the DEA, parole officers, investigators, prisons (which are currently the largest growth industry in the country), and lawyers. It's immense. So, once again, drugs equal money!

Henry Kissinger said to Bob Woodward at the *Washington Post*: "Military men are dumb, stupid animals to be used as pawns for foreign policy."

This statement doesn't directly have anything to do with drugs, but it does reflect the amount of contempt the world leaders (Controllers) have for us. If Kissinger can talk negatively about the military, just think how he sees us -- mere "peasants!"

This comment leads to the Controllers' use of drugs as a tool against its own citizenry. I've done every type of drug known to man, and I'm well aware of their detrimental affects. Anyone who has been down this road will concur with me. But consider, if you will, drugs as a method to undermine the efforts of those who could potentially be "trouble."

What do I mean? During the late 1960s, the protest movement became such a threat to the Controllers that they seriously thought it would crumble their house of cards. So, what did they do? Everyone knows how prevalent marijuana use was during the 1960s. But toward the end of that decade and into the early '70s, harder, more dangerous drugs began hitting the scene, especially in one of the hotbeds of dissent – Haight-Ashbury.

In the span of a few years, the scene went from loving Flower Children to speed freaks, junkies and con men all strung-out and looking for an easy buck.

Another example is the Black protesters who wanted equal rights. Realizing these folks were serious about wanting change, what happened? The Controllers began shipping heroin out of the Golden Triangle in the early '70s and pumping it into the inner cities, right where the protesters lived. Soon we had our first big wave of heroin use in the early-to-mid '70s, and the Cause quietly faded away. Of course drugs weren't the only factor in the demise of these movements, but it was a contributor.

Another example concerns the English Punk Rock movement of the mid-late 1970s. At that time the economic situation in Great Britain was abysmal. Scores of angry teenagers were politically mobilized by a new musical craze -- punk rock. Through the Sex Pistols, Clash, Generation X, Siousxie Sioux and the Banshees and others, this movement actually became dangerous to the English elite.

To counter it, Johnny Thunders, ex-New York Dolls guitarist and quite possibly the most notorious junkie in rock n' roll history (which is saying a lot) and Nancy Spungen (Sid Vicious' girlfriend who was stabbed to death under suspicious circumstances) traveled to England. Thunders joined the Sex Pistols for a total death drag tour, while Nancy set her sights on (and landed) poor ol' Sid. Within months, as Johnny Thunders bragged, every punk rocker in England was a junkie.

Johnny and Nancy, neither of whom had two pennies to rub together, still had unlimited access to smack and turned everyone on that they met. Within less than two years, the Pistols disbanded, Nancy and Sid were dead, and punk rock fizzled into New Wave Music, which was safer, more sanitary, and much more focused on money than revolution.

It's a perfect Hegelian Dialectic at work:

Thesis: dangerous, political punk rock
Antithesis: destructive, readily available heroin
Synthesis: antiseptic, less threatening New Wave music

My final case study involves the marijuana farmers in the hills of Kentucky, West Virginia, and the surrounding areas. These folks are mostly dirt-poor locals who eke out a few extra bucks a year by growing weed up in the hill country. The government stumbled on this phenomenon a few years ago, and realizing they had competition, decided that they'd put an end to the marijuana growers.

Now I'm not advocating the legalization or illegality of marijuana, but here's what happened. The DEA spent hundreds of thousands of dollars to eradicate little thousand-dollar patches way up in the hills of "Deliverance" country. They'd bring in agents, helicopters, and hi-tech heat-sensing equipment just to mess with these dirt farmers.

But those guys in Kentucky are a resilient bunch, so they kept moving deeper and deeper into the woods, setting up more intricate traps and tip-off devices. Realizing they'd never eradicate the marijuana crops, the government took a more novel approach.

Rather than fighting fair, the Feds flooded the backwoods market with Oxycontin (nicknamed "Hillbilly Heroin"). It seems like every partier and pharmacist in the state had a 'script for this stuff. These guys were getting so high on Oxycontin, they didn't care about marijuana any more.

This ended competition for the government; and at the same time they made even money off of the pharmaceutical drugs. Whenever you view the subject of drugs in relation to governments, just remember their fingers are not just dirty – they're filthy.

CHAPTER EIGHT

THE WAR IN AFGHANISTAN: OPIUM AND OIL

Considering how prevalent drug trafficking is in certain political and business circles, we need to ask ourselves why the United States is at war with Afghanistan. To answer this question, one thing must be made perfectly clear.

The Controllers don't go to war over "ideals" such as patriotism, freedom or national sovereignty. Do you know why? Because these people don't give a damn about those concepts. In fact, they hold them in contempt.

So, why are we at war in Afghanistan? Historically, wars have been fought for three reasons: gold, diamonds, and drugs. Today, the two primary incentives to engage in war are oil and drugs. As you can tell, drugs are the constant. With that in mind, let me state that in 1999, Afghanistan produced 4,600 tons of opium, which was 75% of the world's total supply. Their output accounted for 60% of the entire Afghan economy, and was so prevalent that they even surpassed that of the Golden Triangle.

Large portions of the CIA's "black budgets" are derived from drugs (along with arms and money laundering). Afghanistan was thus a very important piece of the puzzle. But then a fanatical religious group, the Taliban, came to power and opium production virtually came to a halt. By the middle of this year, Afghanistan exported less than 100 tons of opium (or 1/50th of their previous production).

Our other motivation for seizing control of Afghanistan is this: inside Russia there exists an immense oil field in the remote Caspian landscape that could produce enough fuel to fulfill the world's needs for over 500 years. There's only one problem. To get this supply to our existing oil lines, we'd have to do away with a tiny roadblock -- it's a country called Afghanistan!

The biggest problem with this scenario is that we're still relying on a form of "old-thought." Fossil fuels are choking our planet. Now, I don't label myself a conservationist (or anything else), but we need to progress past the status quo and start developing alternate forms of energy. If General Motors and Mobil have things their way, we'll soon have a billion cars in China. It's great for the profit margin, but terrible for the planet. It's literally choking us to death.

The other natural resources that Afghanistan has in addition to natural gas and petroleum are coal, copper, and zinc. If we can tap into these resources, we'll become much less reliant upon foreign countries such as Saudi Arabia, which now produces half of the world's oil supply. When you think about it, from the time of the Crusades until the 1920s, the Middle East was nothing more than a sandbox. We didn't care at all about it. But now, this area wields an amazing array of power. The horrifying aspect of their influence is that, by and large, these people are so diametrically opposed to our way of life, they truly despise us. Yet we keep catering to them so the oil doesn't stop flowing. The scenario reminds me of the biggest kid in the schoolyard being terrorized by some scrawny little twerp. It's ridiculous.

Whenever you hear media-talk about the Controllers setting up a "puppet government" in Afghanistan, just remember what's really going on. We're only there for two reasons -- opium and oil. To reinforce this point, I was wondering why, on October 31, 2001, the military said they were actually running out of targets to bomb in Afghanistan. If that's the case, why don't they go in and torch all the opium fields so they'll guarantee no heroin comes out of there for the next couple of years? It's something to think about.

On September 27, 2001 in the Pakistani newspaper, *Unmat*, Osama bin Laden said: "Drug smugglers from all over the world are in contact with the U.S. Secret Agencies. These agencies do not want to eradicate narcotics cultivation and trafficking because their importance will be diminished. The people in the United States drug enforcement department are encouraging drug trade so they could show performance and get millions of dollars worth of budget. General Manuel Noriega was made a drug baron by the CIA and, eventually, he was made a scapegoat ... Is it not that there exists a government within a government in the United States? That secret government must be asked who made the attacks."

I love America and think bin Laden is a rat, but he hit pretty close to the mark with his comment. We should get rid of bin Laden and the Taliban first, then dispense with the Controllers.

CHAPTER NINE

WAR-MONGERS, DEATH-MERCHANTS, & KILLERS: AMERICA'S WAR MACHINE

Before beginning this article, I'd like to make it perfectly clear that I am not an anti-war peacenik that bows to the altar of pacifism. Instead, I take the stance that if any person's family, country, house, or personal being is attacked, they should come out shooting, throwing fists, or dropping bombs. If they don't, that person or nation will get bowled-over day after day with little hope of survival or respect.

With this in mind, I'd also like to note that there are people and leaders in this world that are evil to the core, and counterproductive to humanity as a whole. When these figures threaten us or our sovereignty, they should be dealt with in the harshest terms possible. When viewed in this light, why should we excuse a group of bloodthirsty hit-men from thrusting the United States into another war for the sheer sake of making huge profits for their respective companies, or for furthering the aims of the New World Order Controllers? If the following men have their way, the titles beside their names will ring true with frightening clarity. Why? Because America's War Machine is gearing up once again to feed its bloodlust and greed, and the men below are responsible for lighting its fuse:

Richard Clarke: War-monger, death-merchant, killer?
Paul Wolfowitz: War-monger, death-merchant, killer?
William Kristol: War-monger, death-merchant, killer?
Richard Perle: War-monger, death-merchant, killer?
Dick Cheney: War-monger, death-merchant, killer?
Henry Kissinger: War-monger, death-merchant, killer?
Donald Rumsfeld: War-monger, death-merchant, killer?
Frank Carlucci: War-monger, death-merchant, killer?
James Baker: War-monger, death-merchant, killer?
George Bush, Sr.: War-monger, death-merchant, killer?

(George W. Bush wasn't included because he doesn't make any decisions for himself.)

The list could go on to include those shadowy figures that have these men do their dirty work, but what I'd like to focus on is the visible mechanics of how our War Machine operates (i.e. those who grease its wheels to keep it churning along its course). So, what I'm going to do in this essay is point-out how money and oil interests led us to our current situation, then how the Carlyle Group is leading us into war by using former government officials to DETERMINE public policy.

THE WAR MACHINE

To get things rolling, here's a recent quote from Lt. Colonel Steven Butler that appeared in a Monterey newspaper on 5-26-02. "Of course Bush knew about the impending attacks on America. He did nothing to warn the American people because he needed this war on terrorism." And what did this revelation bring to Lt. Col. Butler? Answer: his dismissal from the U.S. Military.

NBC News weighed in with a similar story, reporting, "Only two days before the September 11 attacks on New York and Washington, President Bush was given a 'detailed war plan' to dismantle Osama bin Laden's network."
I could begin delving into all the "did Bush know" evidence, but instead I'd like to show how various characters in the public eye are tied to the War Machine and the oil industry. One of these men is Richard Clark, who has the following credentials:

Chief of the CSG (Counter-terrorism Security Group)
Member of the Cyber Security Task Force
Member of the Homeland Security Council
Member of the Critical Infrastructure Protection Committee
Coordinator, National Security Council on Counter-Terrorism

In other words, if anyone in America knows about security, it's Richard Clarke. In fact, it's been said that this man worked virtually day and night during 2001 in the CSG, and was exposed to tremendous amounts of information on the threat of impending terrorist attacks. Clarke even commented on the intelligence data he received on the upcoming Al Qaeda attack: "It all came together in the third week of June. The CIA's view was that a major terrorist attack was coming in the next several weeks."
On May 23, 2002, *MSNBC* confirmed that Richard Clarke advised the FAA to issue warnings about possible hijacking threats. And when did

he do that? June 22, 2001. Then, on July 5, 2001, he called a CSG meeting, followed by a get-together with Condaleeza Rice and Bush Chief of Staff Andrew Card. After that, he met again with the CSG, FBI, FAA, and INS (Immigration and Naturalization Services). At these meetings he was quoted as saying, "Something spectacular is going to happen." What do you think he was referring to – the National Tiddlywinks Championship in Hoboken? Hardly.

In that same month (July, 2001), Clarke was also aware of a meeting between the Pakistani and Taliban Ambassadors in Karachi where they discussed rumors of an Al-Qaeda attack on America. That's two months before 9-11. Clarke also knew the ISI (Pakistani Intelligence) Lt. General Ahmad instructed a Mr. Ahmad Uman Sheikh to wire $100,000 to Mohammed Atta, who was considered the mastermind of the attacks.

It seems like a lot is going on, especially when *Newsweek* Magazine reported that on September 10th the Pentagon put its employees on HIGH ALERT and told them to cancel all flights on 9-11. Also, add this little tidbit to the mix. In July, 2001, at the Group of Eight Summit held in Genoa, Italy, plans were already being discussed to oust the Fundamentalist Islamic Taliban from power. And who in America was promoting these plans? Well, they're cryptically referred to as "Team B" and include:

Paul Wolfowitz: Deputy Secretary of Defense
Richard Perle: who holds a National Security policy-making post and attended a Bilderberg meeting in 1985
Paul Nitze: National Security Advisor

Another "Team B" member is the Sunday morning talk-show pundit and propagandist William Kristol. This guy is a CFR member, Bilderberg attendee, and publisher of the *Weekly Standard* which is owned by Rupert Murdoch. To place this publication in context, Rupert Murdoch is controlled by the Rothschild, Bronfman, and Oppenheimer families, who along with Murdoch, are known as the "Billionaire Gang of Four." The Kristol family also owns the publishing company "National Affairs, Inc." on whose board is none other than Henry Kissinger. (His name sure does keep popping up a lot, doesn't it?)

Essentially, then, I've listed these names because oftentimes people in this field refer to those in power as some sort of faceless, nameless entity. Well, I'll give you names. What you have to do is follow-up on them by researching, reading the American Free Press, and finding out for yourself how these war-hawks fit into the puzzle. Right now, it's oil and war. Those are the two primary ingredients to our current situation.

Look at Lynn Cheney, wife of Vice President Dick Cheney. She recently resigned from the Board of Directors of one of America's premier companies – Lockheed Martin. Who are they? Only the world's largest weapons producer that sell F-16's to Oman and the United Arab Emirates, MLRS (Multiple Launch Rocket Systems) to Egypt, and F-16's, C130 transport planes, and P-3 surveillance crafts to Pakistan. (All of these countries, by the way, are in or surround the Middle East.) Her husband, Dick Cheney, was also on the Board of TRW, another huge arms dealer. And Condaleeza Rice was a member of Chevron's board. If you start doing a little digging, you'll find plenty of these 'coincidences.' The only problem is; why won't Dan Rather spell it out like this on the *CBS Evening News*? Maybe the billionaire media moguls don't want you to make the connection! Why? Because war, which results in social unrest and chaos, tends to make people turn to their government for answers, thus laying even MORE POWER in their laps. Do you see how it all comes together?

UNOCAL

Before we proceed any further, we should return to the first phase of this mess, which is the Caspian Sea region where $5 trillion worth of oil and natural gas resources are ripe for the picking. There is also the country of Turkmenistan, which boasts the world's third largest gas reserves, and is in a prime spot to provide oil to the markets of China, India, and Japan. The only problem – there is a troublesome little country near these reserves – you guessed it – Afghanistan. Thus, the key to our current troubles are best explained in economic terms by the Indian Press: "Uzbekistan, Tajikistan, Kazakhstan, and Turkmenistan are threatened by the Taliban that is aiming to control their vast oil, gas, and other resources by bringing Islamic Fundamentalism to power."

Can you see the conflict? The Taliban wanted to control the oil (and opium fields, also), and so did an array of American energy companies. Which ones? Well, there was Amoco, Chevron, Exxon, Mobil, Unocal, Enron, and the UK's British Petroleum. So remember, there's a lot at stake in this part of the world because the biggest industries known to man are energy, usury, drugs, and war. And all four are ready-made to be exploited. Afghanistan produces 75% of the world's heroin supply, there is oil & gas galore, and when nations go to war, they need to borrow money at interest (usury) from the Controller's international banks. Very convenient, huh? As James Dorian stated in the *Oil & Gas Journal*: "Those who control the oil routes out of Central Asia will impact all future direction and quantities of flow and the distribution of revenues from new production." In other words, we're talking about who's going to control the future direction of the world!

The timeline for this debacle began in 1997 when Centgas (Central Asia Gas Pipeline Consortium) proposed a 790 mile pipeline from Turkmenistan through Afghanistan to Pakistan. To convey how important this project is, President Clinton sent his Under Secretary of State Karl Underforth to meet with some Taliban high-rollers in December, 1997. In America, meanwhile, Unocal had tossed their dice and secured 46.5% controlling share in this endeavor.

In January, 1998 the Taliban signed an agreement to let a $2 billion natural gas pipeline be built from Turkmenistan to Pakistan. (Keep an eye on Pakistan; they play a prominent role in this process.) But civil unrest continued to plague Afghanistan, and within one year, by December 1998, Unocal pulled out of the deal, saying they wouldn't invest any more money until an "internationally recognized government" was in place. (Did you notice the words "internationally recognized" – do they sound eerily familiar to something that would fit into the Globalist's New World Order scheme?) Unocal also bailed out of the Centgas consortium, which had as one of its member companies Halliburton. Now think for a second. Who in the current Bush administration is connected to Halliburton (providing him with a $23 million retirement package)? Yup, Dick Cheney!

One of the people who acted in the role of consultant to Unocal was none other than Henry Kissinger. (Here he is again!) Kissinger is also associated with, among other companies, the Daily Telegraph, Hollinger, the CFR (Council on Foreign Relations), the Defense Policy Board, and served as a negotiator with India for the National Security Council. Do you think 'ol Henry K knows what's going on in the world and is up to his eyeballs in it?

Anyway, as you can see, the trouble in Afghanistan began in 1998 with a conflict between Unocal's oil interests and the Taliban's desire to maintain control of that area. Reporter Nina Burleigh described the situation as such: "So many big deals, so much oil; all those big players with powerful connections to the Bush administration. There is a significant money subtext that the American public ought to know about as "Operation Enduring Freedom" blasts new holes where pipelines might be buried someday."

Marty Miller, Unocal Vice President, also weighed in with this assessment. "No other import project can provide such volume of natural gas to the markets of India and Pakistan at a lower price."

Hmmm, now we're getting somewhere. Y'see, India and Pakistan are currently huge markets on the rise, and are slated for even bigger growth in the future due to their ability to be economically exploited. But before Unocal and Centgas could move forward with their plans, they had to overcome one roadblock – the Taliban and those who want to keep this area as their own. So, to ease everyone's fears, an "internationally recognized" government had to be established. To do so, the power-brokers needed to take control of Afghanistan (using terrorism as a guise), while they kept moving eastward in their search for more oil.

PAKISTAN

As I said earlier, the Pakistani government has a crucial vested interest in what's taking place in Afghanistan because this unstable country is the only thing between them and the rich oil fields of Turkmenistan. If the Taliban could be erased from this area, the flow of oil to this country would be dramatically increased. And, considering how close they were to entering a full-scale war with their enemy India, Pakistan is extremely interested in ousting the Taliban (even though they're also the world's largest supporter of terrorism)! To them, a pipeline reaching across Afghanistan would be like manna falling from heaven.

What makes this situation so curious is that the Taliban are primarily a thorn in the side of two major countries – American and the "official" Pakistani government. But guess who worked hand-in-hand to form the Taliban in the first place – the CIA and the ISI, Pakistan's secret service! As the highly regarded *Jane's Defense Weekly* described it, "Half of the Taliban manpower and equipment originated in Pakistan under the ISI" (which is very much controlled by the Fundamentalists).

But similar to America's view of the Taliban, Pakistan's perspective also changed once they saw they were getting out of control. In fact, the only secret service agency NOT to contact our CIA with warnings of the impending 9-11 attacks was the ISI! The United Kingdom did, as did Germany, Italy, Jordan, Egypt, France, Israel, and Morocco.

All of them gave us indications that trouble was on the horizon – all except Pakistan (who was the closest to them). I wonder why? Could it be that they wanted a war with the Taliban as badly as those who control our oil companies and War Machine did? Even more incriminating is that Pakistani General Mahmud Ahmad was in Washington, D.C. from September 4–15, 2001 (during the time of the 9-11 attacks) meeting with a variety of governmental and defense big-wigs. To make matters even more curious, his visit with Condaleeza Rice was altered (censored) in the official White House transcripts. Strange? Indeed.

CHAPTER TEN

THE CARLYLE GROUP

A few weeks ago, James Baker publicly offered advice to the Bush Administration on how they should proceed with their war on Iraq. What he and every newscaster or commentator failed to mention was that Baker is now employed by the highly-influential Carlyle Group, which is the eleventh largest defense contractor in the United States. In essence, then, we have a man trying to influence public policy while privately employed by a company that has a vested interest in activating America's War Machine.

If you're not familiar with them, the Carlyle Group has become a powerhouse in affecting the direction in which our foreign policy takes, especially in regard to war. They accomplish this by hiring former government officials, then investing in private companies that are subject to government change (i.e. the military and telecommunications). Who, you may ask, do they employ to secure their government contracts? Well, check-out this list for starters:

Frank Carlucci	Department of Health, Education and Welfare
	Deputy Director, CIA – 1978-81
	Deputy Secretary of Defense – 1981-82
	National Security Director – 1987-89
George Bush	CIA Director – 1976-77
	Vice President of the United States – 1981-89
	President of the United States – 1989-93
James Baker	Chief of Staff – 1981-85
	Secretary of the Treasury – 1985-89
	Secretary of State – 1989-93
Dick Darman	Former White House Budget Chief
William Kennard	Former Head, FCC
Arthur Levitt	Former Head, SEC
John Major	Former Prime Minister, Britain
Fidel Ramos	Former Philippine President
Afsaneh Beschloss	Treasurer & Chief Investment Officer of the World Bank

Anand Panyarachum	Former President, Thailand
Karl Otto Pohl	Former President, Bundesbank
Louis Vuitton	French Aerobus Company
Park Tae Joon	Former South Korean Prime Minister
Alwaleed Sin Talal bin Abdulaziz Alsaud – Saudi Arabian Prince
George Soros	New World Order/Bilderberg luminary & int'l financier
Fred Malek	George Bush Sr's campaign manager

There is also one other "family" that invested in the Carlyle Group, but I'll keep that as a surprise for a later article. In the meantime, take a look at that list. It's like walking onto a baseball field and having the New York Yankees behind you. The best team money can buy! And I didn't even mention all of the players. Carlyle also employs the former chairman of BMW and Nestle, is interviewing former Clinton cabinet members (to insure that they have both sides of the aisle covered), plus once hired Colin Powell and AOL Time-Warner Chairman Steve Case to speak at a meeting at Washington D.C.'s Monarch House. Plus, if we look at James Baker again, we'll find that he's on the board of Azerbaijan International Oil Company, in which two U.S. oil companies hold 40% of the shares. Who are these two companies? The first is Amoco, who has on their payroll none other than Zbigniew Brzezinski (Trilateral Commission founder, National Security Advisor for the Carter Administration, Globalist supreme, and David Rockefeller's puppet on a string). The second is Pennzoil, who has on their payroll Brent Scowcroft, former National Security Advisor under George Bush, Sr.

But the man that really brought it all together is Frank Carlucci, who holds directorships on such companies as General Dynamics, Westinghouse, the Rand Corporation, and Ashland Oil, plus sits on the board of directors of twelve other companies. Carlucci was also the college classmate of someone very closely related to our current administration's War Machine – Defense Secretary Donald Rumsfeld! What relevance does this association have, you may wonder? I think it is of great importance, for in February, 2001, Carlucci and Vice President Dick Cheney met with Donald Rumsfeld when the Carlyle Group had several billion-dollar defense projects under consideration. (If you haven't guessed, the Carlyle Group fared quite well when all was said and done.) Do you still think these ties don't matter? Philip Agee, in his book "On the Run" details all of Carlucci's CIA connections, many of whom he hired (along with his Pentagon cronies) when he joined Carlyle in 1989. (And all of us know what influence the CIA has, don't we?)

A former Carlyle employee honed-in on these dynamics when he said, "The firm understands that having Bush and Major is like having movie stars around."

It's all about power and access, folks, as Oliver Burkeman and Julian Burger pointed out in *The Guardian* on October 31, 2001. "Carlyle has become the thread which indirectly links American military policy in Afghanistan to the personal financial fortunes of its celebrity employees, not the least the current President's father."

Is the picture becoming clearer? Now we're getting to the bottom of America's War Machine. The Carlyle Group is set to make huge amounts of money from our upcoming military conflicts and weapons expenditures. In other words, when I talk about the War Machine, these folks are at the crux of it. They're the war profiteers that keep its wheels greased!

Dan K. Thomasson, former editor of the Scripps Howard News Service, summed it up best in March, 2001. "Nothing in recent history seems to approach the success this group has had in the wholesale conversion of former high government rank to gigantic profits."

Peter Eisner, Managing Director of the Center for Public Integrity, adds, "It should be a deep cause for concern that a closely held company like Carlyle can simultaneously have directors and advisors that are doing business and making money and also advising the President of the United States."

The Washington Business Journal simply says, "The Carlyle Group seems to play by a different set of rules."

But who is the Carlyle Group? Well, their office is located only a few blocks from the White House, and it was founded by three men:

David Rubinstein – aide in the Carter Administration
Bill Conway – Chief Financial Officer at MCI
Dan D'Aniello – financial executive at Marriott

They named their group "Carlyle" after a New York hotel favored by one of their first investors, the Mellon family. They now have an ownership stake in 164 different companies, have 535 investors, operate in 55 different countries, and have $13.5 billion in capital. International financier George Soros invested $100 million in them, while the

California Public Employees Retirement System dumped $305 million into their laps. They also recently purchased the KorAm Bank, thus accelerating their entry into the highly lucrative Asian markets.

But how did they become so successful so quickly? I'll let the Carlyle Group's company brochure answer that question: "We invest in niche opportunities created in industries heavily affected by changes in government policies." Stated differently, the Carlyle Group buys what it knows best – companies regulated by the government. In fact, 2/3 of their business is either in the defense or telecommunications industries ... those affected by changes in government spending or policy!

And how do they affect these policies? It all revolves around ACCESS! That's the key. Basically, they operate within what is called the "Iron Triangle" – industry, government, and the military. A spokesman for Oklahoma Representative J. C. Watts understood this connection when he said, "Carlyle's strength was within the Department of Defense because they have staff types that work behind the scenes, in the dark, that know everything about the Army and Capitol Hill."

Charles Lewis, ex-Director at the Center for Public Integrity, adds credence to this argument. "Carlyle is as deeply wired into the current administration as they can possibly be."

On May 5, 2001, the *New York Times* described the Carlyle Group as such: "It owns so many companies that it is now in effect one of the nation's biggest defense contractors and a force in global communications. Its blue-chip investors include major banks and insurance companies, billion dollar pension funds and wealthy investors." Hmm, it looks like they have a firm, controlling grip on both the War Machine and the media ... convenient, don't you think?

After reading how deeply established they are as "Insiders," do you think that the Carlyle Group has America's best interests at heart, or their own which entails capitalizing on war? An excellent example can be found in the recent $470 million contract that "United Defense," a Carlyle subsidiary, received. And what did they get it for? To develop the CRUSADER, a faulty, antiquated, horrendous product that was described by Eric Miller of "The Project on Government Oversight" as follows: "The Crusader has been the GAO's (Government Accounting Office) poster child for bad weapons development." The Crusader Project was so maligned that the government was set to drop it completely. But lo and behold, what happened? War was on the horizon, Carlyle pulled a few strings, and welluh – a $470 million contract was thrown Carlyle's way for the Crusader. Funny how things happen, huh?

If that's not bad enough, the Carlyle Group is also the financial advisor to a certain government. Who? Saudi Arabia. In fact, they make nearly $50 million/year training the Saudi Arabian National Guard --- troops that are sworn to protect the Saudi royal family! Now, if all hell breaks loose in the Middle East, and considering that Saudi Arabia is tentative about supporting our efforts against Iraq, who do you think the Saudi soldiers will kill - their own kind – Arabs – or the invading "white American devils?"

If you ask me, we've entered very treacherous waters, all for the sake of making money off of warfare. Regardless of what they say, these men in the Carlyle Group epitomize a very nefarious form of evil via their actions.

CHAPTER ELEVEN

THE BUSH – BIN LADEN FAMILY CONNECTION

When I wrote about the Carlyle Group having an inordinate amount of access to the current administration which is used for their own personal gain, some people may not have realized the general importance of this situation. So, to begin showing you how closely the Carlyle Group is interconnected with both the Bush and bin Laden families, let's start at the beginning.

In the early 1990's, the Carlyle Group (out of the kindness of their heart) chose to take a struggling businessman under their wing and give him a position in their company. But this wasn't just any old job. No, they put this individual on the Board of one of their subsidiaries – CaterAir. That would be commendable in most instances, except that this employee wouldn't be categorized as one of the most brilliant men in the world. But that didn't matter because the person in question who landed this gravy job was none other than George W. Bush. Yup, to keep him occupied until he could be "selected" to his future job as Governor of Texas, the Carlyle Group lent a helping hand.

But lo and behold, one hand quickly washed the other, for after George W. became Governor, he appointed several people to a Board that controlled the money invested by the Texas Teacher's Pension Fund – a total of $100 million! So, this board decides to invest this PUBLIC MONEY with a certain group. Guess who it was. Yup, you're right – the Carlyle Group! In addition, another entity – the University of Texas Board of Regents – invested millions of dollars, too. And guess which way it went. I'll be damned, but it also went to the Carlyle Group. So, let's see – Texas, Bush, money, and the Carlyle Group. A mere coincidence? Who knows? But I'm reminded of that old saying – follow the money. A case in point is Wayne Berman, a Washington consultant and George W. Bush fundraiser who got kickbacks of $900,000+ after Connecticut State Treasurer Paul Silvester pushed tens of millions of dollars of state pension funds to the investment portfolio of a certain group. And which group would that be? Yup, Carlyle!

Are things starting to smell a little fishy? Maybe it doesn't matter that oil companies gave thirteen-times more money to the Bush campaign in 2000 than they did to Gore, and that electric companies gave seven-times more. And this is coming from someone – me – that wouldn't vote for Al Gore if my very life depended on it. (Hell, I wouldn't want to vote for George Bush either if my life depended on it!) The point I'm trying to make is that there are tons of dirty dealings and shenanigans going on behind the scenes that aren't getting reported in the mainstream media.

Don't believe me? Well, how about this one. In December, 2001, Frank Carlucci and James Baker (both Carlyle representatives) met at the Ritz-Carlton in Washington, D.C. for their annual investor conference. Also in attendance were the representatives of another important family that had invested huge amounts of money in the Carlyle Group. And what family were these individuals from? Hold your breath, but it was the BIN LADEN Family. Worse, another famous politician was rumored to be at this same meeting after he SPENT THE NIGHT AT THE WHITE HOUSE with George W. Bush. And who was it that supposedly met with the bin Laden family after spending the night at 1600 Pennsylvania Avenue? Answer: George Bush, Sr.!

Things are getting even stickier, huh? Well, Larry Klayman, spokesman for *Judicial Watch*, comments on this subject. "The idea of the President's father, an ex-President himself, doing business with a company under investigation by the FBI in the terror attacks of September 11 is horrible. President Bush should not ask, but demand that his father pull out of the Carlyle Group."

Tom Fitton, President of *Judicial Watch*, echoes this sentiment. "For the father of our current President to be doing business with foreign governments, there is a clear conflict of interest."

Now some of you may be wondering, "Hey, did I read correctly a couple of paragraphs ago – that the Bush family was doing business with the bin Laden family?" Regrettably, yes you did. Here's the story. Back in the early 1970s when George Bush started his first company, Arbusto Energy, Inc, his first business partner was Salem bin Laden. Yes, Osama bin Laden's brother! This fact is confirmed by the United Kingdom's "Daily Mail" which wrote that Salem bin Laden, "Invested heavily in Bush's first business venture." Salem is also a close friend of Saudi Arabia's King Fahd.

Now some may say, hey, that was a long time ago. Let bygones be bygones. But how does that account, then, for George Bush Sr.'s meeting TWICE with the bin Laden family prior to the 9-11 attacks, the second time being in January, 2000? Or how the bin Laden's have been frequented by Bush, James Baker, and Frank Carlucci over the past few years in Jeddah, Saudi Arabia?

Charles Freeman, President of the Middle East Policy Council, has said of the clandestine relationship, "If there were ever any company closely connected to the U.S. and its presence in Saudi Arabia, it's the bin Laden Group. They're the establishment Osama's trying to overthrow."

This information changes the entire complexion of the "War on Terrorism" doesn't it? I mean, the bin Laden family initially invested $2 million into the Carlyle Group, but that's only what's been 'seen.' A foreign investor with ties to the bin Laden's told the European *Wall Street Journal* on September 28, 2001 that, "The family's overall interest with Carlyle is considerable larger." And according to the *Wall Street Journal* on September 27, 2001, guess who brokered these deals between the bin Laden's and Carlyle? Good 'ol George Bush, Sr.!

So, due to the touchy nature of this relationship, the bin Laden's pulled their investment money out of Carlyle in October 2001. But let's stop for a moment and examine this situation. George Bush has invested money into the Carlyle Group, and is also employed by them. Likewise, the bin Laden's were substantial investors in the Carlyle Group, and have had business ties with George Bush for 30 years since the early 1970s. Now you have to ask yourself, how does the Carlyle Group derive a large percentage of their revenue? Answer: From foreign military contracts and America's War Machine!

Zeroing in on this sinister configuration of forces, the *Wall Street Journal*, on September 27, 2001 in their "Special Report: Aftermath of Terror" section stated: "If the United States boosts defense spending in the quest to stop Osama bin Laden's alleged terrorist activities, there may be one unexpected beneficiary: Mr. bin Laden's family."

Is it starting to sink in yet? George Bush, Sr. is tied to the Carlyle Group and America's War Machine like the spots on a leopard. And guess what his son – the current President of the United States – wants to do within the next month or so – wage another war in the Middle East. And the bin Laden family, former investors in the Carlyle Group, also have a direct family member acting as key player in this scenario – their brother, Osama bin Laden.

Sons, brothers, business ties, investments, the Carlyle Group, huge amounts of profits to be made, oil pipelines running across Afghanistan, and America's War Machine. Do these connections and inter-related "coincidences" stink to high heaven? You better believe they do.

CHAPTER TWELVE

BANKS, OIL, AND DRUG TRAFFICKING: AN OVERVIEW OF MIKE RUPPERT'S "THE TRUTH AND LIES OF 9-11"

Mike Ruppert, a former investigator for the Los Angeles Police Department, begins his *The Truth and Lies of 9-11* videotape by offering a $1,000 cash reward to anyone that can disprove the information contained within his presentation. To date, the money still stands, and no one has been able to dispute even one iota of the wealth of evidence that Mr. Ruppert provides. This is the case because Ruppert unequivocally states that he structured his arguments to avoid speculation, theorization, or hypothesis. In other words, he used the exact same procedure – facts and evidence to build a case - that benefited him as an investigator for the LAPD.

And what has Ruppert uncovered during his research? Well, quite simply that our government no longer serves the interests of everyday American citizens, and that it is now our responsibility to reach out to the REST of America – to those people who still aren't aware of the truth – and fill them in on what's going on. Thus, in this overview, I will show how Mike Ruppert has gathered an astounding amount of evidence pointing to the fact that the 9-11 attacks were part of a larger scheme involving oil, drug trafficking, and the collapse of the American economy. He accomplishes this feat by using the government and the mass media's own statements and evidence against them – exposing the entire charade like the Wizard of Oz behind his curtain.

OIL

In 1998, the head of the Unocal Corporation announced to a House International Committee that it was calling off plans to build a 1,500 mile pipeline across Afghanistan to Pakistan, where United States tankers would then transport the oil to China and Japan, where there exists a huge oil shortage. They would not proceed, he testified, until a "stable international government was established."

Well, four years later, guess what's happening in Afghanistan. Construction on the oil pipeline has begun once again because the "problem" has been taken care of. All we needed to do was bomb the hell out of that country; get rid of the Taliban, and put Hamid Karzai into office as the new head of Afghanistan. (Karzai was, by the way, a former consultant for one of America's major oil companies. Guess which one. Yup – Unocal!) Another funny coincidence is that Henry Kissinger recently took on an advisory role to the Chinese firm that will be importing the oil, plus he also works for a Pakistani firm transporting oil to the Orient. Funny how he's always in the picture, huh.

ZBIGNIEW BRZEZINSKI

For a broader perspective on this situation, we need to turn our attention to Zbigniew the Mad Dog, who wrote a book in 1997 entitled *The Grand Chessboard*. In this work he said that if America wanted to maintain its status as king of the hill, it had to move into the Eurasian area and "manage" its people and natural resources or else anarchy would ensue. And why is this region so important? Well, Zbig states that 75% of the world's physical wealth (including gold and oil) exist in this area, and if America didn't move in, somebody else would. So, what did we do? First off, the CIA created the Islamic Fundamentalist Taliban to keep the USSR from moving south into Afghanistan, Turkmenistan, etc. Then, Goldman Sachs, the U.S. Treasury, the World Bank, and the Federal Reserve looted $300 billion out of Russia. By the 1990's, with a "block" in place around Soviet Russia and depleted of its financial strength, the average lifespan of a Soviet male is now 48 years of age!

So, Russia won't interfere with the oil fields in Eurasia, but then another problem popped-up. The pesky Islamic Fundamentalists started wanting their piece of the pie, so we had to take action against them. The best part is, Zbig knew all of this in 1997, and troops have been getting ready for this battle ever since.

This scenario now leads us to the "big picture," which is as follows: from 1993-2015, oil consumption will double, most of it occurring in the rapidly developing Far East. To keep up with this demand, oil companies will be tapping into reserves in the Eurasian region which dwarf those in the Middle East. So, what we're looking at is one last push to dominate this area. For, whoever controls Eurasia and the Middle East will essentially rule the energy market, and subsequently the world. (If this weren't the case, why do we so adamantly refuse to develop alternative fuel sources?) The final step in the puzzle, then, is to have the United States, the world's final superpower, bow down to the New World Order as the Europeans did with their European Union.

But to pull-off this Grand Deception, we need one final war to put all the pieces (people and countries) in their proper place. So, to get Americans fired-up in a big way, an external threat was created (via the 9-11 attacks), and welluh, the Controllers soon had their support as Osama bin Laden-hatred peaked to a fevered pitch.

ECONOMY AND BANKING

To complicate an already precarious situation, Ruppert contends that prior to 9-11, America was on the verge of a financial collapse and that the Controllers NEEDED this perceived catastrophe to keep their house of cards from tumbling. If one examines the stock market collapse(s), the number of bankruptcies that are occurring (at record rates), and how much of our manufacturing base is being lost overseas (thanks to the GATT and NAFTA treaties), its hard not to concur with this statement.

CIA DRUG TRAFFICKING

As hard as it is to believe for many people, one of the CIA's primary roles is to support the United States economy by bringing illegal drugs into this country. How can this be, you ask? Well, one of the CIA's main responsibilities is to provide much needed cash flow to banks and stock trading houses. If you find this relationship hard to swallow, why did six of the first seven CIA directors come directly from Wall Street, with many others having strong ties to the banking community? What does being an Intelligence director have to do with high-finance? The answer can be found with George Bush, Sr. His father, Prescott, was a financial director for the Brown Brothers Harriman subsidiary (Union Banking Company) that directly financed Hitler before and during WWII by laundering money for the Nazi War Machine.

But let's get back to the importance of drug trafficking and money. In a January, 2001 report, it was disclosed that $1.5 trillion/year is laundered through the world's banking system, and that approximately $500-600 (about 1/3) comes from the drug trade. The CIA's role, then, is to make sure that as much drug money as possible comes into our economy.

Ruppert even goes so far as to say that illegal drug trafficking is the fastest growing industry in America, and that the growth of many multinational companies and international banks was financed through the sale of illegal drugs. And who's the leader in laundering this narcotics money? American banks. To support this claim, Ruppert references a survey of top business and banking leaders. 99 out of 100 of these corporate leaders said that it would be better to keep $500 billion/year of laundered money going through the system than it would be to stop the flow of illegal drugs into our country. For, if we stopped laundering this money, mutual funds would plummet, the stock market would crash, and any possibility of paying off our national debt would be futile (as it already is). We are, regrettably, addicted to drug profiteering in this country.

To further blow your minds, guess what companies are exempt FROM THE LAW in regard to money laundering:

- Banks
- The CIA
- Publicly listed companies that trade on the New York Stock Exchange!

Ruppert backs this up with reports filed by the Government in relation to a United States corporate drug money laundering conference! And if you watch this video, you'll be astounded by which companies were represented at this conference. He also gives examples of how internationally recognized banks buy notorious drug-laundering institutions to get better access to the free-flow of cash, plus names three specific CIA sponsored drug-running operations: Amadeus, Pegasus, and Watchtower. If this isn't enough, Ruppert provides a memo dated February 11, 1982 where Attorney General William Casey tells CIA Director William French Smith how his organization can get away with dealing drugs without having to report it in any official manner. He also has DOCUMENTED proof of $1 billion worth of cocaine being found on a CIA jet in Mexico City, and how DEA Agent Castillo saw CIA planes unloading drugs from 1985-86. Upon reporting his findings DIRECTLY to George Bush, Sr., he was told, "Leave it alone, it's a White House operation!" Can you see what's going on? In no uncertain terms, our very own government is running drugs into our country to poison its own citizens. The CIA and the U.S. Government are drug dealers, plain and simple!

Why do you think we're so obsessed with Afghanistan, a remote, desolate country that is, by all appearances, not very remarkable? To find an answer, you have to see things the way our government does. Before

1980, Afghanistan produced 0% of the world's opium. But then the CIA moved in, and by 1986 they were producing 40% of the world's heroin supply. By 1999, they were churning out 3,200 TONS of heroin a year – nearly 80% of the total market supply.

But then something unexpected happened. The Taliban rose to power, and by 2000 they had destroyed nearly all of the opium fields. Production dropped from 3,000+ tons to only 185 tons, a 94% reduction! This enormous drop in revenue subsequently hurt not only the CIA's Black Budget projects, but also the free-flow of laundered money in and out of the Controller's banks. If you ask me, it seems like these powerful folks didn't like this turn of events (and the easy money being taken out of their pockets). So, to retaliate, we went to war with them, and now guess what's happening. The Afghanistan Northern Alliance, backed by the CIA, chased the Taliban out and re-planted all the opium crops again. Even more horrifying is that while the opium crops were destroyed, the Afghanistan farmers were planting actual FOOD crops such as wheat so that their people could eat. But then the CIA went in, dug-up the wheat, and re-seeded the opium fields. Y'know, when you think about these actions, it's downright sickening. So now the Afghanistan rebels run the poppy fields, and everything is back to normal (albeit a very dirty, corrupt normalcy).

So, with this very interesting foundation laid; Mr. Ruppert delves into the truth and lies behind the 9-11 terrorist attacks, even providing names, such as: the bin Laden-Bush family connection, the Carlyle Group, Israel's Mossad, Colin Powell, General Mahmud and the ISI (Pakistani Secret Service), insider stock trading, the Air Force's deliberate failure to scramble jets, the FBI's Echelon wiretapping program, "Operation Northwoods," and much more.

For the fullest and most complete 9-11 timeline and behind-the-scenes truth of what really happened, I strongly urge you to order this videotape. It's either that, or keep getting snowed by the mass media's controlled lies. The TRUTH is out there; all you have to do is uncover it!

SECTION

THREE:

CONTROL

SYSTEMS

CHAPTER THIRTEEN

THE PSYCHOLOGY OF CONTROL SYSTEMS

Let's examine the current situation that exists in this country between "liberals" and "conservatives." Each side has its supposed "agenda," but when it comes right down to it, these "labels" are all part of a larger shell game.

It's reminiscent of the Wizard of Oz where both sides are doing the dirty work of a hidden figure that is lurking behind a curtain. And although these individuals may disagree on the particulars, they all want the same end, so they use a variety of different means to attain it.

Two of these tactics are distraction and disinformation. The Controllers keep everyone fighting each other instead of focusing their energy on the real enemy. They do it by clandestinely financing each opposing group, then standing back to watch the aftermath as they fight like cats and dogs.

I'll explain myself better by using a trailer park as the setting. Let's pretend that a man named Mr. Thomas runs the park, and collects a fair amount of money from each rented lot. The services he provides are minimal, and the place is falling apart with disrepair. Now, pretend for a moment that this trailer park could be in the Old West where Frontier Justice prevailed. The last thing Mr. Thomas wants is insurrection from the people. If they get upset with him, they'd form vigilante groups and rush the office, then burn it to the ground.

How does Mr. Thomas alleviate this situation? As the folks come in each month to pay their rent, he asks about their gripes. After getting a feel for what's on their mind, he notices there are specific groups that have a variety of complaints. Regrettably, this information is all that he needs. Why? Because Mr. Thomas can then get a few of the "leader-types" and take them aside (in private, of course) and tell them to form groups that will represent their interests and combat the troublemakers. He'll also establish "citizen groups" to "police" the trailer court.

The leaders now have a sense of self-importance and a stake in their "cause," and thus begin implementing their agendas. In no time there are signs and flyers posted all around the trailer court:

- No lawn mowing after 7 PM
- No hanging laundry on clotheslines (due to its ugliness)
- No motor scooters

Some of the people will like certain laws, and others won't. In no time, what will happen? The people from one group are going to be fighting those from another group. You have the mowers, laundry hangers and bikers all aiming their animosities at those who have established a "rule" or "law" that prevents them from realizing their specific vested interests.

As they scream and fight and argue with each other, guess what is also simultaneously happening? All of their attention has been diverted away from Mr. Thomas, the real villain. Every tenant still has to pay rent each month, and when they come into the office, Mr. Thomas naturally tells them he's on their side in the battle. To keep tensions high, though, new "crises" need to be created to insure that the people are kept in a state of constant battle.

How Machiavellian, huh? The people will keep aiming their energies at each other and quit paying attention to Mr. Thomas altogether. Over time, he'll slowly raise their rent and indirectly restrict their freedoms by instigating other groups to make new rules that will "improve their standard of living."

Now, just think what would happen if Mr. Thomas started clandestinely financing each of these groups like our government does via the CIA.

This leads me to a rather funny scenario. Imagine that the *New York Times* ran a headline which read:

"ALIENS INVADING EARTH! Vow To Destroy Our Planet Tomorrow"

One of their star reporters then proceeds to ask a number of groups their opinion of this matter:

Head of the NAACP: "We beg the aliens to recognize the strides we've made with civil rights, and to not discriminate against us."

Head of NOW (National Organization of Women): "Women have come a long way, and we vow to not become second class citizens to the male-dominated alien race."

Jesse Jackson, Rainbow Coalition: "The white Massah ET business-owner must be more tolerant of his under-privileged inner-city ghetto plantation workers."

Head of Planned Parenthood: "The aliens will not tell us how we can use our bodies. The right to abort our children is still our first and foremost choice."

Head of the ADL (Anti-Defamation League): "We'll never forget the Holocaust, and we implore the aliens to help us find some more 98 year-old Nazi war criminals."

Head of the Republican Party: We hope the extra-terrestrials share our conservative family values, and will help us lower taxes and pass a balanced budget amendment."

Head of GLAD (Gays and Lesbians against Discrimination): "We beg these intruders to show tolerance toward our alternative lifestyles, and to accept us into the Boy Scouts."

Head of the Democratic Party: "We want to pass a tax on the fuel that the aliens used to get here, and also another real estate tax on the ground where they've parked their spacecraft."

Do you get it? The world's going to explode in 24 hours and these people are still so myopic they can't see past their little "causes." I don't know. Maybe I'm giving them too much credit. They are, after all, nothing but simple pawns in the Grand Drama ... little marionettes whose strings are being pulled by the Big Boys lurking behind the scene.

So, there ya have it - business as usual.

CHAPTER FOURTEEN

YES, VIRGINIA, THERE IS A NEW WORLD ORDER

Do you think it's conceivable that, considering their sick, evil motives, certain elements of the Secret Cabal could have had pre-knowledge of the terrorist acts on September 11? Before answering, realize there was an abundance of evidence hinting that the Lusitania was going to be sunk, thus "forcing" us into World War I (a war the United States adamantly wanted to stay out of). A couple decades later, Franklin Delano Roosevelt and his elitist handlers were aware that Pearl Harbor was going to be bombed by the Japanese. They allowed it to take place, though, so the American people would be enraged enough to enter World War II.

That's not the end of these horrendous practices ... not by a long shot. During the 1960s, *Operation Northwoods* was a proposed military plan where we would stage *phony* attacks against American citizens right after the Bay of Pigs fiasco to insure our people would get so disgusted, they'd gladly allow us to invade Cuba once again. Luckily, JFK nixed the plan, but it may have cost him his life in doing so.

Propaganda was admittedly used prior to our war against Iraq. You remember the stories about how the Iraqi's were butchering babies in hospitals. Our government confessed that the entire story was a LIE to entice us into that battle. Finally, in Chapter 43, I relay a considerable amount of evidence that points to additional bombs being placed inside Oklahoma's Murrah Federal Building by "inside sources," the ultimate goal being to discredit and ultimately wipe out the Patriot movement.

All of these events were dramatic and grand in scale in order to not only shock the public, but to appeal to their basest instincts of bloodlust and revenge. After the dust settled, our entry into whatever battle was currently being waged could then be legitimized.

I've been saying for years that the Dan Rather State-run news is nothing more than professional wrestling. We have O.J., Jon Benet, the Long Island Lolita, Bill & Monica, then Gary Condit. It's all filled with soap opera drama, sex, violence, and enough titillation to keep the people perched in front of their TV's or buying the latest newspaper and scandal sheet.

But every once in awhile when the Controllers need to move forward and take action, the "play" becomes real and people get killed. Pearl Harbor -- 2,500 dead. Oklahoma City -- 168 dead. The World Trade Center Towers -- 3,000+ dead.

Could it really be possible that the Controllers had pre-knowledge of the catastrophe in New York City and Washington DC? Most people say no, but Brian McWilliams wrote an article in *Newsbytes* on September 27, 2001 that mainstream media has completely ignored. He reported, "Officials at the instant-messaging firm Odigo confirmed today that two employees received text messages warning of an attack on the World Trade Center two hours before terrorists crashed planes into the New York landmarks."

An obvious question is: Why isn't Dan Rather or the *New York Times* investigating these allegations? Why aren't they looking into it closer? What's even scarier is the following scenario: What if the World Trade Center was only a "first step" and an even greater catastrophe was waiting in the wings, like a nuclear warhead dropped on Chicago?

After it drops, people will be freaking out beyond words -- literally going crazy. Worse, what if there was a huge announcement by the media that David Rockefeller (or one of his cohorts) was going to speak the following night on the Dan Rather News, and it was going to be Big Stuff?

So, David Rockefeller appears live beside Dan Rather and says, "Yes, there is a New World Order, and I, along with a secret cabal, are behind it. We admit to it. We run the world and we don't have your best intentions in mind.

"But before you get all riled up, let me make one thing perfectly clear. If any of you malcontents think about getting out of line, we'll make the World Trade Center and Chicago look like a Boy Scout field trip. Yes, we're the one's who masterminded both tragedies. But as I said, don't even think about getting feisty, because if you do, we'll nuke L.A. and kill a million people before you can bat an eye. Then what will you do? There will be so much chaos you'll all start losing your minds. And if we see any trouble after L.A.'s decimated, we'll nuke Dallas and St. Louis, too.

"Then what will you do? Nobody will be safe. We could anthrax entire cities and you'd never know it until it was too late. Or, since we control the entire food distribution network in this country, we'll simply quit shipping to the supermarkets. We'll starve you people to death! Millions upon millions of you will be begging us to ship you dog food!

"So, here's the deal. The New World Order does exist, and we expect you to bow to us and gladly take your implant in the palm of your hand. Yes, Virginia, the New World Order is the Mark of the Beast. So you'd better take it, or we'll start wiping you out tomorrow.

"Just remember, WE have food, and WE have underground bunkers. Now take your implants like good little slavish robots."

CHAPTER FIFTEEN

THE CONTROLLERS AND THEIR EVIL GOALS

Before I show what the Controllers ultimately want (using the United States Government as one of the many pawns to carry out their plans), I'll provide a few quotes that reveal their psychological make-up. While reading these "words of wisdom," ask yourself, do these people have our best intentions in mind? To me, the answer is obvious.

Strobe Talbott, Council on Foreign Relations Member, to *Time* magazine on July 20, 1992 in an article entitled, "America Abroad: The Birth of the Global Nation": "In the next hundred years, nationhood as we know it will be obsolete; all states will recognize a single global authority." He continues, "No matter how permanent and even sacred [nations] may seem at any one time, they are all artificial and temporary."

Dr. Carroll Quigley, author of the frequently quoted *Tragedy and Hope*: "The powers of financial capitalism have another far-reaching aim, nothing less than to create a world system of financial control in private hands able to dominate the political system of each country and the economy of the world as a whole."

Notice the words "private hands."

Zbigniew Brzezinski, former National Security Advisor under Jimmy Carter: "The Technotronic Era involves the gradual appearance of a more controlled society. Such a society would be dominated by an elite; unrestrained by traditional values. Soon it will be possible to assert almost continuous surveillance over every citizen and maintain up-to-date complete files containing even the most personal information about the citizen. These files will be subject to instantaneous retrieval by the authorities."

Pope John Paul II - November 5, 1995: "The United Nations organization needs to rise more and more above the cold status of an administrative institution and become a moral center where all nations of the world feel at home." (The United Nations as a MORAL CENTER? Thanks, Pope John Paul for confirming all the rumors about Papal devilry.)

Edmund Muskie, Secretary of State - July 1980, commenting on official Carter Administration policy concerning the "Global 2000" report and agreeing there should be "the elimination of two billion human beings by the year 2000."

I don't know what the total death count was during the past two decades, but if you look at AIDS, abortion, curable diseases that went purposely uncured, starvation, war, etc., I'd say they did a pretty good job at reaching their goal.

Henry Kissinger, after the 1992 Los Angeles Riots at a Bilderberg meeting in Evian, France: "Today, Americans would be outraged if United Nations troops entered Los Angeles to restore order -- tomorrow they will be grateful. This is especially true if they were told there was an outside threat from beyond -- whether real or promulgated -- that threatened our very existence. It is then that all peoples of the world will plead with world leaders to deliver them from evil.

"The one thing that every man fears is the unknown. When presented with this scenario, individual rights will be willingly relinquished for the guarantee of their well-being, granted to them by their world government."

NOTE: An "outside" force -- could that be terrorists, or invisible biological agents? How about nations with nuclear weapons, or aliens from outer space? Also, Kissinger said the threat could be real or promulgated -- a hoax -- something made-up to create fear so that we'll willingly bow down to them.

President George Bush - September 11, 1990: "Out of these troubled times, our fifth objective -- a New World Order -- can emerge. We are now in sight of a United Nations that performs as envisioned by its founders."

To understand George W. Bush ("Dubya") we need to look back into his family tree starting with his grandfather, Prescott Bush. This man was a Skull & Bones secret society graduate (1917), a United States Senator from Connecticut, and Dwight D. Eisenhower's favorite golf partner.

Prescott was such an insider, he was the man who actually introduced Richard Nixon to the world of politics and managed to get him on Ike's ticket as Vice President.

Dubya's father, George H.W., was head of the CIA during the mid-1970s and also Vice President and President. Do you think there's any chance that Dubya is going to buck the status quo and try to rid our country of the Controller's New World goals?

David Rockefeller (as reported in the French periodical *Lectures Francaises*): "We are grateful to the *Washington Post*, the *New York*

Times, *Time* magazine and other great publications whose directors have attended our meetings and respected their promises of discretion for almost forty years. It would have been impossible for us to develop our plan for the world if we had been subject to the bright lights of publicity during these years. But the world is now more sophisticated and prepared to march toward a world government which will never again know war, but only peace and prosperity for the whole of humanity. The supranational sovereignty of an intellectual elite and world bankers is surely preferable to the national auto-determination practiced in past centuries."

Henry Kissinger (on world armies): "A United Nations army must be able to act immediately, anywhere in the world, without delays involved in each country making its own decisions." God forbid that any country could make its own decision! Also, if you think this scenario is way-off in the future, try this on for size. While we were at "war" in Somalia, our troops -- United States troops -- were under United Nations jurisdiction and command!

With the above information in mind, I'm going to next provide an overview of what these monsters want to do to undermine our fine country. The first thing to remember is that these folks have one primary goal: to retain and expand their power.

Here are the Controller's basic goals:

1) A single, supra-national government.
2) A one-world army.
3) A one-world religion.
4) A one-world economy where they can manipulate every facet of global finance. We moved one step closer to this sorry state in January, 2002 when the Eurodollar was introduced to Europe.
5) Select "elected" leaders who will rise to power and carry out their agenda, while dumping those who don't toe the line.
6) Decide which countries go to war against each other.
7) Create a system in which the citizenry is increasingly under surveillance.
8) Plant microchip implants in us to finalize their control.

Since I've mentioned the Bilderbergs earlier, I'd like to clarify a few points. First of all, when this revolving group of influential world leaders meets at various locations each year, it is still only a "front." Believe me, the real decisions concerning what is about to take place don't happen at Bilderberg meetings, regardless of how secretive they are. These forums are merely another illusion that needs to be stripped away like the layers of an onion.

To really determine who's calling the shots, we need to research groups such as the Council of 13, the Council of 33, and the Committee of 300. Once we transcend the façade, we'll find there are three tiers of control:

1)   Hierarchy level one - Secret societies, European nobility, and royal families such as the Rothschilds, Warburgs, and the English ruling elite.
2)   Hierarchy level two - American dynasties such as Rockefeller, Kuhn, Sachs, Loeb, Lazard, Goldman, Schiff, and Morgan.
3)   Hierarchy level three - Figureheads such as the Bush family.

At level three, we can see the nuts and bolts of how a system of world hegemony is carried out through the interaction of:

- energy (specifically oil)
- finance
- multinational big business
- military
- industry

From these octopus-type tentacles, we see the three biggest industries in the world:

- usury
- energy
- drugs

With the above information in mind, it's easy to determine how we've progressed past the propaganda that's being peddled by Dan Rather, Rush Limbaugh, the *New York Times* and any of the magazines sitting on your local news stand. Another point needs to be repeated and made perfectly clear -- the Controllers don't go to war over ideals because they don't have any ideals other than to maintain and increase their power base. Rather, it's all about control, and keeping the Machine running. They don't care about patriotism, nationalism, or our sovereignty.

The Cold War was largely an excuse for a massive arms build-up between the United States and Russia. Not only did it guarantee that we would base our society and economy upon a military foundation, but it also started the process of incurring a huge national debt (and thus, immense interest payments to the international bankers). If we were such heated enemies with the Soviets from the early 1950s to the mid-1990s, why did David Rockefeller maintain a branch of Chase Manhattan in Moscow since 1927?!!! Something to think about, huh?

Finally, the most frightening aspect of this scenario is that these hidden elitists have already taken over complete control of the United States Government and mainstream corporate media. Let me say it again: they already control our government! If the Controllers were able to execute such a coup here, who's to say they don't control other governments and regimes as well -- even those in Afghanistan or the Middle East!

And if you concur that the Controllers finance both sides of every war, what if they're doing the same thing now, even going so far as to possess knowledge of the terrorist attacks in Washington DC and New York City on 9-11? Hearken back to the quotes at the beginning of this chapter and read how badly the Controllers want a New World Order and how little concern they have for us.

CHAPTER SIXTEEN

COMPARTMENTALIZATION AND THE NEED TO KNOW

Author David Icke has observed with brilliant insight how the Controllers operate. He says those at the top, the elite few, run the show through a concept called "compartmentalization." Information is only provided to people on a "need to know" basis. In the political and military world, this implies that each department or individual is only privy to information that directly addresses their part of the plan. In other words, they do not have access to the big picture.

Here's an analogy. Suppose a certain powerful individual wanted a baseball team to throw game five of the World Series because of a huge gambling loss that he had to repay. He knows he won't be able to pull it off if he confronts the right fielder, catcher, second baseman, three pitchers, and the designated hitter and pays them off. First of all, none of them would be willing to do it because they already make enough money. It's not realistic to think that you could go up to Barry Bonds and say, "I want you to strike out every time you step to the plate."

So, what can he do? The gambler examines all of his options, then finds that the manager is someone who can be manipulated because of his "questionable ties" to an unnamed group that has information on him that wouldn't cast him in the best possible light (maybe some compromising photos, or knowledge of illegal activities). So, he approaches the manager and lays his cards on the table, saying if he doesn't throw the game, these pictures will surface and he'll be publicly humiliated. In return, if he does "act accordingly" and throws the game, not only will the photos be destroyed, but he'll be rewarded at some point in the future.

The manager agrees and as the game goes on, he makes a couple of questionable decisions that keep the game close. Yet, going into the ninth inning, the manager's team is still winning 1-0, and he needs to find a way to lose. His starting pitcher, throwing a two-hitter, is completely on. He's smoking, and has the game well under control.

Surprisingly, the manager pulls him in the ninth inning and puts in a 22 year-old reliever. Now this kid has a rocket for an arm, but he's still immature and easily shaken. He enters the game -- the World Series -- with 60,000 fans cheering him on, and millions watching on TV. Soon the kid walks the first batter, then wham, gives up a home run and the game is over!

Afterward, the media talks to the manager and asks about a couple of his decisions. As for having a slow-runner try to steal second base during a rally, he replied, "The Mets are a strong team. I knew we had to play aggressive baseball."

On having his clean-up hitter bunt in the sixth inning with a man on third: "I thought we'd mix things up a little bit and try to buy a run." Finally, as for putting in the 22 year-old kid in the bottom of the ninth inning: "Our starter was pitching great, but I wanted to keep him strong for game seven. So I figured I'd give him a breather."

The press buys all these answers, and all is well. Now, if you went around and asked the players, coaches, umpires, fans, or owner if the game was fixed, each would say NO. Yet it was still thrown.

Why didn't they know the fix was in? Because they were operating on a need-to-know basis. The hitters were given information on each pitcher (and vice versa), while the coaches were told which outfielders had a good arm in case they wanted to stretch a single into a double. The infielders were told how to defense each batter, and the catcher was prompted on how to deal with every possible pitching strategy.

So, in the end, what happened? The game gets thrown, and not a single person knew about it except the manager! Amazing, huh.

If you don't think this same technique happens to *us* in real life, look at your national news each night. Do you think Dan Rather is telling you the truth? Far from it. I guarantee that in those boardrooms at *CBS News*, there's a group of elite media moguls who decide EVERY night what WE NEED TO KNOW! Not what we SHOULD know, but what we need to know so that we can be better conditioned into accepting their nefarious schemes. We're no different than those guys at the ballpark who got duped because all they had was compartmentalized, need-to-know information.

As you can see, it doesn't take a lot of people to run the world. The Controllers don't need to call the shots for every single person. The only folks who need to be manipulated are those in positions of power who run a department or organization. It's similar to a department head that runs the English Department (or any other department) at a major university.

Every other professor and instructor in that college can be controlled via an array of tools such as the promise (or threat) of tenure, certain course work, scheduling, promotions, and perks (who goes to the Hawaiian literary conference in January, etc.).

If an instructor in the English, Political Science, History or Science Department gets out of line, there are many tactics to either get them back on the straight-and-narrow, or eliminate them completely.

In this sense, it doesn't take a mass of people to control a certain situation or environment. All you have to do is "buy-and-pay for" the key decision-maker at the top. Then the pyramid of control is yours.

In regard to the terrorist attacks on September 11, 2001, we can utilize the same logic. Let's look at what happened:

1)   Planes were taken control of and crashed into the World Trade Center towers.

2)   There are forces in the Middle East, Afghanistan, and Pakistan that despise America.

3)   Somebody, let's say Osama bin Laden, for argument's sake, called the shots to begin this reign of terror.

Taking all of these factors into consideration, how hard would it be to turn the World Trade Center atrocity into an even more tragic event? When you think about it, if Osama bin Laden and the hijackers were only operating on a need-to-know basis, they could easily be bamboozled, or "allowed" to pull off this dastardly feat -- all of which would serve a larger purpose -- the onset of the New World Order.

When viewed in this light, the Controllers don't even need to align themselves with one side or the other. Why? Because they've created both (or *all*) sides anyway! They're the ones manipulating the current "players" already, similar to the manager on a baseball field.

It's all about dividing and conquering -- Islam versus Christianity, America versus Afghanistan, men versus women, black versus white, etc. When you think about it, if you owned both the Oakland Raiders and the Dallas Cowboys and these two teams were competing against each other in the Super Bowl, would you really care who won? Of course not, because you still make out in the end. You get all the money from the fans for their tickets, revenue from the network television coverage, endorsement rights, and whatever other benefits fall your way. Who cares if the Raiders or Cowboys win?

Right now, the Controllers have nearly complete control of the United States government. We're supposed to be the toughest, strongest, most powerful nation on earth. But the Controllers have assumed possession of our government. It's theirs. If they can do that to US, why can't they also control the Russians, English, Australians, and the TALIBAN?!!

If certain nations do get out of line or refuse to play by the rules, what happens to them? They get warred upon! Renegades aren't a problem in the long run because the existing military forces of this earth can eliminate them.

The overall goal of the New World Order, then, is to centralize power into the hands of a global body rather than into separate nation-states. This single ruling body can then be run by a handful of demonic elitists who don't give a damn about us.

How have the Controllers managed to accomplish such a feat? Easy. They infiltrate every country and group there is, ultimately having both (or all) sides covered. If you have X fighting Y, A battling B, and C in a heated struggle with D, it doesn't matter how they go about reaching an outcome if the desired outcome has already been determined.

An added bonus is that while all these groups are fighting each other, they don't have enough time and resources to focus on who the REAL enemy is! As David Icke says, Saddam Hussein is as much controlled as George Bush, and don't you forget it!

Before I end this essay, consider one last point. When John F. Kennedy was assassinated, Lee Harvey Oswald had already been chosen as the scapegoat long before the hit ever took place. The scenario is so outlandish a newspaper even printed an article about Lee Harvey being the lone gunman hours before the hit ever happened! Oh well, why wait until the last minute, right?

What if Osama bin Laden has also been selected as the same type of fall guy to speed up the New World Order's arrival? The Controllers waited around for eight years while Bill Clinton lollygagged and received oral sex in the White House. They knew it was time to get the ball rolling, and old "W" was their man. So, it's easy enough to get Americans to despise a bunch of "filthy ragheads," especially after the attacks on 9-11.

On top of that, it's a given that Osama bin Laden and his kind are a bunch of psychotic creeps. So, why not use them as pawns, or an excuse, to get us rockin' n' rollin' into another war?

In the meantime, we can also start pumping up our surveillance of the citizenry while assuring them that it's okay to take away their rights. After all, it's for the best, right?

CHAPTER SEVENTEEN

NOTES & QUOTES - WE DON'T NEED YOUR EDUCATION

Disclaimer: What follows are some notes and quotes from six books concerning the subject of education. The direct quotes belong solely to the authors and/or persons delivering the quote, and should not be mistaken as my creations. My sole connection to the material below is as a note taker and compiler.

DUMBING US DOWN – The Hidden Curriculum of Compulsory Schooling
By
John Taylor Gatto – copyright 1992
Published by – New Society Publishers

Hannah Arendt – "The aim of totalitarian education has never been to instill convictions, but to destroy the capacity to form any."

John Taylor Gatto – taught in the Manhattan public school system for 26 years, and won the New York State Teacher of the Year Award
....

"Was it possible I had been hired not to enlarge children's power, but to diminish it? That seemed crazy on the face of it, but slowly I began to realize that the bells and the confinement, the crazy sequences, the age-segregation, the lack of privacy, the constant surveillance, and all the rest of the national curriculum of schooling were designed exactly as if someone had set out to prevent children from learning how to think and act, to coax them into addiction and dependent behavior."

"The very stability of our economy is threatened by any form of education that might change the nature of the human product schools now turn out."

"Government monopoly schools are structurally unreformable. They cannot function if their central myths are exposed and abandoned."

"Over the years, I have come to see that whatever I thought I was doing as a teacher ... was teaching an invisible curriculum that reinforced the myths of the school situation and those of an economy based on caste."

THE SEVEN THINGS TEACHERS ARE PAID TO TEACH:

1) Confusion - I teach you to accept confusion as your destiny. Everything I teach is out of context. I teach the un-relating of everything. I teach disconnections – a curriculum full of internal contradictions and lack of coherence.

2) Class Position - The second lesson I teach is that students must stay in the class where they belong. Children are numbered so that if any get away, they can be returned to the right class. Kids can't even imagine themselves somewhere else, because I've shown them how to envy and fear the better classes and how to have contempt for the dumb classes. 99% of the kids are in their class to stay. Everyone has a proper place in the pyramid. You must stay where you are put. I never lie outright, but I've come to see that truth and school teaching are incompatible, just as Socrates said thousands of years ago.

3) Indifference – The third lesson I teach is that children shouldn't learn too much about anything. The lesson of bells is that no work is worth finishing, so why care too deeply about anything? Years of bells will condition all but the strongest to a world that can no longer offer important work to do.

4) Dependence – I teach kids to surrender their will to the predestined chain of command. Rights do not exist inside a school – not even the right of free speech – unless school authorities say they do. Individuality is a contradiction to class theory, a curse to all systems of classification.

5) Intellectual Dependency – Good students wait for a teacher to tell them what to do. It is the most important lesson – that we must wait for other people better trained than ourselves – to make the meanings of our lives. The power to control what children will think lets me separate successful students from failures. Curiosity has no important place in my

work, only conformity. There are tested procedures to break the will of those who resist. We've built a way of life that depends on people doing what they are told because they don't know how to tell themselves what to do.

6) <u>Provisional Self-Esteem</u> - A kid's self-respect should depend on expert opinion. My kids are constantly evaluated and judged. The lesson of report cards, grades, and tests is that children should not trust themselves or their parents, but should instead rely on the evaluation of certified officials. People need to be told what they are worth.

7) <u>One Can't Hide</u> – I teach students that they are always watched, that each is under constant surveillance by myself and my colleagues. I assign a type of extended schooling called "homework" so that the effect of surveillance travels into the households where students might otherwise use free time to learn something unauthorized from a father or mother. Children must be closely watched if you want to keep a society under tight control. Children will follow a private drummer if you can't get them into a uniformed marching band.

"Schools are an essential support system for a model of social engineering that condemns most people to be subordinate stones in a pyramid that narrows as it ascends to a terminal of control."

<u>Socrates</u> – "I will show you how to bring about a feverish city, but you will not like what I am going to say."

------ They didn't. They killed Socrates.

<u>Reasons why school curriculums produce moral, physical, and intellectual paralysis</u>

a) In the early 1900s, the power elite feared a revolution among the industrial poor
b) They were appalled by the immigrants who were coming into this country – the Celts, Slavs, and Italians – plus their Catholic religion
c) The movement of blacks through society after the Civil War

The result was that schools became "prisons" for children – a private training ground to permanently trap underclasses in their place. They wanted to deprive them of any tools for significant advancement.

How schools survive – They exploit the fear, selfishness, and inexperience of children. They don't dare teach them any critical thinking skills.

"Schools have become a replacement for churches in society. Like church, they require their teachings be taken on faith."

Schools are a sorting mechanism that keeps the classes divided. The most important thing they teach is how to obey orders. It is a psychopathic institution that has no conscience – ring a bell, move to a different cell – do your work – ring a bell – move to a different cell – like rats in an experimenter's cage.

"Schools produce formulaic human beings whose behavior can be predicted and controlled."

Schools promote dependence. The by-product of dependence is accumulation. We NEED things to feel secure – drugs, TV, material objects, a sports team, sex, etc.

"If we use schooling to break children away from their parents – and make no mistake, that has been the central function of schools – we're going to continue to have the horror show we have right now."

MIND CONTROL WORLD CONTROL – The Encyclopedia of Mind Control
By Jim Keith – copyright 1997
Published by – Adventures Unlimited Press

The roots of the American educational system are found in Prussia, where compulsory education was born in 1819.

"Prussia set up a three-tier school system in which one-half of one-percent of the population is taught to think. They go to a school called

Academie. Five and a half percent of the population go to Realschulen, where they partially learn to think, but not completely. The lowest 94% went to Volkschulen, where they learn harmony, obedience, freedom from stressful thinking, and how to follow orders."

John Dewey – one of the most influential names in American Education history. "There is no God, and there is no soul. There is no room for fixed, natural law or permanent moral absolutes."

Dewey said that the purpose of public schooling was to "take an active part in determining the social order of the future."

"Man is to be conditioned to accept the circumstances that he finds himself in, not to learn to change them."

"It is only the rebellious public-schooled who must have the devastating effect of individuality brainwashed out of them."

HOW THE ORDER CONTROLS EDUCATION
By Antony Sutton – copyright 1983
Published by – Research Publications, Inc.

"Any group that wants to control the future of American society has to first control education."

"The prime purpose (of education) is not to teach subject matter, but to condition children to live as socially integrated citizen units in an organic society – a real life enactment of the Hegelian absolute State. In this state, the individuals find freedom only in obedience to the State. Consequently, the function of education is to prepare the individual citizen unit for smooth entry into the organic whole."

"The individual is not important. The mere development of individual talent, of individual fitness, mental power, and knowledge is not the purpose of education. The most important task of the educator is to analyze the activities and duties of men within society. The function of instruction is to fulfill these aims and impart to the individual socially desirable ideals."

Eduard von Hartman (German philosopher, late 1800s) – "The principle of freedom is negative in every department of life, save religion alone, and compulsion is necessary. What all men need is rational tyranny, if it only holds them to a steady development, according to the laws of their own nature."

Hegel viewed individuals as valueless cogs to the State.

University Control – "Academic associations are a means of conditioning or even policing academics. Although academics are great at talking about academic freedom, they are peculiarly susceptible to peer-group pressures. And if an academic fails to get the word through his peer group, there is always the threat of not getting tenure. In other words, what is taught at the University level is passed through a sieve. The sieve is faculty conformity. In this century where faculties are larger, conformity cannot be imposed by a President. It is handled equally well through faculty tenure committees and publication committees of academic associations." (The outsider view is weeded out.)

Education is funded by, and a byproduct of, "foundations" – Ford, Carnegie, Rockefeller, etc.

"Parents believe a child goes to school to learn skills to use in the adult world, but Dewey states specifically that education is "not a preparation for future living." The Dewey educational system does not accept the role of developing a child's talents but, contrarily, only to prepare the child to function as a unit in any organic whole – in blunt terms, a cog in the wheel of organic society."

Hegel – "Man finds freedom only in obedience to the State."

Dewey's philosophy – education is used to prepare a person to fit into society rather than develop individual talents. Personal development cannot be achieved by developing individual traits. It must take the form of preparation to serve society.

Education is controlled by controlling CONTENT! The goal is social conditioning of both the teachers and students to be part of a global structure. Social engineering!

The Illuminati – "We must win the common people in every corner. This will be obtained chiefly by means of the schools."

THE OCCULT TECHNOLOGY OF POWER
Published by – Alpine Enterprises – copyright 1974

John Stuart Mill - "A general state education is a mere contrivance for molding people to be exactly like one another; and the mold in which it casts them is that which pleases the predominant power in government – whether this be a monarch, a priesthood, or an aristocracy ... it establishes a despotism over the mind, leading by natural tendency to one over the body."

"The anarchy (possibilities) of private education in which any manner of dangerous ideas could be spread cannot be tolerated."

"The primary purpose of public education is to inculcate the idea that our crucial institutions of coercion and monopoly were created for the public good by national heroes to blunt the past power of malefactors of great wealth."

"Overwhelming financial clout in the publishing industry can induce relatively uniform textbook selection."

"National teacher associations and unions are an excellent power base from which to foster programs of indoctrination."

How Things Work Behind The Scenes – "We obtain sincere, energetic activists to propagate our desires without having to reveal our motives or even our existence. We do not want an educational system that produces hard-driving individuals bent on amassing great wealth and power. Therefore, we discourage education that would develop the potential powers of students to their fullest. "Liberal" education that stresses knowledge for its own sake or even sophistry and sterile mental gymnastics is of no danger to us."

"Education that prepares students to accept a cog-like existence in our military-industrial-social-welfare-regulation system complex is ideal. Progressive education with its stress on 'social adjustment' also produces the conformity we require of our subjects."

"Let only those succeed whose influence could be compatible with our power. Encourage all who would develop the passive or receptive mode of existence. Discourage all who promote the aggressive or active capacities. Build a great cult of salvation through endless education, touting it as the 'democratic' path to success."

The objective of Rockefeller philanthropies as stated in a letter to the General Education Board: "In our dreams we have limitless resources and the people yield themselves with perfect docility to our molding hands. The task we set before ourselves is a beautiful one, to train these people as we find them to a perfectly ideal life just as they are."

SOCIALISM: The Road to Slavery
By Dr. John Coleman – copyright 1994
Published by – Joseph Publishing Company

John Dewey, the father of progressive education, was cited by the Un-American Committee as belonging to 15 Marxist-front organizations.

Dr. William H. Owen – President of the NEA – a speech given at the World Conference on Education – June 23, 1923: "In spite of what we write and say, the world does not believe that education as a form of social control is comparable with armies, navies, and statecraft. We should spend our time and efforts in sharing a constructive educational program that will demonstrate what education can do as a form of social control comparable with armies."

"Outcome Based Education (OBE) has seized control of the schools. Today, instead of having teachers, we have 'change agents' who force acceptance of group views, which they, the facilitators, brainwash into the minds of the students."

THE WORLD'S LAST DICTATOR
By Dwight L. Kinman – copyright 1993
Published by – Solid Rock Books, Inc.

M. J. Blackham – Humorist Magazine – Sept-Oct. 1981 - "If schools teach dependence on one's self, they are more revolutionary than any conspiracy to overthrow the government!"

This passage describes a woman named Anne Herzler who ran for Superintendent of Education in Arizona during the 1980s: "She saw a million people marching in the streets of Paris because the national government was about to take over the schools in France. She saw the people force the resignation of the entire executive branch of the government except the President." She then quotes a woman who had her Ph. D. from Columbia University who wrote:

"Americans are fools. Don't you know there is a world-wide movement to bring all schools under state-control? No government should control education because education must remain in the hands of the people to remain free. Parents have to say how they want their children to be educated. We did not march in Paris for religious purposes. We marched for freedom. You Americans had better wake up or you are going to lose your freedom."

Dr. Pierce – Harvard University – 1973: "Every child in America entering school at the age of five is mentally ill because he comes to school with certain allegiances toward our founding fathers, toward our elected officials, toward his parents, toward a belief in a supernatural Being, and toward the sovereignty of this nation as a separate entity. It's up to you teachers to make all of these sick children well by creating the international children of the future."

W. A. John Johnson – Daily News Digest: "An educational Mafia captured the high ground of American education in the late 1800s. They carefully orchestrated, with a hidden agenda, and deliberately steered the public schools, its teachers and children down a disastrous road to socialism, secular humanism, radicalism, planned failures in reading, writing, suffocation of Christianity, the thrashing of basic values, and the establishment of one of the most powerful and dangerous unions – the National Education Association."

Adolf Hitler – prior to World War II – "Give me one generation of youth and I will take the world."

CHAPTER EIGHTEEN

REVIEW: LAWRENCE DAWSON'S "THE DEATH OF REALITY: How a conspiracy of fools is imposing unreality and laying claim to the destiny of a nation"

Lawrence Dawson begins *The Death of Reality* by claiming that the moral decadence that haunts this country has been politically inspired. In his eyes, the Information Age has created nothing more than an "alternative perception of reality" that supports an ideological agenda of those in power, and ultimately distorts reality. Much of the blame, says Dawson, can be placed at the feet of philosophers such as Ludwig Wittgenstein, who advanced a theory that language is useless as a tool to describe the world. To Wittgenstein, words are "soft and malleable" with meanings that change for every person. In this sense, truth is nonexistent, and reality is only that of personal perception with no absolutes.

But Dawson argues that words, which should mirror objective reality, no longer have defined meanings. They only give "impressions" of an artificial world that is being created by forces that lurk in the shadows. He even uses a quote from U.S. News and World Report (8-7-95) that states, "In the postmodern, post-everything world view, there is no objectivity or truth. Everything is relative."

Dawson goes on to say, "Political forces that rule by deception hide the truth from the people. Political forces that rule by unreality don't even bother. Reality is made "operative" or "non-operative" by political opinion. The people themselves become active defenders of the lie." His words are reminiscent of Ralph Waldo Emerson's famous quote, "Foolish consistency is the hobgoblin of little minds." Dawson continues, "The politics of unreality is the creation of 'truth' which serves a political agenda and does not conform to objective, factual reality."

When I read these lines, I was reminded of a story contained in a book by Jeffrey Tobin entitled *A Vast Conspiracy: The Real Story of the Sex Scandal That Nearly Brought down a President*. He writes about a time in 1996 when Hillary Clinton was embroiled in the Travelgate-scandal, and President Clinton gave his State of the Union Address. During it, he got all teary-eyed and said what a 'wonderful wife and magnificent mother' Hillary was. Afterward, though, he took this very same speech, autographed it, then gave it to Monica Lewinsky (more than likely, before, during, or after she fellated him).

So, in this sense, words don't truly reflect reality, for language can be manipulated to make 'meanings' subjective rather than objective. A teary-eyed President publicly lavishes his wife with 'false praise' to save her political-ass, then races off to his mistress to fool around. Thus, language becomes a tool of those in power to use at their own discretion. In other words, language that suffers from being subjective and plural rather than objective and singular eventually becomes corrupt and loses its capacity to transmit information.

So, let me take a break for a second and ask you this question. "What am I trying to say?" Essentially, the gist of this piece is very simple – listen to what those in power are saying (and also to those in positions to *disseminate* information), then realize that this tool – language – is the most powerful device know to mankind in regard to shaping our behavior. Pay attention to how they use words ... how they twist them ... and how they distort them to their own advantage. Then, last but not least, compare their words to what they actually do ... i.e. talk is cheap ... actions speak louder than words. How many politicians, George Bush being the latest, tell us that they're going to lower our taxes? I don't know about you, but I haven't seen them going down lately. In fact, taxes are at their highest since the mid-1940's (when we had to fight a World War). So, here's the point – LISTEN to what they're saying, and how they use words to condition, manipulate, bamboozle, and brainwash us.

To convey this sentiment, Dawson uses *Alice in Wonderland* as an example: "The difference between Alice's world and the dream world into which she slips is primarily the use of language. In the real world, Alice encounters things as they are called. In both *Wonderland* and *Through the Looking Glass* she encounters a topsy turvy world in which words take on private meanings, become nonsensical, or are used in inappropriate contexts. As Humpty Dumpty tells Alice: Words mean what I want them to mean."

Look around. How many times has language been used to manipulate your emotions, thus causing you to act in a particular fashion? What is essentially happening is that 'reality' is being 'socially constructed' and 'changed' depending upon what the information source hopes to accomplish. Political reality is being created right before our eyes, which Dawson defines as, "ideologically motivated assertions which are immune to contradictory fact."

Dawson continues this train of thought by saying, "When language is authentic, the facts have ultimate authority. When language becomes synthetic, its meanings become fluid."

Why? Because 'meanings' are 'authored' by those who want to promote a certain agenda. 'Meaning' is now in the hands of those in control, making reality not objective or factual, but dependent upon THEIR whims.

Dawson adds to this argument by saying, "The single most common characteristic of the use of synthetic word meanings is that they select out the events which confirm their novel meaning. The synthetic usage is presumed to stand for all concrete examples, while the whole phenomenon is deliberately obscured to prevent real details from discrediting the artificial meaning." In this context, the artificial (invented) meaning becomes 'reality.'

At this point, you must ask yourself, do I want to deal with facts and truth, or am I content to accept the 'perceptions' that are being spoon-fed to me? So, here's another big question – who defines your perception of reality? Where do you get your information? After you arrive at an answer, ask yourself, "Do the people that provide this information to me have my best interests in mind?" If the answer is NO, then ask yourself – what are their motives? Do you want reality to be 'discovered' with a factual foundation or basis, or 'constructed' for you by someone with ulterior motives? Finally, ask yourself, who are these 'constructors' and are they the type of people I trust to present their 'slant' on reality to me?

One must wonder, at this point, how we've allowed this system to reach such a sorry state. The answer lies in the fact that the constructors of social unreality, due to their positions of power, force those who have an influence on 'perception' to bow and conform to their ideological agendas and motivations. It's like a kid with a ball who says, "Either play by my rules or go home." Thus, those who choose to serve the Controllers accept a 'reality' that is based upon how well it serves a certain viewpoint.

To them, reality is the enemy! It must be distorted. Why? Because it's a threat to their conduct! Look at how Bill Clinton used language to blur the lines with his behavior in the Monica Lewinsky Affair. This woman was performing oral sex on him in the Oval Office, doing stripteases for him, and ramming cigars inside her vagina. And he still talked his way out of it!

Another tactic that the Distorters use is this: they shift our focus away from the truth to an alternate point that either supports their views, or distracts us from the truth of a situation. In essence, then, they make a distinction between acceptable and unacceptable realities. To make reality 'favorable' to them, they intentionally distort or suppress the facts of a given situation, or present it in a way that supports their chosen 'angle.' This practice is so pervasive that entire industry's and fields of knowledge have been created to present faulty information in the guise of fact. In this light, we've reached such a sorry state of affairs that not only is the truth ignored; it's treated as if it doesn't even exist!

To better understand this phenomenon, Mr. Dawson has made a distinction between two forms of thought – vertical thinking and lateral thinking. He characterizes vertical thinking as: directed toward specific performance goals by accurately identifying elements in reality; while lateral thinking is shaped by subjective emotions and imposed feelings. In essence, this type of thought does not accept the objective world as it is, but rather makes it what the individual person wants it to be. To these people, truth isn't objective or singular. Instead, there are multiple truths, all of which are dependent upon a certain point of view. One of these 'truths' is as good as any other.

Can you see where this type of thought is leading us? If the Controllers are successful in undermining our language, then they will ultimately be able to erode our beliefs that ANY FORM of externally based, objective 'truth' can be relayed from one individual to another. Truth will no longer be absolute, but a variable based upon personal beliefs.

Taken one step further, if we eliminate the concept of absolute truth, then how can we communicate to each other what we deem important as a form of conduct? Instead of knowing what is right and wrong, the lines are continually being blurred between what is proper and improper. What we've essentially surrendered, then, is the gift of discernment. Without being able to distinguish the 'quality' of one act from another, we begin a troubling process that actually corrupts our thought processes. Look at the world today, especially in light of the many school shootings. Isn't it obvious where this 'perversion of thought' is leading us?

If we conclude that truth does not exist, then we're essentially being held hostage to a form of communication that cannot accurately capture or reflect reality. Plus, if we keep letting the Controllers manipulate our language and define certain terms as THEY see fit (being most beneficial to THEM), then what will this do to how they view our inherent 'rights'? What if our rights no longer imply any individual freedoms, but are construed to represent our service to the State? If we accept this type of rationale, what will result? The answer, from my perspective, is quite clear – the realm of governmental power will continue to grow, and subsequently exert even more influence over us.

But that's not the only thing that is happening. Over the past decade I've noticed a disturbing trend that is ruining our culture – our populace is being weakened as a whole through a variety of subtle techniques (advertising, social conditioning, political correctness, certain 'movements,' etc.). Concepts such as strength, conviction, and belief are seen as detrimental and counter-productive. Instead, the power elite are promoting an agenda of societal weakness that will ultimately result in any fight that we have left being taken away from us. As we move toward this end, remember one thing - as the social conditioners push to weaken us, they will always retain their strength and NEVER deliberately surrender one iota of it (gun control is a perfect example). And what is the 'key' to this weakening process? It lies in one word – conduct. Y'see, the Controllers want us to be TOLERANT of everything, but this tolerance only applies to those acts that follow their patterns of behavior, but not to anything that falls outside of this realm. George Will once described the Democrats as being, "tolerant of everything except speech and thought."

To close this essay, I'd like to reiterate a few important points that Mr. Dawson has brought to our attention. First, the lies being thrown at us are systematically created. What's taking place is not accidental. The people deceiving us do so because that is their purpose within the system. By manipulating communications and the dissemination of information, they ultimately want to create a uniform opinion among the masses that fully supports their control.

Now, what happens if we are perpetually bombarded with doses of unreality? We'll eventually lose our ability to reason through a situation or come to accurate conclusions. Reality will become lost in the shuffle, and we'll accept any pablum or nonsense that the Controllers spoon-feed to us. As sad as it may sound, this transformation has already taken place. Think about it. If there is no basis for truth in our national character, then it doesn't matter what any of us do (our leaders included) because we'll be able to reinvent ourselves on a daily basis. Why? Because, according to those who promote this absurd philosophy, reality isn't objective (fixed), but subjective (fluid and ever-changing). Does this scenario sound familiar? People are now able to escape the consequences of their actions through the clever manipulation of image and LANGUAGE! (Example: could you define what "is" is? I never had sexual 'relations' with that woman, Miss Lewinsky.)

I'll leave you with one final quote from Mr. Dawson's book. "To ignore factual reality by believing it to be otherwise does not mean you are removed from that reality. It only means you suffer it ignorantly."

CHAPTER NINETEEN

REVIEWED: HUGH FOX'S "THE INVISIBLES: A

DIALECTIC"

When I talk about the Controllers, or people that run the world, who do I mean? What does it entail to "run the world?" Well, the first thing we need to know is that when something called "Systems Analysis" and "Corp-Org Models" are used, emotions, personal impact, and human considerations are not part of the equation. How could they be when the brutal realities of this world are so apparent? Look at how the AIDS virus, a man-made disease, is decimating large parts of the world, especially the continent of Africa. Take a second to examine how many fossil fuels are being burned to choke our atmosphere when an alternative - hydrogen energy - is so much more efficient. Consider how many trees, animals, waterways, farms and endangered species get eliminated each day due to "the bottom line."

I could ramble endlessly about these plights, such as how our sickening tax system is destroying the nuclear family, but instead I'll simply say that those who run the world are willing to sacrifice anything, including LIFE ITSELF on this planet, to promote their evil agenda. Hell, hearken back to the Vietnam War and how 57,000 Americans were killed, and who knows how many Asians, for what purpose? To stop the spread of Communism? Hell no! The Controllers wanted to secure "The Golden Triangle" so they could corner the global heroin trade.

Here's another example of how little regard the Controllers have for anything but their own self-serving interests. Directly across from my house is a gorgeous marsh and acres of forest that, when set against an immaculate field, makes one of the most beautiful settings I've ever seen. In fact, I've come to call this area "The Garden of Eden," and when I take my cats for walks at night over there, I'll sit and write as they frolic and play. There are ducks, frogs, rabbits, dragonflies, grasshoppers, deer, and even an occasional bear. But recently, a Texas developer decided he wanted to build a hotel on this land, so the zoning laws were changed, and welluh, thousands of years of natural beauty was decimated within two days. Bulldozers mowed down all the trees, then they were stacked in a huge pile, doused with diesel fuel, and set on fire. I drove by there with a girl I know, and when she saw this atrocity, she almost started crying. How the can these people approve of such a horrendous act?

Now, some of you will naturally say, "The only reason you're upset is because this crime occurred in your own backyard."

In response, I'd have to say, "Sure; that has something to do with it." But this rape and arson of the land is merely a microcosm of the overall disregard that is occurring in the entire world. And, by the end of this essay, you'll see how truly despicable the Controller's are. In fact, the author of *The Invisibles* comments on these inhuman monsters, and how nothing is seen as tragic or horrifying:

"The key to the inner nature of the Invisibles is that they have never been programmed in emotional terms - but merely in terms of success-of-operation-coordinates."

So, before continuing, I should start at the beginning and explain a few things. First of all, to understand the Controllers, I'm reminded of some advice that was once given by a "Mindhunter" - those agents who track serial killers. This detective said that before he could actually capture the animals who became brutally vicious murderers, he had to understand precisely how they thought. The same reasoning applies to those who run the world.

So, let me begin with this question: How do you think David Rockefeller, or one of the other Invisibles, spends each day? They're obviously not digging ditches, sitting in an office deciding who gets a new home equity loan, or punching a clock and working nine-to-five. Him, and those of his ilk, have SO much money that it is no longer the driving force in their lives. Y'see, they OWN money, and control how it's created, distributed, and stored. Thus, those at the very upper echelon of control, those who actually call the shots, spend their time on one primary task - situating the world so that they can perpetuate their realm of control.

Insight # 1: Control breeds the desire to perpetuate, and then increase, one's control.

How does a being continue to control once they've assumed such a position? Does it just happen at random, or by coincidence? Of course not. The planning involved is incredible. One of the techniques used is called Systems Analysis, which is, essentially, a methodology used to examine any given situation or problem. Then, once a decision is arrived at, it is set into motion. During this process, any number of different factors are set in place, all of which can change at any time, and all of which can affect the original proposition. All of these factors are analyzed in relation to how they affect or influence an array of possible outcomes.

In regard to world events, Systems Analysis is used to not only examine each situation, but also to manipulate and direct a set of goals that have already been determined. In other words, this technique is an instrument of CONTROL that is wielded behind the scenes without the knowledge of those being controlled. So, while everyone is worried about a "Big Brother" type scenario with cameras on every corner, the more dangerous type of control is that which cannot be seen.

Insight # 2: To be successful, control mechanisms must be covert - those subjected to them shouldn't even be aware that they are being controlled.

Here's what we need to remember - there are men whose sole function (one that they assumed for themselves) is to manage the world. Thus, if they're able to control the variables and different factors that affect our daily lives without us even being aware of such a force, try to imagine how this contributes to our identities, and to our decision making processes. Many of us believe that a form of "horizontal control" is what keeps the world working. In other words, all of the elements of control are essentially laid flat on a table and exist at roughly the same level. This type of thought would characterize a government where elected leaders are chosen by the people, then serve them in a way that would be most beneficial to everyone in that society.

Now, a second group realizes that horizontal control is merely an illusion that we're conditioned to believe in by our educational system and the media. They can see that the way our system works is more through "vertical control" where there are hierarchies and levels of influence. In this system, a pyramid-like structure exists where those at the top (the few) rule over those at the bottom (the masses).

Finally, a third group sees that although vertical control holds some truth, the reality of our situation is one of "vertical manipulation," a system where control is exercised from hidden quarters and isn't readily explained to those being subjected to it.

Insight # 3: Things are not as they appear to be. To rule effectively, one's apparatus for control cannot be seen by those being subjected to it.

What factors are used in a Systems Analysis model? Let's take, for example, a small Midwestern town where the county commissioners want to build an over-priced new palatial prison. The size of their constituency is approximately 80,000, so the variables that the commissioners would take into consideration are: race, gender, class, religion, political parties, income, residence, education, etc. All of these KNOWNS, then, are used to determine the affect of a certain decision. Now, if this model is expanded to a national, or global level, the Controllers may ask: "What would be the effect of a tax hike or lowered interest rates on a black female Baptist Democrat who lives in an Atlanta hi-rise and earns $18,000/year?" If you multiply this scenario a hundred, thousand, or million fold, then you'll start to see how the world is run. It's nothing but a statistical model that is painstakingly analyzed, updated, refined, and reconfigured to keep abreast of every possible variable.

Insight # 4: Unknown outcomes are a Controller's biggest enemy.

Here is another example of how certain factors can be manipulated to achieve a desired result. Let's say a group of world leaders wanted to examine what would happen to an area if a temporary police state bordering on martial law were implemented. First of all, a very distinct segment of the populace would be targeted as the control group, then systematically and continually bombarded with information that keeps them perpetually disgruntled. When they're brought to the peak of outrage, another injustice (either actual or perceived) is the final straw that sets them over the edge. The target group rebels and begins acting in a "socially unacceptable" manner that triggers violence. After a pre-determined period of time, the "Law" comes in and cracks the whip, establishing martial law across the area.

Now, some may say, that'd never happen. It's only conjecture. Well, less than ten years ago I lived through this precise scenario as it unfolded across an entire city. Do you remember the L.A. Riots in 1992? First of all we had a disgruntled group (the Blacks) who had an ongoing beef with the LAPD, and were primed for action by Spike Lee's *Do the Right Thing*. Then Rodney King got beaten, and the videotape was replayed thousands of times to keep the target group's anger festering. Finally, a trial was conducted and the police officers were found innocent. Incensed, the blacks rioted for three days, then the National Guard, County Sheriff's, State Police, and local police departments set-up what was essentially martial law, complete with curfews, restricted areas, and so forth. So, if Systems Analysis was utilized PRIOR to the riots to examine each divergent scenario, can you now see how things could be mapped-out rather than allowed to simply happen at random, and also how certain situations are manipulated to garner a GUARANTEED response?

Insight # 5: Never allow the average citizen to see behind the scenes.

At this point, I'm going to switch gears a bit and look at a concept that runs parallel to Systems Analysis - the Corp-Org (Corporate Organization) Model. The first area of interest that we need to examine is how prevalent the use of conditioning is in our society. Take for example the use of marketing campaigns that get us to purchase products that we don't even need. Rather than focusing on what is actually required for our survival - that which keeps us alive, like food - these companies create various "needs" in our mind that stimulate our greed and hunger. I just heard on the radio last week how a new "wet" toilet paper is going to be released to the American public. It'll probably also be perfumed, and printed in different fancy colors and designs. The best part is; millions of dollars will be spent to convince us that we need moistened toilet paper.

Someone may now say, who cares if we're tricked into buying pretty air fresheners, or bamboozled into taking our dogs to pet psychologists 'for their own good.' What's the big deal?

Well, if you think about it, how is our personal life, and society in general, molded by this type of subtle conditioning? If you don't believe me, think back to a time one hundred years earlier when advertising didn't play such a prevalent role in our lives. Look at how we've been "seduced" by this deceptive organism. We have teenage and college-aged girls starving themselves to death because we've embraced a culture of thinness. We're also obsessed with youth, so women in their 40's and 50's are having face lifts and tummy tucks, while girls of all ages have boob jobs because flat-chested girls "don't stack up." What a load of bull. In addition, adolescent girls dress like they're 20 years old because "sex sells," while our throwaway, consumer culture has led to rampant personal debt and an environment that is literally exhausted. All because we're told that these are the "things" we need to make us happy.

One hundred years ago we didn't think this way, but we do today. Why? Well, if you take a child that's six months old and sit them in front of a television set for six hours a day (or more), then allow their minds to be poisoned by the public conditioning system (it can no longer be classified as "public education"), then feed them the garbage propaganda on our nightly newscasts, what would you expect? All of these forces combine to do a pretty good job of defining our identity.

Insight # 6: Often-times people, and entire cultures, are fashioned, shaped, and molded without even knowing that such a process is taking place.

So, in light of the Corp-Org Model, everyone is viewed as a consumer, which is why there are always different products being constantly redesigned to fill our 'needs.'

Now, being that the Machine is such a vital part of our Control System, what does it take to keep it running? The answer, of course, is ENERGY, which is the single largest industry in the world. This is why our current Corp-Org way of thinking persists today. Look at some of the wealthiest corporations in the world - Exxon, Texaco, Mobil, and Gulf. What do they all specialize in? Burning fossil fuels. In regard to our homes, what is the largest utility cost that we face? Again, the answer is energy. To get from one place to another, which corporations do we support? Ford, Chevrolet, Dodge, etc. Related to this are the peripheral companies that keep our automobiles running - Goodyear, Firestone, Valvoline, etc. If our cars are too slow, we flock to the airline industry - United, U.S. Air, etc. Finally, to protect our borders, we throw money to an industry that capitalizes on energy - Hughes, Northrop, etc.

Now that we've seen the connection between energy and our economy, we need to analyze how we rely on endeavors that fail to take into consideration the human race or our planetary concerns. How can we still be burning fossil fuels after all these years when hydrogen energy is so much better? By perpetuating this practice, we keep filling our air, water, ground, and lungs with a poison that is destroying us en masse.

With this in mind, the author of The Invisibles contends that this seemingly faulted thinking is all part of a game plan. So, without further ado, here it is:

1) Exhaust planet earth
2) Find new energy sources, such as in outer space
3) Leave planet earth behind
4) Exist in outer space
5) Ultimately destroy the planet and move on

Insight # 7: The Controllers continue to exhaust our planet rather than conserve it because they, the very FEW, have already planned their escape when its usefulness has been depleted.

As the Controllers continue to poison our planet, they're simultaneously examining ways to save their own hides. As Hugh Fox says: "The Invisibles in no way depend on what we consider to be survival conditions for their own survival."

Now, being that we've taken a peek at the Controller's motives, why don't the masses revolt and alter their destiny? The Controllers realize that this reaction is a very real possibility, so they punch a number of factors into their Systems Analysis Model and arrive at a variety of ways to keep the populace appeased and docile.

The three most important variables to keep the American people in line:

1) Economic well-being - If our income, taxes, and cost of living are kept within "acceptable limits," then the citizenry will not cause trouble.

2) Social well-being - If crime rates and the quality of our neighborhoods are maintained, the people will feel safe in their surroundings.

3) Personal well-being - If our family life, our sex life, and our ability to "meet our goals" are kept within acceptable levels, then the masses will remain calm.

Thus, when the Controllers collude with global corporations, American business, industry, government, and the financial centers by calculating the effect of each factor within a Systems Analysis Model, we begin to see that things in our society don't just happen at random. There are hours upon endless hours of planning - and complex strategies - needed to keep the Machine rolling. With this in mind, we find that people can be kept contented with three centers of well being - economic, social, and personal. If you also keep them distracted with sports, gossip, scandals, and the overall rat race; there isn't much they're going to do to rock the boat.

Can't you see? We're seen the same as a company that manufactures bars of soap. But instead of factoring in ingredients, raw materials, cost of production, logistics, and advertising, they plug in social variables, tax rates, crime statistics, inflation, and a slew of other numbers. Thus, by keeping us occupied with the Machine, we don't have the time or effort to get enraged about the sale of our Presidency to the New World Order, blatant assassinations (i.e. Princess Diana), the loss of our input in the electoral process ("Votescam"), the creation of a horrendous disease (AIDS), ongoing CIA mind control experiments, how our guns are slowly being taken away from us, the inception of new laws that continually remove our freedoms and right to privacy, or the way our planet is being decimated and destroyed. But that's all right because at least we have jobs, food on the table, a fairly stable social structure, and a belief that we're the greatest nation of all-time.

Insight # 8: Similar to a reverse-version of Abraham Maslow's famous "hierarchy of needs" model, if the Controllers can manipulate the basic elements needed to keep us satisfied (the least common denominator), and keep us distracted at the same time, then they can continue to chip away at realizing their dream - the creation of a one-world government.

One may now ask, if the Controllers are so ingenious, does that mean they never make mistakes or screw-up? Of course not, but they are aware of those factors that hold the most potential for disaster. They are:

1) Any person (or group) that wants to overthrow the existing order.
2) Any reconciliation between groups usually at odds with each other.

In other words, the Controllers seek to maintain and promote CONTAINED INSTABILITY. Not full-blown anarchy or insurrection, mind you, but enough conflict to perpetuate a Hegelian Dialectic that falls within the desired parameters that have been pre-determined via Systems Analysis. Someone may wonder - why would those in control want a state of constant conflict or strife? Well, because limited wars, limited crime, limited drug use, limited auto fatalities, limited industrial accidents, limited pollution, and limited organized crime all mean that people will always be told that something needs to be done to maintain the status quo (their three centers for well-being). What we're not told, though, is that our status quo is one of deliberate instability - there is always one force being pitted against another - constant tension - and a continual formula of conflict that is being set in motion. And, it is ALL being calculated and implemented behind the scenes, just like the Wizard of Oz.

Another reason for this instability is that whenever there are problems (which is always), the masses will constantly be looking for people to SOLVE these problems. How is this done? By introducing new products, new governmental programs, new investments, and new spending. And what results from this "newness?" People keep consuming, and the Machine keeps rolling!

Insight # 9: Anything that requires "action" is seen by the Controllers as being beneficial to their goals.

What happens if things get out of hand? What if people get so fed up with the status quo that they feel like rebelling, or starting a war? At first glance, such a scenario would seem like a very detrimental thing. But in reality, according to the Controllers, long-term peace is not in the best interest of society (See: *War - The Report from Iron Mountain*). The reason for this is twofold. First, those who rule society view certain segments of the population as "useless," or a tax on our resources. Thus, they need a way to eliminate them. What could be better than war? And secondly, war is the most effective way to stimulate a nation's economy. Plus, from a purely "business" aspect, war allows the Controllers to expand into new markets, rebuild cities that were destroyed (via interest-garnering loans), and to create new consumers (those who were conquered). Also, arms production doesn't require an advertising budget or buyers that need to be convinced of a product's merit. The only thing they have to worry about is distribution - getting the bombs and guns to the area(s) being warred upon.

Insight # 10: The ultimate method of keeping the Machine in motion is via social unrest, uneasiness, and conflict, all of which hold the potential for war. Peace and tranquility are looked upon with disfavor.

To convince us of this system's virtue, the Controller's use "double-agents" and "double-talk" to create an illusion that their programs will ultimately benefit us. A prime example would be the rash of cameras that are being erected in large cities and small towns all across America. As these constant forms of surveillance keep an eye on us, we're told that the ones at each street corner are used to stop red-light runners, while the ones on top of each building are used to combat drug dealers, gangs, or riotous behavior. While some people protest, we get double-talk from newspaper editorials, surveys, phony polls, and TV commentaries that tell us how great this idea is. The end result is that Big Brother slowly becomes more apparent through the implementation of creeping surveillance.

Another example of how double-think affects us is via what we're taught versus the rules under which the Controllers operate. Throughout life, we've been told to be honest, peaceful, virtuous, and fair. Yet look at how those who run the world operate. Do you think they follow, or play by, the same rules that they've told us to adhere to? What I'm trying to convey is this: any time "doubles" are used, different layers of "reality" can be seen. It's similar to peeling back the layers of an onion. Once one is stripped away, other levels still exist beneath it. But we can't stop simply by exposing one layer, for many more are still hidden that we're not even aware of until we keep peeling away at the Controller's veneer. All of these layers, then, are literally "fronts" and "double-fronts" that the Invisibles use to cover their essential CORE.

Insight # 11: By saying one thing in the guise of another, the Invisibles create an illusion where their outer layers conceal the true nature of their inner core.

By now, someone may be thinking, everything sounds so utterly controlled, calculated, and analyzed. What would happen if somebody stepped out of line?

Not only is this an excellent question, but we have a perfect answer that played-out right here in America in the early 1960's when John F. Kennedy was killed right before our eyes. This quote by Hugh Fox is a good starting point:

"There is a truism in espionage circles that runs something like ASSASSINATIONS ARE EASY, PLANNING "NATURAL DEATHS" TAKES TIME. By 1963, the Invisibles had so perfected their technique that there was no longer any need to fake natural deaths. Assassination could look like assassination - only the actual assassin's and assassination game-plan would be projected out on the Invisibles Counter-world in such a way - and on such a *level* - that anyone searching for motivations or logistic links on the straight level of Single - (or even Double) Think would hardly even begin to understand the Logistics of this Invisible Counter-Reality."

Y'see, JFK didn't play by the pre-established, traditional rules that the Controllers set down for him (and other Presidents). A lot of money and time was invested in John Kennedy (see: *The Gemstone Thesis*), but he reneged on his deals and turned his back on the CIA, the Mafia, and all the goals they wanted to accomplish in Cuba, Russia, and Vietnam. Everything had been planned via their Systems Analysis techniques, but Kennedy refused to fit into their "game-model."

How so? Well, Kennedy didn't fall into the Pentagon's fanatical campaigns against Russia or Vietnam (either a perceived "Cold War" or an actual bloodbath in the jungles), thus negating the profitability of their War Machine. In fact, by spring, 1963, Kenneth P. O'Donnell reported that JFK vowed to start withdrawing all troops from Vietnam in the near future.

Thus, what we have is a variety of powerful men who have a vested interest in how certain events unfold. They had created a Corp-Org Model that took into consideration EVERY possible factor that affects a number of outcomes. When things don't work out, the final option was to create a "game-model" scenario to assassinate JFK (the source of their problems) that contained a multitude of variables. By placing numerous false-leads and built-in decoys to divert attention away from (rather than toward) the true killers, a "counter-reality" is thus created similar to the "doubles" mentioned in an earlier section. Look at all the phantom cars, the grassy knoll scenarios, hidden tunnels beneath the freeway, misdirection, patsies, double-identities, and missing evidence. It's incredible! Then, once the kill has taken place, the patsy takes his fall and the surface charade is ended as the link between "visible" and "invisible" disappears.

Insight # 12: Exhaustion will always take precedence over regeneration. Those who try to halt the consumptive nature of the Machine will be duly eliminated.

Now that we've established a basis for how the power elite operate; we need to reexamine the reality of our situation at the present moment. What follows is a brief overview:

1) Power isn't derived from governments, and national boundaries are nothing but an illusion.

2) Supranational companies are the ones who call the shots here on earth.

3) At the top of the corporate-financial power structure are the international bankers.

4) At the head of this power structure - the very men who rule the world - are the chairmen of the world's largest financial structures (i.e. Chase Manhattan).

5) These entities control both war and peace.

6) They are not concerned with conservation, but with depletion.

7) Their overall plan at this stage of the game is to exhaust our planetary resources (kill the seas, destroy the air, poison the soil), then leave earth and move into outer space.

8) The Invisibles, then, are a small group of supra-national inter-related banker-industrialists that set in motion all that happens on earth.

In this sense, we need a new perspective for looking at the world. The concept of sovereign nations is slowly becoming a thing of the past, replaced by global corporations that are controlled by international financiers. If seen in this light, the United States is nothing more than a supranational, government-subsidized business that is interlocked with every other "country/corporation," all of whom are subordinates of the world money interests.

If you doubt that this phenomenon is actually occurring, examine the recent merger attempt between General Electric and Honeywell. Now, both GE and Honeywell are American owned companies, and the merger was to take place on American soil. Plus, the merger had already been okayed by the American Congress. So, everything was set in motion for these two companies to merge, when all of a sudden the deal was denied. Who do you think denied, and ultimately stuck a dagger through its heart - an American regulatory commission or the FTC (Federal Trade Commission)? No, the deal was squashed by the EU - the European Union! A group of Europeans had enough clout and power to tell two American companies on American soil that they couldn't merge. Think about how scary that is!

In essence, then, what we have are national interests bowing to the global Controllers' demands. We are no longer seen as Americans, Canadians, or Australians; no, we're cogs in the Machine that must keep churning away through the process of consumption (consumerism).

Gundrun Tempel, in *The Chairman is God*, comments on how these financiers have become god-like beings. "Every man, woman and child is a mini-market ... we are units in the biggest data bank the world has ever known."

People, the "workable units," are seen as nothing more than insignificant elements of a colossal machine that is hooked-up to a planetary data bank, with layers upon layers of bureaucratic hullabaloo, distraction, illusion, and various modes of conditioning acting as a barrier between us and them. At the other end of this maddeningly complex process, hidden from view, are the Invisibles. If you don't believe me, try to discuss this issue with Mr. David Rockefeller in New York City. Do you think you'll be able to get to him? No! He's untouchable ... out of reach ... invisible. They don't have any need or desire to interact with the "common folk." We're simply cogs in the mega-machine that can be manipulated on a project-by-project basis by a group of elite planners who are hidden from public view.

Insight # 13: People are no longer seen as human entities, but as units or variables in a grand, machinistic design.

The author of this Dialectic ultimately contends that, "The closer we approach the Invisibles, the more invisible they become." He urges us to take hold of this point because once we begin to see who they truly are; they erect a slew of new decoy-realities because they know we're on to them. These added layers of concealment create new counter-realities, and the dialectic process continues to unfold. The very LAST thing they want to happen is how Toto in "The Wizard of Oz" pulls back the curtain and exposes the Wizard's true nature. To them, nothing could be more damaging.

The author concludes with the following sentiment: "Given the general threat of the Invisibles planetary plan, i.e. destruction of the life-support systems, unless this power bloc as a group intends planetary emigration (the possibility of which we cannot entirely ignore), then they must as a group be controlled by a higher power. Perhaps they represent the visible outer shell of the power-nucleus, but the real power must lie within - and then must serve merely as a diversionary cover. The other possibility remains that Rockefeller and the others are not terrestrial at all, but merely extra-terrestrials who have assumed human form and came to earth as merely one stage in an inter-galactic mission whose purpose remains totally unknown to us."

SECTION

FOUR:

THE FEDERAL

RESERVE

SYSTEM

CHAPTER TWENTY

NOTES AND QUOTES: THIS IS HOW OUR FINE COUNTRY WAS DESTROYED IN 1913

The Shadows of Power: The Council on Foreign Relations and the American Decline, by James Perloff (Western Island, 1988):

Felix Frankfurter, United States Supreme Court Justice: "The real rulers in Washington are invisible, and exercise power from behind the scenes."

John F. Hylan, Mayor of New York City, in a March 26, 1922 speech: "The real menace of our republic is the invisible government which, like a giant octopus, sprawls its slimy length over our city, state and nation. At the head is a small group of banking houses generally referred to as "international bankers." This little coterie of powerful international bankers virtually run our government for their own selfish ends."

President Franklin Delano Roosevelt, November 21, 1933: "The real truth of the matter is, as you and I know, that a financial element in the large centers has owned the government since the days of Andrew Jackson.

Cliques that make many of the decisions which affect our country:

- Private schools (training grounds) – Harvard, Yale, Princeton, Columbia

- Exclusive secret societies – Skull & Bones

- Oxford – Rhodes Scholarship program

- Think tanks – Brookings Institute, Rand Corporation

The Council on Foreign Relations, founded in 1921; goals include: world government, centralized power with single authority, boundaries (national) and sovereignty eliminated, increased authority of the United Nations, an international court of justice, and elimination of the "Bill of Rights."

International Bankers – Here is, in a nutshell, how they control the world: They lend money to governments or nations. In order to repay their loans, these governments levy taxes on their citizenry. But not only do the bankers make these loans; they also attach strings to them. In other words, the government grants these bankers a privilege – a "say" in their policy.

The most lucrative event for bankers – WAR – nothing generates more government borrowing faster than war.

To rule a country, one must first establish a monopoly over that nation's money supply by creating a central bank (The Federal Reserve).

Meyer Rothschild: "Let me issue and control a nation's money, and I care not who writes its laws."

Carroll Quigley, 1966: _Tragedy and Hope_: "The powers of financial capitalism had another far-reaching aim, nothing less than to create a world system of financial control in private hands able to dominate the political system of each country and the economy of the world as a whole."

The Federal Reserve: a brief history:

1) The Panic of 1907, an artificially created event; rumors were circulated that all the banks were going under and would lose their money. J. P. Morgan, one of the great influential bankers of all-time, started the rumors.

2) The Federal Reserve Act of 1913 created the Federal Reserve, which now has complete control over interest rates, and also the creation of money (taking this privilege away from Congress). They now control the size of our national money supply, which directly affects inflation, depressions, etc.

3) Although called "federal," the Federal Reserve is privately owned. It has never   been audited.

4) Its policies are not subject to the President of the United States or Congress.

5) It can create – and inflate; has the ability to relax or tighten the money supply as they see fit.

6) Neither the Congress, the President, or the American people can issue money. Only private bankers can do it – and at a PROFIT for themselves!!

7) The United States of America has to borrow money from THEM.

8) To pay off the debt that we owe these private bankers (via the interest on loans), our government had to create the Income Tax (also in 1913!). Prior to 1913, there was no income tax except for a few years during the Civil War and Reparation Period. Our government kept itself afloat by tariffs and excise taxes.

9) Here's the ploy behind the Income Tax – the rich evade it by funneling their money into tax-free "foundations" – the rest of us get manipulated because of a "graduated" tax system. In other words, the more you make, the more the government takes. That way, it's extremely difficult, if not impossible, for people to ascend up the ladder and get into "their league."

1913 – a horrible year – The Federal Reserve (a central bank) was created. This institution loaned HUGE amounts of money to the United States government. To pay off this debt, the Federal Income Tax Law was enacted, which proceeded to STEAL money from the American citizenry. But when the Federal Reserve was created in 1913, they needed to find a reason for our government to start borrowing money from them. They found ... or CREATED ... a reason very shortly thereafter. World War I began in 1914!

President Woodrow Wilson, 1913 – "The New Freedom": "Some of the biggest men in the United States, in the field of commerce and manufacturing, are afraid of something. They know that there is a power somewhere so organized, so subtle, so watchful, so interlocked, so complete, so pervasive, that they had better not speak above their breath when they speak in condemnation of it."

Karl Marx said in "The Communist Manifesto" that a GRADUATED INCOME TAX and a CENTRAL BANK were essential to the formation of a Communist government.

World War I – International bankers profited immensely from it. Banker Bernard Baruch's profits totaled $200 million. Also, shortly after World War I ended, the League of Nations (a predecessor to the United Nations) was formed.

Tactics of the International Bankers – Our nation's original Constitution was written to keep the government out of our hair. This was called a "laissez faire" policy. Government had little or no influence on business, education, religion, or other aspects of our lives. We practiced free enterprise, which meant there was competition. With this philosophy and practice, everyone had a chance to make it to the top.

But then the monopolists entered the picture in the late 1800s – John D. Rockefeller, J. P. Morgan and others – and they eliminated competition. John D. Rockefeller even said "competition is a sin."

They wanted to be able to call the shots via governments, banks and business institutions that were already bought and paid for (controlled). Think about all the monopolies our government runs: education, money (Federal Reserve), Post Office, NASA, military, Court systems, taxation, etc.

Our government is a MONOPOLY – thus, regulation, socialism, and communism are all graduated forms of monopoly!

The Stock Market Crash of 1929 wasn't an accident. From 1923 to 1929, The Federal Reserve expanded the money supply 62%! Think what would happen today if the money supply were expanded 62%.

Congressman Charles Lindbergh – 1913: "From now on, depressions will be scientifically created."

Louis McFadden, Chairman of the House Banking Committee, describing the Great Depression: "It was not accidental. It was a carefully contrived occurrence … the international bankers sought to bring about a condition of despair here so that they might emerge as rulers of us all."

Here's how the Great Crash happened:

1) Plenty of money was made readily available.
2) With lots of money floating around, people bought stocks – the Roaring 20s were a time of great prosperity after World War I.
3) The stocks everyone bought, however, were issued as "24 hour call loans," which meant the money had to be repaid in 24 hours if it was "called" for.
4) So, the New York financiers started "calling in" all their loans at once.
5) Stockbrokers and customers had to dump their stocks to pay their loans.
6) The Stock Market collapsed, which caused a banking catastrophe.
7) All the banks that were not "part" of the cabal also had to pay their "call claims," which exhausted their money supplies and caused them to go under.
8) Only the small investors, not the "insiders," were destroyed.

9)   Paul Warburg, who founded the Federal Reserve, tipped off all the money barons (J. D. Rockefeller, Bernard Baruch, Joe Kennedy, etc.) before the collapse occurred.

10)   All of these men got out of the market before it crashed – selling their stocks while the prices were still high.

11)   Then, when the market collapsed and all the stocks were at rock bottom prices because everyone was broke, they strolled in and bought all of them. This was when their REAL POWER began!

12)   Joe Kennedy's fortune went from $4 million in 1929 to $100 million in 1935!

World War I – This war was devised to get the United States involved in a world conflict, and thus to borrow huge amounts of money. To do this, the Lusitania was deliberately allowed to be sunk by the Germans – 128 Americans died in the process – raising our cockles and guaranteeing that we'd enter the fray.

Joseph Kenworthy, British Naval Intelligence: "The Lusitania was deliberately sent at a considerably reduced speed into an area where a U-boat was known to be waiting and with her escorts withdrawn." This was after the British had already cracked Germany's naval code and knew exactly where all their U-boats were located.

The Federal Reserve Conspiracy by Antony Sutton (CPA Book Publishers, 1995)

Jekyl Island Meeting, 1910 – Here is where the idea of a Federal Reserve Bank was conceived. But if any of the Wall Street names became associated with a Central Bank, the Federal Reserve Bill would surely be labeled with a kiss of death by the American people. Americans at that time were strongly opposed to the concept of central bank, so it was formed in such a way that it seemed like bankers opposed it publicly. But actually, they were the ones who designed and promoted it!

They were so sneaky, even Woodrow Wilson actually thought he was signing a bill that took financial power AWAY from the Wall Street financiers.

Paul Warburg: If anyone asks, "Who were the people who did this?" his name would be the first on the list. Our Federal Reserve Bank was modeled after the German Reichsbank.

The Panic of 1907 – created by the "Standard Oil" crowd. These were the same people who were running the show all along: John D. Rockefeller, J. P. Morgan, etc. In other words, those who benefited most from the Panic (after a Central Bank was created) were the same persons who caused the disaster.

Jekyl Island Meeting attendees:

- Senator Nelson Aldrich – father-in-law of John D. Rockefeller
- Paul Warburg, German banker – founder of Kuhn Loeb and the Federal Reserve
- Henry P. Davison – J. P. Morgan
- Benjamin Strong – Bankers Trust
- Frank Vanderlip – National City Bank
- Charles D. Norton – First National Bank

Woodrow Wilson – Two-thirds of his total campaign funds came from just 7 people!!!

The World Order: A Study in the Hegemony of Parasitism, by Eustace Mullins (Ezra Pound Institute of Civilization, 1985)

League of Nations – a front for the real conspirators – had its origins in three institutions – the RIAA (Royal Institute of International Affairs), The Council on Foreign Relations, and the House of Rothschild.

John Moody – *McClure's* magazine, August, 1911: "Seven men in Wall Street now control a great share of the fundamental industry and resources in the United States." The names he included were: J. P. Morgan, John D. Rockefeller and Jacob Schiff.

Jekyl Island – all of the financiers were emissaries of Baron Alfred Rothschild, who commissioned them to create a Central Bank modeled after the Reichsbank, the Bank of England, and the Bank of France – all of which were controlled by the House of Rothschild!

Six New York banks bought controlling interest in the Federal Reserve Bank in New York. Even as late as 1983, only five banks held 53% of all the shares. These five are: Citibank, Chase Manhattan, Morgan Guaranty Trust, Manhattan Hanover, and Chemical Bank.

American is ruled by FIVE BANKS!!!

A quote from the author: "The World Order rules through a simple technique, Divide and Conquer. Every natural or unnatural disaster among people, every occasion for hatred or greed, is exploited and exacerbated to the limit. The polarization of racial and ethnic groups in the United States is accelerated by a flood of government decrees, originating in foundation "studies," which are designed solely to set American against American. Only in this way can the World Order maintain its iron grip on the daily lives of the people. The World Order also rules by the principle of "1984." No groups of two or more people are allowed to gather unless the World Order has a "representative" present...

"...The World Order adopted the Hegelian Dialectic which regards the World as Power, and the World as Reality. It denies all other powers and all other realities. It functions on the principle of thesis, antithesis, and a synthesis, which results when the thesis and antithesis are thrown against each other for a predetermined outcome. The World Order organizes and finances Jewish groups; it then organizes and finances anti-Jewish groups; it organizes Communist groups; it then organizes and finances anti-Communist groups. It is not necessary for the Order to throw these groups against each other; they seek each other out like heat-seeking missiles and try to destroy each other. By controlling the size and resources of each group, the World Order can always predetermine the outcome...

"...A distinguishing trait of a member of the World Order, although it may not be admitted, is that he does not believe in anything but the World Order. Another distinguishing trait is his absolute contempt for anyone who actually believes in the tenets of Communism, Zionism, Christianity, or any national, religious, or fraternal group, although the Order has members in controlling positions in all these groups. If you are a sincere Christian, Zionist, or Muslim, the Order regards you as a moron unworthy of respect. You can and will be used, but you will never be respected."

Pawns in the Game by **William Guy Carr (Omni/Christian Book Club)**

Jekyl Island, Georgia – The hideaway where the bankers met was owned by J. P. Morgan. When they met, they were called "The First Name Group" because all the attendees were only allowed to be called by their first names (or code names) while addressing each other.

Federal Reserve Act – joined American and European bankers so they could more easily bring about World War I in 1914. This war was fought to enable the International Conspirators a better opportunity to start the Russian (Bolshevik) Revolution in 1917. It was the same with the English Revolution in 1640, the French Revolution in 1789, and the American Civil War in 1860.

Federal Reserve System – 12 total banks by 1946. That year their reserves totaled 45 billion dollars. During World War II alone, they made 42 BILLION DOLLARS in profits!

Vladimir Lenin – "The best revolutionary is a youth devoid of morals."

1912 – The International Bankers and the Grand Orient Lodge of Freemasonry met in Switzerland, where they decided to have Archduke Francis Ferdinand assassinated to start World War I.

New World Order: The Ancient Plan of Secret Societies, by William T. Still (Huntington House Press, 1990)

Financiers of Bolshevik Revolution:

- Max Warburg – brother of Paul Warburg, who founded the Federal Reserve; he was also the head of the German Secret Police during World War I.
- J. P. Morgan & Company
- Rockefeller Oil Company
- Alfred Milner Rothschild
- Jacob Schiff – invested $20 million

Carroll Quigley, 1966 – Tragedy and Hope: "The history of the last century shows that the advice given to government by bankers was consistently good for bankers, but was often disastrous for governments, businessmen, and the people generally."

Vladimir Lenin: "Establishing a central bank is 90% of making a country Communist."

Panic of 1907 – Results: 1) The Insiders made a financial killing, and 2) it "created" the *need* for a central bank.

Federal Reserve Act – Results: It granted control to privately owned central banks in regard to interest rates and the size of the national money supply.

1971 New York Times Magazine – Congressman Louis McFadden, Chairman of the House Committee on Banking & Currency from 1920-1931: The Federal Reserve Act brought about "a super-state controlled by international bankers and international industrialists together to enslave the world for their own pleasure."

We have two governments in this country; one is "elected" and the other is an independent, uncontrolled government of the Federal Reserve.

Have you ever wondered about the National Debt – to whom we owe this money? The answer: We owe it to the banks that participate in and control the Federal Reserve System.

A quote from the author: "More than half of what Americans pay in Federal Income Taxes goes into the pockets of bankers (via interest payments). It is clear that the United States is literally at the mercy of a huge, private monopoly controlled by a handful of undetected men."

The "Black Hand" - The group of people who assassinated Archduke Ferdinand (among others). They were a revolutionary organization affiliated with Freemasonry.

W. Cleon Skousen - *The Naked Capitalist* (1970): "Power from any source tends to create an appetite for additional power ... It was almost inevitable that the super-rich would one day aspire to control not only their own wealth, but the wealth of the whole world."

Descent into Slavery, by Des Griffin (Emissary Publications, 1980): The majority of government bonds are held by people who aren't even American citizens. They're international bankers!

By 1900, it was estimated that half of the wealth in the entire world was controlled by the House of Rothschild.

Jacob Schiff – controlled Kuhn, Loeb, & Company; the top Rothschild agent in the United States who financed J. D. Rockefeller, Edward Harriman (the railroad magnate), and Andrew Carnegie's steel empire; he also provided $20 million directly to the Bolshevik Revolution (which spawned Communism).

World War I – created astronomical debts for every nation involved. "Theaters of War" are always lucrative for those who finance them.

Edwin Stanton – Abraham Lincoln's Secretary of War: "Wars are not fought to defeat an enemy; wars are fought to create a condition."

Treaty of Versailles – Philip Snowden, British Parliament: "It was not a peace treaty, but a declaration of another war."

Treaty of Versailles – Lloyd George: "We have a written document that guarantees war in twenty years."

An Overview of What the International Bankers Did:

1)   They created the conditions to begin World War I.
2)   They made a financial killing from that war.
3)   They also financed the Bolshevik Revolution – by doing so, they took control of Russia.
4)   They manipulated events to create the Treaty of Versailles, plus the Dawes and Young Plans.
5)   They used American loans to re-arm Germany.
6)   While building up the Germans, they also antagonized them (via hyperinflation and high employment) to augment Adolf Hitler's rise to power.

American Business and Hitler's Rise to Power – Ambassador William Dodd to President Roosevelt on August 15, 1936 (3 ½ years after Hitler rose to power): "At the present moment, more than a hundred American corporations have subsidiaries here or cooperative understandings. The DuPonts have three allies in Germany that are aiding in the armament business. Their chief ally is the I. G. Farben Company. The Standard Oil Company sent $2 million here in December 1933, and has made $500,000 a year helping Germans make Ersatz gas for war purposes."

John Swinton – Editor of *New York News* at the annual dinner of America Press Association – 1914: "There is no such thing as an independent press in American … Not a man among you dares to utter his honest opinion … we are tools and the vassals of the rich behind the scenes. We are marionettes. These men pull the strings and we dance. Our time, our talents, our lives and our capacities are all the property of these men – we are intellectual prostitutes."

Fatima and the Great Conspiracy by Deirdre Manifold (The Fatima Crusade, 1982)

Quote from the author: "The United States Federal Reserve Bank is a money dictatorship possessing absolute autocratic powers over the American people and indirectly over the rest of the world."

Quote from the author: "The one fear the Insiders have is of being exposed, and anyone who dares such a venture can expect to be smeared, even to death."

Meyer Amschel Rothschild: "Permit me to issue and control the money of a nation, and I care not who makes its laws."

Sir Josiah Stamp, Director of the Bank of England: "Banking was conceived in iniquity and born in sin ... Bankers own the earth. Take it away from them, but leave them the power to create money, and with a flick of a pen they will create enough money to buy it back again."

One of their tactics: They want ordinary people to think that everything that happens in the world is accidental – that it can't be helped. Now we know differently!!!

Fourth Reich of the Rich by Des Griffin (Emissary Publishers, 1976)

Sir Winston Churchill: "Most people, sometime in their lives, stumble across the truth. Most jump up, brush themselves off and hurry on about their business as if nothing had happened."

John Swinton, Editor of the *New York News*, 1914 – at the annual dinner of the America Press Association: "It is the duty of a New York journalist to lie, to revile, to toady at the feet of Mammon, to sell his country and his race for his daily bread, or what amounts to the same thing, his salary."

David Rockefeller, June 1991 – Bilderberg Meeting: "We are grateful to the *Washington Post*, the *New York Times*, *Time* Magazine and the other great publications whose directors have attended our meetings and respected their promises of discretion for almost 40 years. It would have been impossible for us to develop our plan for the world if we had been subject to the bright lights of publicity during those years."

Quote from the author: "Divide the masses of the people into opposing camps on political, social, racial, economic and religious issues. Then arm and finance those groups and encourage them to fight with each other."

Paul Warburg, Jr., son of Paul Warburg – before the United States Senate, February 17, 1950: "We shall have world government whether or not we like it. The only question is whether world government will be achieved by conquest or consent."

CHAPTER TWENTY-ONE

WHO CONTROLS THE FEDERAL RESERVE SYSTEM?

Now that we know the Federal Reserve is a privately owned, for-profit corporation, a natural question would be: who owns this company? Peter Kershaw provides the answer in *Economic Solutions* where he lists the ten primary shareholders in the Federal Reserve banking system.

1) The Rothschild Family - London
2) The Rothschild Family - Berlin
3) The Lazard Brothers - Paris
4) Israel Seiff - Italy
5) Kuhn-Loeb Company - Germany
6) The Warburgs - Amsterdam
7) The Warburgs - Hamburg
8) Lehman Brothers - New York
9) Goldman & Sachs - New York
10) The Rockefeller Family - New York

Now I don't know about you, but something is terribly wrong with this situation. Namely, don't we live in AMERICA? If so, why are seven of the top ten stockholders located in FOREIGN countries? That's 70%!

To further convey how screwed-up this system is, Jim Marrs provides the following data in his book, *Rule by Secrecy*. He says that the Federal Reserve Bank of New York, which undeniably controls the other eleven Federal Reserve branches, is essentially controlled by two financial institutions:

1) Chase Manhattan (controlled by the Rockefellers) - 6,389,445 shares - 32.3%
2) Citbank - 4,051,851 shares - 20.5%

Thus, these two entities control nearly 53% of the New York Federal Reserve Bank. Considering how many trillions of dollars are involved here, and how the bankers are WAY above our "selected" officials in Washington, D.C., do you think the above-listed banks and families have an inordinate amount of say-so in how our country is being run? The answer is blindingly apparent.

WHERE DOES THE MONEY COME FROM?

We all know that the Federal Reserve CORPORATION prints money, then lends it at interest to our government. But wait until you see what a total scam this process is. Before we get to the meat of this issue, let's remember one thing about the essence of banking -- primarily that money should have some type of standard upon which its value is based.

In the case of America, we operate on what is called a "gold standard" (i.e., our money is backed by gold).

With that in mind, let's look at how money is actually created, and at what cost. If the Treasury wants to print 1,000 one-hundred ($100) bills, their total cost for ink, paper, plates, labor, etc. would be approximately $23.00 (according to Davvy Kidd in *Why A Bankrupt America*). If you do the math, the total cost of 10,000 bills would be $230.00 ($.023 x 10,000).

But here's the catch. Ten thousand $100 bills equal $1,000,000! So, the Federal Reserve can "create" a million dollars; then LEND it to the U.S. Government (with interest) for a total cost of $230.00! That's not a bad deal, huh!

The banking industry calls this process "seignorage." I call it outright THEFT. Why? Well, regardless of the immense profit margin ($1,000,000 for $230), plus the huge interest payments, our government then needs to steal the American people's money to pay off their debts via a Mob-like agency called the IRS.

So the bankers steal from the government, then the government turns around and steals from the people. I'm no genius, but who do you think is getting screwed in this process? We are - the people at the bottom rung of the ladder.

What's worse is that -- now catch your breath -- there's NO MORE gold left in Fort Knox! It's all gone. In other words, the GOLD STANDARD that our financial system was based upon is now an illusion.

We can't convert our money into gold -- only other currency. The entire underlying basis for our money is now a lie -- a sham. The Federal Reserve has become so arrogant that they are a literal MONEY MAKING MACHINE, creating currency out of thin air!

So that's where the Fed gets their money. They literally make it; then lend it to us so they can make even MORE money.

MONEY AS A RELIGION

William Grieder, former assistant managing editor of the *Washington Post*, wrote a book in 1987 entitled, *Secrets of the Temple: How the Federal Reserve Runs the Country* that details how the Controllers have conditioned us to accept this absurd situation.

"To modern minds," he writes, "it seemed bizarre to think of the Federal Reserve as a religious institution. Yet the conspiracy theorists, in their own demented way, were on to something real and significant. The Fed did also function in the realm of religion. Its mysterious powers of money creation, inherited from priestly forebears, shielded a complex bundle of social and psychological meanings. With its own form of secret incantation, the Federal Reserve presided over awesome social ritual, transactions so powerful and frightening they seemed to lie beyond common understanding."

Grieder continues, "Above all, money was a function of faith. It required implicit and universal social consent that was indeed mysterious. To create money and use it, each one must believe, and everyone must believe. Only then did worthless pieces of paper take on value."

Do you get it? MONEY is an ILLUSION! Why? Because the gold standard upon which our money is supposed to be based has been eliminated. There's no more gold in Fort Knox. It's all GONE! Now, money really IS only paper!!! In the past, money was supposed to represent something of tangible value. Now it's simply paper!

Taken one step further, many of us don't even use paper money any more. Many places of employment directly deposit their employee's paychecks into the bank. Once the money is there, when bill time comes around, the person in question can write out a stack of checks to pay them. When they need gasoline they use a credit card; for groceries they use a debit card. If this person goes out for dinner on Friday night, they can charge the tab on their Diner's Card.

But what about the tip? They simply scribble in the amount at the bottom of the check. So far, the person hasn't spent a single dollar bill. Then, if you bring electronic banking into the picture, we've virtually eliminated the use for money. And God forbid, what happens when encoded microchips are implanted into the backs of our hand?

In essence, money has become nothing more than an illusion -- an electronic figure or amount on a computer screen. That's it! As time goes on, we have an increasing tendency toward being sucked into this Wizard of Oz vortex of unreality.

Think about it. Americans as a whole are carrying more personal debt than at any other time in history. And our government keeps going further and further into the hole, with no hope of ever crawling out.

But we have less and less actual MONEY! We are being enslaved by the debt of electronic blips on a computer screen! And 70% of the banks that control this debt via the Federal Reserve exist in foreign countries!

What in God's name is going on? As author William Bramley says, "The result of this whole system is MASSIVE debt at every level of society."

We're being manipulated in a sickening way, folks, and the people doing it are using the ILLUSION of money as their control device. I hate to say it, but if we allow things to keep going as they are, the situation will only get worse. Our only hope ... ONLY HOPE ... is to immediately take drastic action and remedy this crime.

CHAPTER TWENTY-TWO

THE FEDERAL RESERVE SYSTEM MUST BE

DESTROYED

The TRUE terrorists are the international bankers who manipulate our Federal Reserve System for their own personal gain. The Federal Reserve is a privately-owned corporation (not part of our Federal Government), a nefarious cabal of international financiers who lied, connived and ultimately pried the reins of control over our money supply away from Congress.

If we don't return the creation of our nation's money to Congress as set forth in the Constitution and destroy the Federal Reserve System, I guarantee America will no longer be a global super-power by the next decade.

QUOTES

Anthony Sutton (*The Federal Reserve Conspiracy*): "Nothing is more dangerous to the power of the elite than the public discovery and understanding of the private control of the money supply."

Andrew Jackson: "If the people only understood the rank injustice of our money and banking system, there would be a revolution before morning."

H. L. Mencken: "I feel sorry for the man who, after reading the daily newspaper, goes to bed believing he knows something of what's going on in the world."

Did you know that:

• The Federal Reserve is not part of the Federal Government, nor is it an institution run by the United States Government.
• Instead, the Federal Reserve System is an aggregate of private banks owned by international bankers.

151

- Although it is called "Federal," those who created the Federal Reserve took great measures not to call it a "privately owned central bank." Why? Because if they told the truth, the American people would realize that what they instituted was too much like what Karl Marx described in the "Communist Manifesto." The primary tenet of Communism is a central bank. Thus, "Federal Reserve" (a misnomer) sounds more like a governmental agency, even though the terminology was ultimately used to deceive the people.

In essence, the Federal Reserve is a PRIVATE company operated FOR PROFIT where decisions are made behind closed doors and only those who are privy to this process know about the policies beforehand.

Stated differently, since the Federal Reserve is not part of the government, but a private organization OWNED by member banks, they become aware of financial information before everyone else. When they finally make it public (e.g., new interest rates) they're already one-step ahead of the game. Essentially they've rigged the system in their favor!

Picture it like this: How would you like to get a copy of *Fortune* Magazine or the *Wall Street Journal* a month before everyone else so you could make a host of financial decisions? Well, that's what these bankers are doing.

Who is the financial gain derived from? The United States Government! And who PAYS via taxes to support our government? We do! So to me, something sounds fishy about this arrangement. Why? Well, our Constitution, specifically Article 1, Section 8, Subsection 5, gives ONLY Congress the right "to coin Money, and regulate the Value thereof." How did the Federal Reserve; a private company operated for financial gain and controlled by private stockholders, seize control of this crucially important aspect of our government?

Think about how sinister this is. The Constitution -- the most sacred document of our democracy -- says only Congress can create money. But now we have private bankers, NOT elected officials, handling our money supply and reaping huge, perpetual profits along the way.

If you don't believe these FACTS, then take a peek at a Washington, DC phone book sometime. Here's what you'll find. The DC phone book is divided into four sections: a) general information, b) residential numbers, c) the Blue Pages -- United States and District of Columbia governmental listings, and d) business listings.

Now, where do you think the Federal Reserve should be included? If you still think its part of the government, then it should be in Section 3 - - the Blue Pages. But no. Guess where it is? Section 4, under BUSINESS LISTINGS!

Still not disillusioned enough? Well, how about this: the Federal Reserve has NEVER been audited by an independent auditor -- EVER! How many other companies or individuals have been given such carte blanche since 1913 (when it was created)?

In addition, Congress has never investigated the Fed. The Federal Reserve determines its own legislation and is not subject to the President or Congress. Although its board members are "appointed" by the President and "approved" by Congress, the core of them come from the inner sanctum of the Wall Street banking elite, and almost all belong to the Council on Foreign Relations.

This unrestricted power gives the Fed a virtual monopoly over our financial matters, allowing them to control interest rates and the size of our national money supply.

The Fed thus lends money to our government, at interest, and demands repayment. How does that happen? Well, the government instituted a little thing called the Income Tax whereby they take money from our paychecks. And the more they owe the international bankers, the more they pinch from our checks.

You don't believe me? Take a look at the percentage of our income that has been subject to taxation over the past nine decades. Have taxes gone up or come down? We all know the answer to that one -- UP! Finally, now that we've learned that this disastrous situation is actually true, we need to ask: why doesn't the media or at least our college professors tell us about it?

The answer is simple: every member of the mainstream media (CBS, NBC, ABC, CNN, FOX, *Time* Magazine, the *New York Times*, *Washington Post*, *Newsweek*, and *U.S. News and World Report*) is owned by vast multinational corporations, and these corporations are owned by whom? You got it -- the international bankers!

In regard to academia, universities rely quite heavily on grant money from Foundations and state funding. I'm sorry to say that the international bankers control these foundations (e.g., the Rockefeller Foundation), and they have the State in their back pockets. So, is it any wonder that both institutions are mum on the subject? If you were royally bilking the American people out of trillions of dollars a year, would you want them to know about it? Hardly.

THE BASIS OF BANKING

As we all know, barter was the initial form of exchange before money was invented. In other words, if I had a bushel of corn and someone else wanted to trade a hen, we could come to an agreement and make a trade. But since people didn't enjoy carrying live animals and crops with them everywhere, they needed a better system. They decided to give "value" to objects such as seashells, seeds, pebbles, and bones. Of course these items had no "real" intrinsic value other than what a particular ruling body gave them, but their ease of use was apparent. It's much easier trading a purple seashell for a sack of feed than for ten chickens.

Over time, this system also proved inefficient due to the wide array of trading objects being used. A standard was needed, and gold eventually became that standard. Regrettably, this move brought about the inception of banking and usury. Here's why.

Since goldsmiths were the most accustomed to handling this new form of exchange, people began taking their gold to them for safe storage -- to keep it from being stolen, or when it became too bulky to carry around. In return, the goldsmiths gave them promissory notes for their gold.

We need to remember that these promissory notes -- pieces of paper -- had no value in and of itself. It was only PAPER! But since an arbitrary value was established by the goldsmiths (and later the State), these pieces of paper became what is known as "fiat" money. Thus, what originally had no inherent worth (gold and paper) became valuable by someone's decree.

"Fiat" money, then, is nothing more than a promise to repay something at a later date.

So, let's get back to our original thesis. Whenever a person would take their gold to a goldsmith and deposit it, they would be given notes in return specifying a certain amount of "money." But rather than going back to the goldsmith every day to get a chunk of gold, people began using these notes as a form of exchange. It was much easier carrying slips of paper than huge pocketfuls of gold.

The goldsmiths, who were the world's first bankers, soon realized they had tons of valuable gold sitting around and only about 20% of the people ever came back to claim it. They were more content to keep using their paper money.

What could the goldsmiths do with this other 80% of their unclaimed gold? Simple. They started making loans (at interest) because they knew not everyone would "make a run" on them and want their gold at the same time. The obvious benefit to this practice was that they could lend the majority of their accumulation and only keep a small amount on hand. In fact, for every one piece of gold they received, the bankers could issue FIVE notes, or loans.

I'm sure you can see the catch by this point. Only one of the notes was actually backed by gold, while the other four had NO backing whatsoever. So, if you're paying interest to the depositor after he or she gives you one piece of gold, and the depositor banker is receiving interest on FIVE loans in return (at a higher interest rate), there's a definite profit margin to be made, especially if the bankers determine the interest rates!

This practice is called "fractional banking," and via the interest earned on their loans, the goldsmiths became very wealthy men. The major problem today is that there is NO MORE gold left in Fort Knox. It's empty, and as we'll soon see, the entire banking (money) industry is based on nothing more than illusion.

QUOTES

Thomas Jefferson: "I believe that banking institutions are more dangerous than standing armies."

Andrew Jackson (1833, to the shadow banking moguls): "You are a den of thieves -- vipers. I intend to rout you out, and by the Eternal God I will rout you out!"

Andrew Jackson: "If Congress has a right under the Constitution to issue paper money, it was given to them to use by themselves, not to be delegated to individuals or corporations."

Honorable Louis T. McFadden (Chairman of the Banking and Currency Committee): "We have known in this country one of the most corrupt institutions the world has ever known. I refer to the Federal Reserve Board and the Federal Reserve Banks."

Reginald McKenna (Chancellor of the Excheque of England, Chairman of the Board of Midlands Bank, to stockholders in 1924): "They who control credit of the nation direct the policy of Governments and hold in the hollow of their hands the destiny of the people."

Dr. Carroll Quigley (history teacher, Georgetown University, and author of *Tragedy and Hope*): "The history of the last century shows that the advice given to governments by bankers was consistently good for bankers, but was often disastrous for governments, businessmen, and the people."

Dr. Carroll Quigley (on the goals of international bankers): "Nothing less than to create a world system of financial control in PRIVATE HANDS able to dominate the political system of each country, and the economy of the world as a whole."

Senator Barry Goldwater: "Most Americans have no real understanding of the operation of the international moneylenders. The bankers want it that way."

Gary Allen (*None Dare Call It Conspiracy*): "Using a central bank to create alternate periods of inflation, deflation, and thus whipsawing the public for vast profits, has been worked out by the international bankers to an exact science."

Tim Madel, *The Spotlight* (March 30, 1992): "Banks are businesses. Businesses have one reason for existence: profit. Everything the business does is in the pursuit of profits."

AMERICAN HISTORY AND CENTRAL BANKING

When this country was founded over two centuries ago, our Founding Fathers realized the importance of being free from outside influences, especially monetary ones. That's why they saw how crucial it was to print their own money instead of borrowing from the Bank of England.

By engaging in such a practice, America could exist in a debt-free state rather than being controlled and in hock to those whose tyranny they had escaped. But the European and English bankers didn't care for this decision, especially when they realized America's vast financial potential. By pursuing their independence, America was essentially cutting the aristocratic banking families of Europe out of the loop.

In this vein, then, the American Revolution did not take place primarily because of taxation without representation (as we've been taught), but because the European financiers didn't want us to be able to create our own money. By eliminating them and the interest paid on their loans, we didn't allow ourselves to be enslaved by usury and debt. Thus, the American Revolution was actually a battle over who controlled our money!

Regrettably, even though America became a sovereign nation, it didn't take long for the international bankers to get a foothold into our financial matters; the First Bank of North America was founded in 1781. The most disturbing aspect of this institution was that only 20% of the money used to create it came from the United States Government and 80% originated from foreign investors, namely the Rothschilds. Luckily, this bank folded in 1790, and its charter was not renewed.

But the international bankers didn't give up that easily. When they want something badly enough, the best method to achieve it is through war. So, the War of 1812 was, in essence "designed" by the same financiers to send American businesses into chaos so that they'd be forced to form a 2nd Bank of North of America. But due to our hearty nature, the going was tough for those who wanted to infiltrate and corrupt our financial matters. This was particularly true when the Controllers came up against Andrew Jackson, who staunchly opposed any notion of a central bank.

Jackson, who was truly one of the greatest Presidents in our country's history, became such a bane to the international bankers that he was the first Commander-in-Chief to be the target of an assassin. The gunman who tried to kill him was Richard Lawrence, who acted as an agent for the European banking institutions.

Unwilling to abate their efforts to control our money, the Rothschild brothers wrote a letter in 1863 that described the American populace as "the great body of people mentally incapable of comprehending the tremendous advantages that Capital derives from the system ..."

It sounds like they had plenty of respect for us, huh? About as much as they have for us today, which doesn't say a whole lot. Anyway, the Rothschilds were getting so desperate to get a piece of our pie, they resorted to a horrendously despicable act to tear our country apart.

What did they do? Well, they set forces into action that began our Civil War in the 1860s. Now most people aren't aware of this fact, but a group of Rothschild agents in the United States began giving money to each side -- the Union and the Confederates -- to get each sector of the country deeply indebted to them. Their ultimate plan was to have the South secede from the Union, then let each new country rip itself apart to such an extent that they'd be in debt up to their ears. Finally when the bloodshed ended, both new severed, decimated countries would go crawling on their hands and knees to the Rothschild boys to borrow even

MORE money to rebuild. The result: vast amounts of debt, and control shifted from us to them.

Fully aware of their tactics at the time, Abraham Lincoln said shortly before being re-elected to his second term: "I see in the near future a crisis approaching that unnerves me, and causes me to tremble for the safety of my Country; corporations have been enthroned, an era of corruption in high places will follow, and the money power of the country will endeavor to prolong its reign by working upon the prejudices of the people, until the wealth is aggregated in a few hands and the Republic is destroyed."

These were men of courage and conviction. Why don't we have leaders like that today?

Because he stood up and criticized the bankers, Lincoln was assassinated. He wasn't shot because of slavery, prejudice, or Southern loyalties. Lincoln was knocked off by the Rothschilds because he wouldn't let them take over our country's money supply. Thank God for Abraham Lincoln!

THE ROTHSCHILDS

When the 20th century began, it was estimated the Rothschild family owned HALF of the world's total wealth. Think about that for a moment. One family possessed half of everything in the world. Considering that the Rothschilds were ruthless bankers with a penchant for having things go their way, do you think it's safe to say they had some input on what was going on in the world?

Using practices stolen from the Knights Templar, the Rothschilds perfected their banking system on a local level in Europe; then transported it globally to be implemented in various parts of the world. They did this by using secret agents who were paid off via loans, salaries, or appointed positions within a company. Some of the men utilized to undermine our country were Jacob Schiff, J. P. Morgan and Paul Warburg, whose incredible accumulation of power in the United States in the late 1800's was mind-boggling.

Here's the way it worked: The Rothschilds were king of the mountain in Europe, running a majority of the influential banking houses. Then, setting their sights on America, they sent Paul Warburg to our country where he began laying the groundwork to create a central bank patterned after the German Reichbank. Another German to enter this equation was an Illuminati member named Jacob Schiff. Schiff came to

America for the sole purpose of getting control of our financial system. Serving as a direct tool of the Rothschilds, he soon became head of the banking firm Kuhn, Loeb & Company.

More important, Schiff began laying an octopus-like network that connected bankers like J. P. Morgan, Paul Warburg, and the Rockefeller family. One of the perks of being involved in this cabal was access to the Rothschild money, which was demonstrated by the Rockefellers, whose first loans in the 19th century came from the National City Bank in Cleveland.

Guess who owned this bank (and two others) at that time? Yup, the Rothschilds. Over time, these agents, especially J. P. Morgan and Co., ran practically all the banking, oil, steel, and business that took place in America.

At this point, some people may say, "Oh well, that's just American Capitalism at work." And y'know, I'd agree with them if everything was done above board. But these Rothschild-led agents didn't play fairly. Rules didn't matter to them. All they cared about was more power, wealth and influence. So they manipulated industry, commerce, and especially the financial markets.

A perfect example is the Panic of 1907, which was deliberately set into motion by J. P. Morgan's banks and the Rockefeller/Standard Oil people. While thousands of "little people" lost everything they had to this artificially created collapse, the bankers who implemented it reaped enormous rewards due to inside information and foreknowledge. Thus, a few men became even wealthier than they already were, while the majority of hapless citizens were wiped-out.

But the final blow came when certain people ("moles") started whispering that a central bank was needed to prevent another one of these tragedies from occurring. The stage was set for the implementation of a "Federal Reserve" System.

CHAPTER TWENTY-THREE

DO WE WANT TO SAVE AMERICA? THEN DEMAND THAT WE DESTROY THE FEDERAL RESERVE AND DEFAULT ON OUR NATIONAL DEBT

Fact: The privately owned Federal Reserve charges the American people $47 million in interest every hour.

As we have stated previously, the Federal Reserve is not part of our government, but instead a privately owned corporation that makes incredible profits off the money they lend to us at interest. As our country is further strangled by debt to these international bankers, the government continues to steal our money through increased taxation.

The end result is a form of enslavement enacted on the American people by a cabal of Globalists lurking in the shadows.

To save our nation, we must destroy the Federal Reserve System; then default on that portion of our national debt owed to the international bankers. If we fail to eliminate the Federal Reserve or get the Controllers out of our financial affairs, it won't matter what else we do because they'll still have an iron grip on our money supply.

As it stands now, the United States Government pays $360 billion a year in interest payments alone -- that's billions -- 10% of our entire Federal budget. Worse, international bankers represent 37% of our national debt, and two banks (Chase Manhattan and Citibank) control 53% of the New York Federal Reserve. Finally, 7 of the top 10 primary shareholders in the Federal Reserve are foreign entities.

In essence what we have are foreign bankers and two Wall Street powerhouses running our country.

Do you get it? The President, Congress, and voters don't decide what takes place in the United States of America. Foreign bankers and two Fortune 500 financial corporations are in charge of our country's destiny. That is the reality of our situation. And I guarantee you, not one thing will change until we get these Controllers out of our pockets.

How do we accomplish this feat? First, we declare in no uncertain terms that the United States is defaulting on that portion of the national debt owed to anyone other than the American people (i.e. the international bankers).

We simply say, "We're not paying the interest (or the principal) on the money we owe you!" When you think about it, what can the bankers do? If you default on your auto loan or mortgage, what happens? The bank repossesses your car or house. But if we default on our national debt, what are the Controllers going to do? Repossess our country? Not a chance.

The second move America needs to take is to revoke the right to create money from outside entities and return it to those to whom it constitutionally belongs: the Congress. Now I'm no fan of Congress, but anyone is better than the group that controls our money now.

The most obvious benefit of this decision is that rather than borrowing money from the international bankers, then paying exorbitant amounts of money in interest, we can coin our own money without interest.

Y'see, usury is the key to world domination. Whenever a person or country is indebted to another entity, an element of control enters the picture. The more they owe, the less control they have over their affairs. And as it stands now, since we will never pay off our national debt, how can we realistically imagine a day when we'll have control over our own destiny?

It won't happen. Not only are we enslaved through taxation to the government; our government is enslaved to the Controllers via the Federal Reserve. The only solution: destroy the Federal Reserve!

After we return the right to create money back to Congress, we can also eliminate the Federal Income Tax. Don't you think it's strange that the Federal Reserve Act and the Federal Income Tax were both enacted in the same exact year -- 1913? They go hand-in-hand. But prior to that fateful year, there was no Federal Income Tax. Instead, we raised money to pay our bills primarily through tariffs.

Why not do the same thing today? Take a moment and try to conceive of all the products we import. If we slapped a 5% tariff on each and every one of them, we could eliminate the Federal Income Tax without touching one social program.

It's so evident. Of all these products we import, how many can we make ourselves? Nearly all of them. Not only would our own domestic companies benefit from import tariffs (other countries do it; why shouldn't we?), but this transfer of production to the U.S. would strengthen our nation as a whole by reducing our dependence on foreign entities.

The big question, though, is how do we destroy the Federal Reserve System? It's obvious that Globalists like George Bush, Al Gore, Bill Clinton, and Christopher Dodd won't take the leadership role; nor will

Congressmen who are bought and sold by the political contributions to which they are so beholden. There's only one other alternative -- someone OF, BY and FOR the PEOPLE needs to rally every one of us together and return the reins of power to US! If we don't have the resolve to accomplish this, I guarantee the luxuries and rights we now enjoy will be squashed.

But as I said earlier, there is one variable which enters the picture that everyone should know about. When the United States defaults on its national debt, the Controllers aren't going to lie down and take it without batting an eye. We're talking about billions of dollars that they bilk from us each year. This is major league money, and not something they'll brush off lightly.

If they can't repossess our country as banks would a house or car, what else can they do? Well, when a country gets irrevocably out of line, the Controllers only have one other recourse -- WAR!

Here are some of the key secrets that aren't taught to us in history classes. First of all, wars are not primarily started by the masses. The Bolshevik Revolution is a perfect example. Instead, wars are orchestrated by the Controllers to either maintain a balance of power or penalize those nations that don't fall in line with their edicts.

So, if the United States defaults on its national debt and abolishes the Federal Reserve, the Controllers will shortly thereafter declare war on us via all the other nations that are still under their vast umbrella (the European Union, Russian, China, etc.).

I'm sure the first thing you're thinking is: do we really want to enter World War III? Personally, I despise war as much as anyone. But what are our alternatives? To stay enslaved by the New World Order's Federal Reserve in a situation where they continue to control our entire political system? I'd rather fight than cringe, and lash out rather than wallow or hide.

Right now, our political framework is completely unacceptable. We illegally "select" leaders to implement decisions made not in Washington DC, but in New York City and Europe. These policies are made at the upper echelon of the control pyramid, ultimately designed to eliminate our national sovereignty and incorporate us into their much-heralded New World Order.

In this vein, we need to ask ourselves how we feel about paying taxes to a World Government (to be used for projects in China or Zimbabwe). Does this scenario appeal to you? How about our soldiers fighting under the jurisdiction of a United Nations Army that is commandeered by generals in Russia or Europe? How about a World Court located in Saudi Arabia where foreigners who hate our guts convict Americans of crimes? These people would also hand down rulings detrimental to our country, and we'd have to adhere to them.

The main point to remember is this: the Controllers act in ways that benefit their own global interests, not our day-to-day lives. The ONLY way to save this nation is by completely and irrevocably removing them from our political system. If we fail to do so, the United States of America as we currently know it will no longer exist.

This is why we need to destroy the Federal Reserve and default on our national debt. There are no other alternatives. These bloodsuckers have placed a stranglehold around our financial necks and are slowly choking us to death.

By allowing the Globalist international bankers to keep shaking us down, we give them the very thing they crave the most -- power and control. In essence, then, indebtedness equals subservience.

We need to ask ourselves one crucial question: Do we want to remain enslaved to the Controllers, or are we willing to fight for our freedoms like our forefathers did?

CHAPTER TWENTY-FOUR

FINANCIAL ENSLAVEMENT AND THE FEDERAL RESERVE: AN OVERVIEW OF PETER KERSHAW'S "ECONOMIC SOLUTIONS"

Daddy Warbucks himself, Mr. James Warburg, who was the primary architect of America's Federal Reserve Act in 1913, admitted to *Nation* Magazine on February 3, 1932 (right before his death), "I have studied finance and economic and international trade all my life, and now after these recent events, I have come to the conclusion that I know nothing about any of them."

With this quote in mind, I'd like to begin this article by saying that my intent is not to dazzle you with an array of complicated formulas or theories. Instead, I'll simply lay out further evidence as to why the Federal Reserve is the most damaging institution in America, and how its primary goal is to continually grow larger in stature by stealing increased amounts of our hard-earned money. As I've said before, the Federal Reserve is a privately owned for-profit corporation that is operated by the richest men in the world, and it is NOT a part of the Federal Government. These financiers are so arrogant in their positions of power that J.P. Morgan once said of the American people, "God would not have created sheep unless he had intended them to be shorn." I'm sure you can recognize the symbolism – we're the sheep, the wool being shorn is our money, and they've assumed the role of Banker-Gods. Thus, to truly understand what is causing the ills in our society, we need to begin with the Federal Reserve. Why? Well, because, as Robert Hemphill, former Credit Manager of the Federal Reserve Bank in Atlanta said in his testimony before the Senate, "It is the most important subject intelligent persons can investigate and reflect upon."

The men who founded this nation, many of them quite wealthy, were well aware of how dangerous a centralized bank was. In fact, one of the primary motives behind the American Revolution was our Founding Father's hatred of the Bank of England and how they could 'create' notes out of thin air (using the principles of fractional banking); then tax their subjects without giving them proper representation. Does this scenario sound familiar to our current situation in America? The biggest difference, though, is that people during that time only paid 5% of their income to the Crown. Today, a gainfully employed homeowner has approximately 48% of their total income taxed in one form or another. Thomas Jefferson was so outraged by this concept that he said, "The Central Bank is an institution of the most deadly hostility existing against the principles and form of our Constitution."

Many people who are paid to influence public opinion will naturally dismiss this information by calling it 'conspiracy theory.' But the one logical point they can't argue against is that FACTS aren't theories! We can prove that the Federal Reserve is privately owned. We can prove who the primary shareholders are. And we can prove how detrimental it is to the prosperity of this country. If this isn't enough ammunition, listen to what our own politicians have to say about the Federal Reserve:

Senator George W. Malone (to Congress in 1962): "I believe that if the people of this nation fully understood what Congress has done to them over the past 49 years, they would move on Washington, they would not wait for an election ... It adds up to a preconceived plan to destroy the economic and social independence of the United States."

Congressman Wright Patman (Chairman, House Banking & Currency Committee): "In the United States we have, in effect, two governments ... We have the duly Constitutional government ... then we have an independent, uncontrolled and uncoordinated government in the Federal Reserve System operating the money powers which are reserved to Congress by the Constitution."

Congressman Wright Patman (May 5, 1975): "In its sixty-year history, the Federal Reserve System has never been subjected to a complete, independent audit, and it is the only important agency that refuses to consent to an audit by the Congressional agency, the General Accounting Office."

Congressman William E. Simon (in a speech to the House of Representatives on the problems of the Federal Reserve System, April 30, 1976): "I hear no one addressing this danger. Congress does not discuss it. The press does not discuss it. Look around us – the press isn't even here! The people do not discuss is – they are unaware of it. No counter-force in America is being mobilized to fight this danger. The battle is being lost, and not a shot is being fired."

To really get a grasp on how detrimental the Federal Reserve is to our country, we need to look at the basics of banking, usury, and specifically this question: Where does money come from? Author Peter Kershaw provides the best overview of this phenomenon that I've ever come across. The following is a simple step-by-step look at how our monetary system works.

1)   To create new currency, the Fed orders "notes" from the Department of the Treasury's Bureau of Engraving and Printing.
2)   This Bureau prints the money, and subsequently puts it into circulation.
3)   Meanwhile, this same money is also "loaned" to the U.S. Government, who promises to pay back their debt to the Fed.
4)   As collateral for the loan, our Congress puts up the land, labor and assets of the American people. (It's very nice of them to pledge OUR property and services, don't you think?)
5)   Finally, to pay back this loan, a little system was instituted where money is taken directly from our paychecks before we ever have a chance to get our hands on it. It's called taxation.

The most glaring question at this point is: who do you think gets the raw end of the deal? The international bankers? Nah – the last time I checked, the Rockefellers, Warburgs, and Rothschilds were still prominent members of the leisure class. How about the Federal Reserve? Well, they rake in over a trillion dollars in income a year. Plus they're exempt from paying taxes on this income, and they've never been audited once since their inception in 1913. They don't seem to be hurting any. What about the President, Congressmen, and high-level administrators at the Treasury and IRS? Do they feel the pinch? Hardly – they're all pulling six-figure salaries (or more), enjoy lavish expense accounts, and have chauffeurs driving them to work every morning. So, who does that leave as the scapegoat – the one who bears the brunt of funding this system? You guessed it – the American taxpayers! Do you think we should look into changing this system? I mean, there's a lot more of US than there is of THEM!

So, to continue on, the next time it is determined that we need more money in circulation, the Fed essentially creates it out of thin air, and we become the indentured servants that have to pay off these debts. What occurs is that a culture of total fiscal irresponsibility results, which, of course, is in the Controllers best interest because it means we need to borrow even more money from them. How so? Well, let's look at our elected leaders in terms of simple psychology. When they borrow and spend somebody else's money and don't have to pay it back from their own pockets, what motivation do they have to be frugal? Even worse, they get paid very well to spend this money regardless of whether they successfully balance their budgets or not. If this were the business world, every one of them would be fired on the spot. And finally, to add insult to injury, these shysters even get to determine their own salaries, and how much their next pay raise will be!

While all this nonsense is taking place, what do we do? We work forty or fifty hours a week, then get a paycheck that has been raped and pillaged by the very same people that dine on filet mignon and charge it off on their expense accounts. And as you stare in disbelief at your pay stub, can you hear their mocking laughter from Washington D.C., New York City, and other financial centers in Europe?

If you can't see it already, the System that THEY created is parasitical to its core. Why? Because the money that the Federal Reserve creates and puts into circulation (plus the money that is needed to pay the interest on this "loan" to us) comes from the same source – them. Now, the money we earn which is taxed by the government and in turn pays the interest on our "debt" ends up lowering the money supply, thus removing currency from circulation. Realizing that the money supply would slowly dwindle away to nothing if this process persisted, the international bankers came up with a solution. They implore our government (and others) to borrow more money! That way they receive more interest payments, and the cycle keeps repeating itself. The major difference between them and us, though, is how our income is derived. We actually have to go out and work for our pay, while they simply skim money off the top before we ever have a chance to get our hands on it. (That's a polite way of saying that they don't have to actually WORK for their money; instead, a system has been created where they became fabulously wealthy without ever PRODUCING something that benefits society. If you haven't figured it out, the practice of usury does not benefit everyday people.)

In the end, we become so wrapped up in this vicious circle that it creates a troublesome quandary. At this specific date in time, it is now impossible to pay off our national debt because it is higher than all of the money that is currently in circulation! Do you hear what I'm saying? We CAN'T pay it back. The entire debacle is an exercise in futility. So when you hear another politician on TV telling us how we need to raise taxes to pay off the debt, it's an out-and-out lie. These men are nothing more than illusion-spinners for the New World Order. The system has already been irrevocably destroyed, and all they're doing now is using smoke and mirrors to keep us hooked like fish on a line. As it stands now, this problem cannot be fixed within the current parameters that we have erected. And guess what. That's exactly the way the Controllers want it. Why? Well, how would you like someone to be eternally indebted to you paying interest forevermore with no hope of ever paying off the principle? Sounds like easy money to me!

The question we have to ask ourselves now is – why do we even need the Federal Reserve? If we – the United States – can print our own money via the Bureau of Engraving, why should we BORROW it from the international bankers? It is the most cockamamie system ever invented, yet we allow it to continue. When our country was founded, the Constitution gave only Congress the right to create money. And except for the years following the Civil War, our nation existed without a federal deficit. Then in 1913 the Federal Reserve Act was passed, and guess what we're stuck with now - a debt that will NEVER be paid off; and interest payments that increase every year. And even scarier is the fact that our personal debt as a people is five-times greater than the national debt. Think for a moment how much money is being squandered through interest payments. If you buy a house, the first seven years are spent doing little more than paying interest without even touching the principle. And that doesn't include your car payments, credit cards, and whatever other debts you've racked up.

The point I'm trying to hammer home is as such: can you see how unproductive these interest payments are to practically everyone except those collecting the interest? It's wasted money that doesn't create anything other than more debt. Or, as Richard Walbaum wrote in 1992's *The Poverty Trap*: "Our monetary system guarantees that debt must increase regardless of what people, business or government do or do not do, whether or not they balance their budgets."

To further show you how manipulative the banking system is, author Peter Kershaw uses the analogy of a man who wants to sell his motorcycle. His friend agrees to buy the bike, but doesn't want his wife to know about it. So he tells the owner to keep it in his garage, and he'll come by every Saturday to ride it. The owner concurs; then figures, "Hey, I have this bike for six other days of the week when it isn't being used. Why don't I "sell" it to someone else under the same agreement?" In no time he "sells" the bike to seven more people under the same shady

169

arrangement even though there is only ONE valid owner of the bike. This, I'm afraid to say, is the basis of fractional banking. It's a very enlightening insight into the psychology of these world financiers, for what prevents them from creating even more "loans" out of thin air? Nothing does because U.S. Fractional Banking Law allows them to loan out $9 for every $1 on reserve! Think about how easy this system is to manipulate. And the only way a problem could arise is if all nine people went to withdraw their money from the bank at the same time. But the bankers have even made laws to prevent this scenario from occurring.

Peter Kershaw even goes on to say that 97% of all bank transactions are nothing more than simple ledger entries where no money trades hands. Think about it. When you pay your mortgage (principle + interest), do you lay down $700 cash, or do you write a check? The same applies to your monthly car payment, credit cards, or the loan at Sears for your washer/dryer. All that is happening is that numbers are being juggled from one column to another, yet international bankers have become the richest men on earth by capitalizing on this practice. Only 3% of our financial transactions consist of using actual coin and paper!

What, you may wonder, is the result of this practice? Well, as our debts rise, so do our interest payments. To cover these increased expenses, taxes are raised. In the business world, higher interest payments equal higher business expenses, and thus higher prices. I realize that this analysis has been extremely simplified, but if you look back at the last ninety years, have prices, our national debt, taxes, and interest payments gone up or down? The ultimate result is that the everyday person suffers because taxes and inflation continually keep eating into their REAL net worth, not allowing them to get further ahead. This is precisely why it is so hard for people to ascend from one particular social or financial class. It's because the system is designed to keep them where they are! It prevents movement from one class to another.

This framework for social enslavement will continue unabated until we abolish the Federal Reserve and default on our national debt. Or, as author Peter Kershaw tells us, "What we operate on today is not the 'intellect' of confidence based upon tangible wealth and substance, but the 'religion' of 'conviction' based upon blind faith. Without religious conviction, the system collapses! And what is that religion? – a pagan occultic money system."

Larry Burkett, author of *The Coming Economic Earthquake* takes it one step further by saying, "The actual deficits are almost twice as large as those admitted by the government. So why hasn't our economy collapsed? Because the American people still have confidence in the System."

Luckily, a few courageous Americans over the years have tried to alter the status quo. One of them was Congressman Louis T. McFadden, who became Chairman of the House Banking & Currency Committee. On June 10, 1932 in a speech before the House, he described centralized banks as such. "They are not government institutions. They are private credit monopolies; domestic swindlers, rich and predatory money lenders that prey upon the people of the United States for the benefit of themselves and their foreign customers. The Federal Reserve banks are the agents of the foreign central banks. The truth is the Federal Reserve Board has usurped the Government of the United States." (75 Congressional Record 12595-12603)

Six months earlier, on January 13, 1932, Congressman McFadden actually charged the Federal Reserve with treason and tried to have it put out of business. Regrettably, our Congressmen then weren't any braver than they are today, and only five supported him. The House G.O.P. majority leader even mused, "Louis T. McFadden is now politically dead." Sure enough, in his next reelection bid, his opponent received mountains of donation money, while the press slandered McFadden unmercifully and accused him of being "crazy." (It's comforting to know that their tactics haven't changed over the years.) McFadden naturally lost the election, and was the victim of three subsequent assassination attempts within the next few years. His detractors were ultimately successful when McFadden reached his demise in 1936 after being poisoned to death. (James Traficante, an outspoken critic of the Federal Reserve and IRS, better watch what he eats in prison!)

Three decades later, on June 4, 1963, John F. Kennedy issued Executive Order 11110 where he requested the Treasury to start printing "United States Notes." This money was the same as that controlled by the Federal Reserve except that it was created DEBT FREE! Five months later JFK was assassinated.

Hmmm, do you think we've uncovered the key to global domination? Our Founding Fathers led a revolution to keep us from being controlled by the Bank of England, while one of the historically-hidden motives for our Civil War was Abraham Lincoln's adamant refusal to let the Rothschild banking family take control of our monetary system. 'Ol Honest Abe wound-up with a bullet in his head. What do you think – another 'coincidence'?

So, there it is – centralized banking – one of the primary tenets of Karl Marx's *Communist Manifest*. To me, the realities of this situation are clear. We cannot move forward to let America regain its greatness until we eliminate the Controller's iron grip on our financial purse strings. This may be a bitter pill for many people to swallow, but as Samuel Adams said, "It is natural for man to deal in the illusions of hope; but as for me, I want to know the worst; the truth, and prepare for it."

Folks, the Federal Reserve is the most corrupt, debilitating, anti-American institution in this country, and that's the truth. The only question that remains is: are we willing to face it, and then do something about it?

SECTION

FIVE:

TECHNOLOGY

&

INTELLIGENCE

CHAPTER TWENTY-FIVE

AMERICA'S DELIBERATE DEMISE AND CHINA'S ROLE AS NEW KING OF THE HILL

After the catastrophe of September 11, it was evident how many people in this country love and adored the United States of America. We hung flags, cried, rallied together and showed how much this nation meant to us. With this outpouring of support in mind, let me ask you a question: Why are we allowing politicians, international bankers and corporate heads to slowly run this country into the ground? Why?

These monsters don't have respect for sovereignty, nationalism, or freedom. In fact, they have contempt for these concepts.

To prove this point, did you know that Bill Clinton, while still President in 1997, signed Bill # PDD60 that says in case of a nuclear strike on the United States, we must absorb it and not retaliate or launch on warning?

This means we're only allowed to return our own nuclear warheads AFTER our enemy's missiles have already landed on our soil. Think about it. If we can't answer until their nukes hit us, where does that leave our warheads? Sitting in their silos! Instead of the silo's being empty (because the warheads have already been launched), they'll be sitting ducks -- ultimately destroyed because we haven't been given a chance to fight back.

If the above scenario ever does take place, we're all screwed anyway, so what's it matter? Can you see what's happening? Isn't it obvious there are forces at work within our own country ... people who are calling the shots that aren't working in our best interest?

I'm going to say it loud and clear: Unless we do something very soon in a very dramatic fashion, the United States will no longer be the king of the hill. How does that notion settle with you? What if right now we are being replaced as the world's preeminent superpower?

Don't think it can happen? Well, what if one of the Controllers, after declaring that the New World Order does indeed exist and there's nothing we can do about it, then says that our Constitution and Bill of Rights have been declared null and void?

Can't happen? Why not?

Think of the assurances and rights that we've been given in this country ... the same ones we take for granted on a daily basis. Also, consider what a truly remarkable "experiment" the United States has been. For the first time in history, people actually had legal rights to speak and act freely without being crushed by the heavy hand of an overlord. This is the first time in history that a large segment of the population has been able to enjoy the benefits of a middle-class lifestyle. Prior to the founding of this nation, there were primarily two classes -- the elite rulers or kings and the lowly serfs or slaves.

The lower classes were ultimately forced to spend the majority of their time simply trying to stay alive -- raising crops, finding food, maintaining their shelter and clothing their family. Now we actually have "leisure" time!

We're now in the process of being knocked from our pedestals. Regrettably, when Bill Clinton was President and we enjoyed unparalleled economic success, we were experiencing our *fin de siècle*, a French word that means "the end of an era." The Clinton 90s was our heyday, and the end of America's supremacy. And now we're slowly beginning the process of America's deliberate demise.

To reinforce this point, take a look at the British Empire. Before we came along, they were the big boys, the king of the hill. And I'll bet if you had asked them during their reign if they thought they were going to be replaced, they would have laughed at the absurdity of such a notion. They were the British Empire, for Pete's sake -- militarily, economically, and culturally superior to everyone!

But guess what? A bigger fish came along -- the United States of America -- that held the potential to be economically developed, manipulated and exploited one-thousand times more than the British. So, what happened? The English were *deliberately* diminished and America was lifted up on the pedestal. Today, ask any American if we can be beaten militarily, economically, or financially. They'd laugh at such a notion. I mean, we're the American Empire!

Hey folks, listen closely. There's an even BIGGER fish in the ocean. Guess who they are? The Chinese! Consider how many more people and how much more land they have that can be developed, manipulated, and economically exploited. It's dizzying, and it's taking place right now.

I've seen video of some Chinese cities, and if you didn't know better, you'd think you were looking at America! Right now, China is being primed to assume control as the new king of the hill. And when you think about it, do the Controllers care? No! They hate concepts such as nationalism and sovereignty.

The Controllers are only concerned with maintaining and expanding their control and -- the bottom line -- profit margins. Right now, with the largest population in the world, China has the highest potential for future profits. It's scary, but true.

Here's one final thing to think about. I was in the woods last week taking a walk with my cats when I came upon a huge anthill. As my cats chased each other through the bushes and climbed trees, I sat there and stared at this anthill, soon coming up with an analogy. I pictured a bunch of different ants living on this mound -- the tiny black ones, red piss ants, the creepy looking brown ones, and those real big black ones. They're all contained on this hill and pretend for some reason there's no way to leave it.

Also, they're vaguely aware of my presence, especially if I take a stick and start poking around a little bit. There are also rumors among the ants that if I (or any other human) wanted to, we could obliterate their entire anthill -- either by stomping them to death, dousing them with gasoline and setting them on fire, or drowning them with a hose. In other words, they're living in a very precarious situation.

So I'm sitting there watching these ants and I notice that some of them -- the red piss ants -- start attacking the brown ones. At the same time, the little black ones try to destroy the big black ones. And they're not just picking on each other, but actually killing each other. The worst part is; they know I'm watching them, and how, if I chose, I could stomp them to death. Yet they keep destroying one another.

As the carnage continued, I thought, "What a bunch of stupid ants!"

Then it hit me. How are we any different than those goofy ants? We're doing the same thing they are, and we're human beings! Do you realize that with the technology and resources currently available in our world, there doesn't have to be ONE person starving anywhere in the world? (For your information, nearly 100,000 people die EVERY DAY of starvation on this planet.) We could feed all of them if we wanted to.

Also, we now possess the technology to completely eliminate the use of fossil fuels that choke our world. In addition, there are also countless diseases that could be cured overnight, and war could be all but eliminated.

Now don't get me wrong; I'm no head-in-the clouds idealist or socialist. But I am a realist, and here's what troubles me. I find it hard to believe that ADULTS are actually running this world. Yes, ADULTS!!!! What in God's name are we doing? How can grown men and women allow our world to fall apart with war, starvation, disease, and utter sickness?

I'll tell you how -- it's because of a hidden cabal of evil rulers that long for nothing but utter slavishness from us. Government is inherently a power and control game. Those at the top have only two motives -- to retain, and then expand, their power.

What's worse is that the hidden Controllers consider themselves "beyond" responsibility. They don't have to answer to anyone. They feel completely free to do whatever they choose. Are we going to allow them to keep doing so? It's up to us.

CHAPTER TWENTY-SIX

CHINA, THE MOSSAD, AND ARTIFICIAL

INTELLIGENCE

Nearly all the information in this essay comes from Gordon Thomas and his book, *Seeds of Fire: China and the Story behind the Attack on America*. I am merely acting as a conduit to bring it to you, and to encourage you to purchase this book as quickly as possible.

The most explosive book in America right now is Gordon Thomas' *Seeds of Fire*. It is dangerous because it reveals, more than any other book released within the last year, a secretive plot fomented by the Controllers to deliberately undermine America while at the same time enabling China to become the next world superpower.

Aided by the Israeli government, and especially the Mossad, China is undoubtedly this nation's greatest threat – a plotting, inhuman beast ready to strike at us when we've been sufficiently weakened.

Folks, I'm going to say this in the starkest terms possible: our country is being set up to take a mighty fall, and when our economy and military are stretched to their thinnest points, China is going to storm in and give us a royal ass-whipping. Once we're beaten to a pulp and thoroughly defeated, China will reign supreme as the next global king of the hill.

The reason I'm writing this review is (I would imagine) the same as why Mr. Thomas wrote his book and *Dandelion* published it. We're trying to get this information out to the public before it's too late. And believe me; the wheels are being set in motion to implement a massive shift in world power. I've written before about how the Controllers have set their sights on China, viewing it as a huge untapped market waiting to be exploited.

Once that happens and America has been knocked from its perch and loses its vaulted position atop the pyramid of control, try to imagine the resulting consequences. Our standard of living will drop, our influence around the globe will plummet, and somebody else – an entire race of people that view us with disdain – will be the vehicle through which the Controllers will continue to pull their evil shenanigans.

In other words, all of the privileges we've come to enjoy will be stripped away from us and given to China.

Before I get into the actual review of this book, I have to ask you: what will it take to propel us into action before time runs out? The Controllers have already leveled the World Trade Centers, and look at what happened when they did. I don't want to minimize the effects of that atrocity, but believe me, that was only the first step.

The next time they decide to "bring us to our knees," we won't know what hit us. If 9-11 was a slap in the face, stage two of their evil plan will be a full-blown knockout punch. Then what are we going to do? (And if you still don't think that hidden forces were behind the WTC attacks, you better start paying attention. The preponderance of evidence is overwhelming.) I know people who experienced full-blown depression for at least three months after 9-11. How in God's name are they going to cope with an unleashed total assault on our collective consciousness? The effect will be debilitating, if not altogether crippling.

I don't know how loud I have to yell this, but here goes: AMERICA -- HIDDEN FORCES ARE DELIBERATELY LAYING THE GROUNDWORK TO DESTROY THIS GREAT NATION. IF WE DON'T STOP THEM SOON, EVERYTHING WE'VE EARNED AND COME TO ENJOY WILL BE LOST!

Okay, with that introduction in mind, let's take a look at *Seeds of Fire*. A few pages into this book, Mr. Thomas mentions a figure who gained prominence in recent times – Wen Ho Lee – who was accused of passing defense and nuclear secrets to the Chinese. The only problem was -- all charges were dropped by U. S. District Court Judge James Parker because, in reality, Lee was working instead on a program called Project HP that delved into the futuristic concept of Holographic Portals.

These scientists from Los Alamos working at the Lawrence Livermore and Sandia Laboratories were pushing the envelope of "ET technology" and were trying to make contact with existences beyond those on our planet. An authority on this subject and behavioral scientist with sources at the National Security Agency, Dr. Richard Boylan, says that the "nuclear secrets" mentioned in Lee's case were actually code words for secret advanced technology such as antigravity propulsion and psychotronic remote mind-control devices. This type of research goes all the way back to the CIA's infamous MK-ULTRA, which we developed after smuggling Nazi scientists into our country via "Project Paperclip." After letting them loose to wreak havoc, these evil men ultimately wanted to develop the ability to control people. The Russians then further developed these procedures, which the Chinese are now refining and perfecting.

Now, if you're wondering what any of this has to do with China, bear with me. I promise that by the end of this essay, everything will be tied together. Plus, even better, there are new reports surfacing that provide a light at the end of the tunnel and ultimately give us hope. So, although the situation facing us is precarious, it's not all gloom-and-doom.

If we pay attention to what's going on, peek through the veil of illusion and actually take action, we can still save this country.

With that in mind, let's switch our attention to Area 51 for a moment. As almost everyone knows, this once top-secret military base is invariably associated with UFO's and alien technology. And although the government did tinker with "reverse technology" in the past, for the most part, the "little green men from outer space" scenario has been a smokescreen.

What's really going on at Area 51, and other lesser-known installations, is Artificial Intelligence (AI) research. In fact, there's even an AI lab in the "Dreamland" section of Area 51 called "S-4." In this lab, scientists are experimenting with brain implants in relation to robots in hopes that one day, within this half of the century they'll be able to create machines that can actually surpass man via the use of electronic brains.

Kevin Warwick, a professor of Cybernetix at the University of Reading in England, says with confidence, "Machines will one day become the dominant life form on earth." Did you notice that he called machines a LIFE FORM?

So, the big "secret" at Area 51 (and other such places) isn't alien intelligence, but Artificial Intelligence! Warwick continues: "The frontiers of space can be seen in a different way when the frailties and limitations of humans are removed. This will be achieved well before 2050. The human race will probably by then be surpassed by a network of intelligent machines that were created by humans. In doing so these creatures will have orchestrated the destruction of the human race."

Now, if all of the above is true, why don't we simply ask Dr. Wen Ho Lee himself? That's certainly an option, except for one minor detail. In return for being set free and having all charges against him dropped, the government demanded that Lee swear himself to secrecy concerning his research. A convenient little arrangement, don't you think?

Since we've mentioned Dr. Lee again, the next natural step is to examine the Chinese government's relationship to America's military institutions.

If you didn't know it, the CSIS (Chinese Secret Intelligence Service) DID penetrate our installation at Los Alamos, but not with Wen Ho Lee's help.

Instead, they joined forces with an intelligence agency of a different sort – Israel's Mossad! Yes, now we're getting into areas that are very touchy, and extremely dangerous. In fact, Bobby Ray Inman, former CIA head, described Israel as one of a half-dozen countries with a "government-directed, orchestrated and clandestine effort to steal U.S. military and economic secrets."

Could this revelation be true? Israel, the country to which we annually give over $5 billion in foreign aid – our supposed ally - actually spying on and trying to sabotage our nation? Well, it's true, and it gets much worse. To show this country's mindset, Meir Amit, former Director of the Mossad, was quoted in a CIA report on December 15, 1986 as saying, "Mossad should live by the credo 'Israel first, last and always.'"

Well folks, strap on your seatbelts and get ready to hang on because I'm here to tell you in no uncertain terms that China is NOT America's friend, and neither is Israel. I can say that because the Mossad and CSIS – the two most dangerous intelligence forces in the world – have teamed together. And here's what they've been up to.

Israel was the first to obtain Los Alamos secrets. Then, in a move beyond forgiveness, they shared this highly explosive information with China – America's greatest threat. As payment, the Chinese gave Israel their latest military secrets to keep them one step ahead of their Arab enemies in the Middle East.

Now I don't know about you, but the Mossad and the Chinese secret service joining together scares the living hell out of me!

Why? Because Israel is playing both ends against the middle. They sided with the United States for decades because we were king of the hill. But now that they see China slated to replace us, they're switching their allegiance to them while still sucking vast amounts of U.S. foreign aid out of us. Worse, the hidden Controllers are drawing us into a god-awful Middle-Eastern Israeli/Palestinian war that will:

a) Further enrage Arab and Muslim hatred for us.
b) Weaken our military forces by spreading them even thinner (don't forget about India/Pakistan, Afghanistan, etc.)

c) Lead to further economic disaster – the more money we borrow to fuel our War Machine, the more money we need to pay back in interest.

If any of you think for a second that Israel is our friend, you're seriously deceiving yourself. Israel cares about one thing; and one thing only – ISRAEL! Think about it: would an ally hire Jonathan Pollard, a civilian senior analyst at our top-secret Navy Field Operational Intelligence Office in Suitland, Maryland to steal our intelligence reports?

As Thomas wrote in *Seeds of Fire*: "In the time he had spied for Israel, Pollard read and copied and transmitted every worthwhile secret the United States possessed." Keep this sentence in mind, for it reiterates what the CIA's George Tenet said: "Pollard stole every worthwhile intelligence secret we have." Think about this for a moment. The Mossad possesses ALL of our secrets, and they've recently joined forces with the CSIS and are exchanging information with them.

The keys to the future of mankind at both Los Alamos and S-4 (Area 51) are now in the hands of our most dire enemy – China!

How did things get so bad? It all started with a software program created by William Hamilton called Promis (Prosecutors Management Information Systems) that was designed to share information between various databases, and to also track information from other databases by tapping into them.

Hamilton explained to the Department of Justice, "Enhanced Promis has the ability to track every citizen in the United States by accessing their personal data files. The barest details of their lives would be sufficient: a birth certificate, marriage license, driver's license, or employment record."

Promis was obviously a powerful piece of software with the potential to be so all-encompassing and octopus-like in its reach that Deputy Attorney General Lowell Jensen labeled it "one of the greatest discoveries of this century."

Realizing its benefit as an intelligence tool, the LAKAM, operating out of Israel's Ministry of Defense and even more secretive than the Mossad, sent the most notorious spy in the world – Rafi Eitan – to steal it. Eitan (who was the principle figure in setting up the Irangate arms-for-hostages deal) "obtained" a copy of the Enhanced Promis software; then presented it to LAKAM programmers, who deconstructed it. The software was then sold to secret service agencies, terrorists, and financial centers all over the world.

There's only one catch to this story: granted that such an undertaking was not only blatantly ILLEGAL on Israel's part, it was also a betrayal against the U.S. In no uncertain terms, the Israeli's also pulled one final trick. After ripping the Enhanced Promis software apart, they installed a "trap door" before putting it back together again that would allow them to have ANY information on the host system that was using it.

Do you know what this means? Say, for instance, this software was installed into YOUR computer. Because of the back door that nobody knew about when they illegally bought it, the Israeli's could see EVERY FILE on your computer. Every one! So, when the Israeli's began selling the stolen software on the black market, one would wonder why they'd lay such a golden egg into the laps of their enemies. But with the trap door, it becomes evident. They could spy on everything their adversaries were doing! And to whom were they selling it? To name a few: the IRA, England's MI5, the Russian Mafia, the Jordanian government, Switzerland's Credit Suisse Bank (with a wealth of financial data), the Soviet Union's military intelligence, Germany's secret service (BND), and last but not least, the Chinese government, which was intent on breaking into our labs at Los Alamos and unearthing all of our military secrets.

Also on their agenda was Sandia Labs, where we arm our nuclear subs and also do research into time travel and teleportation.

Once again, Israel and China are in cahoots to undermine the United States.

The man who sold the doctored Enhanced Promis software to China's secret service was none other than publishing tycoon Robert Maxwell. He was also instrumental in selling this program to spy agencies all around the world before he got "knocked off" for talking too much and not being able to meet his financial obligations. (Do you remember him drowning after "falling off" his boat a few years ago? The Controllers have a way of eliminating those who become a problem.)

Understanding the ramifications of Israel's role in supplying this stolen, doctored, illegal software to shady organizations all over the world (that THEY and only they benefited from) is crucial. A ruling by the U.S. Congress Judiciary Committee declared in no uncertain terms, "A foreign power – the State of Israel – has been engaged in *active espionage* against the United States by the illegal use of Enhanced Promis software."

What makes this matter even more appalling is that the powers-that-be in our own country knew the Trojan Horse was installed in the back of this software that was sold to spies, criminals, and governments across the world. This invariably leads back to the Israeli secret service and our nation's silence where we made no attempts to prosecute or expose them.

It's truly sickening. John Cohen of the House Judiciary Committee summed it up when he said, "There is a putrid stench that reaches across party lines in Washington and involves cover-ups by various administrations and foreign governments, specifically Israel's. Though tens of millions of dollars have been spent investigating the 'Inslaw Affair,' they have all failed for one reason only. Very powerful people do not wish the truth to get out."

And what is the truth? Well, we'll get to that in time, but before that it's important to realize how world government operates on a daily basis.

It isn't by the "selected" leaders that the Controllers put into office.

It's the secret societies and intelligence agencies that really make the world go 'round. Meir Amit, former Director-General of the Mossad, spoke of transitional administrations. "They are often only temporary stewards of government. The intelligence community often remains in power for a decade, often longer. To understand that is to see the world in a new way - not the world of elected government, but a far more powerful one; the one that lies beneath."

Sean McDade of the Royal Canadian Mounted Police, who performed one of the most extensive investigations into this sordid affair, said of the Inslaw Scandal in a memo to his superiors in 2000, "If made public ... more than one U.S. Presidential administration will be exposed because of their knowledge and complicity." He then went on to indict Israel. "The Israeli Mossad modified the original stolen software by Rafi Eitan, which was the 'first back door.' Later it became a 'two-way back door,' allowing the Israeli's access to top U.S. weapons secrets at Los Alamos and other classified installations in the U.S. The Israelis now possess all the nuclear secrets of the U.S. Compared to this espionage coup, it can be categorically stated that the Jonathan Pollard case is insignificant."

Folks; this information isn't coming from some schmuck sitting at a barstool spouting off. These are credible, reliable sources speaking about Israeli espionage that was so severe it made the Jonathan Pollard case pale in comparison. Yes, the Mossad has teamed up with China to remove our military secrets, all of which are now floating around in a cyber-world of doctored software, back doors, and misguided alliances. And now our greatest enemy, China, is in the driver's seat due to Israel's complicity.

At this point we should take a brief look at the Chinese and see why we should be so suspicious of them. Yeah, this isn't a nation of nice guys.

Instead, they're the ones who sold Iraq the ingredients necessary to develop their hydrogen bomb, specifically large quantities of lithium 6 hydride. But that's not all. They've been dealing arms to Middle Eastern countries for years, and in 1990 alone they sold $300 million worth of military hardware to Syria, Iran, and Iraq. Premier Li Peng even referred to his native China as "the new friend of the Arabs."

During the Reagan administration, China sold the Saudis missiles with a 2000-mile range, plus brokered Silkworm missiles with poison gas warheads to both Iran and Iraq. If you ever wondered where these dirtball countries are getting their explosives and weaponry, a good place to start looking (apart from the United States) is Russia and the People's Republic of China.

But an even better indicator of what type of people rule China can be found in the ruthlessly brutal Tiananmen Massacre in 1989. If you can remember that fateful event, the students in question only wanted two things – freedom and democratic rule. What did they receive for their efforts? A bloody massacre. When the Chinese military retaliated, there were 4,000 deaths and 6,500 people wounded on the very first day alone.

How did the Controller-brainwashed politicians and business leaders react to this atrocious massacre; and all of China's other appalling human rights violations? Well, they gave them MOST FAVORED NATION trading status and started funneling billions of dollars into their economy! Doesn't this reaction seem odd to you, even downright WRONG, especially from a country that supposedly places such a high emphasis on concepts such as equality and rights?

There's only one problem, though; the Controllers who manipulate our leaders like George Bush, Sr., Bill Clinton and now Bush, Jr., don't give a damn about justice or righteousness. Nah, their only concerns are power, money, and a side dish of war as an appetizer.

To them, China isn't a barbaric society with zero regard for individual citizens. Instead, they view it as a huge untapped economic market waiting to be exploited. In fact, during the last decade, Controller-operated companies and governments have invested untold mega-billions into China. Dow Chemicals pumped $56 million into a processing plant, while AT&T laid out an entire communications system for them. That was pretty nice of us, don't you think, especially for a country that holds our values so close to their heart?

The primary devil spearheading this traitorous operation is none other than Bilderberg/CFR luminary Henry Kissinger, who has pumped billions of dollars into the Chinese economy via his company, Kissinger Associates.

Gordon Thomas says of him, "More than any other American, he has been responsible for promoting U.S. investments in China." Kissinger even created the highly lauded American-China Society with former Secretary of State Cyrus Vance. And guess who was on the Board of Directors of this 'association' over the years: Gerald Ford, Jimmy Carter, Richard Nixon, National Security Advisors McGeorge Bundy, Robert McFarlane, and Zigbniew Brzezinski; and former Secretary's of State Dean Rusk, Edward Muskie, Alexander Haig, and William Rogers.

It's good to see that our former public officials have such high regard for the best interests of this country.

Kissinger Associates influence their clients to invest in China. There was David Rockefeller's Chase Manhattan that plunked-down $270 million for a nuclear power plant at Daya Bay, which was subsequently used to make nuclear weapons. Or how about American Express that fronted $138 million for a Beijing office complex, or Atlantic Richfield who laid $170 million for a natural gas field. Aren't you glad these companies are "helping" a country that steals our military secrets and kills anyone who dares speak out against them?

The most grating aspect of this scenario is our continuing lack of resolve in the face of China standing diametrically opposed to what America is supposed to represent. But instead of completely banishing them economically, it's business as usual, with American companies continuing to pour more money into their coffers.

The act that most personifies our intentions toward China was the slaughter at Tiananmen Square. Here's what transpired. George Bush, Sr. was getting ready to invade Iraq, but he wanted full support in the United Nations. The only problem – China was hesitant to give their nod of approval unless they got something in return. So, if the United States took a hard line and denounced the brutal murders that took place at Tiananmen Square, the Chinese would not vote in favor of our Iraqi invasion in the U.N.

In other words, President Bush Sr. sold out in the most abhorrent way possible. China outwardly spit on freedom and any hint of democracy; then we turned around and gave them Most Favored Nation status and the assurance of loans through the World Bank. We also ended all trade restrictions with China, allowed them to enter the World Trade Organization, and welcomed them as part of GATT.

But the Globalist controlled love-fest didn't end there. China forwarded to the U.S. information on their military sales to Iraq that our NSA satellites couldn't locate. By January, 1991, the Pentagon had the exact location of every Silkworm missile site in Iraq, plus all their other weaponry. In addition, we also knew where the lithium 6 deuteride used for making hydrogen bombs was stored (which, by the way, was sold to Iraq by China from a nuclear power plant in Inner Mongolia). In all, when we ultimately invaded Iraq and Saddam Hussein, it was like shooting fish in a bowl – or like adults beating up a six-year old child.

But wait – there's more! When the Chinese government was going to stage "trials" for the students they hadn't already slain (a total mockery of justice), they didn't want the U.S. to give them any problems over the penalties they doled out (many of which were death sentences). So, the Bush administration kept quiet like good little lap dogs while the "rabble-rousers" were unmercifully eliminated. Like the old Chinese saying goes, "kill one, educate one hundred."

Since that time, over a decade ago, what has transpired? Well, we've helped China improve their satellites and given them the know-how to upgrade their missile guidance systems. We're pretty nice guys, huh? We've also given them advance aviation data for their jets and fighter planes. Who do you think was behind the scenes acting as the conduit for these deals? At the time, Joseph Brewer, a Washington analyst, said, "Bush's implicit message to U.S. companies with a total of many billions of dollars invested in China was clear. Despite the massacres, they should regard the situation very much as business as usual. The apologists of Kissinger Associates could not have expressed their positions more clearly than had the President."

Reinforcing this opinion, the *Wall Street Journal* reported in September, 1989, three months after the Tiananmen slaughter, "Kissinger Associates could be on the verge of earning hundreds of thousands from a limited partnership set up to engage in joint dealings with CITIC (a merchandise and banking arm of the Chinese government)."

Three primary individuals took the necessary steps to assure that China got re-certified with Most Favored Nation trading status. They were Henry Kissinger, Alexander Haig, and Prescott Bush (George's brother). Haig remained a player as chairman of Worldwide Associates, Inc., a consulting firm with ties to whom? You guessed it – Kissinger Associates! Through these wheelings-and-dealings, he set-up an array of joint ventures with the CITIC, thus keeping the machine rolling. Prescott Bush, on the other hand, was a consultant for Asset Management International Financing and Settlement, Ltd., where he raised $60 million to invest in joint Chinese-U.S. projects.

At this point, please don't think I'm picking exclusively on George Bush, Sr., and his crony James Baker. No, this traitorous behavior stretches across party lines and successive administrations. Remember, the Controllers don't care about Republicans or Democrats; they merely use them as vehicles to accomplish their goals. As you'll see later in this report, Bill Clinton was guilty beyond words of bending over backwards to facilitate the Chinese. Jimmy Carter (after leaving office) visited the Mainland and suggested that China receive MFN status, which puts tariffs on imports into that country at the lowest possible rate.

Even today, the George Bush Jr. administration is packed with devils doing the Controllers' bidding. What do I mean? Well, look at the former consultants for Kissinger Associates that are currently in the Bush cabinet or on the periphery. First of all, there's Brent Scowcroft, now National Security Advisor, who was formerly the Kissinger Associates Washington office director. Or how about Lawrence Eagleburger in the State Department? Insiders say he's more familiar with the financial interactions between China and America than anyone.

Finally, good 'ol James Baker still pops his head up once in awhile, shaping foreign policy behind the scenes on orders from George Bush, Sr., who no doubt is in direct contact with the Controllers. And if you don't think these individuals play a significant role in determining our foreign policy, check out the December, 2000 CIA report that says George W. Bush is "at best inexperienced in global matters." AT BEST INEXPERIENCED! Do you think the Controllers, with so much at stake, are going to let George W. mess things up for them? Hardly.

Since I've mentioned the CIA, we next need to look at a recently released document entitled, "Global Trends 2015." Here are a few of the CIA's very startling predictions:

1) China's economic growth will be greater than that of all of Europe by the year 2010, while Russia's will only be 1/5th of the United States.
2) China will incite a full-scale trade war by 2010.
3) China will promote various terrorist groups to align and attack the U.S.
4) By 2015, the U.S. will surrender its role as world policeman.

5) By 2015, a MAJOR WAR will break out between the U.S. and China!

6) Finally, a direct quote from the CIA's "Global Trends 2015" report: "China, as it becomes increasingly the NEW SUPERPOWER of the Third Millennium, is likely to provide biological and chemical weapons and 'suitcase' nuclear devices to wage terror against the United States."

Yet all of the devils from Kissinger Associates, the Bilderbergs, the CFR and Trilateral Commission keep telling our government to pump software, hardware, weaponry, computers, and advanced technology into their country. What's going on? We need to wake up quickly or the hammer is going to drop.

What China is doing with the technology we're laying at their doorstep is also very telling in determining what type of society they plan to create. The answer would make George Orwell shudder in his grave. Yes, Big Brother has become such an integral part of China's long-term planning that Gordon Thomas writes, "By the year 2001, technology had become like drug addiction in China."

Here is what the Chinese are currently doing, and intend to do in the future:

- Long before 2010, they would like every street in China to be equipped with closed-circuit television.
- Experimenting with the attachment of microchips to the human brain. Once in place, the authorities could use a device that would read a person's mind and relay the information to a computer. As I'm sure you can imagine; this invasion into the deepest realms of our thought process would be the ultimate surveillance weapon!
- Developing a new radar system that could locate any American stealth fighter plane.
- Privacy International, a London based human rights group, has reported that any foreigner going to China will be entered into at least 300 different databases, all of which will be interconnected. The traveler's every move will then be detailed – e-mails, laptop activity, room service, financial transactions, phone calls, etc. – everything monitored.
- Hundreds of thousands of cameras will be installed on buses, trains, and elevators.

• Residents will essentially be filmed all day long from the time they leave their home. All public buildings, roads, and apartment complexes will also be staked-out with cameras, and new housing projects will eventually have "seeing-eyes" in every room!

• The Chinese government's ultimate goal is to monitor people every second of the day from birth to death; much of this activity arising from technology either purchased or stolen from the United States.

Thomas ultimately says: "In China, surveillance is an integral part of pacification, intimidation, obfuscation, propaganda and control. In its most pernicious form, surveillance is used for behavior modification, including adverse conditioning." Thomas also goes on to say that by the year 2020, Artificial Intelligence will be in full-swing with robots becoming an essential part of the Chinese culture, not only as a part of the work force, but also as observers and snitches!

Not only is Chinese Intelligence obsessed with "obtaining" America's deepest technological, defense, and computer secrets, but they also continue to help Saddam Hussein upgrade his defense network. China is also among the top two purchasers of Russian arms, and reached a peak of $2.7 billion in weapons sales in 1999 (with the volatile country of Pakistan, which was recently on the brink of nuclear war with India, being its primary buyer). Their role is so troublesome that the *New York Times*, on August 20, 2001, quoted the "Conventional Arms Transfers to Developing Nations 1993-2000" report published by the Congressional Research Service, saying: "China can present an important obstacle to efforts to stem proliferation of advanced missile systems to some areas of the developing world where political and military tensions are significant."

But the aspect of Chinese society that Thomas best captures is the difference in outlook between the Chinese and Americans. According to Thomas, the Chinese "Machine" does not care about truth or public opinion, but are much better and more comfortable with censorship and propaganda. Nor do they cater to or create media hysteria when an event takes place. Instead, they simply stand back and observe, then take notes and wait.

Waiting is the key; then at the right moment, they lunge forward and strike.

Thomas writes, "At the core of the Machine – its intelligence, its propaganda – its military leaders, its politicians – is one belief: it despises America's fear of casualties."

From their perspective, every time America enters a war (from Korea and Vietnam to Afghanistan) or needs to "remedy a situation," they always worry about public opinion and body counts. But the Chinese don't place such emphasis on human life. Rather, they teach their soldiers that although America has an array of sophisticated weaponry, they're *afraid of death!*

According to them, we can be beaten in war because we are soft. That's why the Chinese admire the Israeli's. The Jews, in their view, hold this same lack of regard for death. The "individual" does not hold as much importance as does the society or nation.

Thus, the Chinese and Israeli's are linked once again, which brings us to the infamous downing of an American spy plan in May, 2001. When this event took place and was plastered across the daily newspapers, guess who the Chinese invited and promised full-access to inspect the plane and all its sophisticated secrets? A team of Israeli technicians was secretly flown to Hainan Island where the plane was disabled.

Do you see a pattern evolving? But Chinese subterfuge toward the U.S. doesn't end there. On the day of 9-11 – the day America was horrendously attacked – guess what the Chinese were doing? One of their PLA (People's Liberation Army) planes landed at Kabul, Afghanistan, and on board were a team of defense contractors, secret service members and some senior Army officers.

This was on September 11, 2001! And why did they arrive there? To sign contracts giving the Taliban state-of-the-art electronics defense equipment, plus advanced warning and missile tracking systems that helped bring these terrorists into the modern age. Does this action sound like one carried out by a trusted ally of the United States? Hell no, especially on THE DAY we were viciously attacked. Up until then, the Taliban was nothing but a rag-tag operation with a total of 150 tanks, 15 helicopters, 20 bombers, and a few old Russian Kalashnikov rifles. That was it.

But lo and behold, China updated them! So the Taliban received military equipment in return for a promise that the Muslim fundamentalists would not attack their mainland.

Here's another little tidbit of information that might catch your interest. It seems Bill Clinton almost performed one of the few courageous acts of his presidency by considering to put a hit on Osama bin Laden following the attack of our Embassy in Nairobi. But the assassination was foiled because bin Laden had been tipped off – by the CSIS! Bin Laden also made several trips to China in the years preceding 9-11.

But please don't smile favorably on Bill Clinton. Along with Henry Kissinger and the Bush Family, our former president is right up there when it comes to aiding and abetting the Chinese. Here are a few quotes:

General Accounting Office (June 19, 1998): "President Clinton issued waivers on military items valued at $36.3 million and licensing of commercial military exports worth $313 million."

Jeff Garth, _New York Times,_ (October 19, 1998) on how nearly $2 billion in annual trade has been removed from federal scrutiny: "The Pentagon was traditionally the strongest voice against technology exports, and Clinton made several appointments calculated to change the culture. The former president said at that time, 'One reason I ran for President was to tailor export controls to the realization of a post-cold war world.'"

The Cox Report: The thrust of this report revolves around how the Clinton administration helped China get more technology and conveniently paved the way for them to steal and engage in espionage against this country. As Oklahoma Senator James M. Inhofe notes, "As the Cox Report points out, nuclear espionage by China is only one part of the problem. China's efforts to acquire U.S. military-related technology is pervasive. Operating through a maze of government and quasi-government entities and front companies, China has established a technology-gathering network of IMMENSE PROPORTIONS. They are willing and able to trade, bribe, buy or steal to get U.S. advanced technology – all for the purpose of enhancing their long-term military potential. Their success is often determined largely by our willingness to make it easier for them to get what they want."

The following items come from "The Hansen Case: A Trifle Compared to Clinton-China Connection" written by Sam Smith for _Newsmax.com_ on February 22, 2001:

Commerce Secretary Ron Brown: Allowed American-made engines to be sold to China to put into their cruise missiles. The only problem is – this was strictly military equipment; but that didn't matter. Brown got around this little "snag" by reclassifying all the engines as 'civilian.'

New York Times – Clinton took over $2 billion worth of items that we exported to China off the list of things that could come under inspection by our National Security forces. This included nearly 80 supercomputers that could unscramble classified data and also design nuclear weapons. Many of these items were ultimately used by China's military, yet the Clinton administration refused to allow a peep of scrutiny here in the U.S.

President Clinton: Signed National Security waivers to let four U.S. commercial satellites to be set into orbit by the Chinese even though China knowingly was exporting nuclear and missile technology to Iran, Pakistan, and other terrorist countries.

Conclusion to *"The Hansen Case"* (VERY IMPORTANT): "The brunt of evidence was that the Chinese had obtained more American military secrets over the past two decades than had all the previous spies in American history put together! They had basic information on all nuclear weapons systems, they got our most advanced supercomputers, and they gained extraordinarily important information about satellite systems. Some of this knowledge they used for themselves; some they retrofitted and repackaged and sold to other countries like Iraq, where it is used against *our own fighter planes.*"

Smith continues, "While the problem occurred under both Republican and Democratic administrations, it got completely out of hand under Clinton ... a stunning proportion was obtained either as a direct result of political and economic decisions by the Clinton Administration or as a result of what can best be described as premeditated indifference."

Can you see what's going on? The Bush administration, plus Clinton's dog-and-pony show are mere puppets; facilitators who implement decisions from above to prepare China for their showdown with the United States. This is scary stuff, folks, and you may be wondering, when are they going to strike? The answer is simple -- whenever they're ready. And what do they need to get them ready? More and better U.S. technology! Isn't it obvious? We're the ones who are allowing the Controllers to dig our own graves! And while all this occurs, China waits silently, the "ultimate perpetrator" as Gordon Thomas calls them, holding America in contempt for one thing – for being TOO SOFT!

And do you know what? If we keep allowing this atrocity to take place, the Chinese are right -- we ARE too soft because we're not doing anything to stop these preparations for our own demise. It's like your next-door neighbor pointing guns, cannons, bazookas, missiles and bombs at your house; and you just sit there watching it happen, wondering, "I wonder if they're going to attack us?"

Well, you're damn right they're going to lay siege upon you, and if something isn't done to stop it, who is ultimately to blame? We are, for letting it happen.

CHAPTER TWENTY-SEVEN

ARTIFICIAL INTELLIGENCE – THE FINAL

CONSPIRACY

Before I delve into the Controller's ultimate goals (for they are the ones calling the shots), while the "implementers" we see on TV are merely actors filling a role on stage), I'd like to examine one last time a major problem facing this country – foreign aid. The first thing this nation needs to do is stop *all* foreign aid at once, to everyone, and reexamine our overseas policies.

Look at what we do for Israel while they steal our technology and sell it to the Chinese. Thirty percent of all U. S. foreign aid goes to Israel, totaling $3 billion ($1.2 billion for economic aid and $1.8 billion in military aid). We also give Israel $2 billion a year in federal loan guarantees, which comes to a grand total of $5 billion per year, or $13.9 million a day.

Plus, our total aid to Israel from 1949 to date is approximately $96 billion; and this, to the sixteenth wealthiest nation on earth. It's ridiculous, especially when there isn't the slightest inkling of "peace" in the Middle East. I have an idea: Why not give this money to *American citizens* instead!

But y'see, the Controllers don't give a damn about Americans, or for that matter, Jewish or Chinese or Russian or African citizens either. Why not? Because now we're getting to the crux of their motives – the grand finale! Yes, the future of mankind on this planet can be found in Artificial Intelligence! Are you able to see how this phenomenon has turned full-circle? It all began with America's artificial intelligence experiments at Area 51 and other labs, then how the Israeli's stole our technology (referred to as "nuclear secrets") and sold them to the Chinese. The Controllers' ultimate goal is to replace America with the Chinese as the world's next superpower; then begin the process of creating artificial beings on a large-scale.

And why, you may wonder, is America being usurped by the Chinese? It's simple. Americans are still plagued by annoying concepts such as justice, freedom, self-determination, and free will. The Controllers are worried that Americans will not tolerate manning assembly lines where robots are created that will eventually take over this planet. And if America won't assume the lead on a global scale or pull off this coup, how will the rest of the world follow?

They won't. But here's the Controller's safety-valve - their final step in a ghastly Hegelian Dialectic:

Thesis: America – "democracy" – representative of freedom
Antithesis: China – communistic – State controlled
Synthesis: New World Order – Big Brother – robotic subservience

Isn't it becoming clear? To hell with George Orwell's "1984" mind-controlled humans. The Controllers are going one step further by completely eliminating free will altogether (or nearly so), by creating a being that's entirely incapable of experiencing such a concept – the machine! This is it, folks, the final piece to the puzzle – the last line of the stage-play – the FINAL CONSPIRACY!

And what is the purpose behind it all? A couple of incentives are driving this phenomenon. First of all, the Controllers, as their name none-too-subtly implies, are fixated by control! Human beings, thus, are objects to be controlled. But y'see, this control can't be absolute or it would take all the fun out of the game. The Controllers want some degree of resistance just to keep the stage play interesting. I liken them to cats that catch a mouse. Of course the feline could kill the little rodent in a heartbeat; but what do they do instead? They torment, toy with and torture the mouse for hours on end – batting it around, throwing it up in the air, letting it run away, only to capture it again or trap it in a corner. I know this to be true because my cats play this game all the time.

The same rationale applies to the Controllers. They don't want completely mind-numbed robots beneath them because then there'd be no hunt – no chase – no THRILL of MASTERY and CONTROL! Then again, the thought of people rising against them – the MASSES – scares the hell out of them. Even though only a few handful of people control 40% of the world's wealth, there's still that little problem of people getting sick of their shenanigans. And if we ever *did* decide to stage a bloody, murderous, don't-allow-one-Controller-to-live REVOLUTION, guess where they'd be? Dead and buried. Bloody, beaten pulps of mangled flesh and bone. Nothingness. They'd be destroyed.

Death leads us to the flipside of the coin and the final step in every conspiracy since the beginning of time – IMMORTALITY! Realistically, when you think about it, what else is left? If you can control money, politics and people and and have every material object you desire, what is the only thing beyond your control? Death. And in all honesty, considering the supreme egos of men such as the Rockefellers, Rothschilds, etc., don't think for a second that they don't want to live forever. That's the only obstacle yet to overcome.

Before I finish these thoughts, though, I want to delve deeper into the concept of Artificial Intelligence. Of particular interest is an article in the June/July 2002 issue of *UFO Magazine* entitled "What Are They?" by Richard M. Dolan, author of *UFO's and the National Security State*. Dolan refers to an observation made by noted biologist Ivan Sanderson, who said in *Uninvited Visitors* (1967) that aliens may not actually be fully organic beings, but instead artificial life forms.

Think about it. Instead of creatures similar to us who breathe, eat, possess internal organs, and defecate, what if ET's were actually Intelligent Machines? The concept is intriguing, and as you'll see, immensely opens the scope of possibility.

Dolan also introduces us to something called Singularity, which he defines as: "when computer intelligence becomes able to upgrade itself, to reproduce itself continuously, and become SELF-aware!" The process involves "a rapid, exponential increase in computer intelligence, leaving human intelligence in the dust."

Are things starting to become clearer? You're reading the future right here. This is where it's all leading. People from many different fields of research speak of humans attaining the next "level." Well, folks, this is the next level, except humans aren't going to be a part of the picture (at least as we know them).

Gordon E. Moore, Chairman Emeritus of Intel Corporation, came up with "Moore's Law" in 1965 envisioning that "the number of transistors per integrated circuit would double every 18 months in the future." This postulation proved true, for in 1971, the leading integrated circuit had approximately 2,000 transistors. By the new millennium, that number was 42,000,000.

Dolan reinforces the point with this quote: "Once a certain critical mass is achieved in terms of hardware, software, connectivity and storage, machines will develop the ability to foresee their own technological needs and redesign their software."

Are you listening? This isn't science-fiction, folks. This is the stuff that's taking place in hidden facilities like Area 51's S-4 and Los Alamos. Similar to the Manhattan Project A-Bomb that no one knew about until it exploded over Hiroshima and forever changed civilization as we know it, the same type of bombshell is being developed today.

You can disregard it like an ostrich with its head in the sand, or else face the reality of our time. This is where we're going.

Ray Kurzweil, respected Artificial Intelligence researcher, says with confidence: "Things are going to move at a pace beyond what we can now comprehend!" He adds, "It affects the very nature of human intelligence. We'll see intelligence that's derivative of human intelligence, but SUPERIOR TO IT!"

If the above words are starting to alarm you, it's for good reason. Many authorities on this subject see it being a reality by the year 2040, with the initial phases being implemented as early as the next decade. Dolan characterizes the phenomenon as a "godlike level of intelligence residing within machines."

I don't know about you, but this concept scares the hell out of me, especially with a ruthless country like China, or some evil Project Paperclip-type Nazi scientists at the helm. Are you ready to rollover and give these monsters "godlike powers?"

But y'see, the Controllers are playing this all out like a huge Wizard of Oz drama, throwing us a few carrots to chase as if they're the real thing. Why do you think they're so forthcoming with information on Area 51 being a "flying saucer" base? Because it's all a sham. UFOs are only the cover story – a smokescreen. The real story lives with Artificial Intelligence.

Some of you may dismiss this concept as hogwash, saying that humans will always be superior to machines even if a computer can multiply numbers at speeds infinitely higher than us, because in the end, all we have to do is unplug the computer and it's over and done with. Disabled. But what happens when artificial intelligence develops to the point where a machine can walk over and plug itself back in? It might not walk exactly like us, but robots are now able to construct automobiles on an assembly line. Who's to say they won't be able to mobilize themselves enough to plug a simple socket into a wall, or recharge their own power supply? Once they attain that level of sophistication, the machines will even be able to CREATE other machines. Yes, machines begetting more machines, each one evolving to a higher level as these very same machines stamp out their own parts in a factory.

Far-fetched? Once again, return to the assembly line at a GM factory in Detroit. Hell, to an extent, they're already doing it at a rudimentary level.

To combat these self-perpetuation machines, all a human has to do is take a hammer and smash the Frankenstein-like creation to bits -- right? I wouldn't find much reassurance in this notion. Why? Take a look at Steven Spielberg's *AI* sometime when the humanoid's face is simply pulled off like a part inside a vacuum sweeper, then put back in. Do you get it? Machines will know how to repair themselves. Hell, they already know how to do it on other planets; why not here? Once they reach this stage of development, the machines are literally un-killable! They can't be eradicated. Unlike us, when we have a heart pierced by a sword or a brain blown away by bullets, all they have to do is replace their ruined or destroyed parts. It'll be like ripping out the water pump in your car and putting in a new one.

As this nightmare unfolds, two scenarios present themselves.

1)   Scientists will alter our human make-up; then combine it with some form of advanced machine intelligence.
2)   Artificial Intelligence will become so vast and all-encompassing that at this moment in time, we can't even conceive of where it will lead.
3)   Richard Dolan ultimately sees "machine intelligence as something that will be so far greater than ours as to be alien"!

Do you get it? When we see or conceive of "aliens," they're really nothing but our future … or a present form that they've already arrived at that is awaiting us in the near future. So, instead of being far-removed or "different," these crafts from outer space are actually what we'll soon be! There won't any longer be "we" and "they." We'll all be the same, once the machines take dominion over our planet.

Can you grasp the ramifications? Aliens are already a form of Artificial Intelligence. That's why they're able to cross the universe and we cannot. We're not only limited by fossil-fuel burning rockets (at least what is presented to us by the government), but our physical bodies are incapable of traveling such distances because of their limitations. To reach Pluto we'd need a rocket that was so unbelievably huge just to carry enough food to keep us alive, it would be impractical. When coupled with our short life spans (mortality), intergalactic travel is simply a far-flung notion. But what if a machine were in the pilot's seat instead of a human? That completely changes the entire scenario, doesn't it?

Mortality and food consumption are no longer concerns, and once the military and/or NASA break out their next generation of space craft, guess what? The Controllers will be ready to blast off for the stars. The only drawback is: we're not included in those plans!

So, when viewed in this manner, the "aliens" are already advanced beyond us, but the Controllers are aware that if they want to survive, travel beyond this planet is the only alternative. In this sense, Dolan observes, "The natural course of evolution does not give us unlimited intelligence, but the intelligence necessary to exist within a natural ecosystem." If you seriously weigh these words, you'll realize that humans have only progressed to a point necessary to survive on the planet earth. In other words, we've moved forward as far as humans can go. We're able to survive here (at least for the time being), but to reach beyond this level, we require a new form of advancement.

Dolan's insights hit the nail directly on the head. Here on earth, he points out, we've adapted to the temperature, gravity, viruses and elements, but to "live elsewhere, we will need to be modified, perhaps so much that the result would be something entirely different. A new species, created with some of our DNA, would probably be the most logical means of sending biological organisms to distant worlds."

Did you notice that the author didn't say "humans," but transformed "biological entities!" Thus, as pointed out earlier, to copy others already traversing the universe, humans will be altered into a form of advanced machine intelligence. And that's exactly what's happening in our top-secret labs. The Controllers and leaders of world governments won't tell us about these developments for one primary reason – their plans don't include us "lowly humans."

CHAPTER TWENTY-EIGHT

THE CONTROLLERS' ULTIMATE MOTIVES

Here's where we get into the nitty-gritty of the Controller's ultimate motives. The elite desperately need to create a work force of unquestioning slaves to let them survive the coming cataclysm. Whether it be the arrival of a rogue planet or comet, worldwide viruses, full-scale nuclear war, or global warming to the point of burning us out, the Controllers (via access to caches of hidden knowledge) are fully aware that our days on this planet in our current form are numbered. Why do you think they've already built scores of underground bunkers all around the country (and world) and are rapidly constructing new ones in places like Indiana? Is it because of a band of rag-tag terrorists from Afghanistan? Hardly.

The Controllers know that when disaster strikes, the majority of us won't survive. It's happened before to the Mayans, Incas, and on Atlantis, so don't write this scenario off as inconceivable. If it weren't a direct possibility, why would the Controllers be building and updating their bunkers with such fervor? Hell, George Bush even *admitted* to their shadow government preparations in underground bases.

Regrettably, once they're inside of them and the doors are locked, guess who won't have a set of keys to get in? Yup – you and me!

Right now, plenty of people are getting themselves in an uproar about mind control, but those are only short-term worries. Sure, secret service agencies in a number of countries have experimented with mind control (and continue to do so), but when the final conspiracy plays out, there won't be any minds left to control, or humans as we even know them! By mapping our genome/DNA to know what makes us tick and also developing technologies of mind-blowing proportions, a "Brave New World" is on the horizon; but it's not one that would appeal to us in any way, shape, or form.

This is scary, folks. Those of us in our thirties and early forties probably won't see it fully, but our kids and their kids (whatever that means) will. Think about a future where we become sexless machines ... yes, sexless ... why would the Controllers want us to be distracted with something as gratifying and mundane as sexual thought? Think about how much time humans "squander" on being horny. The Controllers can't have that, especially when we won't even need sexual organs to replicate ourselves.

We'll be Machine People, and enjoyment, relaxation or fornication aren't elements of the equation.

Someone may protest, "I'll think about sex if I want to." But in all honesty, you might not have a chance to. What do I mean? Well, picture it as follows. In the future, we're all Artificial Intelligence creations with robotic-machine bodies and computer software minds. The Controllers, of course, at the helm of all this technology, will determine which entities get which software. How do they decide? The answer probably lies in our current status. Ask yourself, if a cataclysmic world event occurred tomorrow, would the Controllers send you an invitation to scurry to their underground bunker to survive? If the answer is no, then it's a safe bet they won't receive anything other than standard Artificial Intelligence slave software.

And what does this entail? First of all, you'll have a limited amount of accessible "memory." A perfect metaphor would be modern-day home computers. If they have three gigabytes of memory and become full, nothing else will fit. The same reasoning applies to our future AI-software brains. The Controllers won't want you to become distracted with thoughts revolving around sex, rebellion, creation, or errant daydreaming. Instead, you'll be a worker, similar to drone bees in a hive. Thus, you'll be programmed to attend work each day, where you'll be plugged into or accessed by a Central Control Computer, or C3.

At work, the C3 will "scan" you and make sure that only what's supposed to be on your software is there … concepts like work, work, and more work. And since you only have a limited amount of accessible memory, nothing else will fit onto your software.

Even more advanced, author Richard Dolan tells us about a procedure known as "Mindscan" where an "entity probes the person's mind telepathically and "sees" their innermost thoughts. This might be interpreted as tremendous psychic power possessed by the entity; but such a thing could easily be done by implants within the alien beings' brain." Not quite convinced? Well, check this out. Right now, chimpanzees can navigate a computer cursor across a monitor by simply using their mind (after, of course, their brain had been implanted with a microchip)!

This madness is occurring *right now*, and is barreling forward with frightening speed each day. What if a maniacal regime like the Chinese –

those with absolutely no respect for human rights or freedom – leaps to the forefront of this movement and gets the Controllers' financial backing? What type of future will await us? I know the answer – one that is as unrewarding and un-human as anyone can imagine.

The Controllers, on the other hand, will be among the few to benefit from this societal and technological transformation (considering their "elite" status). How so? While all the rest of us will be robotic machine-slaves with limited software faculties, the Controllers will capitalize on every technological breakthrough available to them. If you think there's a huge chasm between the "haves" and the "have nots" in the world right now, you ain't seen nothing yet! While the masses will be programmed to complete certain tasks, and that's it, the Controllers will tap into virtually infinite amounts of information. (And remember, information is power if it is acted upon!)

But even better for them is the reality of finally becoming immortal. Y'see, right now every human being is ultimately reduced to one commonality – a physical body which subsequently results in mortal death. But Artificial Intelligence will eliminate the curse of physical death, thus opening the door to an immortal mind. Can you see it? If all the information from our minds can be downloaded onto a computer program, then installed into an AI "body," this mind can then virtually live forever. Sure, the physical parts may wear out, but parts of the "container" can be replaced. The thoughts within will continue indefinitely, thus making that person immortal.

Of course the Controllers won't bestow this privilege on everyone – why should they share their immortality? Do they currently share their wealth, mansions, fancy cars, vacation spots and knowledge with the rest of us "less fortunate" people? Hell no. Why should they give us never-ending life if they don't have to, especially if it would somehow threaten their power?

Folks, I'm going to let you in on a little secret. Do you know what the Controllers are promoting at this moment in time on our planet? The answer: Death. Yup, the Controllers are behind the management of a death-culture that will eventually lay the foundation for our "advancement" to the AI level. What do I mean by a "death culture?" Well, look at our global society for a moment. The man-made AIDS virus is ravaging a variety of locales in our world. Two-thirds of Africa is 35-50% infected with the virus and it is also hitting epidemic proportions in Asia. Nearly 100,000 people die from starvation *every day* on this planet, even though we have the resources, technology, and money to feed everyone.

Then there's the subject of war. Iraq, Afghanistan, Israel and the Palestinians, India and Pakistan, plus a rash of other localized "skirmishes" across the globe. If you analyzed this situation, where do you think most of our wars are taking place -- in the wealthy, affluent countries? Hell no. The wars are being waged in the poor areas. You'd think these downtrodden people could be better served with food, clothes, and medicine, don't you? But what are the Controllers forwarding to them? Weapons to kill each other!

Can't you see it's a death culture ... And, as much as I love this country, guess who's by-and-far leading the way in this sordid endeavor of feeding the War Machine? The USA. In fact, during the year 2000, the United States sold $36.9 billion worth of international arms – 68% to underdeveloped or developing countries. And that's up 8% from the year before. Almost forty billion dollars! $36.9 billion! Half of all weapons sold on the world market come from US! The next highest seller is Russia, at $7.7 billion, while China only sold $400 million – 1/90th of what we dealt. (Data from the "Conventional Arms Transfer to Developing Nations, 1993-2000," published by the Congressional Research Center)

I have to ask you – WHAT IN GOD'S NAME ARE WE DOING?

Thirty-six billion dollars in arms sales – and $30 billion the year before, and $30 billion the year before, and $38 billion the next year, and $38 billion the following year. Think of how messed-up our priorities are. Starvation, poverty, and doing what's right don't register to the Controllers. Instead, huge profits are squirreled away in their pockets every year from this appalling practice. War is hell, but war is also "SELL" (and the Controllers are behind it).

The Controllers are death merchants and death mongers. Peace is a fallacy and doesn't mean a thing to them. Rather, they want to keep all the little people at each other's throats so they can keep the War Machine rolling.

And folks, if you think all this war and terror talk in the media is justification for such a disgusting practice, you need to look at the world leaders whose strings are being pulled by the Controllers. What if all the secret societies that lurk in the shadows around the globe are actually under the domain of one ruling power? Think about it. If Gordon Thomas was able to get such a wealth of information about the Mossad's dealings with the CSIS for his book, *Seeds of Fire*, do you think it's fathomable that those above him aren't aware of what's going on? No way. All these leaders are part of the same plan – the same script – and are carrying out their roles to further promote the War Machine, Globalism, and the Death Culture.

Or, as Eric Jon Phelps, author of *Vatican Assassins* says in an interview with Rick Martin for *The Spectrum* newspaper (May, 2000): "There's no conflict going on with the Arab nations. All of the Arab nations are under the command of Masonic kings or ayatollahs. Saddam Hussein is no enemy of George Bush; they're both brothers, brothers of the lodge."

When Martin says George Bush, Sr. and Saddam Hussein were business partners, Phelps replies, "Sure. That's why they never killed Saddam. They could have easily killed him. The CIA can kill anybody they want to. They could have easily killed Saddam and got out. They could use their own Arab agents in there. Saddam was a very important tool."

It is not implausible that the Death-Merchant Controllers are developing Artificial Intelligence (at our expense) to transcend death and become immortal. With virtually unlimited wealth at their disposal and governmental "black budgets" to also tap into, a future devoid of the human spirit awaits us, with only a few benefiting (if it can even be called that) from the overall scenario. Or, as Richard Dolan says at the conclusion of his article, "What Are They?": "Advanced technology wielded by biological entities may indeed be inherently unstable. But it is not so clear that such a condition applies equally to advanced machine intelligence."

If Mr. Dolan is correct, humanity as we know it will be a thing of the past.

But … as I said earlier in this article, there is hope. Reports are filtering out of China that their economy isn't as healthy as the Controllers wished it to be. In fact, Gordon Chang stated on June 19, 2002 in the *Asian Wall Street Journal* that, "The People's Republic can go from boom to bust in just a few short years." The *NewsMax.com* article in which this was reported goes on to say that "high expectations from the Chinese economy are grossly exaggerated" and "China's economic growth is declining and its banking system is in disarray, posing a threat of destabilization to the international economy."

Thus, similar to the Controllers' grandiose schemes for making Russia into a super-power, China may also prove untenable as a world leader. But it won't be because the international bankers aren't trying.

With high unemployment, inflation, a growing deficit, reckless spending, power grabs and dissatisfaction among the masses, China may not pan out to be such a glimmering diamond in the Controllers' eye. But we shouldn't gloat yet, for if China's (or any other world power's economy collapses), the ramifications will be felt globally, especially here.

So, whether China lives up to the Controller's expectations or not, the research and development into Artificial Intelligence will continue, and the Globalist elite will remain the same. Rome is burning and Noah is building his Ark.

Will we keep on fiddling around as Nero did and disregard the signs of a disastrous, impending storm, or will we take destiny into our own hands and destroy the Controllers? That's what it's going to ultimately take – total destruction. Because if we allow these evil monsters to fulfill their aims, dire consequences await us. Folks, we're not talking any longer about saving this country, or control of our minds. No, the very survival of humanity itself is at stake, for if the Controllers continue to pursue Artificial Intelligence, machines will soon replace human beings.

Everyone needs to ask, "Is this what we really want?" It's time to take action!

To close this article, I'll quote the heralded author Robert Anton Wilson. Hopefully his words will allow you to see a light at the end of the tunnel: "Every conspiracy collapses eventually because of the psychological likelihood that those who are superlatively clever at deceiving others become equally clever at deceiving themselves. Disinformation eats those who create it."

CHAPTER TWENTY-NINE

BIG BROTHER TECHNOLOGY - A BOOT STOMPING ON A HUMAN FACE

George Orwell, author of the infamous novel *1984*, described the horrors of a technological Big Brother future as "a boot stomping on a human face." During the past two months, it has become increasingly clear that all of us are being transformed into mechanistic cogs that more resemble monitored automatons than human beings.

This trend fits part-and-parcel into the Controller's overall goals of global dominance and subservience among the masses. To better understand the direction our society is heading, take a look at what has transpired in the year 2002 alone.

IMPLANTED COMPUTER MICROCHIPS

For years, the dreaded "Mark of the Beast" was spoken about by "crazy conspiratologists" as proof that Big Brother would finalize his quest for control by injecting us with computer microchips. These miniature devices would carry scores of information about an individual that would be retrieved by scanner-like receivers. Over time, no one would be able to buy, sell, obtain a driver's license, log onto a computer, or be admitted into a hospital without the chip.

But, nah, that was all "paranoia talk" the debunkers and unbelievers said. We'd never be implanted with computer microchips that revealed our medical background, family history, financial records, video purchases, brushes with the law, or information about what Internet sites we looked at. This wouldn't happen to us. I mean, America IS the land of the free!

Well, I'm sorry to disappoint all the skeptics, but guess what? The future is now. Applied Digital Solutions recently announced that on April 4, 2002, the FDA granted them permission for the "sales, marketing, and distribution of the VeriChip in the United States." Then, on May 10, 2002, at the VeriChip Center in Palm Beach County, Florida, the Jacobs Family got "chipped" with a "miniaturized, implantable, radio frequency identification device." This chip will have a personalized verification number for each recipient and the information will be stored in a registered database.

Now take a second and let this news sink in. This is the real thing - - the dreaded MARK OF THE BEAST! Folks, this is the beginning of a new era in which we are forfeiting control of our privacy and sovereignty.

Sure, at first these companies will make everything sound tame and benign; but beware! I guarantee that more and more information will be stored on these chips, and they'll be required for more and more activities until the day when all human beings will be FORCED to be injected, probably at birth.

Is this the future you want for yourself?

CLONING

According to the Reuters News Service, on April 24, 2002, Italian doctor Severino Antinori told a television audience there are at least three women in the world now pregnant with "cloned embryos." These impregnations were performed even though the United Nations is "supposed" to draft a document ban on human cloning.

If the Controllers are enthusiastically supporting this movement to further their cause of de-humanization, will that resolution be drafted? At this point we have to ask ourselves, are experiments in bio-technological conception and creation the direction we want our species to be taking?

CYBORGS

On March 22, 2002, Professor Kevin Warwick allowed surgeons at the Radcliffe Infirmary in Oxford, England to implant 3 mm silicon wires into an incision in his left wrist, then attach them to 100 separate electrodes that ran into his median nerve. To perform this first-of-its-kind operation (which cost $715,000), the surgeons sliced into Warwick's forearm, slid connecting wires beneath his skin, then stitched-up the incision.

These wires will then send and receive radio signals from a device that links the subject's nerves to a computer, where they will be recorded. Warwick says the ultimate aim of this operation is "to wire himself up to a ultrasonic sensor used by robots to navigate around objects and to give himself a bat-like sixth sense."

The operative word, in my opinion, is "robot." Think about it.

E-MAIL SPY TECHNOLOGY

One of the most intrusive devices in our modern lives is Carnivore/DCS1000, which uses both hardware and software to read our incoming and outgoing e-mail, including who sent the message, who received it, the body of the e-mail, and also the message subject. Worse, Carnivore can also monitor everything a computer user has ever downloaded, and also their web searches.

It can even go so far as to scan all the electronic traffic from an ISP (Internet Service Provider), more commonly known as a "server."

I don't know about you, but I don't want the FBI, CIA, National Security Agency or any other governmental body looking through what I do, or listening to my telephone conversations. But that is precisely what is going on right now, and we at *Babel Magazine* have firsthand proof of it. We know for a fact that our phone is being monitored and our e-mail transmissions are being read, misdirected, or "munched."

In an article entitled "Stop Carnivore Now," the author says that the FBI could, with their electronic wiretapping equipment:

- Ban any language or content found to be objectionable by interception, deletion, or alteration.
- Monitor the country's communications and target any person who was found or suspected to be a "problem." The judge of who or what is a "problem"? The FBI.
- Invoke mandatory standards for web sites, such as a rating system.
- Shut down or shut off the communications of any one person, website, company, or ISP.
-

The same article continues: "A few years down the road when your phone company, your cable TV provider, radio stations, and cell phone company are all part of your "ISP" and Carnivore/DCS 1000 is installed there, the FBI will have exclusive control of what you can and can't watch, say, or do while using these technologies."

The author concludes, "One of the great powers of the Internet is the fact that it exists beyond the control of any person or agency." Ask yourself this question: shouldn't we keep it that way?

WIDE-SCALE SURVEILLANCE

In March, 2002, Washington DC's Mayor Anthony A. Williams told reporters from the *Washington Times* that the nation's capitol must mimic the actions of cities such as Sydney and London in regard to the expansion of its camera monitoring program. Thus, Mayor Williams plans to eventually make DC comparable to England, where the government now maintains over two million surveillance cameras in city parks, school yards, train and bus depots, intersections, airports, and even in residential neighborhoods.

This plan is a prototype to be used all across the country in every city, town, and municipality. Considering that we already have cameras pointed at us in department stores, elevators, lobbies, malls, banks, gas stations, and at many traffic light intersections, we have to ask ourselves how many more are needed to keep an eye on us. (Not to mention the global tracking satellites that hover above our planet and can photograph you from outer space.)

DO YOU WANT BIG BROTHER?

After reading George Orwell's *1984* and *Animal Farm* and Aldous Huxley's *Brave New World,* many people are overtaken by a sense of dread, yet rationalize the scenario by saying that it's either somewhere down the road in the future, or else couldn't possibly happen at all. But considering the above information (which is literally only the tip of the iceberg), not only is Big Brother very close to becoming a reality; some say it already IS a reality!

If you're still not convinced, rent the movie, *Enemy of the State* with Will Smith, Gene Hackman, an evil Jon Voight, and Lisa Bonet. After viewing it, you'll have a pretty good idea what the Controllers are capable of.

And yet while all this stuff is happening, we sit back, watch, take it all in, and LET it continue! Do we really want Big Brother to know our every move (and thought), keep constant vigilance over us, and ultimately "stomp his boot into our human faces?"

If we don't take action soon, get ready to start cringing, 'cause those guys are going to start kicking!

CHAPTER THIRTY

THE TERMINATOR GENE: WHO CONTROLS THE WORLD'S FOOD SUPPLY? AN OVERVIEW OF TEXE MARRS' "DAYS OF HUNGER, DAYS OF CHAOS"

"Food is power! We use it to change behavior. Some may call that bribery. We do not apologize."
--Catherine Bertini, Executive Director U.N. World Food Program

When one thinks about raising crops, the concept seems pretty simple. Farmers plant seeds, tend to them as they grow, then harvest the end result, whether it is corn, wheat, or alfalfa. But did you know that less than twenty multinational corporations now own the patents to all the seeds in the world?

One of the giants trying to corner, or manipulate this market is Monsanto, based in St. Louis, Missouri. A global leader in agricultural biotechnology, Monsanto is now in a position to control the food chain from seed to supper table. A few other companies such as Dupont in Wilmington, Delaware, W. M. Grace, Bayer, Pfizer, and Archer Daniels Midland have placed the entire control of the world's food supply into the hands of a few companies. In fact, the Rockefeller Foundation controls the patents on seeds for 95% of the earth's major cereal crops.

Why should this statistic alarm you? The answer lies in a little publicized technological breakthrough called "The Terminator Gene." Before delving into the ramifications of this concept, I'd like to present an overview of the "food chain" as it stands now in the world of corporate farming.

To begin with, the above listed companies, along with others in the multinational food network that are maintained by the Controller's octopus-like grip, have a virtual lock on what we ultimately consume. To put it in the bluntest terms possible, these companies plant our food, harvest, warehouse, transport, and eventually sell it. Also, an alarming few corporations also own the EXCLUSIVE patents on many of the seeds sold to farmers.

The Controllers have quietly assumed such a stranglehold over this vitally important industry, as you'll see below, they essentially hold the powers of life-and-death in their hands.

They:

1) Set the crop prices via subsidies and market manipulation.
2) Decide who can purchase and sell the various crops through multinational trade agreements and governmental deals.
3) Control the logistics of food transportation by monopolizing the shipping industry, especially trucking, where independent movers have all but been eliminated. What this means is, if a farmer decides to buck the system, he can keep growing crops, but he won't be able to find anyone to bring his harvest to market. The Controllers have a way of shutting down "troublemakers."
4) Create a slew of regulations that hassle small farmers and/or mavericks out of business.
5) Control fertilizer production (which is an essential element of the overall process).
6) Control the seed market via "terminator genes."
7) Control storage facilities (i.e. grain silos).
8) Refuse bank loans to troublemakers, while granting them (with interest!) to those who are compliant to their demands. These loans are ultimately under the jurisdiction of such New World Order entities as the Federal Reserve Board, the Bank for International Settlements, the World Bank, European Monetary Institute, and the World Trade Organization, among others. The United Nations is also fighting for the ability to levy a "world tax" not only on certain "wealthy" nations, but also on individuals as well. Proceeds will be used to pay for a variety of UN, World Bank, and IMF programs. Thanks a lot!
9) Become more influential on a daily basis with the establishment of corporate farms (as opposed to individually owned ones), and their dominance of meat packing and processing plants.
10) Manipulate agricultural statistics to paint whatever picture they deem necessary, thus never allowing us to truly see where we stand. (Read George Orwell's *Animal Farm* to understand how numbers are continually used to deceive people.)
11) Use satellite technology to monitor the farms and fields.
12) Develop weather modification.
13) Ship American food overseas, thus raising prices domestically.

To really gain control of the food chain, one needs to start at the crux of it all – with the seeds. This is how the cowardly clandestine shadow-dwellers have ultimately decided to control the world's food supply.

Instead of a traditional farmer taking the seeds that he got from his current crop and saving them to be used the following year, now we have hybrid seeds that have been introduced to the farming industry over the years which produce stronger, higher-yielding crops. Over time, farmers didn't see the need to save the "old" traditional seeds and became reliant upon the genetically altered hybrids. Of course, the patents and ownership of these seeds are in the hands of those companies listed earlier -- the Monopolists.

Ken Corbitt stated in the August/September 1994 issue of *Nexxus Magazine* that "total control of the world's seeds and ultimately the survival of mankind itself is now in the hands of an elite cartel of multinational corporations."

What makes this scenario even more terrifying is an earlier-mentioned entity called "The Terminator Gene," which is a "bio-engineered element that mutates a seed's genetic structure, rendering the seed barren and unable to reproduce itself."

In other words, the altered seed will produce a crop -- but for only one year -- and will not reproduce again the following year! Thus, in order to get new seeds, the farmer must go to the corporation that owns the patents on these transformed, genetically altered seeds. These seeds only produce one-time because of the built-in "Terminator Gene" that gives all control to those who own the patents.

Here's the trade-off: farmers are sold high-tech seeds that are sure to produce high-volume crops and can easily stave-off diseases. In return, they have to go back to their seed companies EVERY year and buy more seeds rather than stockpile them because of the internalized terminator gene. Can you see how this situation places every farmer on the planet in a perilous position? What if they do something to enrage the powers-that-be, or buck the system? What happens? Those in control simply refuse to sell them more seed! Don't ya just love the Controllers, and how they always have *our* best interests in mind? To create further dilemmas, the Plant Breeders' Rights Act states that anyone who breaches these patents or refuses to pay royalties on them could face a six month prison term and/or a $250,000 fine.

Geri Guidetti, in a July/August 1998 *Jubilee* newspaper article entitled, "Seed Terminator and Mega-Merger Threaten Food and Freedom" says, "Never before has man created such an insidiously dangerous, far-reaching and potentially 'perfect' plan to control the livelihoods, food supply, and even survival of all humans on the planet." She continues her article by declaring, "Widespread global adoption of the newly patented Terminator Technology will ensure absolute dependence of farmers on multinational corporations."

Jim Hightower, former Texas Secretary of Agriculture, adds, "In their latest scheme, government scientists and corporate profiteers have teamed up to mess up one of Nature's basics: seeds. The geniuses at USDA have used our tax dollars to develop a seed that will not germinate when replanted. Who would want such non-germinating seeds? The seed corporations, of course, since it means every farmer in the world would have to come to them and buy new seeds."

So, what does this all mean? In simplest terms, the Terminator Gene has now placed total control of the world's food supply into the hands of the New World Order. It's that plain and simple. To show the dangers of this situation, I'll close this essay by providing a few quotes from various public and governmental officials that will reinforce the points Mr. Marrs made in his book. They will also show the true aims of the New World Order, and how farmers in the future will be seen as nothing more than serfs, peasants, and sharecroppers. In addition, the very survival of our race is now in the hands of a few devils who truly don't give care about our welfare.

If we don't buckle to their demands and act as they wish us to act (ultimately to be implanted with microchips), they could conceivably cut off our food supply and starve us to death. If this ever happens, we need to ask ourselves a question: who will keep getting food and continuing to live a life of leisure -- us, or them?

And just remember, the New World Order isn't right around the corner. It's already here! Are you ready to welcome it with open arms?

Henry Kissinger, former Secretary of State, at a Bilderberg meeting in the 1990s said "by controlling energy we can control nations, and by controlling food we can control individuals."

Pope John Paul II, as quoted by Father Malachi Martin, declared in *Keys of this Blood*: "By the end of this decade we will all live under the first One World Government that has existed in the society of nations ... a government with absolute authority to declare the basic issues of human survival and human prosperity."

Doctor Carroll Quigley wrote in *Tragedy and Hope*: "There does exist an international network whose aim is to create a world system of financial control in private hands able to dominate the political system of each country and the economy of the world."

Al Gore, former Vice President: "We're continuing to have our spy satellites in the sky; they're there to help us. What we're doing is mapping and monitoring the entire world, including every square inch of the United States."

Larry Bates wrote in *The New Economic Disorder*: "I have said for many years that the term "New World Order" is merely a code word for one-world socialism, with an elite ruling class to govern the rest of us under their demonic system."

Dwayne Andreas, Archer Daniels Midland Chairman, said: "People in the Midwest do not understand -- this is a Socialist country."

John G. Gordon wrote in *Veritas* newspaper, July, 1996: "Rules made by the World Trade Organization made it illegal for the United States to retain sufficient supplies of grain for emergencies. The U.S. was compelled to sell our grain reserves to the rest of the world. The sad reality of all this is that Americans in the land of the free which feeds the world over 80% of its food could actually starve to death while the rest of the world eats."

Congressman Louis McFadden, Chairman of the House Committee on Banking & Currency, in the 1940s said, "The Depression was not accidental. It was a carefully contrived occurrence. The International Bankers sought to bring about a condition of despair so that they might emerge the rulers of us all."

Finally, Larry Bates tells us in *The New Economic Disorder* about a visit to the United Nations: "I couldn't keep still any longer and I blurted out (intending to be facetious), 'Why don't you just take everybody's money, checking accounts, savings accounts, bonds, real estate, and all their other assets and just put everything in one big pile and redistribute it to everybody in the world?'

"Our United Nations guide replied, 'A very good idea -- it's what we are trying to do here.'"

In the same vein, former President Bill Clinton stated at a news conference in Argentina on September 19, 1997: "What I am promoting is the reorganization of the world."

CONCLUSION

Here's one final observation. I don't want Bill or Hillary Clinton reorganizing ANYTHING in my life and world. The big question is: Do you?

CHAPTER THIRTY-ONE

CHEMTRAILS OVER HAPPY VALLEY

On the morning of April 8, 2002 from 6:20 AM to 7:30 AM, Lisa Guliani and I counted eleven different chemtrails being sprayed above the skies of State College, Pa. The culprits of these thick white plumes were military jets flying at approximately 40,000 feet.

This is a regular, alarming occurrence that we've witnessed nearly every single blue-sky day in State College for the past few months.

What are chemtrails, you ask? In order to understand this phenomenon, one must first be familiar with contrails, or condensation trails, which are the pencil-thin white lines we have all seen following in the wake of airplanes. These consist of water vapor, and are harmless.

Chemtrails, on the other hand, are much thicker, and expand across the sky to form X's, O's, and grid patterns. While normal contrails last for less than a minute, chemtrails linger for several hours. As chemtrails puff and spread out, they form a thick white haze that blankets and obscures the sky.

This is not simple skywriting above our heads. Instead, it is a deliberate contamination of our atmosphere by the government for reasons that have not been forthcoming to us. Have any of you noticed that whenever we have a blue-sky day in State College, there are soon military jets flying overhead spreading these white trails? Then the sky becomes whitish, a thick haze forms -- and voilà! -- no more blue sky.

The chemtrail issue has not been reported by the mainstream media. However, it has been addressed by Representative Dennis Kucinich of Ohio, who is in charge of the Armed Services Oversight Committee. He has confirmed the existence of chemtrails and sought to ban them in Section 6 of his House Resolution Bill 2977.

Also, the U.S. Air Force states that chemtrails are being used as part of a program involved with "aerial obscuration."

The reason Kucinich wants to ban chemtrails is because they are composed of biological and chemical ingredients that have detrimental physical effects on people, animals, and the environment. Many concerned citizens nationwide have become ill following chemtrail spraying in their areas. We, too, are concerned because chemtrails may be aggravating or instigating drought conditions here and nationwide due to their stearate component, which soaks up much of the available moisture in areas that are sprayed.

Yet, our attempts to address this issue with Accu-Weather's Expert Senior Meteorologist, Ken Reeves, both Pennsylvania State senators, and the EPA have been futile.

There is cause for concern with respect to this aerial spraying of the population, as those responsible for it have not stepped forward and informed the public as to what is actually going on. Despite repeated requests from concerned citizens nationwide, including independent researchers, journalists and scientists, no answers are being given.

Please note: spraying of uninformed and unconsenting populations is illegal and in violation of the Nuremburg Code and the Environment Modification Treaty, which the United States signed in 1977.

According to William Thomas, one of the first published reporters to break the chemtrail story, "There is zero -- repeat zero doubt -- that chemtrails are an ongoing military operation."

Renowned author Jim Marrs spoke of chemtrails in the April 7 issue of *Babel Magazine*: "There is absolutely no question that someone is spraying chemicals into the air that we all breathe. There is even legislation in Congress attempting to outlaw chemtrails even while government spokesmen deny it is happening."

Therese Aigner, CES consultant and accredited environmental expert/engineer, has analyzed rainwater samples and confirmed that the unusual test results are directly connected with chemtrail aerial spraying. In her results, she determines that the "contaminants would have had to be delivered in large amounts and in concentrated form."

Ms. Aigner also states, "If you look at each one of the parameters, there is consistency here. This would indicate a very controlled delivery (dispersion) of chemtrails by aircraft in your area." Test results show the presence of elements that would not normally be present in rainwater, including barium and aluminum. The official findings can be found at: www.carnicom.com.

This is not merely a matter of concern to us in the Centre Region. The spraying activity is occurring all over the United States, as evidenced by the national database known as ChemtrailtrackingUSA, which monitors and documents all reported chemtrail spraying. The public does not need to be coddled and protected from the truth, whatever the truth may be.

The citizenry has a RIGHT to be made fully aware of what is being sprayed into the air they breathe.

Individual citizen testimonials to Chemtrailtracking USA and also to Chemtrail Central (both sites are accessible via the Internet) cite scores of people reporting ill physical effects following chemtrail activity. Symptoms include, but are not limited to: persistent hacking coughs, upper respiratory and intestinal distress, lethargy, extreme fatigue, pneumonia, dizziness, disorientation, severe headaches, aching joints, nosebleeds, diarrhea, bloody stools, depression, anxiety, nervous tics, loss of bladder control, and dry or burning areas of exposed skin. (*Chemtrails - Frequently Asked Questions,* by Toni Thayer, Executive Director of Blue Skies International.)

Those with compromised immune systems, the elderly, the young, and those in poor physical condition are the first to feel the chemtrail effects.

DID YOU KNOW:

1)   The United States Air Force has a program called "Weather as a Force Multiplier: Owning the Weather by 2025." This program details the MILITARY applications of weather modification.

2)   In his book, *Uncommon Sense,* author George Humphrey states that: "On April 5, 2001, the Senate, with almost no publicity, approved of $4.5 BILLION to 'restore funds for climate change programs.'

3)   In a *Babel Magazine* interview with researcher Jim Marrs, we posed this question to him: What is your position on the chemtrail issue – hoax or not? If we are being inundated by chemtrails, what is the ultimate purpose behind this widespread spraying?

Mr. Marrs responded: "This should be a major issue for the American public as there is absolutely no question that someone is spraying chemicals into the air that we all breathe. There is even legislation in Congress attempting to outlaw "Chemtrails" even while government spokesmen deny it is happening. There are several theories about what this program is all about, everything from mind control to trying to decrease the effects of global warming in order to save the insurance industry, whose collapse could bring down the entire U.S. economy. But none of the theories have yet been proven. It may well be a combination of purposes. The only real fact is that respiratory diseases have increased significantly since the chemtrails began appearing four or five years ago as America has been 'dumbed down'."

4)   Representative Dennis Kucinich of Ohio, who heads the Armed Services Oversight Committee in charge of chemtrail projects for climate control and over-the-horizon radar/radio conduction, introduced House Resolution 2977 that sought to ban chemtrails and other exotic weapons.

So, we respectfully and urgently ask the *Centre Daily Times* and all State College citizens to research the chemtrail issue as we've presented it here and become informed regarding the ongoing aerial spraying being conducted above our heads. We deeply believe this is a matter of grave importance that needs to be confronted and should not be ignored by either the media or the residents of State College.

Our air is the most important resource to sustaining life. We must DEMAND accountability, and we must do it now.

Of course there are many other questions to be answered, such as: who is manufacturing these chemicals and where the military jets are originating from?

So please look up the next time there is a blue-sky day and notice what is happening. Then take photographs and ask questions. Meanwhile, as we continue with our lives, we are all engaging in one similar activity. We are all breathing, breathing, breathing...

CHAPTER THIRTY-TWO

NOTES AND QUOTES: MIND CONTROL

Dr. Jose Delgado (on invisible weaponry) – "More dangerous than atomic destruction, with knowledge of the brain, we may transform, we may shape, direct, and robotize man. I think the great danger of the future is that we will have robotized human beings who are not aware they have been robotized."

Sirhan Sirhan (under hypnosis after supposedly assassinating Robert Kennedy) -
– "Practice practice practice …."
Dr. Diamond – "Practice what?"
Sirhan Sirhan – "Mind control, mind control, mind control, mind control …."

Ford Rowan (_Technospies_ – 1978) – "Computers that can communicate with the brain may help people in all sorts of intellectual tasks. A tiny terminal implanted in a person's brain would give him access to giant computer banks, for instance, and with the miniaturization of computers, an actual computer could be implanted in the brain. From the individual's viewpoint it would become part of his brain, extending his knowledge and memory immensely."

1972 ARPA report to Congress – "The long-sought goal is direct and intimate coupling between man and the computer."

Army classified report (1972) – "It is possible to field a truck-portable microwave barrier system that will completely immobilize personnel in the open with present-day technology and equipment."

DIA report (1976) – Pulsed microwaves can carry "sounds and possibly even words which appear to be originating intercranially."

The London Times – October 17, 1994 – _Bionic Man Comes of Age_ – "Over the past decade," the Times reported, "more than 15,000 people worldwide have had electronic components implanted into their brains. In a procedure confined until recently to the fantasies of science fiction, microchips are now being routinely placed beneath the skull into brain stems. In many cases, these devices are connected to platinum wires, which are fused and buried in the brain."

Dr. Wayne Evans – Army Institute of Environmental Medicine – "In a sense, we are in the same ethical and moral dilemma as the physicists in the days prior to the Manhattan Project. Those of us who work in this field see a developing potential for a nearly total control of human emotional status.

Mae Brussell (1974) – "Many of the current rash of 'senseless killings,' 'massacres,' and 'zombie-type murders' are committed by individuals who have been seen in Army hospitals, mental hospitals or prison hospitals, where their heads have been literally taken over surgically to create terror in the community."

Dr. Corydon Hammond – Professor at the University of Utah's School of Medicine (1993) – "The CIA's cult mind control techniques were based upon those of Nazi scientists recruited by the CIA for Cold Warfare. (Researcher Lenny Lapon estimates in "Mass Murderers In White Coats" that 5,000 Nazi's resettled in the United States after W.W. II).

MK-ULTRA areas of interest – the modification of human behavior and perception through chemical means, the creation of a 'truth serum,' sensory deprivation, religious cults, microwaves, psychological conditioning, psychosurgery, drug experimentation, brain implants, radiation, electroshock, torture, continuous noise (white noise), biological weapons, psychic research, etc.

MK-ULTRA atrocities between 1953 and 1957 - doctors at the Massachusetts General Hospital in Boston injected at least 11 terminally ill cancer patients with uranium 235. During the 1940s, pregnant women were given cocktails of radioactive material in order to study the effects on their fetus. At the Fernald School in Waltham, Massachusetts in 1947, 17 retarded teenagers were given radioactive contaminated meals. In 1962, an Ivy League research team fed radioactive iodide to 760 mentally retarded children (some as young as 1 year old). From 1944 to 1961, entire communities in New Mexico were doused with radioactive lanthanum via open-air experiments. Between 1963 and 1976, 67 prisoners at a Northwestern prison had their testicles exposed to ionizing radiation. The United States Government carried out radiation experiments in at least 33 veteran's hospitals.

Sensory Deprivation test conducted by Dr. John Lilly in 1956 – "Volunteers were immersed in a tank of lukewarm water. The subjects had to wear a particular type of face-mask enabling them to see only blurred light. Under total silence and lack of any stimulation, the subjects suffered mental disturbances. The maximum a volunteer could tolerate these conditions was only three hours. The volunteers reported feelings of unreality and a tremendous loss of identification. They did not know where they were, who they were, or what was happening to them. Due to this enormous mental pressure, most of them abandoned the experiment."

Jose Delgado and the charging bull – "Delgado demonstrated the potential of his Stimoceivers by wiring up a full-grown bull. With the device in place, Delgado stepped into the ring with the bull. The animal charged towards the experimenter – and then suddenly stopped just before it reached him. The powerful beast had been stopped with the simple action of pushing a button on a small black box held in Delgado's hand."

Dr. Jose Delgado (1966) – My experiments "support the distasteful conclusion that motion, emotion, and behavior can be controlled by electrical forces and that humans can be controlled like robots by pushing buttons." He further suggested that, "There would come a time when brain control could be turned over to non-human operators by establishing two-way radio communication between the implanted brain and a computer."

Lincoln Lawrence – describing Radio Hypnotic Intercerebral Control (RHIC) – "It is the ultra sophisticated application of post-hypnotic suggestion triggered at will by radio transmission. It is a recurring hypnotic state, reinduced automatically by the same radio control as the individual is brought under hypnosis. This can be brought into play under many guises. He is then programmed to perform certain actions and maintain certain attitudes upon radio signal."

Charles Hoy Fort – "Almost all people of all eras are hypnotics. Their beliefs are induced beliefs. The proper authorities saw to it that the proper belief should be induced, and people believed properly."

Michael A. Hoffman II (*Secret Societies and Psychological Warfare* – 1989) - "The most amazing thing about the American people is that they are constantly defending their worst betrayers. Who then is modern man? He is a mind-bombed patsy who gets his marching orders from 'twilight language' key words sprinkled throughout 'his' news and current events. Even as he dances to the tune of the elite managers of human behavior, he scoffs with great derision at the idea of the existence and operation of a technology of mass mind control emanating from the media and government. Modern man is much too smart to believe anything as superstitious as that!"

Michael A. Hoffman II (*Secret Societies and Psychological Warfare* – 1989) - Flattery: The First Principle of Mind Control – "Why then does he revere them? Because they flatter him. This is the first secret of mass mind control and can be observed as the foundation stone of virtually every false religion, party, cult, philosophy, system and training. How can modern man free himself when he is told that he is already a demi-god, that the problem lies only in finding a pure enough economic or political system worthy of his high-minded brilliance?"

Michael A. Hoffman II (*Secret Societies and Psychological Warfare* – 1989) - "But if we overthrew them [The Controllers] tomorrow, we would have to write our own scripts. We would have to heal ourselves. We would have to admit the colossal waste and loss of destruction of the past years which our laziness and folly have made possible. We would have to experience the pain of being alive and responsible. WE would have to start acting like men and women instead of as slaves and weaklings."

Charles Fort – "Man deliberately invented the dogma of materialism in order to shield himself from the evidence of what was being done to him by means of psycho-spiritual warfare methods hyped by 'coincidence,' symbolism, and ritual."

John B. Watson – founder of Behaviorist school of psychology – "Give me the baby, and I'll make it climb and use its hands in constructing buildings of stone or wood. I'll make a thief, a gunman or a dope fiend. The possibilities of shaping in any direction are almost endless ... men are built, not born."

Zbigniew Brzezinski – 1968 – *The Technotronic Age* – "The capacity to assert social and political control over the individual will vastly increase. It will soon be possible to assert almost continuous control over every citizen and to maintain up-to-date files, containing even the most personal details about health and personal behavior to every citizen in addition to the more customary data."

Dr. G. Brock Chisholm – Head of the World Health Organization – 1945 address to psychiatrists and government officials in Washington, D.C. – "What basic psychological distortion can be found in every civilization of which we know anything? The only psychological force capable of producing these perversions is morality – the concept of right and wrong. The reinterpretation and eventual eradication of the concept of right and wrong are the belated objectives of nearly all psychotherapy. The people who have been taught to believe whatever they were told by their parents or their teachers are the people who are the menace to the world."

George Estabrooks, Department of Psychology at Colgate University, research between 1940-45 – in 1968, to a reporter from the *Providence Evening Bulletin*: "The key to creating an effective spy or assassin is creating a multiple personality, with the aid of hypnosis."

Other MK-ULTRA atrocities – Black prison inmates were given LSD for 75 consecutive days. Also, the invention of "Torture Trousers" – an electrical torture device made of leather and steel with an electrode fastened to the victim's genitals.

Aldous Huxley – "There will be in the next generation or so, a pharmacological method of making people love their servitude, and producing a kind of painless concentration camp for entire societies."

James Jesus Angleton – the CIA's counter-intelligence director, on the three goals of CIA hypnosis programs – 1) the speedy hypnotic induction of unwitting subjects. 2) the ability to create long-lasting amnesia. 3) the implanting of long-lasting, useful hypnotic suggestion.

George Estabrooks – "I can hypnotize a man without his knowledge or consent into committing treason against the United States."

Dr. Jose Delgado – "The individual is defenseless against direct manipulation of the brain because he is deprived of his most intimate mechanisms of biological reactivity. In experiments, electrical stimulation of appropriate intensity always prevailed over free will."

J. F. Schapitz – Department of Defense – 1974 – "The spoken word of the hypnotist may be conveyed by modulated electromagnetic energy directly into the subconscious parts of the human brain – i.e. without employing any technical devices for receiving or transcoding the messages and without the person exposed to such influence having a chance to control the information input consciously."

Dr. Chris Winter and a team of scientists at British Telecom's Martlesham Heath Laboratories are developing a chip ("Soul Catcher 2025") that, when placed into the skull behind the eye, will record all visual and physical sensations, as well as thoughts. According to Winter: "This is the end of death ... By combining this information with a record of the person's genes, we could recreate a person physically, emotionally, and spiritually." Another of the possibilities of the chip that Winter discussed was the downloading of an older person's entire life experience into a newborn child.

SECTION

SIX:

HISTORY

CHAPTER THIRTY-THREE

DON'T TRUST HISTORY

Here's a concept that I've been intrigued with for quite awhile. The first time it made an impact on me was when I read about it in a book by William Burroughs, the beat writer. Burroughs said, "History does not exist."

At first I was confused, but then he went on to say that everything in life has the potential to be manipulated by those in power to suit their purposes. Burroughs said that the written word is easily altered over time, as are sound recordings via splicing and re-splicing. Photographs can be airbrushed and historical texts are compiled by whoever wins the war. The victor can also go back and destroy a people's existing history and replace it with something that more suits their needs (read Orwell's *1984*). But what about videotape? That's a distinct record of history, isn't it?

Not necessarily so. At the moment of recording it is, but look at the government invasion at Waco and how, through the use of editing, a completely different picture emerged from what really took place. Thus, in a larger sense, anything over time can be altered and "re-made." A perfect example is the Tom Hanks movie, *Forrest Gump*. You remember the scene where he's shaking hands with JFK. It's so real you could easily believe it took place if presented in a different context.

So, Burroughs is basically saying that all of us should be very wary of what is considered history, for it can, and is, being manipulated for very specific purposes, and always has been.

Fdsfds

CHAPTER THIRTY-FOUR

WHY DID AMERICANS FINANCE THE BOLSHEVIK REVOLUTION?

Let's jump right into the fire on this one. The Bolshevik Revolution was not an uprising started by poor Russians (proletariats) against their Czarist overlords. Instead, International Communism was created and financed by American capitalists and European aristocrats, not to help the downtrodden, but to increase their own power and further enslave those who were lower on the socio-economic ladder.

If the above scenario doesn't fit into the historical picture that has been painted for us, the first question we should ask is, "Why doesn't someone in the media point out this discrepancy? In all honesty, with a little bit of research, any journalist in the country could blow the roof off these atrocious misrepresentations. But they don't. Why? John Swinton, former editor of the *New York Times*, said it best in 1914 at the annual dinner of the American Press Association:

"There is no such thing as an independent press in America. Not a man among you dares utter his honest opinion. Were you to utter it, you know beforehand that it would never appear in print. It is the duty of a New York journalist to lie, to revile, to toady at the feet of Mammon, to sell his country and his race for his daily bread, or what amounts to the same thing, his salary.

"We are tools and vassals of the rich behind the scenes. We are marionettes. These men pull the strings, and we dance. Our time, our talents, our lives and our capacities are all the property of these men -- we are intellectual property."

As far as I can tell, the situation hasn't changed one iota in the last 90 years. So, prior to delving into the mechanics of the Bolshevik Revolution, I'd like to string a bunch of quotes before you.

A point about Colonel House: Many people were suspicious of Woodrow Wilson (our country's most weak-spined commander-in-chief EVER) and his administration's reactions during the Bolshevik Revolution. The questions became so probing that a man named Colonel House, one of the shrewdest Invisibles of all-time, told him on November

233

28, 1917, "It is exceedingly important that such criticism should be suppressed."

Russian General Arsene de Goulevitch (*Czarism and the Revolution*): "The main purveyors of funds for the Revolution were neither the crackpot Russian millionaires nor the armed bandits of Lenin. The 'real' money primarily came from certain British and American circles which for a long time past had lent their support to the Russian Revolutionary cause. The important part played by wealthy American banker, Jacob Schiff, in the events in Russia is no longer a secret."

Antony Sutton (*Wall Street and the Bolshevik Revolution*): "International finance prefers to deal with central governments. The last thing the banking community wants is decentralized nations because these disperse power ... Virtually everything the Soviets possess has been acquired from the West."

Gary Allen (*None Dare Call It Conspiracy*): "Communism and Socialism are not a share-the-wealth program, but a consolidate-and-control-the-wealth program ... Communism is not a movement of the downtrodden masses, but is a movement created, manipulated, and used by power-seeking billionaires in order to gain control over the world ... first by establishing socialist governments in the various nations, then consolidating them all through a 'great merger' into an all-powerful world Socialist super state under the auspices of the United Nations."

Winston Churchill: "Lenin was sent to Russia by the Germans in the same way that you might send a vial containing a culture of typhoid or of cholera to be poured into the water supply of a great city. It worked with amazing accuracy."

Frederick C. Howe (*Confessions of a Monopolist*), 1906: "These are the rules of big business: get a monopoly; get society to work for you; and remember that the best of all business is politics."

Henry Davidson [J. P. Morgan partner and CFR member (1912)]: "I would rather have regulation and control than free competition."

TIMELINE

1914-18: As World War I raged on, Lenin had been in Switzerland since 1905, while Leon Trotsky was in New York City writing for a Communist newspaper. Neither went to Russia because the poor huddled masses begged for their help, but only arrived later after being sent by the power elite in Europe and the U.S., as you will soon see.

Meanwhile, World War I left 1,700,000 Russian citizens dead. There were also tremendous food shortages. Their money was practically valueless, they were still battling the Germans across their border, and the government was ready to collapse. In essence, the Russian people were primed for a revolution.

March, 1917: The Czar Nicholas II finally abdicated his throne. Following his departure, Prince Luov arrived on the scene to set up a form of government that he hoped would resemble America's. Shortly thereafter, however, Alexander Kerensky, revolutionary politico, stepped in and did away with Luov's vision. Meanwhile, the Russians kept fighting the Germans while a quarter-million revolutionaries returned to their homeland and toppled Kerensky.

Spring, 1917: Lenin and Trotsky returned to Russia with their pockets full of gold.

July, 1917: Lenin led his first revolution, but was abated by the Russian army.

July 19, 1917: The Russian government arrested Lenin, charging him with being a German spy; he fled to Finland.

November 7, 1917: Lenin returned to Russian and planted the seeds for another revolution.

November 25, 1917: Makeshift elections were held; less than one-quarter of the Russian people voted for Vladimir Lenin.

Realizing he didn't have the public behind him, Lenin sent hordes of gun-toting radicals to make the ruling body of Russia see things in a different light.

As World War I continued, the Rothschild-controlled banks of Europe pumped millions of dollars into Lenin's coffers.

1922 - Russian became a full-blown Communist entity with the State controlling all the resources and manufacturing. This bloody process cost the lives of 28 million citizens. In the same year, famine hit Russia and 5 million people starved to death.

Lenin eventually saw the follies of Marxism and returned most of the state-run resources back to the people. Starvation quickly disappeared.

1924 - Lenin died and Joseph Stalin took over, once more returning State-control to the nation.

Overall, in one short decade, 75 million Russians died due to this insanity:

- World War I - 1.7 million deaths
- Lenin takeover - 28 million deaths
- Starvation - 5 million deaths
- Stalin takeover - 40 million deaths
- TOTAL ------ 75 million deaths!!!!!!!

How could Trotsky, Lenin, Stalin, Kagonovich, and Litvinoff get back into Russia when the government knew they wanted to overthrow it? Max Warburg, head of the German Secret Police, whose brother, Paul, was the founder and first chairman of the United States Federal Reserve Corporation, gave them $5 million in gold and put them, along with 159 other Bolshevik revolutionaries, on a sealed train, guaranteeing them access across the Russian border.

Another item of note is that of all the Bolshevik revolutionaries, over half were Jewish! In addition, of the top 20-30 leaders of this movement, 75% were Jewish. Marx was born in Trier, Germany, and so was Leon Trotsky. The only person of any real significance who wasn't Jewish was Lenin, who was born in Simbirsk, Russia.

MARXISM OF THE ELITE

Karl Marx said: "Political power is the organized use of force by one class in order to keep another class in subjection."

Said Vladimir Lenin upon accomplishing his mission: "Agree to any and every sacrifice and resort to all sorts of devices, maneuvers and illegal methods, to evasion and subterfuge."

The first thing we need to realize about Communism, and even more so about Clinton-like Socialism, is that these movements aren't intended to help the poor, starving, or middle-class (who will eventually be eliminated). Instead, they're created by the ruling class - capitalists and bankers - to perpetuate the reign of those already in control. Power comes from the top down, not from the masses.

Those who promote these concepts always talk about the people in need (the "proletariat"), yet none of the leaders ever come from the poor, or lower classes. Those in charge are always educated and intellectual.

236

Y'see, here's the catch. The great myth revolving around Socialism is that it's created to help the poor -- that the end result is a classless society with no need for a government, police, or army.

But stop for a second and think about something. When was the last time those in power *ever* willingly gave up their positions to let someone needier move in and take over? It doesn't happen, especially when the primary motivating factor behind power and control is to keep it, then extenuate it.

Communism and Socialism don't redistribute the wealth. These forms of government are merely convoluted tools for the super-rich to gain more power. The Bolshevik Revolution was orchestrated not from Moscow, but from New York City, Paris, and London.

In Communism and Socialism, power derives from the State. The first thing you have to do is ask yourself, how much do you trust the State? Before answering, however, ponder the principle tenets of Communism:

1)   state ownership of all land
2)   a steeply graduated income tax
3)   no inheritance from deceased family members
4)   confiscation of all property from political protesters
5)   a centrally run State bank
6)   State run transportation systems, etc

Now, compare these goals to the ones formulated by Adam Weishaupt and the Illuminati in 1776:

1)   abolish all existing governments (to be replaced by a one-world government)
2)   abolish all religions
3)   abolish all private property
4)   abolish all inheritance
5)   abolish the family
6)   abolish nationalism

Although it's not popularly taught in the present day, Karl Marx, who was a member of the "League of the Just," did nothing more than update the demented scribblings of Adam Weishaupt, who founded the Illuminati. In all reality, there's nothing new about the *Communist Manifesto*. The "League of Just Men" was merely an extension of the Illuminati after they were forced to go underground.

While we're on the subject of Karl Marx, it should be noted that he didn't even write the original *Communist Manifesto*. He stole it from a French Socialist named Victor Considerant, who wrote *Principles du Socialisme: Manifeste de la Democratie au Dix Neuvieme Siecle* in 1843.

W. Tcherkesoff, in *Pages of Socialist History*, goes so far as to say that the two works are so similar, the theories, format, titles, and even chapter headings are stolen almost verbatim.

Karl Marx is the same man who supposedly had such a great concern for the lower classes, he dedicated his life to freeing them from their subservience. Yet, Marx came from a well-to-do family. His father was a wealthy lawyer and Karl rarely came in contact with the working class. In fact, Marx never worked a day of physical labor in his life.

One of his few "real" jobs was as a correspondent and political analyst for Horace Greeley's *New York Times*. (As a side note, both Greeley and Clinton Roosevelt (of the infamous Roosevelt political family) both gave money to the Communist League to have the *Communist Manifesto* published.)

Karl Marx survived by leeching off people for most of his life. Three of his six children died of starvation because he never worked, while two others committed suicide. When Marx died in 1883, only six people found it in their heart to attend his funeral.

NOTES ON LEON TROTSKY

When arrested while traveling to Russia to take part in the Bolshevik Revolution, Trotsky was freed by orders given directly by none other than President Woodrow Wilson.

He was given $10,000 traveling expenses by the Rockefeller family before leaving for Russia.

Trotsky was the man who discovered that a variety of Wall Street bankers were up for bankrolling a revolution in Russia.

While in New York City, like Marx, he rarely worked, yet was often seen entering the mansion of Jacob Schiff, who was undoubtedly one of the most powerful men in America at that time.

Trotsky had training facilities, i.e., "boot camps" at the Rockefeller-owned Standard Oil facility in New Jersey.

When he arrived in New York City on January 13, 1917, Trotsky didn't have a job, yet he was able to maintain a top-dollar apartment and ride around in a chauffeured limousine. How was he able to live such a lifestyle? Money was bankrolled to him by Jacob Schiff.

WHY DID AMERICANS FINANCE THE BOLSHEVIK REVOLUTION?

The biggest fallacy concerning the Bolshevik Revolution is that it originated from the people ... from the poor huddled masses. In reality, it was financed by: a) England's Lord Alfred Milner, b) Wall Street bankers such as J. P. Morgan & Company and the Rockefeller Family c) Europe's Rothschild dynasty, and d) German bankers, including Max Warburg, whose brother Paul was the key man in setting up America's Federal Reserve System.

Stop for a moment and digest this information. Money for the Bolshevik Revolution came from super-rich Western financiers, some of whom were Americans! In essence, then, the very core of Communism was a partnership between monopoly-oriented Capitalists and the international Socialist movement.

Could it really be that Americans -- those who should be the most fervently opposed to Communism -- would really finance their arch-nemesis? And if so, who are these people?

The traitorous Americans who turned their backs on this country accumulated their wealth during the latter part of the 1800s through banking, insurance, railroads, and industry. And even though they became incredibly rich through a free enterprise system, they are, in actuality, monopolists who want to eliminate any threat to their dominance. The notorious John D. Rockefeller even went so far as to say "competition is a sin."

It is for this reason that these men were drawn to financing the Bolshevik Revolution. Communism and Socialism are obvious forms of monopolies because the government is the only operator.

Since this is the case, we need to ask ourselves, who are the people who hold control over these forms of government? The answer: international bankers who lend money to the State (at interest), then keep control over a central bank. If you then add clandestine "contributions and donations," bribes, and covert behind the scene deals, you can see how an economic system is manipulated to best suit those who lurk in the shadows.

Worse, these are the same back-stabbers who also had a hand in starting World War I, setting up the criminal Federal Reserve System and the Federal Income Tax in 1913, and who financed the Nazi rise to power before World War II.

Who are these clever people? Surely by now you'll recognize the names: Rothschild, Rockefeller, Schiff, Warburg, Morgan, Harriman...

Max Warburg and Alexander Helphand were the primary Germans who got the ball rolling in Europe in terms of money. Max Warburg is also the man who ran a Rothschild front-bank in Frankfurt, while his brother Paul was instrumental in establishing the Federal Reserve in the United States. Jacob Schiff was a senior partner at Kuhn, Loeb & Company, and was related through marriage to the horrendous Warburg family.

Below are a few specific examples of how money was funneled from the Controllers to the Bolsheviks:

- England's Lord Alfred Milner, who was head of the Round Table founded by Cecil Rhodes (of Oxford's Rhodes Scholar fame and also a front group for the Rothschilds and predecessor of America's Council on Foreign Relations), sank 21 million rubles into the Bolshevik Revolution.

- The American super-industrialist Averill Harriman said in June, 1944 that Joseph Stalin bragged that about 2/3 of all the Russian infrastructure had been built with U. S. aid.

- After Lenin was thrown out of the country by Czar Nicholas II, German bankers led by the Warburg family gave him a suitcase filled with $5 million, put him on a second train and shipped him back to Russia to finish his job.

- The *Washington Post* reported on February 2, 1918 that William B. Thompson, director of the New York Federal Reserve Bank, gave the Bolsheviks $1 million!

- The first Soviet bank was run by J. P. Morgan through his Guranty Trust Company.

One of the most glaring examples of how deeply the United States was involved in assisting the Bolshevik Revolution took place at Petrograd in the summer of 1917. Under the guise of a "Red Cross" mission, 15 Wall Street financiers, their attorneys, and Federal Reserve Director William Bryce Thompson, along with a small group of doctors and nurses, traveled to the nerve center of the Russian revolution. Naturally, the businessmen weren't in Petrograd to wrap wounds and take a patient's blood pressure, and when the doctors and nurses discovered their true motives, they left.

The only problem was -- the bankers & lawyers remained. And why did they stay? Well, Hermann Hagedon, in his biography of William Bryce Thompson, provided photographic evidence that J. P. Morgan cabled Thompson $1 million through a branch office of his City National Bank in Petrograd to support the Bolshevik "cause"! These are American businessmen receiving money from J. P. Morgan (the real-life "Daddy Warbucks") to help push the Communist cause over the top! It's incredible, especially since Morgan's bank was the only one not nationalized after the Bolshevik Revolution. Also, six of those present in Petrograd (three were Wall Street bankers) later became members of America's Council on Foreign Relations in the 1920s.

In essence, the Controllers -- those in England, America, and Germany -- BOUGHT Russia for the paltry sum of $30-40 million. When you think about how much oil, real estate, and minerals are held within that enormous country, it was the sweetest deal of all time.

Some people may protest, "Why would those who supposedly support a Capitalist system want to promote its very antithesis -- Communism?" The answer is simple. What does it matter WHAT a government does if YOU control it?

Can't you see? The Controllers have ALWAYS bought and paid for each side of every conflict. That way they never lose! In regard to the Soviet Union, their motive was clear. After the Bolshevik Revolution took place and a system was set up that epitomized non-productivity and inefficiency, they would always have to rely on the "Capitalists" for a handout (i.e., loans at interest). Thus, whenever it came to money and technology, the Sleeping Bear could always be contained because its very creation came about as a result of the Controllers!

Russia was under their thumb since day one! The same concept applies to our current Welfare state. If we keep down what could potentially be a "threatening" group of people by making them dependent on cash payments and food stamps, they can be contained and made less dangerous.

NOTES AND QUOTES ON THE ROTHSCHILDS, JACOB SCHIFF AND JOHN D. ROCKEFELLER

In the mid-1800's, there was a saying that circulated throughout Europe: "There is only one power in Europe, and that is Rothschild."

The secret to their growing success was a sense of invincibility, for even though they owned factories, businesses, mines, banks, corporations, and were industrial powerhouses, not one of these entities ever bore their name. They could thus do what they've always done -- lurk in the shadows and pull the strings.

Until recently, the British Museum had on display two checks made out from Nathan Rothschild to Karl Marx.

In America, the Rothschild's worked through the banking firm of Kuhn, Loeb & Company, while the J. P. Morgan Company helped finance John D. Rockefeller's Standard Oil Corporation, Edward Harriman's railroad ventures, and Andrew Carnegie's steel factories.

By 1900, it was estimated that the Rothschilds controlled half the world's entire wealth.

With the above information in mind, and considering how prominent the Rothschild family was during the late 1800s, one must wonder why Karl Marx, who supposedly hated Capitalism, never denounced the Rothschilds in *The Communist Manifesto*. The answer is twofold. First, Communism arose out of the Illuminati-type secret societies that flourished during that time, and Marx was, similar to modern-day politicians, nothing but a figurehead who did the bidding of those behind the scenes. Also, how could Marx denounce the very people who not only financed his efforts but would ultimately bankroll a revolution that carried forth his stolen ideas?

The Rothschilds should have been Marx's primary target, but instead they didn't even merit a mention. Doesn't this principle seem to apply to what's going on today? Think about it.

American banker Jacob Schiff went the extra mile to see that the Bolshevik Revolution came to fruition. Schiff was a Rothschild agent who, in the mid-1800s took over control of the prestigious Kuhn, Loeb & Company and who financed John D. Rockefeller, Edward Harriman, and Andrew Carnegie.

Schiff was also the man who GAVE $20 million to the Bolshevik cause. Twenty million dollars!! He also brought Leon Trotsky to the United States without a passport, and when Trotsky was detained in Canada (on an international arrest warrant) HE convinced U. S. authorities to intervene and have him freed. After Trotsky went back to Russia, Schiff secured a large sum of money from the German banker, Max Warburg; then forwarded it to the conspirators in Russia who initiated the Bolshevik Revolution.

Schiff was also instrumental in founding the Council on Foreign Relations, and was a heavy contributor to Woodrow Wilson's campaign in 1912.

In 1925, John D. Rockefeller told his press agent, Ivy Lee, to talk up Communism in the American press so that it would be presented in a favorable light. This public relations drive helped push the U. S. Government to officially recognize Russia in 1933.

The United States illegally gave loans to the Bolshevik Revolution through the Federal Reserve. Averill Harriman and Standard Oil (Rockefeller-owned) also negotiated trade agreements with the Communists and the Rockefeller-controlled Chase Manhattan Bank, along with Lord Milner of London's Round Table, who also lent them money.

In 1922, Chase National Bank established the Russian Chamber of Commerce.

In *The New World Order*, Eustace Mullins writes: "The Rockefeller family is sometimes called the First Family of the Soviet Union."

About David Rockefeller, *Time* Magazine wrote: "As the de facto head of the American Establishment, it has been said that for him the Presidency would be a demotion."

In 1927, Standard Oil built oil refineries in Caucasus, Russia and was guaranteed half of all profits from its output.

For decades we've been told that Capitalists and Communists are enemies (or at least diametrically opposed in their outlooks), but this simply isn't the case. The Rockefellers are a case in point:

1)   Before the Bolshevik Revolution, Russia was the world's number one oil producer -- even ahead of the United States.
2)   After the Revolution, however, due to all the chaos and turmoil, oil production came to a standstill.
3)   Standard Oil stepped in during the next decade and started buying up the Russian oil fields.
4)   Standard Oil also built the Russian's state-of-the-art oil refineries.
5)   In 1926 alone, the Rockefeller-owned Chase Manhattan Bank lent the Russian's $75,000,000.

6)   By this time, with things relatively back to normal in Russia, oil production began once again with the Rockefeller family getting a huge chunk not only from the production, but also from interest on their loans to Russia!

7)   The Rockefellers were essentially the first entity to invest in Russia on a large-scale basis after the Revolution. Their Chase Manhattan Bank helped fund the American-Russian Chamber of Commerce, while this very same bank financed Soviet raw material exports and sold Soviet bonds in the United States.

CHAPTER THIRTY-FIVE

REVIEWED: ANTONY C. SUTTON'S "WALL STREET AND THE RISE OF HITLER"

Have you ever seen news reports on TV that cover remote wars in Afghanistan or Sudan or Egypt, and the scenery is desolate – either sparsely-vegetative mountains or barren deserts? Then you see the residents that live in these areas, and they're gaunt, barely clothed, and look on the brink of starvation because the only thing they have to eat are rats or cactus or dogs or sand. But then the war footage begins, and these people who can barely clothe and feed themselves are sporting bazookas, anti-aircraft missiles, tanks, and hand-grenades. It makes ya wonder – where does the money come from? Sure, some of it is funneled through terrorist groups, but not all of it.

With the above foundation in mind, let's hearken back to Germany in the 1920's. The country had been decimated by World War I, unemployment was rampant, and hyper-inflation virtually made the Deutschmark worthless. Then all of a sudden, an impoverished flophouse artist named Adolf Hitler emerged on the scene and built one of the most imposing war machines in history. By the time he rose to power, the Stock Market had crashed in '29 and the world was in the midst of The Great Depression. So, framed within this context, one has to ask themselves, where did the money come from?

Antony Sutton's *Wall Street and the Rise of Hitler* answers this question in a startling fashion. On the inside dust jacket, the following overview is provided:

"Professor Antony C. Sutton proves that World War I was not only inevitable, it was extremely profitable – for a select group of financial insiders ... Sutton conclusively establishes his thesis: "The contribution made by American capitalism to German war preparations can only be described as phenomenal. It was certainly crucial to German military capabilities."

It continues, "Not only was an influential sector of American business aware of the nature of Nazism, but for its own purposes aided

Nazism whenever possible (and profitable) – *with full knowledge that the probable outcome would be war involving Europe and the United States.* Here is the thoroughly documented account of the role played by J. P. Morgan, T. W. Lamont, the Rockefeller interests, General Electric Company, Standard Oil, National City Bank, Chase and Manhattan Banks, Kuhn, Loeb and Company, and scores of other business elitists in helping to finance the bloodiest, most destructive war in history."

With the above introduction in mind, I'd like to begin this essay by reinforcing the main point of a review that will appear in chapter 39 (see *Adolf Hitler and Black Magic*). In that piece, Trevor Ravenscroft argues that the core of Nazism was founded on occultism and ritual magic. Well, in Professor Sutton's book, he confirms that the roots of Nazism were indeed based upon "neo-pagan societies, the Bavarian Illuminati, and the Thule Society."

Another point that must be made perfectly clear is one involving the responsibility for the Holocaust, and how blame is often shifted away from American and European interests by passing the buck and claiming ignorance. Such claims are simply not true, as can be seen from item 4 of the "Program of the National Socialist German Workers Party":

4 – "None but members of the Nation may be citizens of the state. None but those of German blood, whatever their creed, may be members of the nation. No Jews, therefore, may be a member of the nation."

The above document was published in 1920, more than two decades before the Final Solution began. Also, *Mein Kampf* is littered with anti-Jewish rhetoric. So, if you research this subject and come across individuals who say that they were unaware of Hitler's anti-Semitism, it simply isn't the case. Those in control were well-aware of his leanings, intentions, and inclinations.

With these two points of clarification in mind, I'm going to proceed by breaking this review into six sections:

1) The Financial Octopus
2) The Dawes and Young Plan
3) I. G. Farben
4) American Industrialists
5) Henry Ford
6) Finale

The Financial Octopus

The first point that Professor Sutton wants to make clear is that wide-scale wars and "movements" don't just happen. It takes a tremendous amount of preparation, planning, and behind-the-scenes string-pulling to get them underway. In this vein, he'd like his readers to know that the same group of financiers who funneled money to the Bolshevik Revolution in 1917 and also bankrolled FDR's "New Deal" campaign in the early 1930's were also the same one's to bankroll the Nazi's rise to power. Take a moment and think about the ramifications of this statement. A shadowy cabal of bankers were simultaneously financing a Communist regime; a Fascist dictatorship; and the beginning of American Socialism. I hate to break the news to you folks, but these are the same people who are still running your world today.

At this point, the first question I would ask is: what institutions precisely were responsible for financing the Nazi's? Mr. Sutton provides the answer:

1)   New York's Federal Reserve Bank
2)   Bank of England
3)   Reichsbank
4)   Banque de France

You must remember; when you control the money supply, you're able to control the political machine, and once you control The Machine, you call the shots on which political parties and movements are supported or denied. Thus, these men who ran the above financial centers were the one's pulling the strings on a worldwide basis. But just because they had money didn't allow them to assume total control. No – they needed to pull one more slick maneuver – although they were 'for-profit' bankers, these individuals resorted to donning the uniform of "statesmen" and thus introduced themselves into domestic and foreign policy. As you'll soon see, these people are ingenious in their ability to undermine the System without anyone being the wiser to their shenanigans.

The Dawes and Young Plan

After World War I, the Treaty of Versailles was formulated to force Germany into making reparations for their destruction. The Treaty of Versailles was implemented by a host of international bankers for their OWN benefit, and was ultimately approved and sponsored by the United States government. Out of this treaty, J. P. Morgan orchestrated the Dawes Plan, which was a series of loans made from American banks that ultimately resulted in the formation of I. G. Farben. This super-powerful company came about because Germany diverted some of the money that was intended to pay off their loans into the merger of two chemical and steel companies, thus creating the notorious I. G. Farben Company.

After the Dawes Plan failed, the Young Plan (1928) was implemented. But all this program did was create hyperinflation, send unemployment through the roof, and fill the German people with such abject disgust that it paved the way for Hitler's rise to power. Thus, these treaties and plans that were supposed to return peace to the world instead accomplished the exact opposite. The international bankers turned into manipulative statesmen and reaped huge profits through interest payments, while Germany's war machine and I. G. Farben were created in the process.

I. G. Farben

As money was diverted from loan payments into Germany's re-armament, I. G. Farben, an immense chemical empire, stood at center stage and acted hand-in-hand with the Nazi's. Created in 1925 (three years before the Young Plan was enacted), I. G. Farben became THE powerhouse industrial force in Germany. Now here's where it gets interesting. A man named Max Warburg was on the Board of Supervisors at I. G. Farben; and his brother Paul, founder of the Federal Reserve, was also a member of Farben's American subsidiary.

So, do you see what's going on? American bankers in the guise of statesmen created treaties and plans to loan money to the Germans, who siphoned off the money and formed I. G. Farben. Then - and here's the kicker - Farben set up a slush fund and funneled money to finance Hitler's rise to power. It's all starting to make sense now, huh?

After establishing himself as the Fuhrer, Hitler told I. G. Farben that Germany needed to be self-sufficient in regard to rubber production, gasoline, oils, minerals, and explosives. Within a short time, Farben owned coal mines, electric power plants, iron & steel factories, banks, research units, and chemical refineries.

Farben's monopolistic control of Germany was so vast that Professor Sutton provides these statistics to show their stronghold:

I. G. Farben Production (1942)

Synthetic rubber – 100%

Plastics – 90%

Explosives – 84%

Jet Fuel – 46%

Oil – 100%

Gunpowder – 70%

Gasoline – 33%

Zyklon B – 95%

Yes, you saw that last item correctly – Zyklon B – the poison used to gas the Jews in the concentration camps! Did you ever wonder where it came from? Now you know. I. G. Farben, the company that extorted reparation money and financed Hitler, was the ones who produced it!!

Since I mentioned the American arm of I. G. Farben, I figure it'll be useful to mention which companies had representatives on their Board of Directors:

- Federal Reserve Bank of New York
- Bank of Manhattan
- Standard Oil of New Jersey
- Ford Motor Company

Now, do you know who owned Standard Oil of New Jersey? The Rockefeller Family! And, would you like to know a little tidbit of information? In 1939, when World War II was kicking in full-bore, Standard Oil of New Jersey sold 20 million dollars worth of aviation gasoline to a German company. Who do you think this company was? I. G. Farben! When news reports chronicled Germany's blitzkrieg across Europe and their fighter pilots were decimating cities, a Rockefeller-owned American company was selling them fuel! It makes ya wonder, huh?

American Industrialists

In this section, I'm going to quickly present a few examples that will show one of Mr. Sutton's main contentions in his book – that a variety of American businesses were well-aware of the nature of Naziism, and that they knew a war would result from their preparations. Knowing all this, they still went ahead and profited from their aid to the Nazi's.

So, I'll simply start reeling off a few points from Professor Sutton's book:

The two largest German tank producers were Opel (which was a subsidiary of General Motors and controlled by J. P. Morgan), and Ford A.G.

A few of the industrialists who helped Germany build its War Machine were:

Dupont – armaments

Standard Oil – synthetic fuel products

International Harvester – arms manufacturing

The Kepler Circle was a group of German businessmen who supported Hitler's rise to power before the outbreak of World War II. This Inner Core, as it was called, had representatives on its Board from Wall Street, Standard Oil of New Jersey, and I.T.T. from 1933 to as late as 1944!

Finally, there is strong evidence that after the United States government got into World War II and began mass bombings of Germany, every time the Air Force targeted an area, if an I. G. Farben plant was present, they were instructed BY NO MEANS to destroy it! As you remember, I. G. Farben WAS the German War Machine.

Henry Ford

The strangest and most unsettling information that Professor Sutton presents in his book revolves around Henry Ford, founder of the Ford Motor Company. The author states that not only did the Ford family profit from both the Allied and Axis war efforts, but that Henry Ford was actually decorated by the Nazi's for his service to Nazism!

To back his assessment, Sutton begins by saying that Henry Ford once claimed that there were two classes of financiers:

a)   those who profit from war and use their influence to bring about war for profit

b)   "constructive" financiers

Now re-read statement a) and absorb the full impact of these words. There are men who PROFIT from war and use their influence to bring about war for profit. That's some heavy information! The ramifications of this statement are mind-boggling, and point directly to evidence of PURE EVIL existing in this world. Think about it – the atrocities of war created to pad somebody's pocket. How sick!

Sutton then tracked down a 1938 interview with Henry Ford that appeared in the *New York Times*. Ford is quoted as saying, "Somebody once said that sixty families have directed the destinies of the nation. It might well be said that if somebody would focus the spotlight on twenty-five persons who handle the nation's finances, the world's real war-makers would be brought into bold relief."

Here's a man in the know confirming the existence of a shadowy, conspiratorial, octopus-like group that controls the world from behind the scenes. He continues, "...if these financiers had their way, we'd be in a war now. They want war because they make money out of such conflict – out of the human misery that wars bring."

Now this isn't Joe Schmo drinking beer in some bar and spouting off his mouth. It's Henry Ford, the man who invented the assembly line concept to mass-produce automobiles, and a man who was certainly gifted with inside knowledge of how the System operates.

But Ford was no saint, either, as can be seen from the following details. He was the man who built the Soviet Union's first modern automobile plant in Gorki in late 1930. He also knowingly profited from both sides of the war, for his French and German affiliated plants produced vehicles for the Axis, while his American factories profited from the United States Army. In 1928, Ford merged his German assets with I. G. Farben, while in 1942, Edsel Ford urged his associates at French Ford to arm the German Wehrmacht. In essence, then, Sutton claims that Ford produced vehicles that were used against American soldiers that landed in France in 1944.

If this is all there was to the story, someone could dismiss the above information as being coincidental, or circumstantial. But regrettably, there is more. In *The New York Times* dated December 20, 1922, a headline read: "BERLIN HEARS FORD IS BACKING HITLER," while the subsequent article states, "A rumor is current here that Henry Ford, the American automobile manufacturer, is financing Adolf Hitler's Nationalist and anti-semitic movement in Munich. Indeed, the Berlin Tageblatt has made an appeal to the American Ambassador in Berlin to investigate and interfere."

As I said earlier, there were many people who were either directly or indirectly associated with Adolf Hitler and the Nazi's who said that they had no idea about their anti-Semitic underpinnings. But just remember – this *New York Times* article ran in 1922, over a decade BEFORE World War II even began!

This same *New York Times* article continues, "The wall behind his desk in Hitler's private office is decorated with a large picture of Henry Ford. In the antechamber there is a large table covered with books, nearly all of which are a translation of a book written and published by Henry Ford."

The book that this article referred to is Henry Ford's *The International Jew* which was widely circulated by the Nazi's and translated into a dozen different languages. Adolf Hitler even went so far as to quote sections of this book VERBATIM in *Mein Kampf*!

Doesn't this scare you?

Sutton also takes a quote from Jonathan Leonard's *The Tragedy of Henry Ford* that was relayed by vice president Auer of the Bavarian Diet at a 1923 trial: "Herr Hitler openly boasts of Mr. Ford's support and praises Mr. Ford as a great individualist and a great anti-Semite. A photograph of Mr. Ford hangs in Herr Hitler's quarters …."

Now, if this were the end of the story, it would be damaging enough. But it doesn't end there. The final damning blow to Henry Ford comes from him not only being the most famous of Hitler's foreign backers, but on August 1, 1938, a disturbing photograph appeared in *The New York Times* where Henry Ford is receiving the Grand Cross of the German Eagle from Fritz Heiler and Karl Kapp. Now think of the year – 1938. World War I was about to begin (Germany had already begun its expansion), and its impact would be felt worldwide. But what is Henry Ford doing? He's receiving the highest Nazi decoration that can be given to a foreigner – the first time it was ever awarded in the United States!

Finale

The implications of Professor Sutton's book are so profound that world events can never be seen in the same light again. Rather than unfolding independently and accidentally, it now becomes clear that wars, business transactions, monetary dealings, and back door deals are the order of the day. Instead of things "just happening," this book makes it evident that strings are certainly being pulled from behind the scenes by a cabal of shadowy figures who are more interested in world power and profits than they are about human lives or our best interests.

What we have in effect, then, is an entrenched group of international bankers who worked in unison with big business to create a series of political upheavals that eventually lead to World War I. After this global catastrophe, these very same figures implemented treaties and plans that padded the banker's pockets with huge loan profits while resulting in German hyper-inflation and unemployment. After the Stock Market Crash in 1929, these hidden Controllers eventually backed two world leaders – Franklin Delano Roosevelt and Adolf Hitler.

And what was the motivation for these manipulative machinations? Quite simply, the Controllers wanted another war in Europe. As sickening and repulsive as this is, it's true. THESE ARE THE TYPES OF INDIVIDUALS WHO RUN THE WORLD! This is the truth once you peek behind the veil of illusion.

The infamous Carroll Quigley, author of *Tragedy and Hope* and a professor of International Relations at Georgetown University, summarized the situation very succinctly when saying, "...the powers of financial capitalism had enough far reaching aim, nothing less than to create a world system of financial control in private hands able to dominate the political system of each country and the economy of the world as a whole."

So, what is the end result of this fiasco? Essentially, the Federal Reserve Bank now has a virtual monopoly over the American economy, while groups like the Council on Foreign Relations and the Trilateral Commission determine our foreign policy. The international bankers, controlling all of the above groups, then set the tone by acquiring markets and establishing an economic market base that is run by a tight-knit cadre of individuals that continue to increase taxation, perpetuate wars, manipulate our money, and keep us under their thumbs.

But remember, all of this stuff "just happens," and there's nobody behind the scenes calling the shots.

CHAPTER THIRTY-SIX

FDR AND THE CONTROLLERS: WAR-TIME TRAITORS - PEARL HARBOR

When researchers study American history and try to pinpoint certain time frames that signal the beginning of our "takeover" by the hidden ruling elite, the first glaring example is Woodrow Wilson, by far this country's most manipulated President. While Wilson and his evil cohorts like Colonel House were re-elected to their second term, the Controllers were already searching for another candidate to take his place somewhere down the line.

They found their pigeon in Franklin Delano Roosevelt, whose family had been in banking since the 1700s. In fact, FDR's uncle, Frederic Delano, was one of the original members of the Federal Reserve Board.

FDR was so familiar with elements of the "shadow government" that he said at one time, "Sixty families in America control the wealth of this nation." During the 1920s he held 11 corporate directorships, two law partnerships and was president of a law association.

In his book, *Wall Street and FDR*, Antony Sutton said: "Roosevelt was a creation of Wall Street, an integral part of the New York banking fraternity."

Curtis B. Dall, FDR's son-in-law, went even further with this startling confession: "Most of his thoughts, his political ammunition as it were, were carefully manufactured for him in advance by the CFR-One-World Money Group." Finally, Des Griffin, in *Descent Into Slavery*, characterized the Roosevelt Presidency as such: "In the twelve years during which he occupied the White House, FDR probably did more than any other single politician in history to bring to fruition the plans of the 'Invisible Government' of the international bankers."

KEEPING AMERICA OUT OF WAR?

On October 30, 1940, Franklin Delano Roosevelt assured the American public, "I have said this before, but I shall say it again and again and again: Your boys are not going to be sent into any foreign wars."

Considering how brutal WWII was, and how Americans at that time wanted nothing to do with another European bloodbath, FDR's promise was noble. The only problem was, he didn't mean it. In fact, he was lying through his teeth while uttering these words.

How did I arrive at such a conclusion? In January, 1941, only three months later (and eleven months before the Pearl Harbor attacks), FDR's closest advisor, Harry Hopkins, traveled to England and met with Prime Minister Winston Churchill and told him, "The President is determined that we shall win the war together. Make no mistake about it. He has sent me here to tell you that at all costs and by all means he will carry you through."

During this time, Tyler Kent, who served as a code clerk at the American Embassy in London, unearthed some secret wire transmissions between Roosevelt and Churchill in which FDR disclosed that he intended to bring America into the war.

Mr. Kent tried to reveal these transcripts to the American people, but mysteriously, he was imprisoned until the war was over. The behind-the-scenes deceit was so blatant, FDR biographer Robert Sherwood concluded, "If the isolationists had known the full extent of the secret alliance between the U.S. and Britain, their demands for the President's impeachment would have rumbled like thunder through the land."

Adding fuel to the fire, Henry Stimson, FDR's War Secretary and a Council on Foreign Relations bigwig, wrote in his diary after meeting with Roosevelt in the fall of 1941, "We face the delicate question of the diplomatic fencing to be done so as to be sure Japan is put into the wrong and makes the first bad move -- overt move."

After his next conference with FDR, Stimson wrote on November 25, 1941 (still two weeks prior to the Pearl Harbor attacks): "The question was how we should maneuver them into the position of firing the first shot without too much danger to ourselves. It was desirable to make sure the Japanese were the ones to do this so that there should remain no doubt in anyone's mind as to who were the aggressors."

CRACKING THE JAPANESE CODE

The most damning evidence of FDR's complicity in allowing Pearl Harbor to be attacked was the fact that American Intelligence had broken the Japanese military and diplomatic codes that were used to communicate between Tokyo and its U.S. Embassy as early as 1940. In addition, both Roosevelt and his cabinet knew the exact time and date of the attack from these transmissions.

I realize this is a bitter pill for many people to swallow, but FDR betrayed his country and his soldiers, for our Intelligence knew what the Japanese were doing from hour-to-hour. These cracked codes were then sent to FDR and his Army Chief of Staff, General George Marshall. But cracked codes were only one part of the incriminating evidence against FDR and his cabinet.

* Admiral James Richardson adamantly urged FDR not to move his Pacific Fleet to Pearl Harbor because it was so exposed and vulnerable. And what thanks did he get? The Admiral was released from his position because he would not issue FDR's traitorous orders.

* After decoding their messages, our Intelligence knew that Hawaiian spies had told the Japanese every possible detail about our base at Pearl Harbor.

* A plethora of warnings about this imminent attack flooded in from: Joseph Grew, Japanese Ambassador; FBI Director J. Edgar Hoover; Senator Guy Gillette & Congressman Martin Dies; the Korean underground; and various military personnel such as Brigadier General Elliot Thorpe and Colonel F. G. L. Weijerman.

* U. S. Army Chief of Staff George G. Marshall telegraphed his officers at Pearl Harbor on November 27, 1941 with this odd request: "Hostile action possible at any moment. If hostilities cannot, repeat CANNOT, be avoided; the United States desires that Japan commit the first overt act." How incredible and despicable! What in God's name were they thinking? Our ships were anchored and our planes were grouped together in broad daylight while George Marshall told his officers at Pearl Harbor to wait until the Japanese made the first move! Unbelievable.

* Captain Johan Ranneft, Dutch Naval Attache in D.C., said that on December 6, 1941, Naval Intelligence officers reported that Japanese warships were only 400 miles from Honolulu.

* As the month of December, 1941 began, our Intelligence intercepted the Japanese "Purple" code saying their emissaries in D.C. should eliminate all official papers and evacuate the premises.

* On December 4, Australian Intelligence told U. S. Representatives that Japanese warships and military jets that had dropped from sight a few days earlier were now moving toward Pearl Harbor. How did FDR react? He brushed aside the information as "pro-war propaganda" by the G.O.P.

* U. S. Intelligence tracking the Germans, in addition to British sources, informed FDR's Administration about the attack, but their pleas fell on deaf ears.

* Army Chief of Staff George Marshall and Navy Secretary Frank Knox said they couldn't remember where they were on the night of December 6 -- a day that will live in infamy -- permanently tattooed into every person's memory alive at that time -- yet they couldn't remember. Their whereabouts were later discovered. Both of them were at the White House with one individual. Guess who that was. Yup, FDR! I suppose something like that would be easy to forget, huh?

* Finally, consider this. Although our ships and aircraft were sitting ducks, the U.S. didn't have one AIRCRAFT CARRIER at Pearl Harbor when it was bombed! Why? Because battleships were outdated WWI remnants. To WIN in this theater of war, you needed carriers to transport bombers for flight. So, even though we sacrificed our old battleships and some aircraft, the real strategic aces-up-our-sleeves -- our CARRIERS -- weren't present. We needed them to REALLY keep fighting with.

If you're still not convinced, the following is a telephone conversation between Winston Churchill and FDR that was intercepted by Axis spies in Holland on November 26, 1941 (ten days before the Pearl Harbor attacks):

Churchill: (referring to Japanese warships in the Pacific): I can assure you that their goal is the fleet in Hawaii at Pearl Harbor.
Roosevelt: This is monstrous. Can you tell me -- indicate -- the nature of your intelligence?
Churchill: Reliable.
Roosevelt: The obvious implication is that the Japs are going to do a Port Arthur on us at Pearl Harbor. Do you concur?

Churchill: I do indeed, unless they add an attack on the Panama Canal to this vile business.

Roosevelt: I will have to consider the entire problem. A Japanese attack on us which would result in war between -- and certainly you as well -- would certainly fulfill two of the most important requirements of our policy. (Roosevelt then mentions leaving the White House, adding): What I don't know can't hurt me, and I can't understand messages at a distance.

Let these words stew around in your head for awhile!

CHAPTER THIRTY-SEVEN

FDR AND THE CONTROLLERS: WAR-TIME TRAITORS -- THE ATOMIC BOMB

Edwin Stanton, Abraham Lincoln's Secretary of War, said: "Wars are not fought to defeat an enemy. They are fought to create a condition."

FDR'S REACTION TO FOREKNOWLEDGE OF PEARL HARBOR

Rear Admiral Theobold, in *The Final Secrets of Pearl Harbor* wrote: "The anxiety to have Japan, beyond all possibility of dispute, commit the first act of war, caused the President and his CIVILIAN advisers to disregard military advice [to move the fleet at Pearl Harbor] which would have somewhat cushioned the blow." (Notice Theobold's deliberate use of the word "CIVILIAN" advisers -- those OUTSIDE of government!)

This situation becomes more curious when we examine the reactions of FDR and certain members of his military staff, especially Admiral Stark, who was second in command under FDR. Admiral Stark, when given undeniable proof by Captain Wilkinson that the Japanese were about to attack Pearl Harbor and that they should warn their Pacific fleet, was told that such a move was unnecessary. Peculiar, don't you think?

Worse, FDR and General George Marshall removed most of our air defenses before the attack, and only had one-third of the necessary surveillance planes needed to protect the base in Pearl Harbor. They also refused to pass any information along to military commanders Admiral Husband Kimmel and General Walter C. Short in Hawaii.

But it doesn't end there. When Admiral Richardson, one of the military bigwigs, tried to tell FDR how vulnerable our fleet was in Pearl Harbor, FDR dismissed him.

In the end, as we all know, Pearl Harbor was attacked, 3,300 military personnel were killed, and America was drawn into WWII. But as we've seen, many fingers pointed at FDR, his cabinet, and the Controllers for possible foreknowledge of this atrocity.

An investigation into this matter soon followed, but again events were manipulated behind the scenes. How so?

Of the four-member Roberts Commission, one was Supreme Court Justice Owen Roberts, who was a Globalist friend of FDR, and two were Council on Foreign Relations members (i.e., total insiders). In the end (no surprise), FDR was found free of blame, while Admiral Kimmel and General Short were used as scapegoats and charged with "dereliction of duty."

Now do you see how the System works?

THE YALTA CONFERENCE

In 1945, Winston Churchill, Joseph Stalin, and Franklin Roosevelt (all high-ranking Freemasons) met at Yalta, a Crimean resort in Soviet Russia. The official purpose of this conference was to finalize plans on how the Allies were going to defeat the Nazi's, and also to launch the establishment of the Globalist-oriented United Nations.

It's easy to see from FDR's actions that he was being directed from behind the scenes by those whose ulterior motives reflected an agenda that used America as a vehicle to promote their own aims. For example, two days before President Roosevelt left for Yalta and *seven months* before Japan eventually waved the white flag, FDR received a 40-page report from General Douglas MacArthur.

In these pages, the Japanese gave an unofficial offer of peace on exactly the same terms that the U.S. finally accepted when the war ended. But Roosevelt, acting as curiously as he had on many other occasions, didn't even take this memo to Yalta to show Churchill and Stalin. We have to remember that Douglas MacArthur was one of America's most highly respected Generals, and also a war hero.

Once we realize the powerful role of the War Machine in the global decision- making process, we can see why FDR didn't sign a treaty with the Japanese, but instead decided to push forward and drop the Bomb.

Everyone knew our battle with Japan was over except for the final dance, but the Controllers *had* to take the next step and move to a higher level by placing the atomic equation on the table. When viewed in this light, Churchill evaluated the decision best when he described Roosevelt as knowing he was "a powerless puppet in the hands of the international power brokers." Churchill's words shatter the illusion just a little bit more.

Yes, by 1943 the United States could have ended the war with Japan. But we let it drag on for another year-and-a-half. Why -- when even in March, 1945, five months before Hiroshima and Nagasaki became household words, the Japanese High Command offered America its unconditional surrender? But we rejected it.

Why did we push their offer away? What reason did we give? Believe it or not, our Intelligence said they couldn't interpret the Japanese memo! We broke the most complex of Japanese military codes and knew every step they were going to make, but we couldn't read straight text! Incredible. Also, by that time we had thousands of Japanese prisoners in our internment camps who wouldn't have had any trouble reading this document.

WAR AS URBAN RENEWAL

As repulsive as it may seem, the real reason we perpetuated and prolonged our war with Japan was for urban renewal. Yes, the Theater of War ... the Big Show was nothing more than the creation of a "condition."

Pearl Harbor was the "premise" that lured America into a war that it didn't want to enter. Similar to the Lusitania, the Gulf of Tonkin, and the World Trade Center terrorist attacks, Pearl Harbor served as an "igniter" to incite feelings of nationalism and revenge among the masses. The formula is simple: create an enemy; start a war.

But even as the Japanese dropped their bombs on our sitting-duck battleships, they as well as everyone else knew that America would kick their asses. And we did! Yet veiled in the shadows was the Institute of Pacific Relations -- a Controller front group that continued to push the international banker's goals. So, to create the desired end result, we wiped out huge areas of the Orient (the first of many attacks over the next few decades) and began an "urban renewal" program. Out with the old, in with the new, and the Machine keeps chugging along!

Then we dropped the Bomb, opening an atomic Pandora's Box (elevating us to new levels of horror and fear), began a Cold War with Russia, and spent even more money on the War Machine.

But I think I'm jumping ahead of myself, so let's look at this situation again and ask the question: why did we REALLY attack the Japanese? The answer may surprise you. We declared war on the Japanese not because they were a threat to us, but to set the stage for economic redevelopment.

The Japanese were still stuck in the past and had to be "brought up to speed." Why? Because their country was essentially overrun with old peasant houses that needed to be cleared away.

But how could the Controllers accomplish this goal? Japan was ripe for the taking, but it needed modern factories and other types of economic build-up.

But what could the Controllers do? Ah-ha. When all else fails, there's always the War Machine!

So the Controllers had America attack Japan and totally wipe them out, putting its people into a totally dismal condition. Then, when the Japanese were at their lowest point, completely broke and without hope, the international "developers" zipped in and scooped up the land, using it for their own benefit.

Carroll Quigley, the oft-quoted insider and author of *Tragedy and Hope*, described the situation expertly. He wrote about how American bomber planes "engaged in the systematic destruction of all Japanese cities. The flimsy houses in these crowded urban areas made them very vulnerable to incendiary bombs. On March 9, 1945, the Air Force tried a daring experiment. The defensive armament was removed from 279 B-29s releasing weight for additional incendiaries, and these planes, without guns but carrying 1900 tons of bombs, were sent on a low-level attack of Tokyo. The result was the most devastating air attack in all history, with the loss of only three planes. Sixteen square miles of central Tokyo was burned out, 250,000 homes were destroyed, over a million persons were made homeless, and 84,793 were killed. This was more destructive than the first atomic bomb over Hiroshima five months later."

Now don't get me wrong. I'm not a peacenik bleeding heart by any means, and I certainly don't oppose America "taking care of business" when necessary. But I am irritated when warfare becomes a ruse to accomplish the Controllers' ulterior motives. Sadly, this scam-job is almost always the case, even today.

After WWII ended in 1945, huge amounts of money were pumped into Japan. And what were these funds used for? Well, how about new factories, railroads, storage facilities, import and export docks, urban redevelopment, and office buildings? And more important, where did the money come from to completely rebuild Japan's infrastructure? You guessed it. From the same people who started the war, the same people who profited from the war, and the same people who made a killing after the war. And in case you didn't know, these were also the same people who financed WWI, the Bolshevik Revolution, and the Nazi's rise to power.

These are also the very same people running our world today. Does it make you have affection for them? Do you feel any affinity with them?

In 1945, even before the war had ended, the Controllers were already planning their next succession of moves. They knew America would emerge from WWII king of the hill, so they immediately started providing counter-balances -- one in Japan, and the other in the Soviet Union. In the Japanese they found a slavish worker who was productive, dedicated, didn't question authority, and was easily conditioned.

The result was that over fifty years ago, the Controllers were already planning to undermine America so that it didn't become too powerful.

Do you see the big picture now? Our strong industrially-based economic foundation was being slowly eroded way back then, via the creation of cheap imports from the Orient. Thus, in 2002, instead of being primarily a producing country, we have become a consumer service economy (and hugely indebted to boot).

With imports flooding in over the past three decades from Japan, Taiwan and China (and that's just in the Pacific Rim) plus the crushing effects of NAFTA and GATT, America is rapidly losing its economic grip.

With cheap, subservient labor in Third World countries coupled with open borders, the Controllers keep reaping profits while America is going to wake up one day and cry, "What have we done? We let it all slip away!"

We need to look at who's controlling the world's money, who they're lending it to, what it's being used for, and the motivations behind it. Once we derive this type of knowledge, the overall picture becomes quite clear.

WWII paved the way for the Controllers to enter the Orient. Shortly thereafter, America was at war in Korea, then Vietnam over the Golden Triangle. Now the stage is being set for China to assume its role as the new "king of the hill." We'd better wake up to what's going on before it's too late. The writing is on the wall.

CHAPTER THIRTY-EIGHT

FDR & THE CONTROLLERS: WAR-TIME TRAITORS – RUSSIA AND THE ATOMIC BOMB

In 1943, Franklin Delano Roosevelt and his administration, on orders from the Controllers, began giving the Soviet Union secrets, as well as materials, for building the atomic bomb. Note that 1943 is two years before the U.S. dropped the Bomb on Hiroshima in August, 1945. One of the key players in this outrageous act was Harry Hopkins, FDR's top advisor and Bolshevik admirer. Hopkins played an integral role in giving the Russians both the nuclear materials and blueprints to construct the Bomb.

If you find this information hard to swallow, listen to what Major General John R. Deane said in *The Strange Alliance*: "American aid to the Red Butchers was carried out with a zeal which approached fanaticism."

Air Force Major George Racey Jordan, in his published 1952 diary, revealed even more: "There seemed to be no lengths to which American officials would go in aiding Russia to master the secrets of nuclear fission."

The preeminent historian Antony Sutton, in his book *Western Technology and Soviet Economic Development*, wrote about this disturbing turn of events. "Stalin paid tribute to the assistance rendered by the U.S. to Soviet industry before and during the war. He said that about two-thirds of all the large industrial enterprise in the Soviet Union had been built with United States help or technical assistance."

Finally, Harry Hopkins himself assured a group of Russians at a Madison Square Garden rally in reference to atomic secrets that he was "determined that nothing shall stop us from sharing with you all that we have."

One of the primary sources of information concerning this matter was Air Force Major George Racey Jordan's diary, published in 1952. Major Jordan obtained this knowledge while working as a supply expediter and liaison officer from 1942-44 at the Newark Airport and while serving at an air base in Great Falls, Montana.

Major Jordan meticulously recorded all of the materials that were shipped to the Soviets during his employ -- each of them crucial in building an atomic bomb. It must be noted that most people in America, Major Jordan included, didn't even know what an atomic bomb was prior to 1945 (due, of course, to implicit secrecy). Here is a list of the materials shipped to Russia:

- Graphite – worth $812, 430
- Aluminum tubes (used to cook or turn uranium into plutonium) - $13,041,152
- 834,989 pounds of cadmium metal - worth $781,472
- Thorium - $22,848

In January, 1943 alone, we shipped 11,912 pounds of thorium from Philadelphia to Russia.

Why did the Russians need aluminum tubes to turn uranium into plutonium? But that's not all. We also shipped 1,465 pounds of uranium chemicals and 2.2 pounds of uranium metal (when our ENTIRE stock of uranium metal was 4.5 pounds)!

We surrendered HALF of our entire supply of this crucial raw material to the Soviets! In addition, we also dispatched over 1,000 pounds of deuterium oxide (commonly known as "heavy water") to Russia in November, 1943. Major Jordan also wrote that an incredible amount of materials was being clandestinely shuttled from Alaska to Siberia.

But the story doesn't end there. Thousands of Soviet military personnel and scientists traveled to the U.S. in large numbers to visit our labs and bases. This was DURING WWII! Major Racey also recounts how he came upon questionable briefcases delivered to the Russians that had road maps to industrial sites and also classified military bases. One of them was to the Aberdeen Proving Grounds, a highly sensitive locale that was crucial during WWII.

Along with the maps were engineering and scientific papers, and reports from HARRY HOPKINS including the words "uranium," "cyclotron," "proton," and "deuteron." Their briefcases also possessed maps for "Oak Ridge, Manhattan Engineering District."

Hmmm, do you think that had anything to do with the secretive "Manhattan Project?" Guess it wasn't so hush-hush after all.

Below is the annual total aid we gave to Russia while we were in the midst of WWII:

- 1942 - $1,422,853,332
- 1943 - $2,955,811,271
- 1944 - $3,459,274,155
- 1945 - $1,838,281,501

The total: $9.6 billion. Yes ... 9.6 BILLION dollars in aid to the Soviet Union!

But once the war was over, did the aid end? Not by a long shot. General Leslie R. Groves lists the variety of items sent to post-war Russia:

- 121 merchant ships - $123 million
- 1,285 trains - $103 million
- trucks and buses - $508 million
- tractors - $24 million
- telephone equipment - $33 million
- generators - $222 million

Well, lo and behold, on September 23, 1949, guess what happened? The Soviets tested and exploded their first A-bomb -- only four years after we did. For a long time I wondered how they could have developed this technology so quickly. Here was an ass-backwards country that had been decimated by WWII AND the ravages of Communism. They were broke, hurting, starving, and hardly in any position to make this fantastic leap into the nuclear age ... unless ...!

Des Griffin, in *Descent Into Slavery*, summed it up best when he wrote, "It was only when the Russians exploded their first atomic bomb in 1949 that the thunderous reality of where the Reds obtained their atomic secrets dawned on Major Jordan; these atomic secrets had come straight from the White House!"

The big question is, why? Why did the United States government find it so imperative to finance the Soviet War Machine during and AFTER the war and hand them our nuclear secrets before we had even fully developed the Bomb ourselves? The answer might surprise you.

WE didn't, of our own volition, give them anything. Instead, FDR and his cabinet, and later Harry Truman, were mere "implementers" for the Controllers, who were behind everything.

The Controllers "created" Communist Russia in the first place by financing Lenin's "Bolshevik Revolution" during Woodrow Wilson's administration. Then, after WWI, which everyone knew would lead to WWII (due to the type of treaties that were put into place) the Controllers realized when the A-bomb was dropped, there would only be one "king of the hill" -- America. Why? Because every European country was decimated, while the USA remained unscathed. We were at the top of our game both economically, and also in regard to production. No wonder our confidence soared. We were the greatest, strongest nation in the world and everyone knew it.

But having one force mightier than any other is a tremendous threat to the Controllers. Mere bankers, they could easily be thrust from their seats of power if a nation set its mind to it.

To prevent such a thing from happening, the Controllers always plan ahead and make sure they have a "back-up" to offset the winner of a certain war. And how do they determine who ultimately wins the war? Simple. They control the money and thus the loans. If a huge influx of money is suddenly cut off, how can a country's War Machine keep churning ahead? Without loans, it's hard to buy or manufacture tanks, bombs, aircraft, guns, and uniforms.

Realizing that America would emerge victorious, the Controllers already began planning for a nation to act as a balance: someone to offset the USA's vast dominance in every area. That nation happened to be the Soviet Union. Thus, preparations were being made before WWII had even ended.   Now do you see why we were funneling so much money and supplies into post-war Russia immediately after the war was over? The Controllers knew it was imperative to "even things out" quickly before America grew even more dominant.

The same goes for our willingness to give our atomic secrets to Russia even before we dropped our own A-bomb. God forbid that America lasted too long as the only nation with nuclear capabilities.

Don't you see? That would make our dominance too one-sided; thus, Russia was our atomic balance.

A secondary effect also resulted from the U.S. building up Russia's nuclear arsenal. It began a "Cold War" that lasted for over thirty years, up to Reagan's presidency. The Cold War created an overwhelming "fear factor" -- bomb shelters, "Red" scares, rehearsals of children instructed to crawl under their desks, apocalypse rumors, etc.

The Cold War also led to the beginning of huge deficit spending to make sure one side didn't get more weapons than the other.

By building a larger War Machine, we had to keep borrowing more money from whom? You guessed it -- the Controllers! The further we were in debt, the more control they gained over us. Also, with an "enemy" (the "Commies"), America had a way to "justify" all this outlandish spending.

In the end, the Controllers stayed in power. America became massively indebted, Russia eventually crumbled, and the people of this country focused their attention on a "created" enemy -- the Soviets.

Everything was "balanced out" and the only winners were those who lurked in the shadows pulling all the strings!

CHAPTER THIRTY-NINE

ADOLF HITLER AND BLACK MAGIC: THE REAL REASON BEHIND THE NAZI PARTY'S RISE TO POWER – A REVIEW OF "THE SPEAR OF DESTINY" BY TREVOR RAVENSCROFT

The atrocities of World War II – a soldier's leg ripped from his body as screams and blood fill the air ... innocent citizens led into crematoriums that are pumped full of poison as they gag for breath ... a 19-year-old boy's chest wracked by shrapnel ... blitzkrieg storm troopers piercing a pregnant woman's abdomen with their bayonets ... houses destroyed by falling bombs ... prayers in a foxhole... orphaned children crying for their deceased parents...

A battle-scarred sergeant vomiting uncontrollably as his buddy's face is ripped-off and an eyeball lies unblinking in the mud ... loved ones never to be seen again ... horror-laden nightmares ... machine guns blasting holes in the souls of men you'd never met before ... and people literally melted into the pavement as an atomic bomb explodes.

At the center of this abomination stands one man – Germany's Fuhrer. Since his death more than half a century ago, more books have been written about Adolf Hitler than any other person. While researching this enigmatic figure, every author eventually confronts the same question: What caused Hitler to follow such an evil course? A plenitude of explanations have been given over the years – a tyrannical father, an incestuous relationship with his mother, Hitler's resentment of his ancestors possibly having Jewish blood, schizophrenia, and so forth. But none of these theories zero in on the true source of this man's madness. The true, underlying cause of Adolf Hitler's evil is: he was willingly possessed and controlled by The Great Beast – Satan himself.

Before I proceed with Mr. Ravenscroft's analysis of Adolf Hitler, I'd like the reader to be aware of two important facts that the Controllers of this world don't want you to know. First, there is so much more going on around us that cannot be seen by the human eye that is never appreciated or realized due to our lifetimes of conditioning and the barriers erected by "reason" and "logic."

In other words, there are a wide array of forces at work that have a remarkable impact on the decisions we make, the directions we take, and the lives we lead.

The second disclosure concerns the public and not-so-public figures that determine the immediate destiny of this world. These personages, akin to Adolf Hitler, are systematically deceiving, exploiting and manipulating the populace to such negative ends that at some point everyone must become aware of their motives and put an end to this destructive path. These leaders deal in secrecy, are aligned with negative forces, and don't (even for a second) have our best interests at heart. Instead, they view mankind and the planet itself as something to be controlled and dominated. After reading this analysis, I hope the picture becomes clearer.

Mr. Ravenscroft begins *The Spear of Destiny* by stating that the men who ran the Nuremberg Trials never properly identified the true "core" of Nazi evil – that at its heart lies the practice of black magic, rituals, rites, and initiations.

The truth, he said, was forwarded by a Viennese philosopher named Dr. Walter Johannes Stein who served Winston Churchill during the war. Stein made a startling observation. Decisions made at the highest political levels to explain Nazi (and other) atrocities as "mental aberrations" were nothing more than a smoke screen. At their core was one striking similarity: these men were consumed by and doing the work of hidden, evil forces.

To expose this phenomenon, Ravenscroft begins by taking a closer look at Adolf Hitler's "flophouse" years that were supposedly spent in poverty and anonymity. In reality, Ravenscroft tells us that Hitler actually spent this time as a "training period" where he gained a wealth of knowledge and plotted his future course.

One aspect of Hitler's life that is not particularly promoted by biographers or historians is the fact that the future Fuhrer was a voracious reader. He was so curious for knowledge that he devoured books on history, the Roman Empire, religion, the occult, psychology, meditation, and astrology.

As opposed to the stumblebum politicians of today (Bush, Clinton, Reagan, etc.) who are merely empty vessels parroting what their Controllers want them to say, Hitler actually did his research. His flophouse years as a struggling artist selling watercolor paintings were not wasted, as popular history leads us to believe.

274

Rather, this time was the most productive (in relative terms) of his life. During these years, Hitler became a student, spending day after day in libraries and bookstores studying occultism, political theory, philosophy, and ritual magic.

Hitler realized that to "educate" himself, he couldn't rely on what was being spoon-fed to the masses in the halls of primary and secondary schools. He was so adamant about this belief that here is how he described his elementary teachers in *Mein Kampf*: "They had no sympathy with youth; their one object was to stuff our brains and turn us into erudite apes. If a pupil showed even a small trace of originality, they persecuted him relentlessly."

So Hitler set out on his own course, making one of his primary pursuits the study of past German philosophers. He read Lessing, Schelling, Goethe and Fichte, and each page in his books was scribbled with meticulous notes and comments. He also discovered Arthur Schopenhauer, who said that conceptual thought could never arrive at ultimate truths, and that reality was only unearthed through the Will.

Likewise, Hitler burned through the pages of Hegel, who announced that the laws of morality didn't apply to monumental figures of world history.

But the philosopher who had the most impact on Hitler was Friedrich Nietzsche. In his book, *The Genealogy of Morals*, Nietzsche tells us that evil is actually good, and good is evil. Nietzsche, who eventually lost his mind to syphilitic insanity, characterized modern man as being weakened by society and paralyzed by the industrial revolution. He wanted to re-discover a time that predated our current form of stifled consciousness, even going so far as to say: "to call the taming of an animal its 'improvement' sounds almost like a joke."

Mirroring Nietzsche's beliefs, Hitler also longed for a time that heralded a people who weren't constrained by morals, customs, or societal mores. He didn't even want God in the picture. Instead, both Hitler and Nietzsche looked to a Viking-type man who would re-emerge through the exertion of his Will and reign supreme with total freedom. Hitler was so enthused about this force of Nature that he boasted, "The Superman is living amongst us now! He is here! Isn't that enough for you? I have seen the New Man. He is intrepid and cruel. I was afraid of him."

Anyone familiar with Hitler must realize that for him to make such a statement (and admit his weakness and fear) implies that his vision of the new Superman must have been horrifying. But did Hitler actually *see* this Being, or was it a manifestation of his own psychosis, megalomania, or delusions of grandeur? To answer this question, we need to find out who Hitler, the person, was.

The first thing everyone should know about this man is that he was a drug addict. Most of us are aware of the fact that Hitler was a rampant speed-freak throughout his final years, but less attention has been paid to his formative years that were mentioned earlier. While struggling, painting and studying, Hitler began using psychedelics (especially an early form of peyote), to achieve a state of higher consciousness. In fact, this may be one of the biggest secrets that Mr. Ravenscroft tells about Hitler.

It seems that he came to accept his world-view through drugs and transcendent consciousness while a bum on the streets of Vienna. He even summarized his goals by saying, "The aim of human evolution is to attain a mystic vision of the Universe."

Another aspect of Hitler's personality that has been revealed in various sources, but not capitalized upon to the fullest, was his bizarre sexual appetites. His practices and behaviors were so unnatural, in fact, that one begins to see what a truly deranged and twisted little man he really was.

What specifically do I mean? Picture this scenario. Hitler is sitting in a secluded fortress in Germany teeming with megalomaniacal visions to the point of being insane. On the walls of his fortress are the most graphic photos of naked women that could be found at that time. Seething with hatred, he remembers back to his less-affluent days when he would pay the cheapest hookers in town to whip him like a dog.

Embittered, he realizes there is nothing he can do about his unbridled lust. To compensate, he explodes at his counterparts for being liars or for trying to betray him. These reactions are nothing more than symbolic projections of what is hidden inside him and ultimately leads to his sadistic hatred of humanity.

Not only have I read in more than a couple books (especially a biography entitled *The Psychopathic God*, by Robert George Leeson Waite) that Hitler was impotent and only had one testicle, but he also loved to have women urinate and defecate on him.

At the core of this man's personality were a slew of unleashed perversions that were the crux of his clairvoyant and mediumistic powers. The only way Hitler could get off was by creating pain in others, or even more so, by being the recipient of this sexual degradation. Do you get it? The only women who excited Hitler were the crazy ones with a touch of "hysteria" – the ones who'd whip him and humiliate him by urinating on his naked body, or defecating on him.

Hitler even fell in love with his own niece, Eva Braun, driving her to suicide. She is described as being nothing more than a groveling slave.

Hitler also believed he had been Klingsor, a practitioner of black magic, in an earlier life. Klingsor wanted to become a member of the Grail Order during King Arthur's time, but he wasn't able to master his lusts and desires. Disgruntled that he couldn't attain his dreams, he went off the deep end and castrated himself.

Thus, unable to get rid of the sexual yearnings that caused his downfall, he decided to banish the drives he couldn't overcome by Will itself. When Amfortas, who guarded the Grail, discovered what Klingsor had done, he banished him forever from the Order. This rejection so infuriated Klingsor that he began harboring an insatiable lust for revenge against Amfortas, the Order, and the Grail itself. He turned all the knowledge he had acquired during his youth toward black magic and the forces of evil, vowing to destroy the souls of those he encountered rather than trying to save them.

With the above information in mind, we need to ask ourselves what image in our collective consciousness best captures the maniacal madness of Hitler. The answer can be found at the notorious Nazi rallies where Hitler ranted and raved in front of thousands of his mesmerized followers.

The Fuhrer was so charismatic, Joseph Goebbels, the Nazi Minister of Propaganda, said at one point, "I recognize him as my leader quite unconditionally ... He is so deep and mystical. He knows how to express infinite truth ... He seems like a prophet of old."

Think for a second about what is being conveyed by this disclosure. Adolf Hitler, a reincarnated black magician who obsessed over women defecating and urinating on him, stood before legions of devoted followers, some of them so enamored, they saw him as a prophet.

What led to these mystical powers? One of the answers can be derived from a single word – Will. I'm sure all of us are familiar with the image of Hitler standing before a crowd with his arm extended in a Nazi salute. Hitler's Will was so strong, in fact, that well after every other general allowed their arm to fall from exhaustion, Hitler's was still extended – his Will extending beyond anyone's he had ever met.

Hitler was so fond of these rallies that he affectionately called them "Feasts of Blood." Try to place yourself at one of these events – throngs of hypnotized followers hanging on their leader's every word ... rivers of manic energy ... scores of torches lighting a darkened arena ... while fanaticism and hysteria filled the air. The crowd became mesmerized as Hitler's entire 'Being' was absorbed by forces beyond his comprehension or control.

Spellbound, Hitler became so obsessed with his oratory prowess, he commented in *Mein Kampf*, "The power which has always started the greatest religions and political avalanches in history has from time memorial been the magic power of the spoken word."

But there had to be something beyond being simply a great statesman. What Hitler accomplished with the majestic symbolism, the fervent crowds, and unbridled devotion went beyond the realm of being a skilled orator.

Alan Bullock's *A Study in Tyranny* probably comes as close to capturing the 'hidden variable' at the source of his power as anyone. He writes: "His power to bewitch an audience has been linked to the occult arts of the African Medicine Man or the Asiatic Shaman; others have compared it to the sensitivity of a medium, and the magnetism of a hypnotic."

By mentioning the occult arts, Mr. Bullock has allowed us to confront the core of Adolf Hitler and the Nazi Party's power. This generally ignored aspect was so influential, Hermann Rausching, in *Hitler Speaks*, quotes a heartfelt woman's warning to Adolf Hitler during his ascent to prominence. "My Leader, don't touch Black Magic! As yet both black and white are open to you. But once you've embarked on black magic, it will dominate your destiny. It will hold you captive. Don't choose the quick and easy successes. There lies before you the power over a realm of pure spirits. Do not allow yourself to be led away from your true path by earthbound spirits which will rob you of your creative powers."

But Hitler didn't heed her warning, as can be seen from two of his direct quotes:

1)   "We are at the outset of a tremendous revolution in moral ideas and man's spiritual orientation. A new age of the magic interpretation of the world is coming, an interpretation in terms of Will and not the intelligence."

2)   "I am founding an Order. It is from there that the final stage in human mutation will emerge – the Man-God!"

For someone with such lofty goals, Hitler needed an enormous amount of external help from forces outside his control to actually reach the pinnacle of world power. The first of these factors was German's defeat in World War I. Crushed, humiliated, and impoverished, this once proud country now stood downtrodden, virtually wiped-out by the Treaty of Versailles.

The German economy was in such poor condition and inflation so high, an old joke used to be told that epitomizes their plight. A robber saw an entire wheelbarrow filled with German money. So, what did he do – steal the Deutschmarks? No. He tipped over the wheelbarrow, poured out the money, and stole the wheelbarrow!

Thus, being at their lowest, Germany looked to the future for a savior who would enter their lives and lift them out of their emotional and economic depression. Amazingly, all the planets were aligned just right and an historic zeitgeist took place as Adolf Hitler entered the political landscape. It seemed as if this little downtrodden tramp with his sexual perversions and messianic visions had been delivered by some sort of external force.

But without Germany's defeat, there would have been no place for Adolf Hitler in our public consciousness. He needed defeat to make his ascension, and a force beyond Hitler used him as a tool to wreak further havoc after the already catastrophic consequences of World War I.

As this congruence of time and place unfolded in post-war Germany, Hitler joined forces with a group called the New German Workers Party. To most people, even those who have studied European history, this bit of information may seem significant. But this tiny group, especially its founding members, went on to form one of the most explosive political forces of all time.

And the reason? All forty original members were initiates in Germany's most powerful occult society – The Thule Gesellschaft.

At the core of the Thule Society was a man named Dietrich Eckart who is called the spiritual founder of Naziism. Eckart was a morphine addict who experimented with psychedelics and spent time in an insane asylum. Adolf Hitler considered him the single most important figure in his life.

Eckart considered himself to be the reincarnation of a 9th century historical figure Bernard of Barcelona. Eckart was also a central figure in the Thule Society, a group whose reason for existence was to prepare the way for an Anti-Christ who would take over the world. After searching for and then finding this new German Messiah who would seek to destroy the world as we knew it, Eckart said (echoing John the Baptist): "Here is the one for whom I was but the prophet and the forerunner." Before Eckart died, he initiated Hitler into the Thule Group by using a sadistic, Luciferian magic ritual from the 9th century.

At the core of the Thule Society was a group of Adepts who became the inner circle of the Nazi Party. They believed themselves to be guided by historic destiny, and practiced black magic. By doing so, they summoned a host of bizarre Beings from beyond, such as Klingsor, and tried to capitalize on these manifestations as a source of power.

The Thule Society's occult interactions extended to every facet of German life. Like the hidden tentacles of an octopus, its members were judges, cops, professors, those of high-society, doctors, businessmen, scientists, and aristocrats.

Other influences also helped shape the Nazi Party and Adolf Hitler:

"The Protocols of the Wise Men of Zion" was a Russian document (possibly forged) stating that the Jewish people had a secret plan to take over the world. It was precisely the tool needed to fuel the German people and their innate anti-Semitism.

Houston Stewart Chamberlain was another one of Hitler's gurus who said "the birth of a new race is dependent upon a homogenous group of people in historic circumstances whose souls come together as one, for the sole purpose of bringing about the new Messiah."

His views were similar to the Essenes, although this holy group awaited the arrival of Jesus, while the Nazi's longed for his evil counterpart.

Madame Blavatsky was a Russian mystic who founded The Theosophical Society and wrote a mystical document entitled, *The Secret Doctrine.*

Aleister Crowley was a member of the magical "Golden Dawn." Known as the Great Beast 666 of Revelations, Crowley was once called "the wickedest man alive" by the English press.

Freemasonry also influenced Hitler, although he distrusted this organization. He once said that "they have developed an esoteric doctrine, not merely formulated it, but imparted it through the medium of symbols and mysterious rites."

The Edelweiss Society, an offshoot of Crowley's "Golden Dawn," also awaited the coming Nordic Messiah. Hermann Goring was one of its members.

Karl Haushofer was another guru who instructed Hitler on how to attain higher degrees of initiation into the secretive orders. In essence, he led the Fuhrer through the hierarchies of evil, which at their core espoused three things:

a)   an opposition to human development
b)   the awakening of Luciferian motives
c)   a halt to the evolution of human consciousness

None of these goals were utilized for positive means, but were instead used to promote an array of Luciferian ideals.

The Vril Society, also named "The Luminous Lodge," was Hitler's next initiation after the Thule Society. This group's sole purpose was to research its Aryan origins and then recapture the magical powers that had been lost over time.

The notorious Heinrich Himmler took control of the Vril Society and turned it into the Nazi Occult Bureau. This organization, tapping into elements of Aleister Crowley's Templar Order, also housed the Black Order of the SS. Himmler got so involved in the occult that he became Hitler's doppelganger ("double"). Doppelganger is defined as an "endless capacity to counterfeit and dissemble, to make something look what it is not, and to feign benign reasons and moral justifications to cover up evil motives."

Now that we've examined the various occult sources that influenced Adolf Hitler and his Nazi regime, the ultimate question is this – what did they hope to accomplish? We already know that each of these groups was searching for a new Messiah who would lead the German people back to glory. But where did they get such an idea?

To find an answer, we need to look once again at the inner core of the Nazi Party. The men who ran this show were all-consumed by Satanism, practiced black magic and were led by their master adept, Dietrich Eckart. The crux of their belief system was as follows: according to the Thule Legend, many eons ago, the island of Atlantis vanished due to a catastrophe. Although a majority of its residents perished in this disaster, some of them, along with their ancient secrets, survived and migrated to the European continent.

These secret doctrines focused on man's origins on this planet and how humans are the product of a breed of Atlantean Spirit Beings who bred with other lower races on earth. It seemed that while still on Atlantis, these Beings prospered until they became interested in harnessing the powers of ritualistic black magic. These practices led to their involvement in an area of forbidden knowledge that ultimately resulted in their downfall – the tinkering with and perversion of human reproduction.

By letting loose a whole host of horrifying forces, catastrophe befell them, but not before a new sub-race was created.

These sub-races, then, along with a few of the original Spirit Beings, relocated to various parts of the globe and began repopulating the planet. Several differences existed between God's originally created Spirit Beings and the resultant sub-races. The primary variation involved the way these figures interacted with their surroundings.

The Spirit Beings enjoyed a mystical communion with their surroundings that was based on a form of telepathy. The new creations, on the other hand, relied on logic, reason and their five senses. They were eventually able to master the physical world, but by doing so, they lost their magical powers and cut off their perceptions.

The original Spirit Beings also believed in reincarnation, alternate consciousness, magic and spirituality, and the Will was the primary force in the universe. Conversely, the sub-races (prototypes for Western man) eliminated magic as a part of reality and relied more on reason, materialism, and science.

In terms of modern man, it's easy to see how the sub-races evolved into the creatures we are now. Most of us stumble through life in a state of unawareness, accepting our sentences due to our conditioning. We sleep at night, then slave away during the day, too distracted and blinded to realize the workings of an invisible spirit world.

Over time, the memory of our magical beginnings was forgotten and replaced by ignorance and denial. Although our ancestors enjoyed an existence of multi-consciousness, we've willingly been reduced to accepting our paltry three dimensions. Although we've been taught to only believe in what we're told, our forebears allowed messages to enter from beyond, and they were receptive to letting these messages guide their actions.

As Adolf Hitler learned these ancient secrets, his Will steadily grew stronger. Convinced that he was the last in a line of Spirit Beings who could evolve into Supermen, his ultimate goal was to reinvigorate the Aryan race that had resided on Atlantis! During this pursuit for Pure Will, Adolf Hitler became a Magician Supreme who tapped into an Evil Hierarchy of spirits that led to the rise of his Nazi Party.

When we examine the various influences and motives behind the Nazi Party, along with the destruction that occurred during World War II, we can only come to one conclusion. More negative forces may have been unleashed upon humanity over the course of this war than at any other time in our history.

Although Hitler was wounded in World War I, he managed to survive several assassination attempts, countless betrayals and a multitude of bone-headed tactical errors. In fact, Hitler had to survive, or the effects of WWII wouldn't have been so atrocious. We *needed* to see humanity at its lowest and ugliest ... to see the demonic forces unleashed to the fullest, and to realize there had to be a better way.

Think about what happened during World War II. If you ever wondered what Satan's fury looked like, take a glance at the carnage on those battlefields, or at the repercussions resulting from the dropping of two atomic bombs. This is what the face of evil looks like. We *needed* to see it to decide whether we wanted to change our path in the future.

But did we? Not a chance. Shortly after WWII, we began a Cold War, entered the Korean War, barely survived the Cuban Missile Crisis, killed a president, entered a god -awful war in Vietnam, and continue to fund and support various wars worldwide. So much for moral salvation.

Do you think that after all the things I've listed above someone would realize that the path we've chosen isn't the most optimal for mankind? If we have come to the conclusion that something is obviously wrong, then we need to look at those forces that are running the show and ask ourselves if they have our best interests at heart. Do they?

The answer is no. Do you remember a quote I gave earlier associated with the doppelganger – specifically, "an endless capacity to counterfeit and dissemble, to make something look what it is not, and to feign benign reasons and moral justifications to cover up evil motives"? This characterization captures exactly what is going on in our society today in terms of the government, media, and the entire Control System.

We need only look around to note that nearly every segment of our existence is riddled by a doppelganger – an alternate reality that doesn't accurately reflect the truth. Those who have firmly entrenched themselves in positions of power have an "endless capacity" to mislead us, to lie, and to make every piece of the puzzle appear different than it really is.

The Controllers who exert a huge amount of influence over all our lives are following a systematic path of secrecy and deceit. Everything about them is a lie. Get it? A LIE! The people who run the world, similar to Adolf Hitler and his cronies, are evil to the core and embrace the same dark secrets as the Nazi's.

The reason these words are hard to swallow is because of one important concept: reason as opposed to secrecy. The Controllers realize there is much more to life than what we see with the human eye. They're well aware that invisible forces interact, guide and communicate with all of us on a daily basis. But because the knowledge imparted from these forces would undermine their stranglehold of control, they keep filling our minds with notions that reinforce reason, logic, and science to lead us away from the total realm of possibilities.

Thus, while we're urged to follow the same stumblebum path as did the Atlantean sub-races, the Controllers keep tapping into their sources of hidden knowledge. In this manner they're continually able to keep their underhanded regimes in power.

If you don't believe me, think for a second about the secrecy that penetrates our culture and government. The first thing you need to do is look at our presidents – George W. Bush was a member of Skull & Bones while attending Yale. This group is one of the most secretive societies in existence and is literally a breeding ground for future high-ranking government officials. His father was the head of the CIA. Does anything else need to be said about secrecy when those three letters are mentioned?

Bill Clinton, like nearly every president for the last 70 years, was a Freemason. Have you ever tried to penetrate the veil of secrecy surrounding those people? Then, how about all the clandestine organizations that meet in private outside the glare of the media's eye – the Council on Foreign Relations, the Trilateral Commission and the Bilderbergs. Shall I continue?

How about all the government documents we'll never see, not even through the Freedom of Information Act because they're classified "TOP SECRET"? Then there are the hidden mind control projects being carried out by shadow factions of our government, the secrecy surrounding UFO's, the black military projects, etc.

The government is supposed to be a servant of the people, but the "servants" are lying, concealing, cheating, and involving themselves in so many underhanded, corrupt, and outright EVIL practices, they've essentially gone way past being our rulers. They are now our Overlords who won't stop at anything until *we* become the servant/slaves to their black magic regime.

The people who run this nation and have aligned themselves with the New World Order are the Sons of Darkness. Their only motives are the pursuit of evil. Sure, they'll lie through their teeth at every turn and try to make themselves look like benign caretakers who are only trying to help "the people." But believe me, these men and women are inspired and led by the spark of Satan.

So, when it comes to explaining what made the Nazi's tick, all the reasons are listed except the real one. Hitler was motivated by EVIL. That's the key. And evil needs a source.

What is that source? Lucifer. And once you realize that Lucifer and his fallen angels actually do exist, then you must also come to another conclusion – the one that the world rulers MOST FEAR – the flip side of evil is PURITY, and the source of purity is GOD. And guess who hates God more than anyone – Satan!

Here it is in a nutshell, folks – the Controllers are evil, and they're ruled by Satan. Whenever one of their own makes it into the public consciousness (Stalin, Richard Ramirez, etc.) by committing an especially atrocious deed, the Controllers need to discount the true source of this EVIL. So they peddle a bunch of psychologists, academics and sociologists before you on TV and explain that this particular act was due to family, society, genetics, drugs, mental illness, etc. But they'll never say the truth – that the act resulted from SATAN.

And why won't they admit that Satan exists? Because if they do that, then they also have to admit the existence of another Being – God. You see, the Controller's primary goal is to eliminate God. If they admit that Satan exists, then they also have to admit God's existence. They fear that more than anything. That, my friends, is the KEY to everything!!!

In conclusion, I'd like to deliver a final quote from Mr. Ravenscroft's book that sums up this essay: "The representatives of the Western world simply refused to admit what their defeated enemies were really like. Their strange beliefs, inhuman practices and horrible crimes could only be explained in psycho-analytical terms as mental aberrations. Western science, which had produced an Atom bomb, denied the very existence of evil and spoke in terms of behaviorism and a relativity of morals. The religion of the West, which had reduced God to a simple carpenter from Nazareth, could make no sense of men who worshipped the cosmic Anti-Christ and gained initiation into a supersensible world through rites of ritual sacrifice.

"Those who knew kept silent. The leaders of the Occult Lodges and Secret Societies linked with power politics in the Western hemisphere had nothing to gain by exposing the Satanic nature of the Nazi Party. Such a serious public investigation into occult rites and initiation knowledge might have unveiled spiritual realities which they themselves sought at all costs to keep hidden from the mass of mankind."

CHAPTER FORTY

THE BUSH FAMILY AND NAZI BLOOD MONEY

Have you ever wondered how Adolf Hitler, a destitute artist who lived in flophouses, was able to become Germany's preeminent Furhergod in the 1930's and 1940's? I mean, how many near-homeless people are you aware of that have had such good fortune befall them? As many of you know, the Nazi phenomenon was not accidental. Instead, Wall Street bankers (among others) were the hidden financiers behind their meteoric rise to power. Even more regrettable is the fact that our current President's family were among those who bankrolled and profited enormously from the German War Machine.

Authors Webster G. Tarpley and Anton Chaitkin, in *George Bush: The Unauthorized Biography*, sum up the situation as such: "By deciding that Prescott Bush [George W. Bush's grandfather] and the other directors of the Union Banking Company were legally FRONT MEN FOR THE NAZIS, the government avoided the more important historical issue: In what way were Hitler's Nazis themselves hired, armed and instructed by the New York and London cliques of which Prescott Bush was an executive manager?"

So, before getting into the nuts-and-bolts of this article, I'll begin by saying that what you are about to read is not "new" information. It is readily available from a wide variety of sources, so please don't think my intent is to break new ground. Rather, my purpose is to provide an overview of how Dutch Intelligence and U.S. Government files 'confirm absolutely' a direct link between Prescott Bush, the Thyssen Family, and death profits derived from our second world war. They derived this blood-money via the Union Banking Corporation (UBC), where Prescott Bush and his father-in-law George Herbert Walker joined forces with German manufacturer Fritz Thyssen and bankrolled Adolf Hitler prior to, and during, WWII.

Now, even though plenty of other companies helped the Nazis (like the Rockefeller's Standard Oil and Chase Bank, plus prominent American auto makers), Prescott Bush's interests were much deeper and sinister. Not only was there a monetary link, but also business ties that were much more involved.

What I'm trying to say is this: a good portion of the Bush Family's financial foundation was established through their assistance to Adolf Hitler. Can you feel the ramifications of this statement? The current President of the United States, plus his father (an ex-President, V.P., and CIA Director) rose to the top of the American political ladder because their grandfather and in-laws aided and abetted the Nazis. The questions I want to ask right now are:

1) Why won't President Bush admit to these family crimes?
2) Why won't the media directly question him about these abhorrent acts?

Naturally, some may not believe that the Bush Family directly assisted the Germans, in essence committing treason against their own country. But sadly, it's true. To prove it, let's start at the beginning.

In 1922, W. Averill Harriman, the infamous railroad magnate, traveled to Berlin where he met with members of the Thyssen Family to set-up a branch bank. And who became the President of this bank? George Herbert Walker, Prescott Bush's father-in-law. Two years later, in 1924, the Union Banking Corporation (UBC) was created to join forces with Fritz Thyssen's "Bank voor Handel en Scheepvaart." And who was appointed to DIRECTLY MANAGE UBC? Prescott Bush. Even better for Prescott was the fact that George Herbert Walker gave him a tremendous break in 1926 by making him vice president and managing partner in Brown Brothers Harriman. And who did Prescott bring along with him to this firm? A handful of his Yale classmates from Skull & Bones. Plus, Prescott Bush was only one of seven shareholders in UBC.

At this point you're probably thinking, what's the big deal? Nothing seems out-of-the-ordinary. This is nothing more than business as usual. But appearances can be deceiving, as we'll soon find out. Y'see, right at the end of the Roaring Twenties, something happened that, when viewed in the context of Prescott Bush, puts everything in perspective.

Authors Tarpley and Chaitkin once again in "George Bush: The Unauthorized Biography": "The great financial collapse of 1929-31 shook America, Germany and Britain, weakening all governments. It also made the hard-pressed Prescott Bush even more willing to do whatever was necessary to retain his new place in the world. It was in this crisis that certain Anglo-Americans determined on the installation of a Hitler regime in Germany."

And who would be one of the key figures to initiate the change of the guard in Germany? The Bush Family's business partner – Fritz Thyssen. This, I believe, would be a good time to take a look at what type of crowd the Bush's were running around with. Fritz Thyssen was the first man to get the newly-formed Nazi Party off the ground by giving them $25,000 in the mid-1920's. In 1931, he joined the Nazi Party, and soon became close friends with Adolf Hitler. Over the years, Thyssen came to be known as "Hitler's most important and prominent financier" and became one of the primary figures in his rise to power. Thyssen was fascinated by Hitler, as he boasted, "I realized his orator gifts and his ability to lead the masses. What impressed me most, however, was the order that reigned over his meetings, the almost military discipline of his followers."

By September, 1932, Thyssen invited a cadre of German manufacturers to meet with Hitler, and all walked away overjoyed after he answered each question to their 'utmost satisfaction.' Thyssen was so overt in his praise and support that he even wrote a book entitled, "I Paid Hitler" where he comes clean about the role he played in Nazism since October, 1923.

Fritz Thyssen was also influential in establishing the "German Steel Trust" which was founded in 1926 by Wall Street high-roller Clarence Dillon. And who was one of Dillon's cohorts on this project? Prescott Bush's father, Sam Bush. Thus, Fritz Thyssen became one of the men at the core of Germany's War Machine due to his position at German Steel. His family also owned a slew of banks (on the sly, of course) that allowed the Thyssens to move their money from Berlin to Holland to New York City. That way, after World War II came to a close, they wouldn't have to surrender their profits!

But I'm jumping ahead of myself. Y'see, the Thyssen Family established three highly important banks during the 1920's:

1) August Thyssen Bank – Berlin
2) Bank voor Handel en Scheepvaart – Holland
3) Union Banking Corporation (UBC) – New York City

Now we're starting to get somewhere. Why? Because the Thyssens received their initial financing from two places to start their War Machine operations: Brown Brothers Harriman, and UBC. And who were key figures at both of these places? George Herbert Walker and Prescott Bush! Thus, UBC was set-up to transfer funds between Manhattan and

Germany via Thyssen's Dutch banks. The Thyssen's got assistance in this endeavor from the Dutch Royal Family, who cooperated to hide their accounts in a variety of Dutch banks. This point is significant, for the chief perpetrator was Prince Bernhard. And what did he go on to create? Answer: the infamous Bilderberg group during the 1950s!

UBC, then, became a secret pipeline for Nazi money as it went from Germany to Holland to the USA. And when they needed to replenish their supplies, Brown Brothers Harriman shipped their funds right back to Germany. Are you starting to see how this operation worked? UBC received the money from Holland, and Brown Brothers Harriman sent it back out. And who was on the Board of Directors of both companies? Yup, Prescott Bush! He was the Nazi's primary money launderer!

Their practices became so blatant and injurious to Americans that on October 10, 1942 the U.S. Government ordered the seizure of all Nazi Germany banking operations in New York City that were being conducted by Prescott Bush. UBC, with Bush as its director, was charged under the "Trading with the Enemy Act" and all their stocks were seized. And do you remember who I said owned all these stocks? There were only seven people – Prescott Bush, three Nazi financiers, and three Americans.

But the crackdown didn't end there; not by a long-shot. On October 26, 1942, the government ordered seizures of two other front companies that were run by Prescott Bush for the Harriman Banking firm:

1) Holland-America Trading Corporation
2) Seamless Steel Equipment Corporation

Then, on November 11, 1942, ANOTHER company managed by Prescott Bush and George Herbert Walker was seized under the "Trading with the Enemy Act" – Silesian-American Corporation. I don't know if you'd agree, but if our government went to those lengths to shut down the Bush Family's operations, I'd have to say they were involved in some seriously nasty business.

John Loftus, who I quoted at the beginning of this article, said of this traitorous situation: "It is bad enough that the Bush Family helped raise the money for Thyssen to give Hitler his start in the 1920's, but giving aid and comfort to the enemy in time of war is treason. The Bush bank helped the Thyssens make the Nazi steel that killed Allied soldiers."

Tarpley and Chaitkin, in *George Bush: The Unauthorized Biography*, said it even more succinctly: "The President's family fortune was largely a result of the Hitler Project."

Still not convinced? Well, how about this. The Union Banking Corporation, which Prescott Bush ran, in unison with Fritz Thyssen's German Steel Trust, produced the following percentages of the Nazi War Machine:

- 50.8% pig iron
- 41.4% universal plate
- 36% heavy plate
- 38.5% galvanized steel
- 45.5% pipes and tubes
- 22.1% wire
- 35% explosives

All the above materials are needed to build tanks, fighter planes, guns and bombs – roughly 1/3 of the entire German War Machine – all of it bankrolled by not only an outward Nazi in Fritz Thyssen, but also the Bush Family as well.

Anyway, if you're not disgusted enough already, let's jump forward a few years. The war ends in 1945, and Fritz Thyssen subsequently dies in 1951. Upon his death, the remaining shareholders at UBC liquidated their stock (these were the same assets frozen by our government under the "U.S. Alien Property Custodian Act" in 1942 and not given back until 1951). And guess who one of the beneficiaries was. You got it – Prescott Bush! And how much money did he receive? $1.5 million. Coincidentally, Mr. Bush took these profits and instantly plunged it into starting his own business. Convenient, huh? Worse, Prescott Bush's cohorts (the same Wall Street backstabbers that financed Hitler) are also the same ones that (over time) made George Bush Sr. CIA Director in the 1970's and put him and his son into the White House! Now do you see why Dan Rather and the *New York Times* aren't giving you this information?

To confirm the above details, new information surfaced in 1996 that came from three different sources: a) Dutch journalist Eddy Roever b) U.S. Freedom of Information Act S.S. files and c) Alien Property Custodian Archives. The information derived from these sources paints an even nastier picture of the situation. It seems that UBC in New York

City was owned by the Thyssens. Thus, the Bush Family's primary banking facility was owned by, and their boss was, one of the most notorious behind-the-scenes Nazis of all-time! The big question at this point is, was Prescott Bush aware of his Nazi links and business dealings? Considering all the information brought out in this article, I'd have to say that as DIRECTOR of UBC, it was HIS ultimate responsibility to oversee every investment, including who they were made to and where they went.

Another interesting note is that the Rockefeller Family also invested heavily in the Nazi War Machine. As it turns out, UBC was an essential element for the laundering of dirty money that was derived from the Rockefeller's investments in Germany during the war. This scenario becomes even more interesting when we find that the Rockefeller's bank – Chase Manhattan – wound up with 31% ownership of the Thyssen Group after WWII!

This point is very important for TBC (the Thyssen Group) is the largest industry in Germany today, worth $50 billion. They're so huge that they even bought out the Krupp Family, who was infamous weapons suppliers for the Nazis. In essence, they are one of the richest companies in the world, and where did their start-up money come from? The Nazis!

What we have then are links to the three major secret trade organizations in the world. Prince Bernhard, who founded the Bilderbergs, enabled the Thyssen Family to launder their money through Holland while the Rockefellers bought nearly 1/3 controlling interest of Thyssen (David Rockefeller founded the Trilateral Commission). And finally, Brown Brothers Harriman and UBC, through which Nazi money was funneled into America, was largely formed by Yale's Skull & Bones members, all of whom were instrumental in forming the Council on Foreign Relations (CFR). Are you beginning to see how all of these organizations are interconnected like the giant tentacles of an evil octopus?

Finally, in regard to the Bush Family, we've discussed in this article how the Bush Family fortune was mounted on the back of Nazi blood-money. Plus, in a prior article that I wrote (See chapter 11) we discovered that the Bush Family has also enjoyed business relations with the bin Laden family for the past thirty years, and both belonged to the Carlyle Group. Knowing this, what type of loyalties and decisions do you think George W. Bush will make - those that benefit everyday American citizens, or those made by his puppet-masters? If you ask me, I'd say we're in trouble.

CHAPTER FORTY-ONE

NOTES AND QUOTES: "THE ROCKEFELLER FILE" BY GARY ALLEN

NOTE: The data included in the following article pertains to the time the book was published by '76 Press in 1976. Some of the company names have changed and/or have been purchased by other companies.

Walter Cronkite - *CBS Reports*: "The Rockefellers are the epitome of the nation's permanent Establishment: governments change, economies fluctuate, foreign alliances shift -- the Rockefeller's prevail."

On September 29, 1916, the *New York Times* called John D. Rockefeller America's first billionaire.

The Rockefellers protect their money via Trusts and Foundations. Ever since 1913 when the Federal Income Tax was implemented, Congress allowed the wealthy elite to protect their money so it wouldn't be subjected to the same enslaving taxation that hinders the rest of us. By placing their money in Trusts and Foundations, these wealthy individuals give up "ownership" of their properties, but they ultimately retain control of it via positions on each foundation's Board of Directors. Thus, they don't have pink slips or titles because their assets are in trusts, yet they ultimately keep control while not having to pay income, probate, estate, or inheritance taxes. Pretty sneaky, huh!

When this book was written, the Rockefellers controlled at least 200 trusts/funds, but the number could well be in the thousands if one uncovered all the complex layers of their financial empire. Because of all these complexities, they virtually pay no taxes. In fact, in 1970 Nelson Rockefeller testified before a Judiciary Committee and stated that although his income was 33 million dollars the year before, he paid NO INCOME TAXES.

He then admitted that his actual income was 198 million -- *not 33 million.* But the particulars were the same -- no income taxes paid by one of the richest men in America.

The Rockefeller Estate in Pocantico Hills consists of over 7,500 acres and has 70 miles of private roads, 75 buildings, and underground bunkers with underground entranceways so the "help" can enter without being seen by the owners. It employs 500 persons full-time to maintain the grounds.

The Rockefellers own a significant portion of America's top 50 companies: IBM, Chase Manhattan, Mobil, Kodak, GE, Texas Instruments, and Exxon.

Their money is used to control the government, big business, energy, banking, the media, religion, and education.

John D. Rockefeller once said "competition is a sin." He deduced that the only efficient way to run anything was via a monopoly.

When John D. started his oil business in 1859 as a small fry, he used bribery, coercion, violence, spies in his competitor's workplace, and a variety of financial schemes to one-up the next guy. Within 30 years, by 1890, 90% of all American crude oil was refined by his Standard Oil Company.

John D. eventually controlled two of the most valuable commodities on earth, money and fuel -- thus giving him the ability to create financial or energy crises whenever it best suited his (or the Controllers) interests.

Here are some of the companies that are under the Rockefeller umbrella:

- Chase Manhattan -- not the largest bank in the world, but one of the most influential.
- The largest controlling block of stock in at least 21 major corporations, including United Air Lines, Northwest, Long Island Lighting, and Atlantic Richfield.
- Majority control in IBM, Mobil, Texaco, IT&T, Westinghouse, Boeing, International Paper, Sperry Rand, Xerox, and National Steel.
- Transportation companies under the Rockefeller corporate thumb: Penn Central, TWA, Eastern Airlines, United, Delta and Northwest.
- Other corporations where they have financial interest: AT&T, Motorola, Honeywell, General Foods, and Burlington Industries.

When someone owns a powerful financial institution, they can make loans to specific companies and governments, then call the shots for these entities and make them jump through hoops. If they don't toe the line, they don't get the money. This is the gist of high-finance in a nutshell, and one of the primary reasons why we still don't have gasoline-free cars in this country. No one's lending money (or enough of it) to the companies that are trying to find alternative-source automobiles.

The Rockefeller web envelops 37 of the top 100 industries, 9 of the top 20 transportation firms, 1 utility company, and 3 of the 4 largest insurance companies.

The *Washington Post* once described the Rockefellers in these terms: "The power of the family fortune is beyond measure."

Quote from the author: "Philanthropy is the essential element in the making of Rockefeller power. Philanthropy generates more power then wealth alone can provide."

In the early 1900's, John D. Rockefeller was the most hated man in America, his reputation worse than that of Scrooge. So, what did he do? He hired a public relations firm to re-make his image.

How so? Well, whenever 'ol John D. would walk around in public, he carried dimes and threw them to all the little street urchins (of course, only when camera's were there to catch the moment).

Here's the way foundations work: Once someone like the Rockefellers donate money to one of these entities (or *creates* a foundation themselves), they assume control of it and have this foundation spend money on *their* companies to bring them even more wealth!

It's great for them because it's all a big cycle of donating money (tax free), then waiting for this money to be incorporated back into their own companies to generate more profits. John D. called it "The Principle of Scientific Giving"!

The Rockefellers also supported the passing of a bill on graduated income tax in 1913 because they found ways to avoid it! While the rest of us keep supporting THEIR governments by paying taxes, we're also kept DOWN because we can never rise to their level. Why? The answer's easy -- we're playing on an uneven field.

A graduated income tax also keeps competitors at bay because they have to continue paying taxes (they haven't risen to the elite level yet), while the Rockefellers hide their money in trusts and foundations. Thus, their assets are non-taxable, then passed from generation to generation, perpetuating the family's king-of-the-hill status.

The Rockefellers then use groups like the CFR (Council on Foreign Relations) to carry out their governmental plans.

Fred Gates, who was in charge of the Rockefeller's General Education Board, said in *Occasional Paper No. 1*: "In our dreams we have limitless resources and the people yield themselves with perfect docility to our moulding hands."

In regard to higher education, the Carnegie and Rockefeller Foundations provided two-thirds of all endowment funding to colleges from 1900-1933. Who do you think controls these institutions of higher learning? They have become a quasi Ministry of Education, exerting a high degree of control over their curriculum and what is taught.

Author Gary Allen states: "I believe those who control education will, over a period of several generations, control a nation."

Allen goes on to say that, considering all the money the Rockefellers have given out over the past century, "we have been unable to find a single project in history of the Rockefeller Foundations which promotes free enterprise. Almost all of the Rockefeller grants have been used directly or indirectly to promote economic and social collectivism, i.e., socialism-fascism."

He continues: "The easiest way to control or eliminate competitors is not to best them in the marketplace, but to use the power of government to exclude them from the marketplace."

And how does one do that? By controlling the government!

John Franklin Campbell once wrote in *New York Magazine*, "Practically every lawyer, banker, professor, general, journalist, and bureaucrat who has had any influence in the foreign policy of the last six presidents -- from Franklin Roosevelt to Richard Nixon -- has spent some time in the Harold Pratt House (home of the CFR)."

George Wallace (former Presidential candidate) said: "There isn't a dime's worth of difference between the Democratic and Republican parties."

Admiral Chester Ward, U. S. Navy; described the goal of the CFR as the submergence of U. S. sovereignty and national independence into an all-powerful one-world government.

James Warburg (February 17, 1950), CFR Member, testifying before the Senate Foreign Relations Committee, said: "We shall have world government whether or not you like it -- by conquest or consent."

The Trilateral Commission, in the *Triangle Papers* released between October 1973 and December 1974, said their four major goals were:

1) Renovation of the world's monetary system. (Nearly the entire European continent just switched their currency to the EU in January, 2002.)

2) Loot the United States of their resources for radicalization of the "have-not" nations.

3) Step-up trade with communist countries. (In the 1990s, both NAFTA and GATT were passed by the United States Congress.)

4) Create energy crises for greater international control. (Think back to the gasoline and fuel oil disasters last year when gasoline prices rose to nearly $2.00 a gallon.)

<u>Dr. Medford Evans</u>: "Energy makes the world go 'round. Who controls what makes the world go 'round controls the world."

<u>Thomas Jefferson</u>: "Since acts of tyranny may be ascribed to the accidental opinion of a day, but a series of oppressions, begun at a distinguished period, unalterable through every change of ministers, too plainly prove a deliberate, systematic plan of reducing us to slavery."

When John D. Rockefeller had almost total control of the oil industry in the early 1900s, his favorite way to topple a competitor was from the inside. He'd plant spies (bugs) in their offices or bribe certain employees to undermine the firm's operations.

The Rockefellers' influence in Presidential politics began in 1894 with the election of William McKinley, but they didn't really start determining policy until FDR was elected in the 1930s. That's when they got their hands filthy stinking dirty.

The New Deal wasn't implemented to help business and the stock market recover from the effects of the Great Depression, but to drag it out for a few more years. The reason? They wanted to keep the stock market on a downswing so they could buy more shares at lower prices.

CHAPTER FORTY-TWO

A REVIEW OF "THE REPORT FROM IRON MOUNTAIN ON THE POSSIBILITY AND DESIRABILITY OF PEACE"

TELEVISION COMMERCIAL: Are you sick of war? Tired of all the blood and carnage and killing and dead bodies? Well then, why not try the new mind-control implant pacifier that is Government approved and State sanctioned? Hurry up and get yours today – no more wars and no more fighting – just a life filled with mind-numbing subservience and unquestioning dependence. Don't be the last person on your block to get implanted. It's "1984" and "Brave New World" all wrapped up in one!

In 1961, a committee called The Special Study Group was assembled by high-ranking officials of the Kennedy Administration (including Robert McNamara, Dean Rusk, and McGeorge Bundy). This 15-member group, comprised of academicians, scientists, a sociologist, historian, lawyer, businessman, a member of the military, psychologists and an economist, first met in August of 1963 and completed a 2 ½ year study to determine the problems that would confront the United States if permanent peace ever became a reality.

War in the context of population control was already the subject of two studies by this point – the Gather Report in 1957, and Hubert Humphrey's ambitious report in 1962. But neither of these would have as far-reaching an impact as the one written in March, 1966 at Iron Mountain. Located near Hudson, New York, Iron Mountain was an underground nuclear facility for a number of influential American companies, including Manufacturers Hanover, Shell and Standard Oil (the famous Rockefeller-owned entity).

The Special Study Group primarily wanted to answer two questions: 1) What is the function of war in society, and 2) Is war necessary in terms of social stability? The answer they arrived at was that *lasting peace is not a benefit to society!*

If this verdict fills you with shock or surprise, the following quote from their report may fill you with even more horror: "War fills certain functions essential to the stability of our society; until other ways of filling them are developed, the war system must be maintained and improved in effectiveness."

This group also arrived at a few other startling conclusions. For example, rapid advances in medicine are a hindrance (due to increased longevity), poverty is both necessary and desirable, and our military forces are a form of social welfare (like Social Security or Medicaid).

Now that you've been "enlightened" as to what helps society and what is detrimental to it, your next question should be: what was the goal of this report? The answer, in simplest terms, is: the Special Study Group wanted to arrive at a long-range plan in which they could establish an "optimal" number of lives that could be "forfeited" each year to the War Machine.

Now that it is becoming clearer that war is an entity, almost a living organism, we need to look at its impact on society as a whole. To do so, we should realize that war has been the predominant factor in nearly every culture since the beginning of time.

War is the common thread that has governed nearly every society in history, even our own today. We need to understand, however, that war entails much more than soldiers killed on a battlefield or bombs being dropped on a village. It affects us in many other ways, such as bomb shelters and children hiding under their school desks in the 1950s; flower children, hippies and agitators battling the police in Chicago, 1968; or the Berlin Wall's destruction changing the face of Europe a decade ago. Ramifications from the Civil War in the 1860s even included brother-fighting-brother on American soil.

Wars do not take place by accident. They don't just "happen." Rather, the people who run the world -- the Controllers, industrialists and international bankers -- are the ones who determine all the variables that revolve around war. In this regard we need to look at war as something that isn't caused by a conflict of interest between two opposing factions (this is only a symptom that can be manipulated by the money-interests) but as a means to further the agenda of those in Control.

In this sense, the nations and players (We the People!) are merely pawns on a chessboard that the Controllers can move around to further their own self interests.

War isn't a random act that simply "breaks out" because of some sorry excuse-for-a-reason that we read about in the newspaper. No, there is most certainly a logical plan behind every war, and our reaction or philosophy toward this method of "global enterprise" is our most telling indicator as a people.

Do we really want to give the Controllers the authority over life and death? These people are the height of arrogance and ruthlessness; and worse, they don't give a damn about our personal well-being. But when it comes to marching our teenagers off to war to pad their pockets or further their self-interests, they don't seem to have a problem. From their perspective, individual lives cannot be a consideration when they decide to kill. And they'll have us believe anything to get the masses supporting them. We'll slaughter each other over freedom, territory, revenge, religion or a supposed future threat by some country that we've never even visited.

But guess what? It's all a ruse! All of the above concepts, and countless others, are nothing but a smoke screen (propaganda) that allows them to place more value on the State (implying their vested interests) than on a citizen's life.

If we view this phenomenon in terms of Hegelian Dialectics, it will become much clearer. To begin this analogy, we'll take a thesis: a group of people who think that everyone should wear blue clothes and sing songs about flowers. Another group, the antithesis, thinks everyone should wear orange clothes and sing songs about bumblebees.

As the years go by, antagonism builds between these factions, but nothing ever gets out of hand. Then someone says, "Hmmm, if we can create a tremendous problem between these two groups and then lend money to each side so they can fight each other, we'll be able to make a hefty profit in the process. In addition, when the war is over, both sides will be completely depleted and broke, so we'll lend them more money to rebuild -- but only on the condition that we get to make a few POLICY decisions for them."

So, when all is said and done, one force (thesis) was brought into conflict with another force (antithesis), resulting in a third force (synthesis). And what was the end result? Now everyone in these two groups wears purple polka dot clothes and sings songs about alligators (all the while paying huge interest payments to the Controllers while forfeiting their sovereignty and freedom). Now bring Communism, Capitalism, religion, oil wells, and so forth into the equation.

Do you see how war works? War is the ultimate conflict pitting one "ideology" against another, with the victors (the Controllers, not the citizenry) in the driver's seat to promote their own agenda.

With this analysis in mind, one needs to ask, "How do the Controllers keep getting away with it?"

Here are a few of the insights that *The Special Iron Mountain Study Group* arrived at. First of all, war is by far the most electrifying event that will ever befall a nation. Even a minor skirmish like the Gulf War (where the United States was guaranteed victory) had the people clamoring with excitement. When you think about it, what else could bring all of us together like a good enemy? It's just "professional wrestling," folks. The Controllers know that people need something to hate (human beings, organizations, or concepts). So, what do they do? They give us enemies (either real or created) – something or someone to kill.

Look around at people going crazy with activity. There's always more to do and we never seem to catch up because there are never enough hours in the day. We need more money, more time, more rest, more energy ... Do you know what this cycle of MORE MORE MORE is called? It's THE MACHINE! The Controllers need the Machine to keep us all so consumed by the mundane activities of daily life, we can't just stop, catch our breath and look around and say, "Hey, wait a minute, the Machine has made us nothing more than rats running around in a laboratory maze!"

And when we do have some down time, we need to be "involved" in things like who's in first place in the National League, who scored the most touchdowns, how can I lose weight to look like the movie stars on magazine covers, what's happening on the daily soap opera, and so forth. It's the Machine – the never-ending cycle of nonsense that overloads our brains, consumes our lives and makes things so overwhelming, there's no time to notice the big picture.

So, the Controllers exert a tremendous amount of effort into not only keeping the Machine running, but also in not letting us peek behind their veil to see how they're manipulating this Machine (like the Wizard of Oz). If, however, life (or the Machine) becomes too routine and blasé, what can they do? They can kick-start the System (our economy) and also give us all a jolt of adrenaline by starting a war! All of a sudden, our apathy has been washed away and everyone is charged up again ... kind of like an old battery that slowly dies in your flashlight. All ya gotta do is hook that baby up to the battery charger (start a war), and welluh! The citizenry is once again filled with fervor and life.

At least for the time being, all our attention is focused on what makes us so great over everyone else (our blue clothes and flower songs are much better than yellow clothes, etc.). Once again we're all brought together ... at least until the war is over and the Controllers can start their Hegelian Dialectic all over again (this time on us).

302

(Remember, everything in life can be explained via this simple formula – thesis – antithesis – synthesis).

The Controllers know that without the existence and threat of war, they'd lose their ability to govern us. Why? Because a government's primary role is that of protector. They need to "watch over us" against an array of threats (whether they're real or imaginary).

If the Controllers are unable to maintain the credibility of this threat ... i.e., keep war on the front burners of people's minds ... then they'll eventually lose their stranglehold on us.

The Controllers don't want us to be like coyotes in the desert – ever alert, ever vigilant and ever aware. Instead, their intent is to pacify and stabilize us. Man can't be sovereign, independent, and ultimately free. No – we need to be dependent on them – passive – sacrificing our own self-sufficiency and personal responsibility to an entity whose sole existence is the necessity of government.

We The People have to be dependent, and also fearful. Without this threat of violent retaliation, how could entities such as a police force, the IRS, or our Court System ever survive? We need to cower beneath our Controllers – and war is the ultimate fear tactic. In fact, this analogy is so vitally important to the Controllers, the way they became victorious in war becomes a symbol of how they will eventually control their citizenry.

If you don't believe me, look at Joseph Stalin's tactics before, during, and after World War II, and the resulting Cold War Russia.

War not only lays the basis for a nation's laws; it becomes a symbol of what can happen to people if they get on the "wrong side" of the power base.

To keep this vicious cycle in existence, the Controllers realized long ago that the War Machine is dependent upon another machine – the propaganda machine. To keep the people "true" to their control, they need a "cause" or a reason for their allegiance. How do they accomplish that? By constantly keeping an enemy in front of the populace.

These enemies can take a variety of forms, but the largest and worst must be "formidable," at least in appearance, so that its threat to people seems real. In this regard, the more complex a society is, the more imposing the enemy has to be.

A good example would be two warring tribes in Africa attacking each other with spears, versus our post-Cold War situation with the UN and NATO approved treaties, anti-ballistic missiles, Star Wars, nuclear weapons, and so forth. War has become a complicated business.

In this sense, the "reality" of a threat to any nation determines how much energy is expended on preparing to do battle with this enemy, and also how much money is funneled into this pursuit.

Thus, even though war is the epitome of chaos, it ultimately becomes the model for a nation's stability. Without this threat, the concept of government would not be possible. Why? Because a citizenry's acceptance of political authority is based upon fear of the resulting punishments -- violence, imprisonment, retribution, etc.

So, as you can see, the main ingredient in this formula is an enemy (real or imagined) that instills enough fear in the people so they allow themselves to be subjugated. Without this threat, the reality of government would slowly disappear.

Once people accept the notion of a government that influences and "guides" their lives, the other factor that must be considered in this equation is money. When the Iron Mountain Report was written in the mid-1960s, the War Machine accounted for ten percent of the world's total economic output. If one considers what a truly staggering figure this is (literally tens of billions of dollars), they'd realize what an integral part of our lives war has become.

Even scarier is the concept of eliminating the War Machine. To do so would dramatically undermine the economic base of nearly every country on earth. I'm not saying I support this God-awful development, but I am pointing out a very real dilemma. If we did away with the War Machine, the world would be cast into such dire financial straits, it would make the Great Depression look like child's play.

This is the corner we've backed ourselves into, folks. The War Machine – death, destruction, and armed preparations – is the basis of our economy. Check out the highest paying jobs and you'll find them in the aerospace industry and at the companies that do contract work for the military. If we pulled the rug out from beneath their feet, our nation would almost instantly go into a nosedive.

So, whenever the economy seems a little sluggish and things are dragging along, what eventually happens? People lose their jobs. They get disgruntled and quickly turn their attention to the "cause" – government. Realizing human nature, what is the first thing the Controllers do to give the economy a boost? Start a war and revitalize not only the citizen's pocketbooks, but also their spirits.

In this context, there is no other force that even remotely comes close to giving a jolt to employment, output, and consumption as the onset of war. And if the war is large enough, we can get the economy buzzing.

Here's the way our System operates. It's all based upon CONSUMPTION. To keep the Machine rolling, people need to consume. In other words, Capitalism = Consumption. And to consume, we need to produce. If people aren't producing (as good little worker bees), they won't be able to consume. Without consumption, the Machine slows down; people get distracted and unsettled; then eventually turn their attention to the source of Control. In other words, idle hands lead to unsettled minds, and the last thing the Controllers want us to do is think about anything other than keeping the Machine on track.

Can you see how they keep us in line? We need to keep busy, we need to be distracted (with spin-doctored news stories, sports, TV, drama, etc.), and we need to be afraid of retaliation if we step out of line.

The System is set up quite nicely, don't you think? We keep the Machine rolling so we can pay our taxes, bills, rent and mortgage while the Controllers profit through interest payments, taxation, and ownership. And if anyone rocks the boat, the law's heavy hand will topple them.

Now that we've established an economic basis for war, we also need to realize that this entity operates outside the normal parameters of supply and demand. What do I mean? In our daily lives, people have "demands" for certain items – food, clothes, toilet paper, and so forth. Someone then determines what these needs are and supplies a product or service to fill that demand. This give-and-take is the basis for our economic system.

When left to its own devices, this relationship lays the foundation for the entire capitalist system.

But even though war is a tremendous economic shot in the arm, essentially it creates an "artificial demand." How so? Well, when was the last time you went to the store and said, "Hmm, today I need toilet paper, bologna, milk, and ... oh yeah, I'll buy some war products?"

Consumers don't need or demand war, nor can they purchase it.

In this light, war is seen as "wasteful" and ultimately unproductive to the overall good of society in terms of capitalism. Rather than filling the people's needs, all of the resources injected into the War Machine are geared toward one goal – destruction. In this regard, we've transcended the traditional rules of supply and demand. Instead of letting the free-market decide what is produced and consumed, all decisions are now subject to central control.

So, the government supersedes the backbone of free enterprise by becoming the primary decision-maker instead of allowing it to rest in the hands of the free-market forces.

Before anyone accuses me of being short-sighted, I must admit that without war, many of our technological advances would not have been introduced (at least not until much later). Advancements in the modern-day assembly line were a direct result of firearms being mass-produced during the Civil War. The production of warships in World War I lead to advancements in architecture. We must also consider how far we've come with medicine, electronics, and everyday products such as the lawnmower (which arose out of military drawings made by Leonardo da Vinci).

Without these technological advances and the existence of a long-established War Machine, it's safe to say that the development of our current global super-states would not have been possible. Naturally, world powers have existed for millennia, but none compare to what is in existence today – a super-state inching closer toward a one-world government.

In all likelihood, this phenomenon would not be possible without the industrial and technological advances that our warring nature developed. Thus, in a twisted, ironic sense, war, the height of destruction, became historically progressive; and our production would not have been possible without these conflicts.

As strange as it sounds, war, which ultimately rips a society apart, also stabilizes it economically. The trade-off, though, is that with each technological step forward, society surrenders more of its sovereignty and freedom into the hands of a growing political presence that has now become monstrous in its proportions.

Before you jump to conclusions and say, "Hey, wait a minute, this whole War Machine sounds pretty good ... at least it keeps people in line," let's look at the reality of how the Controllers view war in social terms.

First, poverty must be perpetuated in order to meet certain ends. Not only are the lowest social classes maintained to keep picking the cotton, cleaning toilets and driving the taxi's, but they're also not eliminated because of one important factor – who else would we ship off to war? Before you dismiss this argument, look at it in the context of the Vietnam War. This "conflict" epitomized the class system in this country, and the way we distinguish between the haves and the have-nots.

If you could pull some strings and defer (like Bill Clinton and so many others did), then you could remain safe. But if you weren't lucky enough to have connections, you were shipped off to the jungles of Viet Nam to get your mind messed-up or your brains blown out. So, as you can see, there is an incentive to keep the class system alive and well in this country.

You would think that since the lower classes greatly outnumber the elite, somewhere along the line they would rebel and try to overthrow their Controllers. But ya see; war (and its ever present threat) is what maintains this system. If the Controllers can perpetuate and make credible a *threat* from outside that only *they* can save us from, then a "protective" type relationship has been established. The scenario is similar to the tactics used by organized religion. Religious leaders tell their congregation that the only way to salvation is through the Church. If they don't follow the Church's dogma, they'll be overtaken by evil.

It's the same with government. By creating an external threat, they can step in and say the only way to stay alive (and be safe) is through *them*. They're the authority figure that has been established to look out for our best interests.

In reality, though, the threat of war also lays the groundwork for what happens if the populace steps out of line. Without these threats, both internal and external, the Controllers would never be able to maintain their positions of power.

Are you beginning to see the psychology of control? Doesn't it feel like you're being subtly or covertly manipulated at every turn? War not only perpetuates class distinctions, but also generational ones too.

What do I mean? If we reverted to a time when "survival of the species" was determined by physical prowess, then the elderly would undoubtedly be wiped-away by the young. It only seems natural that a twenty-year old kid would "cast aside" an eighty-year old man if it meant that his status or standard of living was elevated. But look at the Viet Nam war. Who was shipped off to the jungles? Twenty-year old kids. And who sent them? Old men making decisions in well-protected institutions. Thus, if the young get too out of control for the Old Guard (like they were starting to do in the late 50s with the Beat Generation, James Dean, and rock n' roll with Elvis Presley, Jerry Lee Lewis, Chuck Berry, Buddy Holly and Little Richard), what is one alternative? Start a war and decrease their numbers and influence. That way, they can still maintain CONTROL and retain their positions of power. Luckily, the kids in the 1960s rebelled and set a precedent, ultimately saying "we're not going to take your nonsense any longer." And, except for minor "skirmishes" like the Gulf War, we have yet to enter another major conflict.

Since I've mentioned rebellion, another purpose the War Machine has historically served is to maintain control by "herding" social misfits into the military. Although this technique isn't as prevalent today, if you've ever watched movies or TV from the 50s and 60s, you'll notice that whenever a "JD" (Juvenile Delinquent) gets out of line, the first threat is to send them to juvenile hall or the Army. Thus, if someone was labeled a social misfit, unfit to become part of the Machine, or was a "danger" to the status quo, all they had to do was ship them off to the Army to "get their head straightened out." Today, since we've eliminated the mandatory draft, all we do is send these same people to prison.

So, now we need to get down to the nitty-gritty of this subject. Some people say that war is necessary for the continuation of our species because it allows the strong to survive while eliminating the weak (natural selection). And, if you want to know the truth, I agree with that assertion up to a certain point. Why? Because one of the basic credos of economic theory is that with mankind as a whole, we have unlimited wants, while we're surrounded by limited supplies. Look at concepts such as real estate, gold, food, and consumer products. If left to his own devices, man would consume endlessly. The problem arises when we're confronted with the variable of limited supply.

In this context, we need to examine man in a historical sense before the advent of supermarkets and department stores. To feed, clothe and shelter one's family, man needed to enter the wild and fend for himself. If, due to a number of factors (droughts, etc.) the crops or wildlife were in especially low abundance, the tribe needed to find other ways to survive. Or, what if all their needs were being met, but in another locale a different tribe's crops and livestock were wiped out by disease, flooding, pestilence, etc.? What would this clan do to survive? Invade the other tribe and attempt to steal their food, women, tools and animals?

After this skirmish ran its course, the invaded tribe would naturally harbor animosity toward their invaders, and at some point in the future they'd retaliate. The cycle will endure and the end result would be a war society. The only positive factor, if it can be called such, is that "survival of the species" will become the established order. In other words, the strong will live, while the weak will perish.

Over time, mankind will evolve according to natural selection; the genes of the strong will be passed on, while those of the weak will be eliminated. Until that time when man is able to live in peace instead of killing each other like rats, this is the reality of our existence.

If we adhere to the above synopsis, we would conclude that, due to war, man's evolution is based on natural selection and survival of the fittest. But I'm here to say that this analogy is only correct up to a certain point; then it stops being applicable. In other words, war itself, like a living organism, has evolved to the point where our species will still survive as it kills itself off; but it will no longer evolve. Why? Contrary to the past when practically the entire tribe or society was engaged in war (for pure survival reasons), the physically stronger endured while the "inferior" were eliminated.

If you look at war in the context of history, you discover that those who led mankind in war were the same persons who became its leaders in times of peace. Or, a pre-existing ruler led his people into battle by leading the charge. Thus, even if a leader weren't physically large (e.g., Napoleon) he still had to have the courage and guts to lead his troops.

But as war "evolved" in recent times, a strange turn of events took place. Look at it this way. Did John D. Rockefeller, J. P. Morgan, or a billionaire banker sitting in a New York City skyscraper go to World War I, World War II, the Korean War, or Viet Nam? Of course not. They sent into battle those who were young and strong - a farm boy from South Dakota or a ghetto kid from Watts were the ones who were drafted. In this sense, those who are the physically strongest are also the same ones who are being eliminated.

Now can you see why humans are no longer on the cusp of the evolutionary scale? In the past, war was a means for the strongest to survive because they were the ones who led their people into war and endured. But today, war demands that the most physically able perish, while those who are the craftiest, deceitful and most evil perpetuate themselves through a multitude of control mechanisms. So -- yes, we will keep surviving, but at the moment, war by no means is allowing us to evolve. All it is doing is strengthening the grip those in power have over us.

Considering everything I've written up until this point, we need to ask ourselves one last question. How do the Controllers, after concluding that war is essential to the stability of society, justify its perpetuation in regard to a one-world government that will supposedly operate without borders or war? The answer will shock you, but there is only one alternative to war, and that is enslavement.

SLAVERY, one may gasp! We could never return to those times. I hate to break the news to you, folks, but we're already well on our way to a form of technological mind-control slavery via the use of implants.

Regrettably, the Controllers have concluded that for the New World Order to become a reality, there are no other alternatives to war but slavery. Y'see, war is a form of eugenics where certain "types" or "classes" of people are perpetually eliminated. But war is so costly, bloody, and disorderly that it ends up being very threatening to the powers-that-be.

War demands a huge sacrifice from people, and at some point they might rebel and turn on those who are commanding them to kill (ever hear of "friendly fire"?). So, what can they do? They find a much neater, simpler and more efficient way to keep people in line. And what is that? Implant technology!

Before anyone jumps to conclusions and yells, "People will never stand for it! They'll never allow themselves to be implanted. There's no way we could be forced into doing that," they'd better think again.

What about our tax situation? A homeowner in this day and age is forking over nearly 50% of their take home pay in some form of taxation. Who's holding a gun to our heads and forcing us to do it? No one, but we're still doing it. What makes an implant any different, especially in light of the way fear tactics can be utilized?

What do I mean? Well, not everyone in society will NEED an implant. What'll happen is this: One day, a bunch of "bad seeds" will be herded-up and collectively implanted, then strolled before the American public on TV. Everyone will see these brain-dead automatons that look like Jack Nicholson at the end of *Cuckoo's Nest* and gasp in horror. Then a caption will appear on the screen that says, "If you don't stay in line, you could be next."

Just imagine how ideal this situation would be for the Controllers. Not only will all the law-abiding citizens be mortified into toeing the line, but those who don't will be "numbed" into submission and complacency.

Think of it -- no more street violence, no more crime, no more prisons, and everyone does their job. Man, the Controllers sure do have it all figured out, huh? The people will be kept under control and they won't have to worry anymore about overpopulation.

Wait a second, you're probably thinking. How are the Controllers going to keep our birth rates down? The solution is simple – through eugenic management. In other words, only those who are deemed "privileged enough" will be able to reproduce, and only then through artificial insemination. Y'see, with the genome now mapped-out, the Controllers will know exactly what type of genes are needed to make a good little (human) worker bee.

And what happens if people don't follow these rules? You implant them! Or the Controllers can always dangle the threat of an "economic downturn." If you control the money, you control the means of production and capital. Without food for their families, people will resort to almost anything – even implants. Or, what if you're not even able to buy food without an implant to run over the scanner? What would you do then? Your kids are screaming for food and milk and you can't buy anything for them because the cash register won't let you check out without an implant it can scan. You say to hell with it and leave in a huff, but your kids keep screaming night and day, so you return to the store to buy some food and milk. Again the cash register wants to scan your implant.

Without it, you can't buy anything. Your kids keep screaming. They're starving. What other alternative is there? How many of us will eventually get the implant?

If you think this scenario is hogwash, consider for a moment how widely fear is used on a daily basis to condition us. Did Russia ever invade our country? No, but we lived in fear of them (the Cold War) for four decades. Or, how many people do you know who have ever been imprisoned by the IRS for not paying their taxes? Probably none, but we keep paying those damn taxes out of fear.

Now do you know what I'm trying to say? This analogy could go on indefinitely.

So, there you have it. Mind control implants as an alternative to war – they're safe, orderly, and efficient – a sophisticated form of slavery. All our behavior patterns can be controlled, and society can live in peace like a great big happy family under the watchful eye of the New World Order. Welcome to the future!

CHAPTER FORTY-THREE

JONESTOWN: MASS SUICIDE, OR MASSACRE?

Nine hundred and thirteen dead bodies lying in rows in the middle of a Guyanese jungle as helicopter cameramen transmit the ghastly images to an American TV audience. Nine hundred and thirteen bodies, mostly black, many of them children, dead from drinking poisoned Kool-Aid. Nine hundred and thirteen human beings that were so devoted to a fanatical religious cult leader, they willingly committed suicide for him. On November 18, 1978 - 913 casualties catapulted Jim Jones into the same league as Charles Manson, Jeffrey Dahmer, and Ted Bundy.

This is the cover story that was relayed by mainstream media. But did you know that when this story was first reported, the headline ran as follows:

"Cult deaths in South American jungle: 400 die in mass suicide, 700 flee into jungle."

A week later, the body count had mysteriously jumped to 913 when 505 new bodies were "discovered." When asked about these discrepancies, "official sources" first said that it came about because the Guyanese government couldn't count correctly. They realized how ridiculous that excuse sounded, so they recanted and came up with a new explanation. The miscount resulted from bodies being stacked atop other bodies. But when you think about it, 408 bodies were initially found, then 505 more a week later. Does that mean that 408 bodies can completely cover 505 bodies? Also when researchers looked into this matter and examined 150 aerial and close-up photos, they noticed that not one body was piled atop another.

To reiterate this point, the next time you see photos of the death scene at Jonestown, you'll see that all of the bodies are aligned in neat rows, face down, with few exceptions. The most striking, unreported aspect of this situation was that nearly 90% of the deceased had apparent syringe marks on their bodies, while others had bullet wounds or evidence of strangulation.

Other peculiarities were the signs of "drag marks" in the earth near the victims, as if they had been dragged to their final resting spot; then laid in rows. Another oddity concerning the death scene was that Jim Jones' hand gun, which he supposedly used to kill himself after all the others had died, was found lying about 70 yards away from his body. Also, when the bodies were examined, it seems that none of the corpses exhibited the telling signs of cyanide poisoning (called *cyanide rictus*) that is common to this type of death.

If the members of Jim Jones cult didn't commit mass suicide as was reported, what was behind this atrocity? Without beating around the bush, Jonestown was part of a thirty-year MK-ULTRA program that was run by military intelligence and the CIA.

The U. S. Embassy at Georgetown, Guyana essentially had every position filled with CIA operatives. (If you researched this claim, you wouldn't find it very surprising, considering the nature of that spy operation.) Also, many of the members in the upper echelon of the Jonestown hierarchy had shadowy family histories, including associations with Navy Intelligence, warfare research, Navy missile development, and financial dealings with I. G. Farben (the infamous Nazi conglomerate).

Researchers who have investigated this phenomenon have even gone so far as to say that Jonestown wasn't only associated with the CIA, it WAS the CIA! Once you get past the smoke screens and secrecy, it appears that spooks were lurking behind every corner, their dirty little hands pulling the strings of all the bit players. Here is a list of the drugs that were recovered at Jonestown, all of which are MK-ULTRA mainstays:

- 11,000 doses of thorazine (to induce trances)
- sodium pentathol (truth serum)
- chloral hydrate (a hypnotic)
- demerol (depressant)
- thallium (to fog mental activity)

It was also estimated that between 26 million to 2 billion dollars in assets were recovered from a variety of Jonestown bank accounts, properties, and investments. How did the Reverend accumulate so much wealth?

It surely wasn't from cashing little old lady's Social Security checks at the beginning of each month. Hell no.

In addition to being a secret mind-control/genocide experiment, Jonestown was also a cover for illegal drug smuggling and gun running. Folks; Jonestown wasn't a quaint little refuge that a few hundred religious-minded people ran away to. It was a full-fledged mind-control concentration camp that had all the earmarks of a CIA experiment gone awry.

Instead of studying their Bibles, praying, and living in utopia, these people were the subjects of psychological testing, isolation techniques, drug use, brainwashing, torture, and mind games. Why do you think none of the corpses had autopsies performed on them by a qualified physician? One of the reasons is that they would have discovered all the drugs that were being funneled into these people.

This argument is reinforced when you consider that chief medical examiner Dr. Mootoo testified before a Guyanese grand jury and said he felt that all but three of the people who perished at Jonestown were murdered and only two had committed suicide. If this is the case, why didn't the Guyanese government blow the whistle on the CIA? The answer is simple. They covered it up because certain Guyanese officials received over 2 ½ million dollars that had been lifted from the camp. That kind of money silences a lot of tongues.

If Jonestown was not, in fact, the culmination of a mass suicide effort, then how did all these people die? The first clue can be found in this tidbit of information. In the fall of 1978, two forces were performing "training exercises" in the Guyanese jungles. The first was the British Black Watch Troops and the second was the American Green Berets. Both of these groups are trained in the art of commando-type covert killing.

Eyewitnesses at the airstrip where Congressman Leo Ryan flew into and tried to depart saw zombie-like men with guns who emerged from a tractor-trailer and started shooting at Congressman Ryan and the three journalists traveling with him.

These assassins also delivered the final death blows to those who were already wounded and lying on the runway. Could it be that these hired mercenaries were the same ones who injected and killed the first 408 Jonestown members, then rounded up and executed the 505 others that escaped into the jungle? It seems plausible; especially when Congressman Jones and his journalist counterparts had traveled to Guyana with the intention of exposing the Jonestown mind-control secrets.

In 1973, the CIA was hauled in front of Congress and promised that the horrors of their MK-ULTRA program would be immediately stopped. Of course, that never happened. The CIA simply altered the nature of their experimentation and focused on a different batch of victims. When Congressman Leo Ryan and three journalists visited Guyana, what did they find? A total freak show – drugs, religious insanity, a fanatical guru, mind control, manipulation, and quasi-slavery. They realized that once these people returned to the States and reported their findings, heads would roll as far as the CIA was concerned.

So, there was only one alternative – send in a crew of zombie killers and wipe out the whole bunch of them. And that's what they did. Nine hundred and thirteen murders – a jolt of horror to the public consciousness as they turned on their TV's and saw this atrocity – and in the end, business as usual for the CIA.

Joseph Holsinger, aide to Congressman Leo Ryan, called Jonestown a "mind-control experiment." Their visit to Guyana was a peek behind the curtain of what was really going on in the jungles of South America. It exposed the truth about the CIA's continued mind control activities, and ultimately led to the demise of over 900 innocent people.

Joyce Shaw, who was a former member of the Jonestown cult, dismissed the mass suicide story; instead calling the aftermath of what happened in Guyana "some kind of horrible government experiment, or some sort of sick racist thing ... a plan like the Germans to exterminate blacks."

CHAPTER FORTY-FOUR

NOTES AND QUOTES: THE OKLAHOMA CITY

BOMBING

"People who shut their eyes to reality simply invite their own destruction."

-- James Baldwin

<u>The Oklahoma City Bombing</u>, compiled by: Al Hiddel and Joan D'Arc, *Paranoia Magazine*, Summer, 1995: "CNN and the New York Times both reported the statement of an Army friend of bombing suspect Timothy McVeigh, who says that McVeigh told him that he had some sort of microchip device implanted in his backside while serving in the Persian Gulf.

"According to seismogram reports from the University of Oklahoma Geological Department in Norman, OK, there were two surface waves on the morning of April 19 -- one at 9:02:13, then one at 9:02:23 -- ten seconds later. When asked what this meant, Dr. Ken Luza said there were two detonations of a bomb, not one."

<u>John Stadtmiller</u>: "With the fertilizer bomb story, they [the government] keep increasing the size of the bomb. It started out being a thousand to fifteen hundred pounds. Now they're up to two tons. But, even still, that type of blasting device is a low-yield, low-frequency device not capable of doing the type of damage that was done to the Federal Building."

OKLAHOMA DAMAGE REPORT

Quotes from: Brigadier General Benton K. Partin (retired), *Paranoia Magazine*, Fall, 1995. "The damage pattern on the reinforced concrete superstructure could not possibly have been attained from a single truck bomb without supplementing demolition charges at some of the reinforced column bases.

"The pattern of damage would have been technically impossible without supplementing demolition charges at some of the reinforced column bases (a standard demolition technique).

"Blast through air is a very inefficient energy coupling mechanism against heavy reinforced concrete beams and columns.

"The entire building in Oklahoma City could have been collapsed with relatively small demolition charges against the base of columns and with even less explosives if linear cavity cutting charges had been used. I know of no way possible to reproduce the apparent building damage without well-placed demolition charges complementing the truck bomb damage."

Reassessing Oklahoma City: The Truck-Bomb Hoax, by Cletus Nelson, from *You Are Being Lied To,* The Disinformation Company, Ltd., edited by Russ Kick:
"Within 48 hours of this atrocious tragedy, the Justice Department had already broken the case."

ANFO - Ammonium Nitrate mixed with fuel oil to create a combustible "slurry" device. It would be physically impossible for an ANFO bomb to have destroyed the many steel-reinforced concrete columns that were situated far from the bomb site.

To reinforce the theory that explosives were used INSIDE the Federal Building, columns B-4 and B-5, which were in direct proximity to the blast, remained standing, while column A-7, which stood some 60 feet from the Ryder truck, was mysteriously demolished. The much closer columns are still standing, while the much larger column A-7 is down. These facts are sufficient reason to know that columns B-3 and A-7 had demolition charges on them.

ANFO (ammonium nitrate) is a poor choice for breaking reinforced concrete.

August 1996 FEMA study: "4,800 pounds of ANFO would have been virtually unable to have caused the so-called 30-foot crater in Oklahoma City."

Leaked Pentagon study that appeared in *Strategic Investment Newsletter*: "The destruction of the Federal Building last April was caused by five separate bombs."

318

1997 Air Force *Elgin Blast Effects Study*: "The final study could not ascribe the damage that occurred on April 19, 1995 to a single truck bomb containing 4,800 pounds of ANFO and instead suggested that other facts such as locally placed charges within the building itself may have been responsible."

Samuel Cohen (physicist who created the neutron bomb): "I believe that demolition charges in the building placed inside at certain key concrete columns did the primary damage to the Murrah Federal Building. It seems to me that evidence has gotten much stronger in favor of internal charges, while the ammonium nitrate bomb theory has fallen apart."

Justice Department Inspector General's Office (IGO) publicly questioned the shoddy practices and overt bias of the FBI. They also rebuked the FBI for engaging in "unsound science."

United States Government Technical Manual Number 9-1910 issued by both the Army and Air Force: "ANFO couldn't possibly produce a shock wave capable of mangling the building's concrete supports."

Dr. Randall Heather on Oklahoma City's Channel 4: "It's actually a great stroke of luck that we've got undefused bombs." (He was commenting on the undetonated charges that were located and defused once rescue efforts were underway *inside* the Murrah Building after it was crumbled.)

KFOR TV, 11:31 EST: "The FBI has confirmed there is another bomb in the Federal Building. It's in the East side of the building. We're not sure what floor, what level, but there is definitely danger of a second explosion."

Radio logs and transcripts of Oklahoma City police and fire department personnel show the discussion of removing additional explosives. "Reports of up to four bombs have surfaced."

Ian Williams Goddard - April 19, 1995: "As widely reported on CNN and TV stations across the nation, up to four primed bombs were found inside what remained of the Murrah Federal Building." (He suggested that highly powerful non-ANFO explosive devices were detected INSIDE the building.)

Attorney Charles Watts, who was in a Federal courtroom directly across the street from the Murrah Building, to *Media Bypass*: "We heard an explosion that knocked everyone to the floor." As the Vietnam veteran hit the deck, he alleged he "felt a second detonation more powerful than the first.

"If ANFO is physically incapable of causing the level of damage sustained by the Murrah Building, and if evidence shows that more than one explosion occurred on April 19, 1995, one must at least consider the existence of a more far-reaching conspiracy than the one sanctified by the mainstream media.

"The Federal Government possessed prior knowledge of an imminent terrorist strike on the Murrah Building."

Only TWO members of the ATF were in the building at the time of the explosion -- two of seventeen employed there!

A man was told by a BATF agent that "we were tipped off by our pagers not to come to work that day." His employer willingly confirmed this controversial claim.

ABC's *20/20* reporters provided substantial proof that local fire department officials were instructed by the FBI five days before the blast that "there were some people coming through town they should be on the lookout for."

The Executive Secretariat's Office at the Justice Department received a call 24 minutes BEFORE the explosion announcing that "the Oklahoma Federal Building had just been bombed."

Conclusion: These two events [The World Trade Center Bombing in 1993 and Oklahoma City in 1995] have provided the impetus for a State-sanctioned war against anti-government dissent that has produced a chilling effect on certain forms of political activism in this country ever since.

Result: Repressive anti-terrorism laws, Internet surveillance, and crackdowns on politically suspect dissent groups.

CHAPTER FORTY-FIVE

NOTES AND QUOTES: THE FREEMASONS, LUCIFER, THE NEW WORLD ORDER AND BEYOND

Cheque Mate: The Game of Princes – The New World Order: Dark Conspiracy or Benevolent Master Plan – How It Affects You and the Sovereignty of America, by: Jeffrey A. Baker (Whitaker House, 1993)

Hegel: "History teaches us that man learns nothing from history."

Franklin Delano Roosevelt: "In politics, nothing happens by accident. If it happens, you can bet it was planned that way."

Jeffrey Baker, author of this book: "Unfortunately for America, the Princes have well-insulated themselves from mass exposure to the public at large through control of the propaganda that we call news. I do not believe that Dan Rather, Tom Brokaw, or Peter Jennings are maniacal men with evil intent. They are, if you will, utopian dreamers so enamored with their own intelligence that they are blinded by their own "illumination," and professing themselves to be wise, they become utter fools."

Manley P. Hall (famed Masonic writer who says the legend of Atlantis is central to the teachings and philosophies of all secret societies): "Freemasonry is a shadow of the great Atlantean Mystery School which stood with all its splendor in the ancient City of the Golden Gates where now the turbulent Atlantic rolls in unbroken sweep."

Ignatius Donnelly (noted Atlantis authority, 1882 – in comparing the Great Flood from the Bible with the destruction of Atlantis – he says they are the same event): "The deluge plainly refers to the destruction of Atlantis and that it agrees in many particulars with the account given by Plato. The people destroyed were, in both instances, the ancient race that

321

had created civilization; they had formerly been in a happy and sinless condition; they had become great and wicked; they were destroyed for their sins – they were destroyed by water."

William Still (*New World Order*): "Information about Atlantis is still possessed by the highest initiates of the secret societies."

Manley P. Hall (*The Secret Destiny of America*) – Plato wrote about Atlantis in 400 B.C., and his information was taken from accounts given by Solon, who was the father of Greek democracy. Solon learned about Atlantis by studying with priests in the Temple of Isis in Sais, Egypt. In 595 B.C., these priests took Solon to an underground cave where the Nile flowed. There they got on a boat and sailed to an island where they saw artifacts that were left by the "Lost People." In the remains of this society, they found laws that were inscribed on columns that were intended to guide mankind. This information became the basis for the secret societies and mystery religions that ensured.

Albert Pike (accomplishments):

- Grand Commander of the Supreme Council of Freemasonry from 1859-1891
- Civil War General for the Confederacy
- Counterpart of the famous spiritualist Madame Blavatsky
- One of the original architects of the Ku Klux Klan

Albert Pike (in a letter to the 23 Supreme Councils of the World, July 14, 1889): "That which we must say to the crowd is we worship God, but it is the God that one adores without superstition. You may repeat it to the 32nd, 31st, and 30th degrees --- The Masonic religion should be, by all of us initiates of the high degrees, maintained in the purity of the Luciferian doctrine. If Lucifer were not God, would Adonay (Yahweh) and his priests calumniate him?"

Manley P. Hall (*The Lost Keys of Freemasonry*): "When the Mason learns the key to the warrior on the block is the proper application of the dynamo of the living power, he has learned the mystery of the Craft.

322

The seething energies of Lucifer are in his hands and before he may step onward and upward, he must prove his ability to properly apply energy."

1930s – more than three-quarters of Americans owned their land without owing money or rent on it.

1990s – less than 10% of Americans own their land, and those who do are burdened by incredibly high real estate taxes, school taxes, property taxes, etc.

A general theme indicating the way things are going in this country: History has now become multiculturalism – nationalism is being replaced by globalism. We aren't encouraged how to think, but what to think. There are no longer any absolutes or clearly-defined distinctions between right and wrong, only gray areas in-between. Bill Clinton was a perfect example of how "gray areas" took precedence above all else.

General Accounting Office – The average American now pays 48% of everything he or she earns in one form of taxation or another.

By stealing everything that Americans make through progressive taxation, the Controllers have eliminated the possibility that we will ever attain their wealth or status.

Lucifer – Eliphas Levi – Albert Pike and the Masonic Lodge: A Study of Freemasonry and Its Relationship to Occult and Satanism, by David Carrico (Emissary Publications, 1991):

William Schnoebelen (*Masonry beyond the Light*): "Set (Lucifer) is the acknowledged god of Masonry."

Edith Starr Miller (*The Occult Theocrasy*, 1933): "The real masonry of the Cabalistic degrees which is in touch with all secret societies, Masonic as well as non-Masonic, have been able to state that Luciferian Occultism controls Freemasonry."

Ralph Epperson (*The New World Order*): "The Masons know that they must conceal their horrible secret from the people. That secret is simply the fact that certain of their members worship Lucifer."

Eliphas Levi – [Cabalist, Magician, Aleister Crowley thought he was Levi reincarnated. (*The Book of Splendors*)]: "Satan is not the ruler of the realm of shadows, he is the agent of light behind a veil. He is of service to God, he performs God's work: God has not rejected him, for he holds him still in his hand ... what is the Devil, then, in the final analysis? The Devil is God working evil."

William Guy Carr (Commander of the Royal Canadian Navy, on Albert Pike): "While Pike was Sovereign Pontiff of Universal Freemasonry and Head of the Illuminati during the 1870's, he revised and modernized the ritual of the Black Mass celebrated to emphasize the Luciferian and Satanic victory achieved in the Garden of Eden and over Christ to end his mission on earth. Lucifer is worshipped as The Giver of the True Light; the fountain of All wisdom; and as the greatest of all Supernatural Beings."

Des Griffin (*Fourth Reich of the Rich*): "Albert Pike was an evil genius of the first magnitude. He was a man of many talents who invariably used his abilities to destructive ends. He was very literate; being able to both read and write in 16 ancient languages. He was an avowed worshipper of Satan by name who practiced necromancy and all forms of sorcery."

Albert Pike (*Morals and Dogma*): "Lucifer, the Light-bearer! Strange and mysterious name to give the spirit of Darkness! Lucifer, the Son of the Morning! It is he who bears the Light."

Albert Pike (in a speech to the 23 Supreme Councils, June 14, 1889): "The true and pure philosophical religion is the belief in Lucifer, the equal of Adonay (Yahweh); but Lucifer, God of Light and God of Good, is struggling for humanity against Adonay, the God of Darkness and Evil."

Albert Pike: (*Morals and Dogma* – on how members in the lower ranks of Masonry are deliberately lied to about the true meaning of the Masonic symbols) – "The Blue Degrees are but the outer court or portico of the Temple. Part of the symbols are displayed there to the initiate, but he is intentionally misled by false interpretations. It is not intended that he shall understand them, but it is intended that he shall imagine he understands them. Their true explanation is reserved for the Adepts, the Princes of Masonry."

New World Order: The Ancient Plan of Secret Societies, by William Still (Hunting House Publishers, 1990):

Copin Albancelli (1908 – showing the distinction between lower-level and upper-echelon Masons):

- Lower level Masonic motto: "To the glory of the Great Architect of the Universe."
- Upper level Masonic motto: "To the Glory and Love for Lucifer! Hatred! Hatred! Hatred! To God, accursed, accursed, accursed!"

Manley P. Hall said that the origin of all secret societies was on Atlantis. There, the Atlanteans formulated the "Great Plan" that would guide human events through the next millennia. One part of the blueprint concerned America's special destiny. "Time will reveal that the continent now known as America was actually discovered and, to a considerable degree, explored more than a thousand years before the beginning of the Christian era. The true story was in the keeping of the Mystery Schools, and passed from them to the Secret Societies of the medieval world."

Following the Illuminati 666 – The New Age Movement, by William Josiah Sutton (By: William Josiah Sutton (The Institute of Religious Knowledge, 1983):

Albert Pike [The only Confederate General with a statue on Federal property in Washington D. C. (*Morals and Dogma*)]: "Masonry is a search after Light. That search leads us directly back, as you see, to the Kabalah."

Fifty of the original fifty-six signers of the Declaration of Independence were Masons who were also involved in Rosicrucianism, astrology, secret societies, numerology, Tarot, and the Cabala.

Albert Pike was a Prince Adept of Freemasonry, and also a Palladist, which is a secret society that openly worships Lucifer.

Albert Pike: "Yes, Lucifer is God, and unfortunately, Adonay (Yahweh) is also God, for the eternal law is that there is no light without shade, no beauty without ugliness, no white without black. For the absolute can only exist as two Gods: darkness being necessary to light to serve as its foil as the pedestal is necessary to the statue, and the brake to the locomotive."

The Gods of the Lodge, by Reginald C. Haupt, Jr. (Victory Publishing Company, 1990)

Albert Pike (*Morals and Dogma*): "Every Masonic lodge is a temple of religion and its teachings are instructions in religion."

Gnosis – Superior wisdom; knowledge of mysteries and spiritual truths.

Fourth Reich of the Rich, by Des Griffin (Emissary Publications, 1976):

Original Writings of the Order of the Sect of the Illuminati: "The great strength of our Order lies in its concealment; never let it appear in any place in its own name, but always covered by another name, and another occupation."

Illuminati Requirements: – (a) always remain hidden behind the scenes, (b) never let your true identity and purpose be known, (c) keep the truth hidden from the people

International bankers: For years they made tons of money off every nation by financing each of them in wars against each other. There is only one winner in every war – the bankers!

Des Griffin: "The men who conceived the diabolical conspiracy as laid out in the Protocols were not atheists; they were members of the Illuminati, followers of the original 'light bearer,' Satan the Devil. They were worshippers of Satan. This is the plan of Satan.

Excerpts from "The Protocols of the Learned Elders of Zion" (translated by Victor Marsden):

- "The best results in governing are attained by violence and terrorization, not by academic discussion."
- "The ruler who is governed by the moral is not a skilled politician."
- "Great national qualities like frankness and honesty are vices in politics."
- "The political has nothing in common with the moral."
- "We must not stop at bribery, deceit, and treachery when they should serve towards the attainment of our end."

Henry Ford: "The only statement I care to make about the Protocols is that they fit in with what is going on. They are at least sixteen years old, and they have fitted the world situation up to this time. They fit it now."

Two phrases that frequently appear in the "Protocols":

- Goyim – "human cattle": a slur used to categorize all people of every race or creed who aren't members of the Illuminati.
- Agentur: all of the agents who are used by the Illuminati.

General Douglas MacArthur: "History fails to record a single precedent in which nations subject to moral decay have not passed into economic and political decline."

Boston Tea Party: all of the participating members were Freemasons who belonged to the St. Andrews Lodge in Boston.

Benjamin Franklin: Joined his first American Masonic Lodge in 1731 – Lodge of St. John in Philadelphia. He printed the first Masonic book ever released in America (*Constitutions*). He was also a Grand Master of the Nine Sisters Mason Lodge in Paris.

George Washington: also a high-ranking Mason.

Des Griffin: "In order to establish how deeply the secret societies have penetrated politics, it is necessary to understand how the history of the twentieth century has been molded by a hidden power group. This group is not necessarily aligned to either the left or right wings of the conventional political movements which have taken the public role in shaping world events in the years since the end of World War I. It operates within both capitalism and communism and has as its ultimate goal a politico-spiritual vision which transcends both these materialistic systems which are used to control the masses."

The World's Last Dictator, by Dwight L. Kinman (Solid Rock Books, Inc., 1993)

Antony Sutton (*America's Secret Establishment – An Introduction to the Order of Skull & Bones*) commenting on the philosophical outlook of the Controllers: "We're going to use the Hegelian Dialectic process to bring about a society in which the state is in absolute and total powerful control, a new world order where the state is absolute and the individual can only find freedom in blind obedience to the state."

John Rankin (U. S. Representative on the floor of the House of Representatives): "The United Nations is the greatest fraud in all history. Its purpose is to destroy the United States."

David Rockefeller: "We are on the verge of a global transformation. All we need is the right major crisis and the nations will accept the New World Order."

Malachi Martin (*The Keys of This Blood*): "At the round table of international politics, no ruler could command, no government could function without the nod of the Roman Pope."

Alice Bailey (*A World Problem*, 1950): "A new world religion is on its way to externalize the earth. It is the Masonic ritual, the role of the solar angel."

Albert Pike (July 13, 1889): "Lucifer is god ... Pure philosophic religion is the belief that Lucifer is the god of light and the god of good."

Albert Pike (*Morals and Dogma*): "The Masonic religion should by all of us initiates of the highest degrees be maintained in the purity of the Luciferian Doctrine."

Dark Majesty: The Secret Brotherhood and the Magic of a Thousand Points of Light, by Texe Marrs (Living Truth Ministries, 1992)

A. K. Chesterton (*The New Unhappy Lords*) – "A conspiracy of worldwide dimensions does exist and unless we manage to defeat the conspirators, no matter how great the odds against us, we shall have nothing to pass on to our successors except the certainty of enslavement."

Texe Marrs: "The men of the Secret Brotherhood are not like you and me. They believe in magic. Theirs is the strange and bizarre world of ritual alchemy, the recitation of mantras, of words of power, the study of esoteric philosophies, and the mysterious display of arcane New Age symbols ... no one would suspect for a moment what actually goes on in the deep, dark recesses of their diabolical minds ... The Secret Brotherhood holds you and I in utter contempt. Their deceitful actions will demonstrate their contemptuous attitude toward us. All their lives they have been taught the necessity of deceiving the masses."

Robert Anton Wilson (*Cosmic Trigger II*): "Language and hypnosis form the foundation on which humans create worlds of consciousness and of fantasy ... Very few people know how to dehypnotize themselves."

Albert Pike (on why the average Mason doesn't know what his group represents): "They do not know because we lie to them."

Manly P. Hall: "Freemasonry is a fraternity within a fraternity – an outer organization concealing an inner brotherhood of the elite."

Adam Weishaupt (founder of the Illuminati in 1776): "Reason will be the only code of man. This is one of our greatest secrets. When at last Reason becomes the religion of man, then will the problem be solved."

Bertrand Russell (famous 20th century philosopher, who wrote in *Impact of Science on Society* (1953): "Education should aim at destroying free will so that after pupils have left school, they shall be incapable throughout the rest of their lives of thinking or acting other than their schoolmaster would have wished.

CHAPTER FORTY-SIX

Civilization, History, and the Decline of the West: An Overview of Samuel P. Huntington's "The Clash of Civilizations and the Remaking of World Order"

Civilizations

Samuel P. Huntington, one of the elite architects of the New World Order, wrote an article in the summer of 1993 for the Council on Foreign Relations premier publication, *Foreign Affairs*, where he said, "The central and most dangerous dimension of the emerging global politics would be the conflict between groups of differing civilizations."

This simple passage was the key to Huntington's seminal 1996 work, *Clash of Civilizations*, which was the first to lay the foundation for our current global-war environment. Because Russian Communism had finally withered away due to its inherent fallibility as a political system, those at the top of the Control pyramid needed to create a new enemy to keep their conflict-oriented Hegelian Dialectic chugging along its course. Stated differently, Michael Dibdin wrote in *Dead Lagoon*: "There can be no true friends without true enemies. Unless we hate what we are not, we cannot love what we are." This simple sentiment – psychology 101 at its most simple – is the central tenet of the Controllers divide-and-conquer strategy that they've used to keep their subjects at each other's throat since the beginning of time. It's the oldest trick in the book, and one that capitalizes on mankind's suspicion of those different than themselves.

Thus, as the New World Order media pundits tell us on a daily basis, the most dangerous enemies we have today are those from different civilizations. Similar to the perpetual war culture of George Orwell's *1984*, we've gone from having the Germans/Nazis/Japanese as our primary enemy in the 1940's to the Soviets during the Cold War. Along the way, we also had the Koreans as our enemy in the 1950's, the Vietnamese in the 1960's and early '70's, plus the Libyans, Nicaraguans, and Serbs.

But since these enemies have outlived their usefulness and fallen to the wayside, the global planners needed another villain to raise our ire.

So, why not exploit the concept of hating those who are culturally different than we are? This process began nearly ten years ago with the publication of Samuel Huntington's CFR article, and was quickly advanced by another NWO blueprint-maker, Zbginiew Brzezinski's *The Grand Chessboard.*

Huntington's work, which will be the primary focus of this article, begins by asking: what precisely is Western civilization? The famous historian Carroll Quigley answers by telling us that in 500 A.D., there was no such concept as Western civilization. But, a thousand years later – in 1,500 A.D. – Western civilization had grown to full flower and was the most dominant force on earth. As its influence grew, the Europeans moved into other countries, invaded them, and tried to affect how other parts of the world were ruled (i.e. imperialism). Regrettably, Huntington informs us that today Western civilization is rapidly on the decline and will, within less than five centuries, pass from existence!

The actuality of specific "civilizations" did not even come into prominence until the 1700's when the notion was advanced by French intellectuals who differentiated nomadic savages from those who were "settled, urban, and literate." According to these French thinkers, society could only progress if mankind became more civilized. One of the most monumental results of this paradigm-shift was the Industrial Revolution, which forever changed the face of our planet in regard to production, consumption, the environment, human interaction, and our general psyche.

At the time when these societal shifts were unfolding, civilizations were by-and-large geographically separated. Due to travel and communication limitations, the only contact the majority of people from one civilization had with another was via war (the conquering and/or elimination of one people by another), or through enslavement (example: Africa to America). Today, though, with the advancement of mind-boggling technological advancements, eight distinct, globally-interrelated civilizations have emerged:

Oriental
Indian
Islamic
Russian
Western
Latin
African
Jewish

Most of these civilizations have at their center a "core" country whose dynamics come to represent the overall whole. These dominant core countries within each civilization change over time, as can be seen in Western civilization with France, England, and then the United States filling this role over the last three centuries. The same can be said for the Orient, where Japan was once the leader, while today China is quickly assuming that role. On the contrary, some civilizations such as Islam do not have a dominant core country to lead the helm; a fact which is very evident today as Western leaders warn us of an elusive "reign of terror" and "axis of evil."

Historian Arnold J. Toynbee has even gone so far as to outline the stages of each civilization, which I will reproduce in the context of the United States of America:

1) Creation as a response to great challenges. (Our American Revolution due to immense dissatisfaction with England's rule from across the sea.)
2) A period of growth where control of the environment is produced by a creative minority. (The Founding Fathers - a group of inordinately talented men.)
3) Times of trouble. (Our Civil War, and now a potential post-9/11 world war.)
4) Rise of a universal state. (New World Order.)
5) Disintegration. (Western civilization as we know it today eliminated.)

The United States was thus formed by a collection of like-minded people with a common religion, language, history, morality, and form of government. But this foundation – the Constitution, Declaration of Independence, and our Bill of Rights – is being systematically usurped and destroyed by the Globalists. This travesty will be the primary cause for our eventual downfall unless the people of this country are strong enough to retain what made us great in the first place.

Adda Bozeman, in *Strategic Intelligence and Statecraft*, said of this phenomenon: "International history rightly documents the thesis ... that the destiny of each linguistically and MORALLY UNIFIED COMMUNITY depends ultimately upon the survival of certain primary structuring ideas around which successive generations have coalesced and which thus symbolize the society's continuity."

To better convey this concept, I've often used the analogy of an automobile and its oil. If a car owner keeps their oil pure and clean, it will literally run forever. But if they ignore this vital component and allow their oil to get dirty, or if outside elements are added to impair the car's performance, soon it will break down alongside the road. (The old adage about oil and water not mixing is certainly true.) These negative external influences in relation to our country would be: rampant illegal immigration, increasing U.N. rule, the rise of super-national corporate infiltration of government, trade agreements like NAFTA and GATT, or the emergence of a world court system. The result, of course, would be the eventual loss of our national sovereignty, and ultimately our country as a whole.

So, the question we need to ask ourselves is: what are we as a country and a civilization, and what do we want to become? If certain trends continue unabated as they have been, it's fair to say that the United States is embarking upon a road that is leading to ruin, not resurgence.

Historical Paradigm Shifts

If the study of world empires shows anything, it is that those who are "king of the hill" don't remain there forever. Look at the Assyrians, Babylonians, Egyptians, Ottoman, Persian, Roman, and British empires. You will find that those at the pinnacle have always been toppled, and history does indeed repeat itself. One of the reasons why certain societies ascend upward or defeat another in battle is due to technological breakthroughs which gives them a unique advantage over everyone else. The type of ammunition used by the North in opposition to the South in America's Civil War is a perfect example of why the Union won. Thomas Kuhn, in *The Structure of Scientific Revolution*, applies this concept to a shift in the way we view our physical world because new information or data replaces the old. He writes, "To be accepted as a paradigm a theory must seem better than its competitors, but it need not, and never does, explain all the facts with which it can be confronted."

In the 20th century we saw three such historical shifts. The first took place with World War I, which was deliberately staged by the Controllers to rid Europe of its old-style rule of kings, princes, royal families and scattered sovereign nation-states. What the moneyed-elite desired was a destruction of the past power-structure, replaced by those who were groomed in the Round Table-Oxford-New World Order style government. Building upon this notion, WWII was deliberately fomented

336

from the ashes of WWI and the League of Nations so that the United Nations could emerge as a new global power.

Franklin Delano Roosevelt said that WWII would "end the system of unilateral action, the exclusive alliances, the balances of power, and all the other expedients that have been tried for centuries – and have always failed."

In essence, then, what resulted from these two wars was a dramatic shift in the way our world was governed. Whereas a multitude of distinct nation-states existed independent of each other prior to the Great Wars, they were eventually 'collectivized' by global treaties and organizations. By the early 1950's, coinciding with the creation of Cold War hostilities, the world was divided into three camps. On one side we had the United States – democratic and capitalistic, on the other was Communist Russian; while every other country was a minor player in the shadow of this bi-polar rule. During this four decade Cold War, America and the Soviet Union competed for the soul of every other third world country in terms of philosophy, governing style, business ventures and weaponry.

The third shift of the 20th century came about with the fall of Communism (symbolized by the Berlin Wall coming down) and cemented when George Bush Sr. gave his famous "New World Order" proclamation on three different occasions. When this change in political perspective took place, our world moved beyond bi-polar rule and found itself with one remaining super-power and unrivaled king of the hill – the United States of America.

The primary problems facing this nation today aren't terrorists with 12th century mindsets or elusive weapons of mass destruction supposedly hidden in Iraq. No, the true cancer eating away at us is the collective thought of invincibility on the part of the American people. We've become so confident in our position that American cannot be beaten at anything (especially war) that any suggestion to the contrary seems laughable. In other words, I'm afraid to say that we now consider ourselves the end-all and be-all of everything. But as Samuel Huntington says with frightening clarity, "Societies that assume that their history has ended are usually societies whose history is about to decline."

This quote is reminiscent of one given by Arnold J. Toynbee in *A Study of History* where he described the English middle class in 1897 and their inflated notions of "Pax Brittanica" – "As they saw it, history for them was over, and they had every reason to congratulate themselves on the permanent state of felicity which this ending of history had conferred on them."

But guess what. The British Empire fell, and in this vein, America is a mature society (as opposed to a lean, mean, young and hungry society), and it is in decline due to deterioration from within. When these symptoms surfaced in the past, one of two things resulted:

1) The country in question was invaded and severely beaten. If we become immersed in a world war on multiple fronts and all our troops are on foreign soil, what would prevent Russian or China from sweeping onto our shores and giving us a whooping?

2) The society rots from within. If you don't think we're completely rotten on the inside, take a few moments to look at how the 'selected' leaders of this country have absolutely sold us out to the Controllers. It's appalling. In this sense, we're as rotten as ancient Rome was in every conceivable way.

Plus, due to the deliberate erosion of our borders and the inception of cultural-elements contrary to what made this country great; we're following a path leading to a less-than-optimal outcome. Or, as Samuel Huntington tell us, "History shows that no country so constituted [with a cultural core] can long endure as a coherent society. A multicivilizational United States will not be the United States; it will be the United Nations."

Balance of Power

As the Cold War came to an end, so did the way our world was structured. Although America and the West are still atop the control pyramid, Samuel Huntington warns us that our relative power in relation to other countries is plunging. "Power is shifting from the long predominant West to non-Western civilizations. Global politics has become multipolar and multicivilizational." [As opposed to a bi-polar structure that existed between the U.S. and USSR.]

To prove that Western dominance is on the decline and that Asian and Islamic civilizations are becoming more influential, we first need to look at the concept of power, which Huntington defines as, "The ability of one person or group to change the behavior of another person or group." Taking this notion one step further, Huntington adds, "The power of a state or group is normally estimated by measuring the resources it has at its disposal against those of the other states or groups it is trying to influence."

This point is extremely important, for Huntington proceeds to give a plethora of data to prove that the West's influence is declining. His findings are as follows:

Share of the Total World Military by Civilizations

Western	1900	43.7%
	1991	21.1%
China	1900	0.4%
	1991	25.7%
Islam	1900	16.7%
	1991	20.0%

If you combine the military manpower of China and the Islamic nations it totals 45.7%. Thus, these two entities comprise nearly one-half of the world's entire troops!

Share of the World Population under Political Control of Civilizations

Western	1900	44.3%
	1990	13.1%
	2025	10.1% (estimated)
China	2025	21.0% (estimated)
Islam	1900	4.2%
	1990	13.4%
	2025	19.2% (estimated)

These numbers are truly frightening. In two decades, world populations under the political systems of Western civilizations will only control 10% of the world, while China and Islam combined will control over 40% of the world. Plus, as the above statistics show, they will also possess over 45% of the world's armies.

Territory under Political Control of a Civilization

Western - 1900 - 38.7%
- 1993 - 24.2%
Islam - 1900 - 6.8%
- 1993 - 21.1%

Share of World Gross Economic Product by Civilization

Western - 1950 - 64.1%
- 1992 - 48.9%
China - 1950 - 3.3%
- 1990 - 10.0%
Islam - 1950 - 2.9%
- 1990 - 11.0%

Share of World Manufacturing Output by Civilization

Western - 1928 - 84.2%
- 1980 - 57.8%

These numbers show quite clearly that the West's prominence is waning and that our two primary threats – China and Islam – are on the rise. What should be most alarming to Americans is that our manufacturing base has been absolutely decimated during the past ten years and shipped overseas to countries with cheap labor that are exploited by multinational companies. Whereas power shifted from Europe to America following WWII, it is yet again being transformed, as Samuel Huntington points out. "The successors to Regan, Thatcher, Mitterand, and Kohl will be rivaled by those of Deng Xiaoping, Nakasone, Indira Gandhi, Yeltsin, Khomeini, and Suharto. The age of Western dominance will be over." And who is peddling this power to other foreign countries? Answer: the Controllers via their international corporations and unfair trade agreements that have done immeasurable harm to this nation.

One of Huntington's greatest strengths in *Clash of Civilizations* is his ability to show how we've reached this weakened state. As we saw in the previous section, Western civilization began in 700-800 A.D. and arose out of European Christianity. By 1500 A.D., Europe was the world's dominant power center, but it began losing its edge in the 1700's with America's secession from England. The main reason we rose to such prominence was due to our advanced technology. One of the results of this scientific superiority was that the West was better able to wage war than anyone else. The only problem was, while they were battling other civilizations, the royal families were also fighting each other. As Huntington so succinctly describes the situation, "Among European states peace was the exception, not the rule." Today, Western countries no longer fight each other, but they do something equally as dangerous – they allow their multinational companies to sell its technology to foreign countries!

After the World War I, European kings, queens and princes were replaced by international federations, organizations and groups, but as Huntington points out, its prominence is waning. In fact, as can be seen from hot spots such as the Middle East, Korea, and the anti-war protests across Europe, the brunt of this backlash is being directed at the United States. Worse, rather than continuing to be subjected to Western edicts and/or expansion, other areas of the globe are becoming more proactive and attempting to call their own shots.

This desire for independence is naturally causing growth pains for the New World Order elite, and is the direct cause of the 9-11 terrorist attacks and our upcoming war in Iraq (and beyond). Y'see, similar to the restructuring of Europe that took place after World War I and II, the NWO leaders are also pushing to rid the Middle East, Eurasia, and Korea of their royal families, princes, and sheiks; ultimately to be replaced by leaders more receptive to a "universal state." Thus, the arena of war no longer sets Western nation against Western nation in order to counteract the advances of rulers like King Phillip II, Louis XIV, Frederick the Great, Napolean, the German Kaisers, or Adolf Hitler. Rather, it now entails a clash of civilizations set-up by the Controllers to actualize once-and-for-all their New World Order blueprints.

The New World Order

As non-Western civilizations continue to gain more prominence on the global stage, their financial and military presence becomes more obvious. China and other Oriental nations are perfect examples of a new economic force, while North Korea's threats to expand their nuclear arsenal reveal a new player in the game. The problem in regard to the United States is that we are being deliberately set-up to take a fall. How do I arrive at this conclusion? One of the major indicators that rarely get mentioned in the media is the way in which we use our resources. What do we do with the billions of dollars raised through taxation of the American people? Do we use it to strengthen our borders, prop-up our industrial base, and reinforce our infrastructure to be the best in the world? No, our political leaders (guided by their New World Order puppet-masters) are sending more and more of it outside our borders via foreign aid, foreign weapons build-ups, and as enormous payoffs to foreign nations for the use of their military bases (Turkey is a perfect example).

The big question is; who is making these decisions – our Congressmen and President? Of course not. They're being made by the elitists who belong to the CFR and Trilateral Commission, or meet yearly with the Bilderbergs or at the World Economic Forum in Davos, Switzerland. These individuals – bankers, international businessmen, government officials, intellectuals, and media moguls – do not act in the best interest of the United States.

<u>2003 attendees of the Davos Conference</u> (largely unreported in the American mainstream media)

> John Ashcroft – U.S. Attorney General
> Bill Clinton – Former President of the United States
> Christopher Dodd – Connecticut Senator
> Orrin Hatch – Utah Senator
> Colin Powell – U.S. Secretary of State
> Bill Richardson – New Mexico Governor
> Laurence Summers – President, Harvard University
> Tommy Thompson – Secretary of Health and Human Services
> Christine Todd Whitman – EPA Administrator
> Richard Sergay – Senior Producer, ABC News
> Stephen Case – Chairman, AOL Time-Warner
> Alexander Higgins – Associated Press Bureau Chief
> Thomas Fenton – CBS News
> Jim Bitterman – CNN
> Peter Sutherland – Chief Executive BP Oil, Bilderberg luminary
> Yosef A. Maiman – Former Mossad agent
> Bill Gates – Microsoft
> Thomas Friedman – New York Times
> Ross Perot – Former presidential candidate
> George Soros - Interpol

Instead of taking actions which benefit this country, their aim is to further their own Globalist goals. Their power is incredible, as Samuel P. Huntington admits in startlingly honest terms. "Davos people control virtually all international institutions, many of the world's governments, and the bulk of the world's economic and military capabilities."

Did you read those words? This is the 'smoking gun' admission of a New World Order power hierarchy. Whenever people say this is all conspiratorial nonsense, all they have to do is read the above words. This is one of their own architects laying it on the table!

To further incriminate his cohorts, Huntington goes on to say that although nation-states still have some control over their own destiny, they are losing importance and will soon be replaced by international institutions which will have the "right to judge and to constrain what states do in their own territory." To those who don't realize it, this is precisely the definition of what a NEW WORLD ORDER is! This international ruling body will assume the role previously performed by sovereign nations, with a Globalist bureaucracy directing the citizenry, not a duly-elected government.

Of course we have already taken quite a few steps toward this Orwellian nightmare with the establishment of the United Nations, European Union, IMF, etc., and the New World Order elite realize that to maintain their positions of power they need to promote a concept called "Universalism." In other words, whenever a conflict presents itself outside of their sphere of influence, the Globalists try to bring the troublemaker into their stable.

Huntington describes their aims and tactics as such: "The West is attempting and will continue attempting to sustain its preeminent position and defend its interests by defining those interests as the interests of the WORLD COMMUNITY."

One of the ways they like to do this is by easing non-Western civilizations into their economic system via loans or aid packages through the IMF and World Bank. But Georgi Arbatov, a long-time Russian politico, CFR member, and author of The System: an Insiders Life in Soviet Politics, likened the IMF crowd to "neo-Bolsheviks who love expropriating other people's money, imposing undemocratic and alien rules of economic and political conduct and stifling economic freedom." In other words, they suck OUR money out of our pockets, then dole it out to those will further their self-serving goals. In reality, this practice is nothing more than Global Socialism with those at the top acting as plantation owners, while we slave away to keep them in power. It's a sick little game that we shouldn't keep falling for.

To insure that they keep the upper hand and can further pursue their Globalist aims, the Universalists preach non-proliferation to the masses. In this sense, any nation that doesn't belong to the New World Order clique is absolutely forbidden to acquire atomic weapons. Naturally, though, if you're an Islamic sect that sees America, Israel, China, France, and Russia with nukes, you want to secure some of your own! In their eyes, non-proliferation only benefits the Controllers, while keeping them in a lessened state.

Now I'm by no means advocating giving atomic weaponry to Saddam Hussein, the North Koreans, or Islamic Terrorists in Afghanistan. Rather, I'm simply pointing out that the real basis for our upcoming war in the Middle East and beyond revolves around this very issue. The Controllers want to preserve the status quo and expand their power base, while those without such weapons see proliferation as the only way to 'equalize' this situation.

The Controllers counter this stance by once again falling back on economic blackmail as a way to prevent arms proliferation. But the big question is: how long will this practice endure? If North Korea is any indicator, our planet is quickly becoming a very dangerous place, with nuclear bombs diffusing the Controller's power and opening it up even more so to a multicivilizational world war. And, if anyone has noticed, this trend is already taking place with the Controllers on one side and the Axis of Evil on the other – Iran, Iraq, Syria, Libya and Sudan. (By the way, Huntington had already identified this Axis of Evil in 1996 – five whole years before George W. Bush labeled them after the 9-11 terrorist attacks. Coincidence, or an insight into the long-term planning objectives of the New World Order elite? You decide!)

China

Which country will man the helm and be the recipient of the Controllers good graces to lead our world into the 21st century? If history repeats itself and is any indicator, we need to learn a few lessons about nations on the rise and their behavior. Samuel Huntington encapsulates in the following quote what all Americans should be wary of. "Every other major power, Britain and France, Germany and Japan, and the U.S. and the Soviet Union, has engaged in outward expansion, assertion, and imperialism coincidental with or immediately following the years in which it went through rapid industrialization and economic growth. No reason exists to think that the acquisition of economic and military power will not have comparable effects in China."

Here it is folks – China – America's greatest threat - a Confucian civilization that has never known freedom in the entirety of its history - a culture that advocates yielding to authority, a structured hierarchy, surrender of individual rights, consensus, meekness, and the State over personal freedom. This is a country that flaunts absolute power and frowns upon checks and balances while telling its people to bow in subservience. This is a civilization so diametrically opposed to our own that I'd almost liken them to something alien. The Chinese possess, quite literally, everything that the New World Order crowd craves – a conditioned, freedom-less populace and an iron-fisted, tyrannical government. And if you think this characterization is inaccurate or too strong, simply hearken back to what happened at the Tiananmen Square student uprising. The Chinese military swooped down and killed with a vengeance, and those protestors not eliminated on the spot were executed shortly thereafter without a trial. These are vicious, bloodthirsty leaders that won't bat an eye at further enslaving their people. Here is the perfectly docile, unquestioning automaton citizenry portrayed in George Orwell's *1984*, yet with an obedient army of millions and plenty of newfound Western technology. Forget about Afghanistan and Iraq. They're only precursors being used to prime the pump. Then, when we're sufficiently weakened, BAM, the Chinese will lay us out and land the final death blow! If this description is still not enough, ask yourself this question: would your life be freer under Chinese rule? The answer is obvious. If the Chinese leaders haven't respected freedom of speech or individual rights for the last few thousand years, what makes you think they'll start now?

The primary reason why China has become such a force to be reckoned with is because the Controllers have been inundating them with enormous amounts of Western technology for the past decade from both the private and public sectors. This includes computer hardware and software, satellites, military technology and weaponry, and the means of advanced production for their factories. The growth of their gross domestic product has more than doubled in twenty years from 6% in 1972 to 13.5% in 1993, and as Kishore Mahbubani wrote in the CFR's *Foreign Affairs* January-February 1995 edition, "The Chinese economy will become the world's largest early in the twenty-first century."

Mahbubani continues, this time speaking of the entire Pacific Rim. "With the second and third largest economies in the world in the 1990's, Asia is likely to have four of the five largest and seven of the ten largest economies by 2020. By that date Asian societies are likely to account for over 40% of the global economic product."

Malaysian Deputy Prime Minister Anwar Ibrahim concurs, telling the *International Herald Tribune* on January 31, 1994, "Asia's increasing prosperity means that it is now in a position to offer serious alternatives to the dominant global, political, social, and economic arrangements."

These words are coming from political leaders and CFR members that the global elite listen to intently. And what they are saying is that Asian civilizations are primed to assume a leadership role on the world stage, replacing us as king of the hill. Folks, the writing is on the wall. This is going to happen. Why? Because the New World Planners have funded and provided for their economic independence so that they can expand their influence, maximize profits, and capitalize on cheap, docile Asian labor. Not only does this phenomenon strengthen the Pacific Rim, but it also weakens our manufacturing base in the United States at the same time. It is actually cheaper for companies in this country to import steel manufactured in China and ship it across the ocean than it is for them to produce it domestically. There is something seriously wrong with that equation, and the result is that our economy falters while the Asians become more self-reliant and primed to move forward.

Samuel Huntington observes, "East Asian economic development is altering the balance of power between Asia and the West, specifically the United States."

The most immediate danger of this situation is obvious: the stronger and more independent China and the Orient becomes, the less control we have over their activities. Plus, their increasing energy demands will have to be met one way or another. This dilemma opens up the possibility of a truly horrifying scenario which I will address in the following section.

In the meantime, Samuel Huntington adds more perspective to this situation. "China's increasing needs for oil are likely to impel it to expand its relations with Iran, Iraq, and Saudi Arabia as well as Kazakhstan and Azerbaijan. Such an arms-for-oil axis, one energy expert observed in 1994, won't have to take orders from London, Paris, or Washington anymore."

As China and its Asian counterparts are moved to the forefront by the Controllers, we need to examine how these changes will affect

America. The most profound explanation comes from Samuel P. Huntington, who says in the starkest terms possible, "China's emergence as a major power will dwarf any comparable phenomena during the last half of the second millennium." Lee Kuan Yew, Singapore's first Prime Minister, concurs, "It's not possible to pretend that this is just another big player. This is the biggest player in the history of man!"

Is the importance of this upcoming change starting to hit you yet? The Controllers want to run the world through China, and they're setting the stage with non-Western arms proliferation in North Korea, Pakistan, Iraq, Iran, India, and China. Once the Red Army officially takes control of the Asian theater, Japan will, out of necessity, side with them. Huntington also points out that others with hostile feelings toward the U.S. will side with them. "In politics a common enemy creates a common interest. Islamic and Sinic [Chinese] societies which see the West as their antagonist thus have reason to cooperate with each other against the West."

Hearken back to the statistics provided a few pages earlier showing that nearly half of the world's military manpower will belong to the Chinese and Muslims and you will realize the magnitude of what we're up against. It is truly horrifying. To make matters worse, take a look at the following two quotes by Samuel Huntington to determine how the Chinese feel about us:

"The most important group in China with an antagonistic view toward the U.S. is the military."

"By the mid-1990's Chinese officials and agencies routinely portrayed the U.S. as a hostile power."

Please remember, these opinions are coming from a *New York Times* best-selling author and one of the New World Order's most lauded academics. The Chinese threat is for real, so what can we do about it? Huntington arrives at three possibilities:

1)   Wage war against China be victorious
2)   Accept a lesser role on the global stage and allow China to become king of the hill
3)   Stumble blindly into a world war and get severely trounced

Our World Today

As this overview comes to a close, the final territory we need to cover is the world's current hot spots – Eurasia and the Middle East. America's most recent interaction with the Islamic world occurred when the Russians invaded Afghanistan in 1979. This event had vital historical importance for not only did the United States give armaments and technological aid to the Afghan rebels, but the USSR's humiliating defeat was one of the factors ultimately leading to its demise. The ramifications of that war continue to reverberate to this day, for although Saudi Arabia was Afghanistan's primary backer, the fledgling Taliban and Al Qaeda were trained by the ISI (Pakistan's secret service) and our own CIA. Pakistan also served as a conduit for U.S. money and weapons to the Muslims.

Thus, a seemingly beneficial link was established between the U.S. and Islamic world, but if we jump ahead to 1991's Gulf War and our invasion of Iraq, problems start to arise. Even though the Muslim world supported America's intervention (at least on the surface), they also saw the battle between Kuwait and Iraq as an inter-family squabble to be settled among themselves. A fitting analogy would be Iran attacking our Southwest after Texas and Oklahoma got into a tussle.

Another factor that strained this situation was the Bush Administration, via U.S. Ambassador April Gillespie, giving Saddam Hussein the okay to invade their neighbor by telling him, "We have no opinion on Arab-Arab conflicts, like your border disagreement with Kuwait." Worse, it was later discovered that the story of 300 premature babies at Kuwait's Maternity Hospital that were supposedly removed from their incubators and slaughtered by Iraqi soldiers was completely untrue and nothing more than a propaganda stunt to sway public opinion. As Samuel Huntington explains, the Arab world saw our Iraqi invasion as nothing more than a means to protect our self-interests (oil), plus a way to keep them under our thumb. Worse, as the U.S. soundly whooped the Iraqis, the Muslim world felt a sense of humiliation in that their civilization was once again defeated by the West. And last but not least, the Arabs feel that the United States blatant favoritism of Israel over every other Muslim country is patently unfair.

Two years later, in February 1993, our World Trade Center was bombed for the first time, and then on September 11, 2001 tragedy struck with the infamous terrorist attacks. The world changed that day, and the machinations for the Controllers to move forward with their New World Order agenda were ignited.

Thus, if you stick with me, we'll take a look at how this debacle is playing out. First of all, the power elite realize that problems face both of their Cold War super-powers – the U.S. and USSR – none the least being that they are 'mature' societies with low birth rates, aging populations, sluggish economies, and no continuing vigor to expand their territories (despite how the media portrays American imperialism). Compared to other hungry countries like those in Asia, India, or the Islamic world, the U.S. and Russia are seen by the Controllers as being satisfied with the status quo.

So, wanting to lay a New World Order foundation in these other countries before they got too strong while minimizing the risk of monumental personal losses, the Controllers came up with a grand scheme. First of all they baited the American people into finding a new enemy – the Muslims - by allowing three airliners to crash into our Pentagon and World Trade Centers. We naturally wanted revenge, so a *Wag the Dog* scenario unfolded complete with widespread flag-waving and conditioned patriotism. Soon we were bombing an invisible enemy (Osama bin Laden) in Afghanistan to take back the poppy fields for the CIA (heroin), and the natural resources for the Controllers' oil companies.

Not content with a mere takeover of Eurasia, the war-hawks next pushed America into invading Iraq (and beyond). Now, if you remember the Controller's motivation behind World War I – to rid Europe of its old-world governing system of kings, princes, and royal families – well, the same rationale applies to the Middle East where they want to replace the sheiks and oil families with those more receptive to their Globalist game plan.

But world sentiment is against the war, as it is even within our own borders. So, the Controllers can either rally support via another outrageous catastrophe reminiscent of 9-11, or they can 'allow' the U.S. to invade Iraq and the Middle East and do their dirty work for them. But things are already on shaky ground in America. Our national debt is skyrocketing once again, layoffs continue in the manufacturing field, the economy is stalled or in reverse, our stock market is anemic despite rock-bottom interest rates, and oil prices are through the roof. In addition, a war with Iraq and our subsequent 'restructuring' will cost upwards of $100 billion. But the Controllers don't care, for once America's usefulness has been outlived and we've rid the Middle East of their royal families and old-style rulers, the door will finally be opened for China –

the next king of the hill – to waltz through. And what will we do about it? I'm not sure, but consider that we'll be broke, unable to get loans from the international bankers, and our military will be exhausted. At this point everything will become clear as we finally see how we had been set-up for a double sucker-punch from the Muslims and Chinese.

The final outrage will occur when people look back upon this event, for remember, the victor always writes the history books. That new king will be China, and they'll put forth the same line that was used on Germany after World War II – the Nazis were aggressors who wanted to expand their territory and were hated worldwide. But nowadays, think about who is being called the aggressor, the imperialist, and is invoking global hostility. We are, and our President is even being characterized as another Adolf Hitler. Can't you see what's going on? We're being set-up to take a fall, only to be written off as another militaristic Nazi Germany-like aggressor.

The only question remaining is: will we do anything about our predicament before it's too late? Do we have the intestinal fortitude to fight back against this impending atrocity, or will we roll over and play dead? If we choose to do the latter, then please remember these haunting words written by historian Carroll Quigley in *The Evolution of Civilizations*: "A civilization, no longer able to defend itself because it is no longer willing to defend itself, lies wide open to 'barbarian invaders' who often come from another younger, more powerful civilization."

America, it is now time to lay aside our complacency and apathy and summon the courage that made this nation great. If we fail to do so, we're finished. It's that plain and simple.

SECTION SEVEN:

THE

AMERICAN

PRESIDENCY

CHAPTER FORTY-SEVEN

WHO CONTROLS THE AMERICAN PRESIDENCY?

At this moment in time, the American people have NO say-so in determining who their next President will be. Zero. None. Zilch! How can I make such a drastic statement? Well, if reading the articles on *Votescam* later in this book don't convince you; then check-out this observation by noted researcher Susan George: "Economists generally agree that if 55% or more of a given market is controlled by four or fewer companies, then an oligopoly exists."

An oligopoly is defined as "control by a few competing sellers of the amount and price of a given product or service to a large number of buyers." Thus, in regard to the 'selection' (as opposed to 'election') of our President, there are three organizations which determine not only who is chosen for that office, but also its Cabinet and policies. They are the Council on Foreign Relations, the Trilateral Commission, and the Bilderbergs. In this sense, the United States has gone from being a democracy to that of an oligopoly. We're the bamboozled 'buyers' who are getting suckered by the illusion provided to us buy the 'sellers.'

In this chapter I'm going to lay a groundwork that will show how the three above-listed organizations have controlled the Executive Office from the Nixon and Carter Administrations all the way up to the current one. The most disturbing aspect of this phenomenon is the virtual lock these groups have on our highest office.

In other words, how would you feel if every president in the last fifty years was a Hare Krishna, a plumber, or belonged to the Knights of Columbus? Would it unnerve you, or make you think something suspicious was taking place? It should, for this is exactly what's going on today, only the three main groups involved are the CFR, the Trilateral Commission, and the Bilderbergs, all led by the nefariously scheming David Rockefeller.

So, before I begin, please allow me to run a few quotes by you to set the stage:

Sir William Pitts, addressing the House of Lords in England, 1770: "There is something behind the Throne greater than the King himself."

Felix Frankfurter, former U.S. Supreme Court Justice: "The real rulers in Washington are invisible, and exercise power from behind the scenes."

Abraham Lincoln: "If destruction be our lot, we ourselves must be its author and finisher."

Walter Bernays (*Propaganda*): "Those who manipulate the unseen mechanism of society constitute an invisible government which is the true ruling power of our country. Our minds are molded largely by men we have never heard of."

THE COUNCIL ON FOREIGN RELATIONS, THE BILDERBERGS AND THE TRILATERAL COMMISSION

The CFR was formed in 1921, and one of its early influential members, Colonel Edward Mandell House, Chief Adviser to President Wilson, exerted an extremely heavy hand on three policy areas that America is still suffering from today:

1) The establishment of a Federal Income Tax
2) The establishment of the Federal Reserve System
3) Our entry into the League of Nations (a precursor to the United Nations)

Two of the main financial contributors to the CFR were the Carnegie and Rockefeller Foundations. (The second name is very important to remember, as you'll see.) The CFR became such an important force in American politics that ever since the early 1940s virtually every candidate for President has been a member.

The CFR's primary goals are to:

1) Establish a single government with global power
2) Eliminate national boundaries
3) Increase the United Nation's domain

To support this point, Rear Admiral Chester Ward, former Judge Advocate of the Navy from 1956-1960, commented: "The purpose of promoting disarmament and submergence of U.S. sovereignty and national independence into an all-powerful and one-world government is the only objective revealed to about 95% of the 1,551 members in 1975."

The *Wall Street Journal* stated in its *Notable and Quotable* section on April 10, 1991: "In the postwar years, the Council [on Foreign Relations] has continued to represent an invaluable way for many Washingtonians to tap the enormously important New York business and intellectual community."

What does this mean? The answer is very important because the "supposed" elected leaders that we place in Washington, DC *don't* make the decisions that affect our lives. Rather, the *real* shots are called in New York City, and even Europe. Thus, the direction our government takes isn't determined in the halls of Congress or the Oval Office, but instead in New York City by international bankers and the heads of multinational businesses.

This, I'm sorry to say, is the key to power in our country.

The trend to filling an Administration's cabinet with CFR members is startling, as the numbers below reveal:

- Nixon - 115 CFR members
- Carter - 284 CFR members
- Reagan - 257 CFR members
- Bush - 382 CFR members
- Clinton - 17 of his top 19 Cabinet members were either CFR or TC

The third group, the Trilateral Commission, was formed in 1973 by Zbigniew Brzezinsky and David Rockefeller, and is at the top of the "financial brotherhood." Regrettably, the Executive Branch is below them. An excellent description of this group is provided by Antony C. Sutton and Patrick M. Wood in *Trilaterals Over Washington*:

1) The Trilateral Commission was formed primarily by David Rockefeller.

2) Its members are chosen by David Rockefeller and four assistants.

3) They're financed by David Rockefeller and the Kettering and Ford Foundations.

State the authors: "Without being accused of hastiness or bias, one can reasonably conclude that David Rockefeller is the power behind the Trilateral Commission and presumably stands to gain the most from its activities.

"The essential point to hold in mind ... is that a global multinational corporation (Chase Manhattan owned by David Rockefeller) is in control of a power vehicle that controls the United States government. In 1976 the American voter thought they had elected Jimmy Carter. In fact, they elected Chase Manhattan."

Holly Sklar, in the introductory chapter to a book about the Trilaterals titled *Trilateralism: Managing Dependence and Democracy -- An Overview*," states the chief goal of this commission: "The people, governments, and economies of all nations must serve the needs of multinational banks and corporations."

How is this information settling with you thus far? Well, don't worry -- it gets scarier.

Senator Barry Goldwater, in his book *No Apologies*, called the Trilateral Commission, "David Rockefeller's newest international cabal."

Since I mentioned Zbigniew Brzezinski earlier, a few quotes from him are appropriate to convey where these people are coming from. These are culled from *Between Two Ages*, which is one of the Trilateral Commission's most important books:

"Marxism is simultaneously a victory of the external, active man over the inner, passive man and a victory of reason over belief ... Marxism, disseminated on the popular level in the form of Communism represented a major advance in man's ability to conceptualize his relationship to the world ... Marxism supplied the best available insight into contemporary reality."

Hmmm, if I didn't know better, I'd say Zig the Mad Dog actually LIKED Marxism and Communism! And to think; he was David Rockefeller's right-hand man, and also a key member of Jimmy Carter's Cabinet. Something smells fishy to me.

Zig's views on how he sees the world are further represented in *The Technetronic Era*: "The nation state as a fundamental unit of man's organized life has ceased to be the principle creative force: International banks and international corporations are acting and planning in terms that are far in advance of the political concepts of the nation-state."

How much more obvious could it be? The Controllers want to diminish; then virtually eliminate national sovereignty and the Constitution, replacing it with a new framework determined by THEM -- unelected global financial leaders! Is this what you want?

Adding fuel to the fire, the *Washington Post* published a piece in 1976 that said "Trilateralists are not three-sided people. They are members of a private, though not secret, international organization put together by the wealthy banker David Rockefeller ... But here is the unsettling thing about the Trilateral Commission. The President-elect is a member. So is the Vice President-elect Walter F. Mondale. So are the new Secretaries of State, Defense, and Treasury. So is Zbigniew Brzezinski, who is a former Trilateral Director and Carter's next National Security Advisor, and also a bunch of others who will make foreign policy for American in the next four years."

Can't you see? It's the same people over and over again who are calling the shots for us regardless of who the President is. It's the international bankers on Wall Street and in their New York City offices, and to a lesser extent, the heads of multinational corporations. These men and women aren't Democrats or Republicans, but members of the CFR, TC, and the Bilderbergs.

In fact, at a 1974 Bilderberg meeting, seven of the eighteen Americans present, or 39 percent, were either Rockefellers per se, or Rockefeller agents. When you examine these organizations, what do you find? The CFR's former Director was who? David Rockefeller! Who co-founded the Trilateral Commission? David Rockefeller! And who controls nearly 40% (of the American invitees) to the most powerful group of all, the Bilderbergs? David Rockefeller!

Following is some information published by Robert Goldsborough, President of the American Research Foundation that was provided to him by Mark Jones in 1992: "Just four men, through their interlocking directorates on boards of large corporations and major banks, controlled the movement of capital and the creation of debt in America."

What position did Mark Jones hold prior to disclosing this information? He was the financial advisor to John D. Rockefeller himself!

DAVID ROCKEFELLER AND HIS FAMILY CABAL

Who is David Rockefeller? For starters, he is a billionaire, the Chairman of Chase Manhattan Bank (arguably the most influential financial center in the world), one-time director of the CFR, co-founder of the Trilateral Commission, and also a perennial attendee of the highly-secretive Bilderberg meetings. A September 7, 1962, *Time* Magazine article described David Rockefeller as "the prime mover in banking that controls the course of world economic affairs and history."

Those accolades aren't too shabby. But to really understand David Rockefeller, you must first become acquainted with the creator of their family fortune, John D. Rockefeller. In *Titan: the Life of John D. Rockefeller*, author Ron Chernow says, "If he'd lived in the Middle Ages, he'd have been the Pope at Rome."

Similarly, in *The Rockefellers* by Collier and Horowitz, the dynasty's dominance is unmistakable: "Among the power elite whose rule stretched from Wall Street to Washington, the Rockefellers were without peer."

At the apex of the Rockefeller pyramid is Chase Manhattan Bank, an octopus-like financial network with over 50,000 branches and affiliates worldwide. "Worldwide" is the operative word, for the Rockefeller's loyalty isn't, by any means, to the United States, but to their global interests. Did you know that the first American banks to open in Moscow and Peking were Chase Manhattan? In addition, Chase Manhattan financed the building of the largest truck factory in history. The only catch is; it wasn't erected in America, but along the Kama River in the Soviet Union. Do you remember the Soviet Union -- our arch enemy, the Evil Empire, Communism, Stalin, and the Cold War?

With the above information in mind, we need to ask ourselves, what do the Rockefellers want? The best answer can be found in Gary Allen's book, *The Rockefeller File*. Their motive is to "use American money and know-how to build up your competitors, while at the same time use every devious strategy you can devise to weaken and impoverish this country ... The goal is not to bankrupt the United States. Rather, it is to reduce our productive might, and therefore our standard of living."

A case in point is China, who is set to replace the United States as the world's next superpower. Let's examine what's going on with this situation. Who has given them their status as "Most Favored Nation?" We have! Who is providing all the technological know-how to bring China into the 21st century? We are! Who is giving China all their computer parts? We are! And who continues to engage in unbalanced trade agreements with China where their products flood into our country unabated, while ours are subject to tariffs and governmental regulation? We do! When added to how messed-up the NAFTA and GATT agreements are (orchestrated by the Globalists), you have to scratch your head and wonder what forces would be at work to deliberately undermine our country. Is it US -- the American people -- doing it, or monsters and snakes lurking behind the scenes?

John D. Rockefeller HIMSELF, in his autobiography, *Reminiscenses*, reinforced this point when he said, "One of our greatest helpers has been the State Department in Washington. Our ambassadors and ministers and consuls have aided to push our way into new markets to the utmost corners of the world."

Do you know how they became a world power? Can you see the behind-the-scene machinations taking place? China's going to become the next world super-power because they're the largest unexploited economic market in the world. And when this transformation takes place, our importance and status will be lessened, as it currently is right now. The United States is a cow being led to a slaughterhouse by the New World Order!

But other world affairs are also being affected by the Globalists' manipulative ways. A perfect example is given by the noted economic historian Dr. Balthus Freihofner. He said, "It's a long-familiar Rockefeller practice to build a financial empire on predatory oil deals."

We need to look at our war in Afghanistan and the real reasons behind it. One of the keys is the oil lying beneath the Caspian region of Russia. The only problem with getting this buried oil to the existing pipelines is a little country standing between them ... Afghanistan.

But their bamboozling doesn't stop there. It also directly affects domestic policy, as John F. McManus points out in *The Insiders: Architects of the New World Order.* McManus says: "One of the more sinister tactics employed by Socialists to gain economic control of the people involves accumulating huge national indebtedness. Paying interest on the debt then gives the government leaders the excuse to impose more and more taxation."

Think about it. We pay over $300 billion per year in interest on our National Debt. If you divide this sum by all the working people in this country, the total comes to $3,000 per person per year to simply pay the interest alone. Can you see how counter-productive this situation is, both to our country and its citizens – every one of us? What could each of us do with an extra $3,000 per year? We're getting screwed in a big way. Do you know what's even more sickening? In 1976, the largest bank in the United States -- Chase Manhattan -- which generated huge profits throughout the year, filed their taxes. Guess what percentage of their income they paid in U.S. taxes. Zero percent. Yes, zero percent!!!

Why don't we ever hear about any of this nonsense? Quite simply because the Rockefellers are part of a hidden network that runs the world. Don't believe me? The notorious Bilderbergs met at Vermont's Woodstock Inn years ago. Guess who owned the lodge? Yup, Laurance Rockefeller. They also met at a resort in Williamsburg, Virginia. And who owned that one? You got it -- the Rockefeller family.

But wait. Shouldn't the media let us in on this terrible little secret? Fat chance, as Peter Borsnan so exquisitely relayed in his November 25, 1978 article in *The Nation* entitled "Who Owns the Networks?" He said: "Chase Manhattan and the other Rockefeller Institutions are among the largest holders of Network stock with substantial interests in all three networks (ABC, CBS, and NBC)."

Borsnan then went on to say that if a particular institution holds at least 5% of a company's stock, they can wield great influence or even outright control. At the time that article was written, Chase Manhattan controlled 14% of CBS stock. Now do you know why we never hear any of these dirty little secrets? If YOU owned the media, would YOU expose your dirty dealings? Of course not. And neither does the New World Order. They're no dummies, and they don't plan on changing their tactics now.

CHAPTER FORTY-EIGHT

NIXON, CARTER, REAGAN, BUSH, CLINTON, AND BUSH: ALL BOUGHT, SOLD, AND CONTROLLED

The Executive Office is completely at the beck and call of the Controllers. Hidden forces in New York City and beyond (the Bilderbergs) call the shots in our country, determining not only who gets "selected" but also who will be in their administration, and what policies they will adopt.

JOHN F. KENNEDY

To his credit, JFK was the last American President who wasn't totally controlled by the shadow powers. But his Administration didn't start that way. In fact, according to Anthony Lukas of the *New York Times*, 63 of the 82 members of JFK's State Department were chosen from the CFR (Council on Foreign Relations). In Kennedy's cabinet specifically, the Secretary of the Treasury, the National Security Advisor (McGeorge Bundy), CIA Director, Assistant Secretary of Defense, and Under Secretary of Defense were also CFR.

Furthermore, Kennedy's Secretary of Defense, Dean Rusk, joined the CFR in 1952 and was also the chairman of a certain foundation. Can you guess which one? Yup, the Rockefeller Foundation!

The respected economist John Kenneth Galbraith said it best: "Those of us who had worked for the Kennedy election were tolerated in the government ... but foreign policy was still with the Council on Foreign Relations people."

To illustrate how the President's cabinet was CHOSEN for him, before JFK took office, he chose Robert McNamara as his Secretary of Defense. Then, at a gathering of his cabinet members, Kennedy was told that McNamara had just entered the room. Befuddled, Kennedy had to ask which one he was prior to being introduced to McNamara. He didn't even know what he looked like!

Luckily, JFK came to his senses and realized the horrors surrounding him. Regrettably, his rebelliousness and decision to break free from the Controllers also guaranteed his death. After threatening to break the CIA into a thousand pieces and scatter them to the wind, and after vowing to stop the War Machine by pulling out of Vietnam, he sealed his fate.

But I commend President Kennedy for all he did -- especially the guts it took to deliver a speech at Columbia University only days before being killed. "The high office of President has been used to foment a plot to destroy the Americans' freedom, and before I leave office I must inform the citizens of this plight." *(Ed. note: the authenticity of this statement is still a matter of debate. While some highly-noted researchers claim that it is true, others doubt its veracity.)*

Kennedy had courage and an independent, free thinking mind. Do you know what that bought him? Death! The Controllers said, in essence, "Don't mess with us!" And I assure you that NO American President ever did it again. They KILLED the King in broad daylight one afternoon in Dallas, Texas. Not only was the act atrocious, but also symbolic. Those bullets that pierced Kennedy's skull are still speaking loud and clear today.

If you don't believe me, listen to this quote given by JFK's brother, Robert: "All of us will ultimately be judged on the effort we have contributed to building a New World Order."

On the surface, it may sound as if RFK was supporting the Controllers, but read his words again: "We're going to be judged on what we do to help build a New World Order." Like his brother, RFK was intent on bucking the system and would probably have won the Presidency in 1968.

To stop his juggernaut, the Controllers put a bullet in his head in the summer of '68 in Los Angeles. That day was the VERY LAST that we've ever had any hope for an American Presidency free from the influence of the New World Order. Every occupant in the White House since then has been bought and paid for.

The situation quickly deteriorated during the Johnson Administration. As the *Chicago Tribune* reported in September, 1964: "David Rockefeller, President of Chase Manhattan Bank, briefed President Johnson today on his recent meeting with Premier Nikita Khrushchev of Russia."

It seems Rockefeller and Nikita talked about trade and credit, but the big question is: since when do bank presidents meet with foreign heads of state to talk about high-finance, then report back to the President of the United States? Doesn't this scenario seem a little weird?

RICHARD NIXON

In 1946, Richard Nixon was a small-town California lawyer who had never held public office. He was then "chosen" to run for Congress and won after receiving money from certain forces in New York City. By 1947, one year later, he wrote a bill for the United Nations to have the ability to "enact, interpret, and enforce world law." By 1952, only six years after being a "nobody lawyer" in Southern California, Nixon was Vice President of the United States!

You may wonder how this shady, somewhat unlikable person could have had such a meteoric rise to prominence. The answer lies with a man named Prescott Bush. (Hmmm, Bush ... why does that name ring a bell? I guess because Prescott was George Sr.'s father.)

Prescott Bush was Dwight Eisenhower's favorite golf partner and the man who was not only responsible for getting Nixon into politics, but also for securing Tricky Dick's slot as the Vice President.

Eight years later, Nixon ran for President against John Kennedy. As he was drawing up his platform at the Republican Convention, he was suddenly called away to Chicago to meet with someone at their apartment to work out a few "details."

Who was this individual? Mr. Nelson Rockefeller himself. Why would Nixon do such a thing? He already had the nomination sewed-up. Why would he meet with the Governor of New York while he was a Presidential nominee right in the middle of the Republican Convention? It's so strange that Senator Barry Goldwater described it as "Grant surrendering to Lee."

Nonetheless, Nixon lost to JFK in 1960, then lost a gubernatorial race in California to Pat Brown in 1962. Dejected and seemingly washed up, the candidate walked away, uttering his famous line, "You won't have Richard Nixon to kick around any more."

To save his career, Tricky Dick realized he needed something to spice up his portfolio. So in the early 1960's he joined an influential group. Guess which one it was. Yes, the nasty old CFR!

Still down on his luck, Nixon proceeded to pay a visit to someone in New York City. Guess who? Mr. David Rockefeller. Shortly thereafter, Nixon had not only moved to the Big Apple, but became a member of Nelson Rockefeller's law firm, and also lived in an apartment building owned by Rockefeller. Nelson ended up becoming Nixon's "employer, benefactor, landlord and neighbor."

He also worked for a man named John Mitchell (later to be part of his cabinet), who was the personal lawyer for a certain individual. Yup, Nelson Rockefeller. I'm not sure, but doesn't it seem as if the Rockefeller family was exerting an inordinate amount of influence on poor 'ol Tricky Dick?

Amazingly, the washed-up Nixon re-emerged and was running for President again in 1968 against Hubert Humphrey. And guess what organization BOTH candidates belonged to? The CFR. The same applied to the 1972 election where both Nixon and McGovern were CFR members. As George Wallace said, "There's not a dime's worth of difference between the Democratic and Republican parties." How true.

Nixon, of course, won the election in '68, and Pat Robertson relays an interesting story about this time period in his book, *New World Order*. The tale is told by former secretary of the Navy William Mittendorf, who served as Nixon's finance chairman in 1968. Mittendorf said the morning after Nixon won the election, at 5:30 AM, two people entered his hotel room to choose his Cabinet. One of them was William Rogers. And the other? Nelson Rockefeller.

Nixon's Commerce Secretary, Federal Reserve Board Chairman, HEW Secretary, Housing Secretary, U. N. Ambassador, and MANY others were all members of one distinct group. The CFR! He also offered the post of Treasury Secretary on two different occasions to the same person, who twice turned it down. Guess who that person was: David Rockefeller!

Spiro Agnew was also selected as Nixon's Vice President. Before he was nominated, Agnew had been the National Chairman for a certain candidate's presidential campaign in 1968. Who was the candidate? Nelson Rockefeller!

But the most blatantly nasty selection for his cabinet was Henry Kissinger. Let's take a moment and examine this man a little more closely. For starters, Nixon only met Kissinger one time prior to granting him the highly important position of Director of National Security, and that was at a casual dinner party. But y'see, Kissinger brought some clout to the table, for he was the five-year personal advisor on foreign affairs for a very prominent man. Who is that man? You guessed it. Nelson Rockefeller. Thus, it was Mr. Rockefeller who urged Nixon to appoint him, as author J. Robert Muskin discloses: "It was principally because of his long association with the Rockefellers that Henry Kissinger became a force in the Council. His influence is indirect and enormous -- much of it through his Rockefeller connection."

On November 1, 1971, *U.S. News & World Report* stated: "It was on the advice of Governor Rockefeller, who described Mr. Kissinger as 'the smartest guy available,' that Mr. Nixon chose him for his top adviser on foreign policy." In fact, after he was selected to fill this post, the Rockefeller's gave Kissinger a $50,000 check as a gift to cover his moving expenses to Washington, D.C. What a nice bunch of guys, huh!

Finally, according to Associated Press Writer Deb Reichmann (February 11, 2002), "Just before he left government, Kissinger had all the phone records moved from his office at the State Department." Guess where he moved them? To a vault at David Rockefeller's estate in New York!

But that's not the end. During the first year of his Presidency, Nixon came up with a program called his "New Federalism." Where did he get this title? From a book written by someone close to him. Who is that "someone"? Nelson Rockefeller!

Now, where do you think Nelson Rockefeller's head was at during this era? In an October 1975 interview with *Playboy* magazine, he said, "I'm a great believer in planning. Economic, social, political, military, total world planning." Hmmm. WORLD PLANNING and the Rockefellers. Do you think that has anything to do with the New World Order, or is it just a coincidence?

The amount of control by the outside forces was so extreme that Mike Culbert wrote an article in the Richmond, California *Independent-Gazette* on June 27, 1974 in reference to his discussions with Charles Colson (a member of Nixon's cabinet). Stated Culbert: "There is a de facto 'secret government' operating nationally and internationally and involved in the highest circles of the U. S. government, exercising an impact over domestic policies and economics ranging between extreme influence to, at times, outright control. This extreme influence to outright control naturally includes the Presidency. The de facto 'secret government,' much of whose intellectual -- and financial -- muscle are to be found in the New York office of the CFR, the great tax-free foundation, and certain international firms and corporations."

As we all know, the Nixon Administration melted down and he was bounced from office. Things could have gone better, but his successor, Gerald Ford (a member of the totally corrupt Warren Commission), attended two top secretive meetings prior to being "annoointed" President. What type of meetings were they? You guessed it - Bilderberg meetings! But that's not the worst part of this scam-job. Do you remember whom Ford chose as his Vice-President? Good 'ol Nelson

Rockefeller. And if Sarah Jane Moore or Lynnette "Squeaky" Fromme (on two different occasions) had known how to shoot their guns, we would have had a Rockefeller in the White House! Scary, huh!

JIMMY CARTER

To understand Jimmy Carter's phenomenal rise to public office, we first must return to his home state of Georgia. Which family has much of its personal investment property in Atlanta, Georgia? Answer: the Rockefellers. Their influence in this city (home of Ted Turner's AOL Time-Warner mind control brainwashing psychic driving CNN TV network) is so vast that David Horowitz, in his book, *The Rockefellers,* said, "Atlanta is Rockefeller Center South."

In 1971 David Rockefeller invited the virtually unknown Jimmy Carter to eat with him at Chase Manhattan Bank in New York City. The year before, in 1970, he was transformed from a simple peanut farmer into being the Governor of Georgia.

Their interaction continued in 1973. Laurence Stern, reporting in the *Washington Post* on May 8, 1976, said that Jimmy Carter met with two individuals in London and was told that he would be given the go ahead to win the Presidency.

Who were these two individuals? One was Lord Rothschild, and the other was David Rockefeller! This story is corroborated by a 1973 *London Times* article that said while in London during the autumn of 1973, Carter met with another visitor who was forming an international commission and wanted someone to fill the slot of Presidency in the White House.

The commission they formed was the Trilateral Commission, of course. And the person Carter met with? David Rockefeller! Now do you think there are no behind-the-scene interventions by very powerful and secretive men? Carter met with the Rothschilds and Rockefellers!

But David Rockefeller wasn't the only man to take Carter under his wing. There was also the mad dog Zgibniew Brzezinski. On May 23, 1976, *New York Times* reporter Leslie H. Gelb wrote: "Brzezinski was the first guy in the Community to pay attention to Carter, to take him seriously. He spent time with Carter, talked to him, sent him books and articles, educated him." In other words, Brzezinski became his mentor -- making and molding this virtual "unknown," then SELECTING him as the President! Sixteen years later, they did the same thing with another relative "unknown" -- Bill Clinton.

Can't you see? THEY have much more influence than WE do in regard to whom will occupy the White House.

In fact, in 1973 (three years before the election), Zig decided what the WINNER of the next election needed: "The Democratic candidate in 1976 will have to emphasize work, the family, religion, and, increasingly, patriotism ..."

My question is: Why is HE deciding anything for us, let alone what OUR President needs in order to win?

The *Far Eastern Economic Review*, quoted by Howard Zinn in his book *A People's History of the United States* confirms this point. He writes: "Peter Bourne, Carter's former Deputy Campaign Chief, has said David [Rockefeller] and Zbig [Brzezinski] had both agreed that Carter was the ideal politician to build on."

I don't know about you, but doesn't this "arrangement" seem pretty twisted? Since when do David Rockefeller and Zbigniew Brzezinski decide who the ideal President will be? Shouldn't WE do that? Worse, after they chose him, he ends up winning, too!

The manipulations keep going; in 1973, David Rockefeller and Zbig formed the Trilateral Commission. These men wanted a Trilateral in the Oval Office in '76, so they went through a list of all the Liberal Democrats and decided who would best fit the "suit."

Zbig was quoted as saying at the time: "It was a close thing between Carter and Askew [Florida Governor], but we were impressed that Carter had opened up trade offices for the state of Georgia in Brussels & Tokyo. That seemed to fit perfectly into the concept of the Trilaterals."

Again, why is Zibgniew Brzezinski making these decisions, especially ones that are furthering THEIR global interests? Worse, after he helps to decide WHO will be President and what policies are implemented, he then becomes part of the Cabinet!

Senator Barry Goldwater, a man definitely in the know, describes the situation: "David Rockefeller and Zbigniew Brzezinski found Jimmy Carter to be their ideal candidate. They helped him win the nomination and the Presidency. To accomplish this purpose, they mobilized the money power of Wall Street, the intellectual influence of the academic community -- which is subservient to the wealth of the great tax-free foundations -- and the media controllers represented in the membership of the Council of Foreign Relations and Trilateral Commission."

Ladies and gentlemen, Barry Goldwater isn't any run-of-the-mill Joe 6-pak sitting on a barstool spouting off about politics. He was one of the most knowledgeable senators we've ever had. And in the above paragraph, he essentially outlined how the 1976 presidential election was rigged by forces hiding behind a cloak of secrecy.

A big question now is: what part did Jimmy Carter play in this scenario? Was he fully aware of the machinations taking place behind the scenes? Instead of giving a direct answer, we'll let this drama unfold on its own.

To get the ball rolling, let's begin with a speech Carter gave in Boston on February 17, 1976, nine months before the election: "The people of this country know from bitter experience that we are not going to get these changes merely by shifting around the same group of insiders. The insiders had their chance and they have not delivered."

I agree. So far; so good.

A couple of weeks before winning the election, Hamilton Jordan, one of Jimmy Carter's aides, said, "If, after the inauguration, you find a Cy Vance as Secretary of State and Zigbniew Brzezinski as head of National Security, then I would say we failed. And I would quit. But that's not going to happen. You're going to see new faces and new ideas."

Hmmmm, I like his spirit, but guess what? Cyrus Vance DID became the Secretary of State. But before doing so, he was the Chairman of the Board of a very famous foundation. Can you guess which one? Yup, the Rockefeller Foundation!

And Zbig DID become the Head of National Security. And can you guess what organization he belonged to? The CFR. Zbig is also co-founder of the Trilateral Commission with ... you guessed it ... David Rockefeller!

Things are really starting to look bad now, especially when we consider that the head of the CFR during Carter's Administration was David Rockefeller. Also, Carter's Vice President, Walter Mondale, was CFR, as were those who filled his top three posts:

- Secretary of State - Cyrus Vance
- Secretary of Defense - Harold Brown
- Secretary of the Treasury - Michael Blumenthal

Also, his CIA Director was CFR, as were the Secretary of HEW, HUD, his National Security Advisor, and the Ambassador to the U.N. In all, and listen closely, the TOP 19 positions in Carter's Cabinet were held by Trilateral Commission members. These are all extremely powerful posts and constitute nearly one-third of the TOTAL United States membership in the Trilateral Commission. Think about how scary that is.

One out of every three people in Jimmy Carter's cabinet belonged to the TC. Why didn't he just fess up and call his Administration the CFR/TC? It would have been more accurate. Add that the fact that every single person that was instrumental in constructing Carter's foreign policy was a previous member of the Trilateral Commission. Not 10% or 50%, but 100%!

Even Paul Volcker, the Chairman of the Federal Reserve, was a former employee of a famous bank. Guess which one? David Rockefeller's Chase Manhattan! This administration was so infiltrated and corrupted by outside forces, on the July 1977 cover of the *Atlantic Monthly* is a cartoon picture of Jimmy Carter and David Rockefeller in a wooden tub, with the headline reading, "Carter Revealed: He's a Rockefeller Republican." Are you finally starting to see the full picture?

In his book, *New World Order,* Pat Robertson tells the following story: Lou Sheldon was a pro-family advocate and friend of Jimmy Carter. Prior to Carter winning the election, these two discussed what type of people they would like in Carter's cabinet.

"[Lou] Sheldon arrived at the Carter residence to find the next President barefoot and in blue jeans. They greeted each other warmly and Sheldon proudly presented the booklet [with a roster of names and resumés of persons they wanted in their cabinet]. Carter took it, read it, and began to cry.

"When he got back to Virginia Beach, Sheldon said, 'Jimmy was so touched by all the work that we did that tears came to his eyes.'

"I said, 'Lou, you are wrong. The reason he cried is because the appointment process is out of his hands, and he is not going to appoint any of his [own] people.'"

Not ONE person Jimmy Carter wanted in his Cabinet was appointed! Not one. They were all selected for him. Are you starting to get a sick feeling in your stomach?

RONALD REAGAN

After Ronald Reagan beat Jimmy Carter in the 1980 election, you would think there couldn't be two more opposite candidates. Carter was a liberal Southern Democrat and Reagan, a Hollywood Conservative Republican. Surely, the same people who infiltrated Carter's cabinet would never be able to do the same with 'ol Ronald Reagan, would they?

This doesn't seem to be the case. In 1980, two months before the November election, a party was thrown for Reagan in Middlesburg,

Virginia. Reagan sat in the seat of honor, of course, and beside him to his right sat a very important man. Guess who that person was: David Rockefeller, head of the CFR & Trilateral Commission.

Somewhere along the line, Reagan was told that his bid for the Presidency on the Republican ticket would be thwarted unless he chose George Bush as his Vice President. He did so, and soon was bombarded by heaps of money by ... guess whom. David Rockefeller.

Ironically, a few months after being inaugurated, Reagan was nearly assassinated by John Hinckley, Jr. Who do you think was VERY close friends with the Hinckley family, even dining with them shortly before the assassination attempt? George Bush himself!

Coincidence? You decide, especially in light of the fact that Nelson Rockefeller came within a breath of being the President if Squeaky Fromme had known how to shoot a gun.

Although he claimed to not be an insider, Reagan's cabinet was packed with CFR and/or TC members, including his Campaign Manager, CIA Director, Chief of Staff, and Secretaries of State, Treasury, Commerce, and Defense. It appears the lyrics may have changed, but the music was still the same.

GEORGE HERBERT WALKER BUSH - THE ULTIMATE INSIDER

Briefly, here is George H.W. Bush's biography:

1948: Graduated from Yale, where he was a member of Skull & Bones, the most notorious collegiate secret society in existence and breeding ground for future CFR and CIA members. (Note: Bush would later be on the CFR's Board of Directors, and also a member of the Trilateral Commission.)

November 29, 1963: Six days after JFK was assassinated, J. Edgar Hoover, head of the FBI, sent a memo to the State Department saying that Texas Special Agent W. T. Forsythe briefed "Mr. George Bush of the Central Intelligence Agency" about "problems with the JFK assassination."

Following is a quote from Kris Millegan's article, *Everything You Ever Wanted To Know, But Were Afraid To Ask* that appeared in *ParaScope*: "Many researchers contend that George Bush has been with the CIA since the early 1950s, and that one of his jobs was to consolidate and coordinate the worldwide narcotics industry, the largest industry on earth. Some say that one of the reasons behind the Vietnam "Police Action" was a cover for the consolidation of the "Golden Triangle."

1967-70: Texas Congressman, two terms

1971-3: U. S. Ambassador during the Nixon Administration

1973-4: National Chairman, Republican Party

1974-5: U. S. Liason to China under President Ford; Board of Directors on the Atlantic Council of the United States

1975: CIA Director

1979: According to plan (the following year he would make his first run for the Presidency), Bush stepped down from both the CFR and TC. Concerning this move, David Rockefeller told Sidney Blumenthal of the *Washington Post* on February 10, 1988, "Even though he has resigned, he hasn't walked away from them." In fact, on March 19, 1981, less than two months after entering the office of Vice President, Elder Bush spoke before the Trilateral Commission in Washington, D.C.! Also, the next day he was supposed to confer with them again in the White House, but that's the day Reagan was shot.

1980: When Bush, Sr. ran against Ronald Reagan in the Republican Primaries, he received the highest contributions allowed by law from the following people: David Rockefeller, Edwin Rockefeller, Helen Rockefeller, Laurance Rockefeller, Mary Rockefeller, Godfrey Rockefeller, and a number of other Rockefeller relatives and employees.

1981: Vice President of the United States

1988: Elected as President of the U.S. by defeating Michael Dukakis

1989: Guess who was listed as a new member in the CFR's annual report? Michael Dukakis!

George H. W. Bush's Cabinet: All CFR members

- Secretary of Defense - Dick Cheney
- Secretary of the Treasury - Nicholas Brady
- National Security Advisor - Brent Scowcroft
- Attorney General - Dick Thornburgh
- CIA Director - William Webster
- Federal Reserve Chairman - Alan Greenspan
- Joint Chief of Staff - Colin Powell

(Do any of these names sound familiar … like maybe these people are part of the current administration?)

September, 1989: Boris Yeltsin journeyed to America and visited two people. Whom was the second person he met? Answer: President George H.W. Bush at the White House. But whom was the FIRST person he met? David Rockefeller in New York City at the CFR headquarters!!!

BILL CLINTON

Before discussing the specifics of Bill Clinton's career, we need to know that his home state of Arkansas has long been known to be the stronghold of a prominent family for many years. In fact, one member of this famous family was not only elected as the Governor of Arkansas in 1967, but was also the first person to notice Bill Clinton and take him under his wing.

The individual in question? Winthrop Rockefeller! It seems like that name keeps popping up over and over and over again.

After graduating from high school, Bill Clinton took an internship under Arkansas Senator J. William Fulbright, who was a U. S. Senator for 32 years. He also sponsored the "Fullbright Act of 1946" which was responsible for sending American students overseas to study. In fact, Fullbright was a Rhodes Scholar at Oxford, a staunch advocate of the United Nations, and is described as a "strong internationalist," another name for a *globalist*.

After high school, Clinton attended college at Georgetown, where the noted Illuminati insider Professor Carroll J. Quigley (author of the premier CFR book *Tragedy and Hope*) mentored him. Clinton's "training" continued with a Rhodes Scholarship at England's Oxford University, which is home for "The Round Table" and the number one training ground for New World Order recruits.

He then received his law degree from Yale University, home of Skull & Bones and the Bush Family's favorite school.

Clinton returned to Arkansas, which as I said earlier was ruled for years by the Rockefeller banking family. At age 29 (an amazingly young age), he became the state's Attorney General. Shortly thereafter, he rose to become the Governor and then joined an infamous organization in 1988.

Which group could it be? Of course -- the Trilateral Commission! Then in 1989, he became a member of yet another group. Can you guess which one it was? You got it -- the CFR! Are you noticing a theme, or a continuous thread that keeps running through each successive administration? Finally in 1991, Clinton was secretly invited to the crème de la crème meeting of them all -- the Bilderberg meeting -- in Baden Baden, Germany. There, it was decided that he would become the next Democratic nominee for the Presidency.

Regrettably, Clinton won the 1992 election and during his first inaugural speech, he mentioned and thanked only one person by name. Do you know who it was? Dr. Carroll Quigley, one of the premier insiders of all time, and noted CFR authority.

So Clinton entered the Oval Office, and soon his Cabinet was LOADED with CFR, TC and Bilderberg members, including his National Security Advisor, Vice President, Secretary of State, Secretary of Defense, Chairman of the Joint Chiefs of Staff, CIA Director, Treasury Secretary, Chairman of the Council of Economic Advisors, Secretary of the Interior, and HUD Secretary.

Is everything finally clear? The same people -- the CFR, TC, and Bilderberg members keep running the American Presidency regardless of whom *they select*!

The same applies to our current President, George W. Bush. And if you don't believe me, leaf back and take a look at the people in his father's cabinet. They're practically IDENTICAL to who now fills those seats. Every one of them is bought, sold, and controlled.

CHAPTER FORTY-NINE

An Overview of Gerald Carroll's "Project Seek: Onassis, Kennedy, and the Gemstone Thesis"

During the 1970's, a document called *The Gemstone Papers* was circulated throughout the underground. The author, Bruce Roberts, encouraged his readers to pass this thesis along however possible. "The only way to spread this information here in America is hand-to-hand. Make one, five, ten, one-hundred copies - or whatever you can - and give them to friends, pols, or media groups. The game is nearly up. Either the Mafia goes - or America goes."

The Gemstone Thesis contends the following: During the early 1900's, Aristotle Onassis and Joseph Kennedy became extremely wealthy men - Onassis from cornering the shipping lanes and running opium - and Kennedy from bootlegging whiskey during Prohibition. Along the way, these men joined forces to further each other's career. In the 1950's, Onassis' cohorts kidnapped Howard Hughes and replaced him with a double, then assumed control of his empire (which was built upon the defense and aviation industries).

Onassis, via his mob connections, was instrumental in giving John F. Kennedy the presidency in 1960. Indebted to Onassis, John Kennedy and his brother Robert nonetheless double-crossed the kingpin and his Mafia counterparts after Joe Sr. suffered a heart attack in 1961. Onassis retaliated by destroying Camelot (do you remember that famous assassination?), then ran off with Jackie O. Gerald Ford and the Warren Commission covered up the entire affair by naming Lee Harvey Oswald as the lone-killer (patsy). Robert and Teddy Kennedy were well aware of these circumstances, so the former was also "hit," while the latter's political career was destroyed at Chappaquidick.

The Gemstone File, a sordid expose of these shenanigans, fell into Richard Nixon's hands. Paranoid about his long-standing mob connections, he soon became entangled in the Watergate debacle and was "brought down" by Katherine Graham of the Washington Post. With Tricky Dick out of the picture, Gerald Ford was rewarded for his services by being given the non-elected position of President of the United States of America.

This tale concludes with *Hustler* Magazine's Larry Flynt. The illustrious porn king became interested in The Gemstone Files during the mid-1970's, and offered one million dollars to anyone that could reveal the truth behind the Kennedy Assassination. Prior to releasing the Gemstone Files to a national audience in *Hustler* Magazine, Flynt was crippled by a gunman's bullets. Months later, a censored version of the Gemstone document was released.

With this timeline in mind, I'd like to expand upon the particulars. Before doing so, though, I'll begin with an introduction to the Gemstone Files that appeared in the February, 1979 edition of *Hustler* Magazine written by editor John G. Clancy:

"Throughout history, whenever new voices become powerful and commanding, there is a traceable pattern of violent response. Whether from the right or left, there is a stealthy, savage reaction, like a shaft of ramrod steel. From Jesus Christ to Chile's Salvador Allende, the markings are clear. Action calls forth reaction, and nowhere is this more clear than in the savage history of our own country: Abraham Lincoln, Huey Long, John Fitzgerald Kennedy, Robert Kennedy and all the others whose cries for justice have been stilled by the staccato burst of a gun. These are the facts of our political life. Sudden death is not just an overtime in professional football.

The article that follows, the Gemstone File - a condensation of a thousand-page manuscript - may be considered by many to be a work of madness. But remember, through all the ages, all innovative works of genius have been thought to be the products of insanity. One need only reflect on the spectacle of Galileo recanting before the church. It was madness - they said - for him to advance the notion that the earth moved around the sun. And they were right: It was madness, even though he was correct. The astronomer's thinking was madness because it upset the settled scheme of things and could be demonstrably proven for all to see. For that reason, Galileo's idea had to be dismissed and done away with - perhaps, just like the Gemstone File.

No doubt reasonable men will say that the factual essentials of the Gemstone File are simply preposterous - because they go too far and encompass too much. That may be true, but it should never be overlooked that the hellish vision this article contains may well bear the germs of truth, virulent though they may be."

Aristotle Onassis, Joseph Kennedy, and John D. Rockefeller

One of the Gemstone File's main contentions was that Aristotle Onassis was the "crowned head of the Mafia." It also states that Ari made his fortune by transporting opium, especially after the United States outlawed it in the early part of the 20th century, causing prices to increase tenfold. Being an extremely profitable venture, Ari made a killing by transporting drugs; then focused his attention on the oil business by joining forces with John D. Rockefeller. The Gemstone File claims that in 1934, these two titans reached an agreement where Rockefeller would refine the oil, while Aristotle shipped it. Ari knew that whoever ruled the shipping lanes would become inordinately wealthy, for not only would he control the oil market, but drugs, arms, and war-supplies, also. John D. Rockefeller, on the other hand, had an interest in recapturing the oil industry after the government forced him to break-up his monopoly at Standard Oil in the early 1900's.

While embarking upon these pursuits, Ari was also involved with another historical figure - Joseph Kennedy. Old Man Kennedy, of course, made his fortune by being a bootlegger during Prohibition. Being that booze was illegal in this country, Kennedy struck up a deal with Ari where Mr. Onassis would ship the contraband into Boston; then Joe Sr. would sell it. Having a long-term association with the Mob, Joe Kennedy felt right at home dealing with Ari. To show his gratitude, in 1937, Joe Kennedy, while Chairman of the United States Maritime Commission, sold a fleet of surplus ships to Aristotle. With these ships, Onassis would build his empire.

Joe Kennedy's decision to sell these ships to Ari was quite controversial being that the world was quickly barreling toward World War II. But war was exactly what Ari, Joe, John D., the Roosevelts, and I. G. Farben wanted. What better way was there to make a quick buck than selling oil, arms, and drugs to both the Axis and Allied Forces? And don't forget how much dough John D. and Kennedy made off the Stock Market Crash (see "This Is How Our Fine Country Was Destroyed In 1913"). While we're on the subject of World War II, here's a final side-note - the notorious I. G. Farben, manufacturer of the Zyklon B gases used in Nazi death camps, was also the largest heroin producer in Germany between WWI & WWII. A nice bunch of guys, huh!!

Howard Hughes

The story associated with Howard Hughes is a rather brief, but vitally important key to this story. Y'see, Hughes may have become the wealthiest man in the shortest amount of time during the 20th century. By cornering the aviation and defense industries, he literally came into money hands-over-fist. If you think about the top dollars paid to the likes of Northrup, McDonell Douglas, Hughes, etc., you'll understand where his wealth originated. Plus, Hughes was smart enough to get past America's tax laws by setting up the tax-free Hughes Foundation.

Hating the concept of taxes, and seeing what a cash cow Hughes was sitting upon, Aristotle Onassis decided to kidnap Hughes in 1957 and replace him with a double. That same year, Onassis took final control of the Mob; then ran the Hughes Empire as another arm of his growing illegal operation. Hughes, on the other hand, became a secluded heroin addict who finally died in 1971.

The Kennedy's

As mentioned in the timeline, Joe Kennedy Sr. and Aristotle Onassis became "business partners" in the early 1900's, each of them furthering the other's career. During Prohibition, when obtaining alcohol was difficult, Mr. Onassis transported huge shipments of booze into Boston for Kennedy to sell illegally. In return, Joe Kennedy laid the foundation for Onassis' Empire by selling him a fleet of U. S. surplus ships while he was Chairman of the U. S. Maritime Commission in 1937. This single act made it possible for Ari O. to become one of the single wealthiest men on the planet. In return, Onassis promised that the two men would continue "helping" each other, and that someday a Kennedy would be put in the White House.

So, to begin this section, let's set the stage with the following scene. This year is 1957, Dwight Eisenhower is the President, and JFK is a New England Congressman with a promising future. Three years before the next presidential election, Joe Kennedy Sr. took his son John onto Ari O's yacht for a little "discussion" reminding Ari of his promise. Someday a Kennedy would be in the White House.

Onassis felt very confident about this election in that he owned both candidates. Y'see, Richard Nixon, who would be the Republican nominee, was bought and paid for years earlier by Howard Hughes, who had recently been kidnapped by Onassis. Nixon had countless "dues" to be paid because of his Mob connections, and was thus already in the bag. JFK, on the other hand, was well aware of his old man's ties to not only Ari, but also his history of mob-related dealings during Prohibition. If you doubt this analysis, ask yourself how John Kennedy could have possibly had a very tumultuous affair with Judith Exner, who was the girlfriend of Sam Giancana, quite possibly the most notorious mobster in the country at that time. People just don't have "flings" with Mob girlfriends out of the blue. There has to be some sort of connection. In the end, we know it's true because without the Mob pulling Chicago for Kennedy in the 1960 election, he never would have defeated Nixon.

Now, here's where things get sticky. In 1961, Joe Sr. suffered a stroke and slipped out of the picture. JFK and Bobby were, in essence, free ... now able to call their own shots. They knew what kind of men their father ran around with, and they were well aware of his deal with Ari. In all honesty, they could have been on the cusp of a true Kennedy presidential dynasty. First John would serve until 1968, then Bobby from '69 to '76, and finally Teddy from '77 to '84. The Kennedy's could have conceivably held the Oval Office for 24 years!

But what do John and Bobby start doing? They welch on the agreement Joe made with Ari and started going after Organized Crime! I'm sure all of us have seen the infamous newsreels where Jimmy Hoffa is sitting before the Senate and Bobby Kennedy is grilling him. But instead of letting well enough alone, the Gemstone File contends that the Kennedy's double-crossed Ari and began the most extreme family bloodbath in U. S. history.

Why would the Kennedy brothers commit what was essentially political suicide? It's difficult to gauge their motivation, but on the surface, it almost appears to be a case of idealism run rampant. I mean, here are the Kennedy boys - JFK is president and his younger brother Bobby is Attorney General. The old man is now incapacitated and no longer pulling their strings, yet they have all these mobsters, Teamsters, crooked politicians, corrupt billionaires, and creeps like the CIA and J. Edgar Hoover to deal with. Plus, the media created a "Camelot" setting for them - Jack could get laid any time he wanted with any woman he desired, even Marilyn Monroe, and the public, by and large, adored this youthful, handsome, entertaining president. If he bucked the system and went after the Mob, what could possibly happen? He was the President after all - indestructible, invincible, and untouchable.

Ari O. didn't buy into this rationale for one second. He got double-crossed, and didn't like seeing this good guy/bad guy scenario being played out by two rich kids from Massachusetts. So, being that the Kennedy boys welched on their agreement, Ari put a hit on them. Considering how many others were infuriated by John's actions, it didn't take long to find a multitude of recruits to help pull off the "killing of a king."

The first black mark against Kennedy came with the Bay of Pigs fiasco. Not only did Kennedy blow it, then blame the debacle on the CIA (who he later said would be "broken into a thousand pieces and scattered to the wind"), but the Mob and Ari O. were losing tons of money ever since Castro took over Cuba and shut down the casinos. In those days, Cuba was a terrific playground (popularized by Ernest Hemingway) attracting scores of wealthy tourists that boozed and gambled and spent their dough freely. Once Castro shut down this market, many people felt the pinch.

In all likelihood, I don't think the Kennedy brothers knew what they were dealing with at this point. Sure, they were trying to clean up the System and get rid of the crooks, but when you start going after the Mob and the CIA, idealism doesn't get you very far. On the other hand, Ari, a long-time drug dealer, was extremely street smart and realized that there was supposed to be "honor among thieves" and a "criminal code" where ya stuck to your deals and didn't screw over certain people. What made things worse was that Ari was the one who put JFK into office over Nixon, and now Kennedy blew the Bay of Pigs. Tricky Dick would have surely carried out their plans in Cuba and given the gambling and booze profits back to the big boys.

So now we've reached the year of 1963, and plans are set in motion to knock-off Kennedy. But what were the reasons? Why kill a sitting president?

1) Kennedy undoubtedly wanted to get the United States out of Vietnam - a situation he inherited from Dwight Eisenhower. The first question people should ask is: why were we even in Vietnam? What made that tiny country so important? Did we really need to stop the spread of Communism so badly that we'd sacrifice 57,000 American lives, plus shatter countless others?

Well, the real reason we were in Vietnam had little to do with "Communism." What certain people actually wanted to do was corner, or take control of, "The Golden Triangle" so that they could monopolize the opium fields and resultant heroin trade. Hell, the drug trade became so vitally important that heroin was even being shipped back to America in the coffins of our dead G. I.'s!

Vietnam was also crucially important to the War Machine and the immense amount of money that could be derived from it. So, it all reverts back to the standard tricks of the trade - illegal drugs, running guns, and control through fear and violence.

2) Clean up and convict the Mob

3) Drastically lessen the CIA's influence. Don't forget, this was an agency that was established less than two decades earlier by heavy-hitters like Allen Dulles and all the Nazi creeps he smuggled into this country via "Project Paperclip" after World War II.

4) Kennedy's inability to take back Cuba so that the Mob could recoup its gambling profits.

5) Finally, the Kennedy Administration had plans to investigate the financial dealings of Howard Hughes, which would have been disastrous to Ari being that they kidnapped and replaced him with a double in 1957.

With the above list in mind, it isn't hard to see Ari O's motivation in knocking off the King. After the Kennedy's enacted a full-out assault and reneged on their father's deal, Ari counter-attacked by bringing Camelot to its knees. Try to look at the situation in this light. Here was JFK on top of the world - he's a star, he's the President, he's getting women galore and he feels indestructible. Likewise, Ari has become so wealthy and so assured of his hold over the cops, the press, the FBI & CIA, plus the legal system, that he was convinced that he could kill Kennedy in broad daylight. If he was successful, from that day forward the Mob and the United States Government would become one in the same. So, what we have here are two tremendously powerful forces at work, and two inflated, very confident egos. Each was at the top of their game, but Ari had one advantage.

According to *The Gemstone File*, in October of 1963, only one month before her husband was assassinated; Jackie O. spent two weeks on Ari's yacht! Think about this! Ari was LIVING the mobster's creed - kill your enemy, then steal his woman. Worse, the author contends that not only did Jackie begin an affair with Aristotle, but she also knew that he planned on whacking him. Jackie didn't know the exact time or date, but she was aware of what was going on. Why do you think she exhibited such superhuman calm after such a horrendous event as a public assassination? I mean, her husband's brains were blasted into her lap, and Jackie O. was cool as a cucumber.

If this all sounds too incredible, I'd like to relay a story that I read years ago. The tale takes place at Jackie's wedding, and while speaking with an old friend during her bridal dance, one that she hadn't seen in years, the man says, "I can't believe you fell in love and got married so quickly since the last time I saw you." Upon hearing this statement, Jackie leans forward and whispers in the man's ear, "My dear, whoever said that I was in love?"

Anyway, as we all know, Kennedy got ambushed and killed in Dallas, and Lee Harvey Oswald became the fall guy/patsy. What most people aren't aware of was that two days later, who was in attendance with all the mourners at the Kennedy mansion? None other than Aristotle Onassis! Think about how wild this is! What in God's name was Ari O. doing at the Kennedy's house? Why would HE be there?

Things are starting to get a little fishy, huh? By this time, Mr. Onassis is the crowned head of the Mafia, the world's (supposedly) richest man, a global powerhouse, and he just snagged the President's wife! Plus, he had the sitting president also in his pocket, for soon after the assassination, LBJ was threatened by Ari himself. "There is no conspiracy. Oswald was a lone nut assassin. Get it, Lyndon?" Ari then reminded him that if he pushed things, there was a good possibility that Air Force One would have an "accident" some day. When LBJ finally died in 1971, some of his final words were, "You know, fellows, it really was a conspiracy ..."

Bobby Kennedy was well aware of what transpired, and who killed his brother. Still being full of piss and vinegar, there were hints made that he would expose the real "conspiracy" of killers behind his brother's assassination. So, to "silence" this problem, Bobby was killed in Los Angeles during his 1968 Democratic Primary Campaign --- a slot he was sure to win. Similar to Lee Harvey Oswald, Sirhan Sirhan was the patsy.

Prior to his "role" in the assassination, Sirhan wrote what is a classic example of psychic driving mind control.

"My determination to eliminate RFK is becoming more of an unshakable obsession. RFK must die, RFK must be killed, RFK must be assassinated. RFK must die, RFK must be killed, RFK must be assassinated. RFK must die, RFK must be killed, RFK must be assassinated. RFK must die, RFK must be killed, RFK must be assassinated ... Robert F. Kennedy must be assassinated before 5 June 68, Robert Kennedy must be assassinated ..."

Seeing what happened to his two older brothers, Teddy Kennedy was terrified and vowed to be obedient to Ari O., even giving him his blessing to marry Jackie. The only problem was Mary Jo Kopechne, a key organizer of RFK's campaign, who stumbled upon too much "touchy" information and considered exposing it. To keep her in check, and to also destroy any possibility that Teddy would enter the White House, Chappaquidick drove a stake through any future presidential hopes for Teddy. What had once looked like a six-term Kennedy dynasty in the Oval Office had now petered to nothingness.

Nixon, Ford, and Watergate

With the Kennedy boys out of the way and Lyndon Johnson's usefulness depleted, America needed to "elect" a new president in 1968. Of all the fine citizens in this country, who's the best person we could come up with? Richard Nixon! Yup, 'ol Tricky Dick himself.

So, how does Mr. Nixon fit into the "Gemstone" picture? Well, like all of the major players in this scenario, Nixon had Mob ties out the kazoo. Where Joe Kennedy was tied to the Prohibition-era gangsters, and, according to Bruce Roberts, Gerald Ford's real father had a background in Organized Crime, Nixon was also connected to the likes of Bebe Rebozo and Carlos Marcella. In essence, then, from 1960 to 1976, America's Presidency was characterized by very strong organized crime ties.

Richard Nixon first entered the "Gemstone" picture in the mid-1940's when Howard Hughes "bought" his first politician, Nixon, by giving his brother Donald a $200,000 non-repayable loan for the 1946 California Congressional race. Nixon's career progressed rapidly as he became Dwight Eisenhower's Vice President for eight years, beginning in 1953. A temporary blow came in 1960, though, when he lost his presidential bid to JFK. Three years later, naturally, Kennedy was killed, and Gerald Ford would cover-up the assassination as head of the Warren Commission.

By 1968, Nixon was elected as our esteemed President, and by 1969 he read an early version of *The Gemstone Files*. Already looking forward to re-election, Nixon realized that the powers-that-be had loads of dirt on him, especially in regard to his Mob ties. Fearful that this information could be "leaked" to the Democratic National Committee, the seeds for Watergate were planted.

Over time, the Controllers came to see Nixon as a loose cannon that had to be eliminated. So, what was originally a non-eventful break-in at the Watergate Hotel became President Nixon's downfall. Leading the charge for Nixon's head (at least publicly) was none other than Katherine Graham, who was in charge of *The Washington Post*. As you'll see later in this book (see: *Votescam*), you'll discover that Nixon threatened to revoke Graham's FCC license at a television station she owned in Florida due to her failure to report on the widespread fraud in Dade County. (Former Attorney General Janet Reno also played a prominent role in concealing the illegal voting practices.)

Also, being that Katherine Graham was known as "the most powerful woman in America," and was a member of both the CFR and the Bilderbergs, she was certainly in a position to implement a "downfall" if the Controllers deemed it necessary. Thus, Ms. Graham became a "Deep Throat"-type figure that fed information to Woodward and Bernstein. With the writing on the wall that his "crucifixion" had been successfully orchestrated, Nixon finally resigned after David Rockefeller sent Henry Kissinger into his office with these final words: "Resign. Right now." This, of course, occurred at the infamous meeting where Kissinger and Nixon knelt down and prayed together!

The wildest part of this entire scenario, according to Bruce Roberts, was that the notorious 18 1/2 minutes of "missing time" on the Watergate Tapes is of Nixon ranting about those "assholes Roberts, Onassis, and Howard Hughes." Now do you know why this portion of the tape was mysteriously "erased?" Anyway, Gerald Ford was rewarded for his "loyalty and subservience" in covering up the Kennedy Assassination by being awarded the Presidency after Nixon got knocked off his pedestal. By agreeing not to spill the beans, Nixon was granted a full pardon by Mr. Ford. In all, The Machine kept rolling without missing a beat.

Conclusion

The final piece to this puzzle concerns an unlikely character - Larry Flynt of *Hustler* fame. It seems that Mr. Flynt wasn't actually shot by a "right-wing moralist" that disagreed with his magazine's content, but was actually "brought down" because of a reward he offered in January, 1978. Y'see, Flynt said he'd pay $1 million to anyone that could prove there was a conspiracy behind Kennedy's assassination. Flynt already had "The Gemstone File" in his possession for at least three years since his magazine became nationally renowned, and certain forces realized that he could make things very uncomfortable for them. So, to prevent the publication of a very damning expose that had *The Gemstone File* at its center, Flynt was shot and crippled. In February, 1979, *Hustler* Magazine finally ran a "Gemstone" article, but its version was watered down, sanitized, and heavily censored, thus not stepping on any of the wrong toes.

The rest is history - and business as usual.

CHAPTER FIFTY

An Overview of Michael Collins Piper's "Final Judgment: The Missing Link in the JFK Assassination Conspiracy"

JFK, The Atomic Bomb, and Israel's War Machine

"Israel need not apologize for the assassination or destruction of those who seek to destroy it. The first order of business for any country is the protection of its people."

Washington Jewish Week, October 9, 1997

In March, 1992, Illinois Representative Paul Findley said in *The Washington Report on Middle East Affairs*, "It is interesting – but not surprising – to note that in all the words written and uttered about the Kennedy assassination, Israel's intelligence agency, the Mossad, has never been mentioned."

Considering that the Mossad is quite possibly the most ruthless and efficient intelligence agency in the world, it is peculiar that they have never been scrutinized in relation to the Kennedy assassination, especially when practically every other entity in the world (short of Elvis impersonators) has been implicated. But that all changed in January, 1994 with the release of Michael Collins Piper's *Final Judgment*. In this book, Piper says, "Israel's Mossad was a primary (and critical) behind the scenes player in the conspiracy that ended the life of JFK. Through its own vast resources and through its international contacts in the intelligence community and in organized crime, Israel had the means, it had the opportunity, and it had the motive to play a major frontline role in the crime of the century – and it did."

Their motive? Israel's much touted Prime Minister David Ben-Gurion, who ruled that country from its inception in 1948 until he resigned on June 16, 1963, was so enraged at John F. Kennedy for not allowing Israel to become a nuclear power that, Collins asserts, in his final days in office he commanded the Mossad to become involved in a plot to kill America's president.

Ben-Gurion was so convinced that Israel's very survival was in dire jeopardy that in one of his final letters to JFK he said, "Mr. President, my people have the right to exist, and this existence is in danger."

In the days leading up to Ben-Gurion's resignation from office, he and JFK had been involved in an unpublicized, contentious debate over the possibility of Israel getting nuclear capabilities. Their disagreement eventually escalated into a full-fledged war of words that was virtually ignored in the press. Ethan Bronner wrote about this secret battle between JFK and Ben-Gurion years later in a *New York Times* article on October 31, 1998, calling it a "fiercely hidden subject." In fact, the Kennedy/Ben-Gurion conversations are still classified by the United States government. Maybe this is the case because Ben-Gurion's rage and frustration became so intense – and his power so great within Israel – that Piper contends it was at the center of the conspiracy to kill John Kennedy. This stance is supported by New York banker Abe Feinberg, who describes the situation as such: "Ben-Gurion could be vicious, and he had such a hatred of the old man [Joe Kennedy, Sr., JFK's father]." Ben-Gurion despised Joe Kennedy because he felt that not only was he an anti-Semite, but that he had also sided with Hitler during the 1930's and 40's. [We will touch upon this aspect of the story later in this article].

Anyway, Ben-Gurion was convinced that Israel needed nuclear weapons to insure its survival, while Kennedy was dead-set against it. This inability to reach an agreement caused obvious problems. One of them revolved around Kennedy's decision that he would make America his top priority in regard to foreign policy, and not Israel! Kennedy planned to honor the 1950 Tripartite Declaration which said that the United States would retaliate against any nation in the Middle East that attacked any other country. Ben-Gurion, on the other hand, wanted the Kennedy Administration to sell them offensive weapons, particularly Hawk missiles.

The two leaders thus engaged in a brutal letter exchange, but Kennedy wouldn't budge. Ben-Gurion, obsessed by this issue, slipped into total paranoia, feeling that Kennedy's obstinance was a blatant threat to the very existence of Israel as a nation. Piper writes, "Ben-Gurion had devoted a lifetime creating a Jewish State and guiding it into the world arena. And, in Ben-Gurion's eyes, John F. Kennedy was an enemy of the Jewish people and his beloved state of Israel." He continues, "The 'nuclear option' was not only at the very core of Ben-Gurion's personal world view, but the very foundation of Israel's national security policy."

Ben-Gurion was so preoccupied with obtaining nuclear weapons that on June 27, 1963, eleven days after resigning from office, he announced, "I do not know of any other nation whose neighbors declare that they wish to terminate it, and not only declare, but prepare for it by all means available to them. We must have no illusions that what is declared every day in Cairo, Damascus, and Iraq are just words. This is the thought that guides the Arab leaders ... I am confident ... that science is able to provide us with the weapons that will serve the peace and deter our enemies."

Avner Cohen, in *Israel and the Bomb*, published by Columbia University Press, reinforces this sense of urgency by writing, "Imbued with lessons of the Holocaust, Ben-Gurion was consumed by fears of security ... Anxiety about the Holocaust reached beyond Ben-Gurion to infuse Israel's military thinking." He further adds fuel to this point by pointing out, "Ben-Gurion had no qualms about Israel's need for weapons of mass destruction," and "Ben-Gurion's world view and his decisive governing style shaped his critical role in instigating Israel's nuclear progress."

Kennedy, on the other hand, was adamant in his refusal to promote Israel's ascension to the nuclear stage. Avener Cohen, in *Israel and the Bomb*, stresses, "No American president was more concerned with the danger of nuclear proliferation than John Fitzgerald Kennedy. He was convinced that the spread of nuclear weapons would make the world more dangerous and undermine U.S. interests." Cohen continues at the end of this passage, "The only example Kennedy used to make this point was Israel."

Realizing that Kennedy would not change his mind, Ben-Gurion decided to join forces with Communist China. Both countries were greatly interested in creating nuclear programs, and so began their secret joint dealings. Working in unison through intermediary Shaul Eisenberg, who was a partner of Mossad gun-runner and accountant Tibor Rosenbaum, Israel and China proceeded to develop their own nuclear capabilities without the knowledge of the United States.

If you find this scenario improbable, I strongly urge you to read Gordon Thomas' excellent book, *Seeds of Fire*, where he exposes how the Mossad and CSIS (Chinese secret service) have conspired on many occasions to not only steal American military secrets, but to also doctor U.S. intelligence programs such as the Justice Department's PROMISE software. This instance, I am afraid to say, is but the first where echoes of the JFK assassination can still be felt today reverberating through our post

9-11 world. The danger of Israel developing the Bomb in unison with China became a highly volatile situation, and was closely monitored by the CIA.

Intent on pursuing this path, the Israeli's constructed a nuclear facility at Dimona. When Kennedy demanded that the U.S. inspect this plant, Ben-Gurion was so incensed that he erected another PHONY facility that held no evidence of nuclear research and development. (Does this scenario sound eerily familiar to the game we're playing with Saddam Hussein in Iraq right now?) Fully aware of their shenanigans, though, JFK told Charles Bartlett, "The sons of bitches lie to me constantly about their nuclear capability."

Avner Cohen, in *Israel and the Bomb*, reiterates this claim by saying that Ben-Gurion had taken the nuclear issue so closely to heart that he, "concluded that he could not tell the truth about Dimona to American leaders, not even in private."

Dr. Gerald M. Steinberg, political science professor at Bar-Ilan University's BESA Center for Strategic Studies in Tel Aviv, weighs in by saying, "Between 1961 and 1963, the Kennedy administration placed a great deal of pressure on Ben-Gurion in the effort to pressure for acceptance of international inspection of Dimona and Israeli abdication of their nuclear weapons. This pressure apparently did not alter Israeli policy, but it was a contributing factor to Ben-Gurion's resignation in 1963."

To convey how serious this situation had become in modern terms, look at what is happening in Iraq with United Nations security teams inspecting the royal palaces and bunkers for nuclear weapons and materials. This matter is so urgent that our nation is on the verge of war. Forty years earlier, the heat that JFK was placing on Ben-Gurion was equally as strong as what George Bush is laying on Saddam Hussein today.

In *Israel and the Bomb*, Avner Cohen reinforces this point. "To force Ben-Gurion to accept the conditions, Kennedy exerted the most useful leverage available to an American president in dealing with Israel: a threat that an unsatisfactory solution would jeopardize the U.S. government's commitment to, and support of, Israel."

The pressure on Ben-Gurion was so immense that he ended up leaving office. But Kennedy, in true pit-bull style, didn't let up on Ben-Gurion's successor, Levi Eshkol, as Avner Cohen reports. "Kennedy told Eshkol that the U.S. commitment and support of Israel 'could be seriously jeopardized' if Israel did not let the U.S. obtain 'reliable information' about its efforts in the nuclear field. Kennedy's demands were unprecedented. They amounted, in effect, to an ultimatum." Cohen concludes this thought by asserting, "Kennedy's letter precipitated a near-crisis situation in Eshkol's office."

In the end, as we're all aware, Kennedy was assassinated in November 1963; but less known is that China conducted its first nuclear test in October, 1964. What makes this event more profound is Piper's claim that even though Israel said its first nuclear tests took place in 1979, they actually occurred in October, 1964 along with the Chinese! If this is true, other than August, 1945 when the United States dropped atomic bombs on Hiroshima and Nagasaki, October 1964 may have possibly been the most dangerous month in 20th century history.

Let's return, though, to JFK's assassination and the direct results of it in regard to the Jewish lobby, American foreign policy, and the militarization of Israel. To understand how powerful the Israeli lobby is in this country, venerable Senator J. William Fulbright told CBS *Face the Nation* on April 15, 1973, "Israel controls the U.S. Senate. The Senate is subservient, much too much; we should be more concerned about U.S. interests rather than doing the bidding of Israel. The great majority of the Senate of the U.S. – somewhere around 80% - is completely in support of Israel; anything Israel wants; Israel gets. This has been demonstrated time and again, and this has made [foreign policy] difficult for our government."

Do you hear what Senator Fulbright said? This isn't a crazy conspiracy theorist or a KKK anti-Semite. It's a much-respected U.S. Senator saying that about 80% of the Senate is in Israel's hip pocket. Adding clout to this argument is Rep. Paul Findley, who was quoted in *The Washington Report on Middle East Affairs* in March, 1992, "During John Kennedy's campaign for the presidency, a group of New York Jews had privately offered to meet his campaign expenses if he would let them set his Middle East policy. He did not agree … As the president, he provided only limited support of Israel."

To understand how important Kennedy's decisions were during his short-lived presidency, we need to look at the issue of campaign finance. Considering how influential the Israeli lobby is in the U.S. Senate (hearkening back to the words of Senator Fulbright), they had to have been enraged when President Kennedy genuinely wanted to cut the knees out from under the current campaign finance methods because it made politicians so reliant upon the huge cash inlays of special-interest groups. Regrettably, Kennedy did not have the time to implement this program, and to this day our political system is still monopolized by lobbyists from the very same special-interest groups. One can only imagine what changes would have occurred in regard to our foreign policy had Kennedy eradicated these vipers and blood-suckers from the halls of Congress.

Tragically, Kennedy's ideas never came to fruition, and his heated battle with Prime Minister Ben-Gurion over whether Israel should be allowed to develop a nuclear program was ultimately lost. The reason why is that Lyndon Baines Johnson, who Kennedy intended to drop from his ticket in 1964 due to his extreme dislike for, had a complete reversal in foreign policy. As you will see, not only did Israel's nuclear program move ahead unchecked; they also became the primary beneficiary of our foreign aid.

But this absolute turnaround would not have occurred if Kennedy would not have been assassinated. Up until LBJ became president, Kennedy dealt with the Middle East in a way that most benefited the U.S. His primary goal – and one which would most keep the peace – was a balance of power in the Middle East so that each and every nation would be secure. This decision adhered to the Tripartite Declaration which the U.S. signed in 1950. But under the Johnson administration, this fragile balance was overturned, and by 1967 – only four years after Kennedy's assassination – the U.S. was Israel's main weapons supplier, and OUR best interests were put well behind those of Israel!

As Michael Collins Piper writes: "The bottom line is this: JFK was adamantly determined to stop Israel from building the nuclear bomb. LBJ simply looked the other way. JFK's death did indeed prove beneficial to Israel's nuclear ambitions and the evidence proves it."

Reuven Pedatzer, in a review of Avner Cohen's *Israel and the Bomb* in the Israeli Newspaper *Ha'aretz* on February 5, 1999 wrote, "The murder of American president John F. Kennedy brought to an abrupt end the massive pressure being applied by the U.S. administration on the government of Israel to discontinue their nuclear program." He continues, "Kennedy made it quite clear to the Israeli Prime Minister that he would not under any circumstances agree to Israel becoming a nuclear state." Pedatzer concludes, "Had Kennedy remained alive, it is doubtful whether Israel would today have a nuclear option," and that, "Ben-Gurion's decision to resign in 1963 was taken to a large extent against the background of the tremendous pressure that Kennedy was applying on him concerning the nuclear issue."

If you're still not convinced; how about some numbers? In Kennedy's last fiscal budget year of 1964, Israeli aid was $40 million. In

LBJ's first budget of 1965, it soared to $71 million, and in 1966 more than tripled from two years earlier to $130 million! Plus, during Kennedy's administration, almost none of our aid to Israel was military in nature. Instead, it was split equally between development loans and food assistance under the PL480 Program. Yet in 1965 under the Johnson administration, 20% of our aid to Israel was for the military, while in 1966, 71% was used for war-related materials.

Continuing in this same vein, in 1963 the Kennedy administration sold 5 Hawk missiles to Israel as part of an air-defense system. In 1965-66, though, LBJ laid 250 tanks on Israel, 48 Skyhawk attack aircrafts, plus guns and artillery which were all offensive in nature. If you ever wondered when the Israeli War Machine was created, this is it! LBJ was its father.

According to Stephen Green in *Taking Sides: America's Secret Relations with a Militant Israel*, "The $92 million in military assistance provided in fiscal year 1966 was greater than the total of all official military aid provided to Israel cumulatively in all the years going back to the foundation of that nation in 1948."

Green continues, "70% of all U.S. official assistance to Israel has been military. America has given Israel over $17 billion in military aid since 1946, virtually all of which – over 99% - has been provided since 1965."

Can you see what's happening here? Within two years of JFK's assassination, Israel went from being a weak, outmatched member of the volatile Middle Eastern community that was not allowed to develop nuclear weapons to one that was well on its way to becoming a undeniable military force on the world stage. John Kennedy adamantly put his foot down and refused to allow Israel to develop a nuclear program, while LBJ bent over backward to facilitate and bolster them. Or, as Seymour Hersh wrote in *The Samson Option*, "By 1968, the president had no intention of doing anything to stop the Israeli bomb."

The result of this shift in focus from the Kennedy to Johnson administration is, in my opinion, the PRIMARY reason behind our current troubles in the Middle East which culminated in the 9-11 attacks and our upcoming war with Iraq (and beyond). I have a great deal of confidence in this statement, for as Michael Collins Piper points out, here are the results of John F. Kennedy's assassination:

1)   Our foreign and military aid to Israel increased dramatically once LBJ became president.

2)   Rather than trying to maintain a BALANCE in the Middle East, Israel suddenly emerged as the dominant force.

3)   Since the LBJ administration, Israel has always had weaponry that was superior to any of its direct neighbors.

4)   Due to this undeniable and obvious increase in Israel's War Machine, a constant struggle has been perpetuated in the Middle East.

5)   LBJ also allowed Israel to proceed with its nuclear development, resulting in them becoming the 6th largest nuclear force in the world.

6)   Finally, our huge outlays of foreign aid to Israel (approximately $10 billion/year when all is said and done) has created a situation of never-ending attacks and retaliation in the Middle East, plus outright scorn and enmity against the U.S. for playing the role of Israel's military enabler.

In Israel's, and especially David Ben-Gurion's eyes then, what were their alternatives – to remain weakened (or at least balanced) in relation to their neighbors and handcuffed by JFK's refusal to bow to their will, or KILL the one man standing in their way to becoming dominant in the Middle East, the recipient of huge amounts of military aid, and one of the premier nuclear forces in the world? It's something to think about. Also, while these thoughts are running through your head, ask yourself this question. If Kennedy, LBJ, and all subsequent administrations would have adhered to the 1950 Tripartite Declaration and did everything in their power to maintain balance in the Middle East instead of pushing Israel to the forefront, would our Towers have been attacked on 9-11, 2001, and would we be on the verge of a possibly catastrophic war today? It's certainly something to ponder.

THE CIA'S ROLE IN JFK'S ASSASSINATION

Quite possibly the most important court trial of the 1990's (yes, even more relevant than O.J.) was E. Howard Hunt vs. *The Spotlight* newspaper.

Although I won't delve into the circumstances surrounding it, juror Leslie Armstrong told *The Spotlight* in their November 11, 1991 issue, "Mr. Lane [representing the defendant] was asking us [the jury] to do something very difficult. He was asking us to believe John Kennedy had been killed by our own government. Yet when we examined the evidence closely, we were compelled to conclude that the CIA had indeed killed President Kennedy." This information is extremely important to 20th century history, yet the mainstream media gave it virtually no coverage due to its explosive nature. I suppose they were saving everything to see if O.J.'s glove fit.

The vital point being made, and one confirmed by the Church Committee in 1975, was that a conspiracy to assassinate President Kennedy did exist, and that it extended directly into the U.S. Government. To fully understand the ramifications of this information, one needs to be aware of what the CIA has been doing since it formed out of the OSS after WWII. Although time prevents me from engaging in a lengthy discourse, you should research "Project Paperclip" where Nazi scientists were secretly relocated to America after the war. You can also investigate the CIA's illegal mind control experiments, their illicit drug tests on unwitting subjects, their drug trafficking activities, how they've successfully infiltrated the American corporate media, and their assassinations of various world leaders. In other words, these guys have, and still are, dirty up to their eyeballs.

To fully understand not only this branch of Intelligence, but also the broader spectrum of how our world works, we need to realize that what is depicted on the nightly news is not an accurate representation of reality. Rather, the true impetus, or driving force behind our global political system, is rarely ever seen by the American public. The real decision-makers lurk in the shadows, plotting and planning, then using their 'operational arms' such as the CIA, Mossad, other intelligence agencies, and Organized Crime to do their bidding. As Michael Collins Piper tells us, these groups – the money launderers, drug dealers, killers and crooks – are the only entities able to operate outside of societal laws and mores. The Controllers – international bankers, heads of multinational corporations, and top ranking members of secret societies – "guide" our world, then use their "implementers" to carry forth their decisions. Politicians are one of the "guises" used in front of the scenes, while the CIA, Mossad, and Mob take care of their dirty dealings far-removed from public scrutiny. I'm sorry to say, but this is the way our world operates.

One of the primary reasons that John F. Kennedy got assassinated was because he dared to interfere with this tenuous framework of power. More specifically, JFK, realizing how out-of-control these various agencies were, wanted to rein them in and bring them all under one roof, giving his brother Bobby jurisdiction over all of them. He also planned on getting rid of master-manipulator J. Edgar Hoover (who was very aware of their plans, but out of sheer self-interest had no incentive to uncover the truth about Kennedy's murder). To make matters worse for himself, Kennedy fired CIA Director Allen Dulles, who was one of the dirtiest backroom wheeler-dealers of all-time. (Incredibly, Dulles would later serve on the Warren Commission! Talk about having the deck stacked against you.)

Arthur Krock wrote in *The New York Times* about this battle between Kennedy and the CIA on October 3, 1963, saying that the CIA "represents a tremendous power and total unaccountability to anyone." Krock also referred to someone close to Kennedy in the White House who said that if anyone ever tried to takeover the U.S. Government, it would be the CIA, and that JFK was no longer able to keep them in reins. Now remember, this was only a month-and-a-half before that fateful day in Dallas.

Reinforcing how out-of-control the CIA was at this time, attorney and researcher Mark Lane wrote in *The Spotlight* on February 17, 1992, "President Kennedy sent Henry Cabot Lodge, his Ambassador to Vietnam, with orders to the CIA on two separate occasions and in both cases the CIA ignored these orders, saying that it was different from what the agency thought should be done. In other words, the CIA had decided that it – not the president – would make the decisions as to how American foreign policy should be conducted."

Is this situation starting to become clearer to you? Can you see to what proportions the CIA had grown? Kennedy was treading through very treacherous waters, but the straw that broke the camel's back was only reported years later by *The New York Times* on April 25, 1966. It seems that Kennedy was so intent on exercising his ELECTED powers and not allowing them to be usurped by power-crazed individuals in the intelligence community that he threatened to "splinter the CIA in a thousand pieces and scatter it to the wind." By uttering these words, Kennedy's fate was sealed, for now he had struck at the very core of the Controller's power center!

In essence, Michael Collins Piper points out that Kennedy had done, or intended to do, four things that filled the CIA with rage:

1) Fired Allen Dulles.
2) Was in the process of founding a panel that would investigate the CIA's numerous crimes.
3) Put a damper on the breadth and scope of the CIA.
4) Limit their ability to act under National Security Memoranda 55. Colonel Fletcher Prouty spoke of the CIA's reaction. "Nothing I

had ever been involved with in my entire career had created such an uproar. NSAM 55 stripped the CIA of its cherished covert operations goal, except for some small actions. It was an explosive document. The military-industrial complex was not pleased."

One of these incensed individuals was CIA Chief of Counter-Intelligence, James Jesus Angleton. Assuming this post in 1954 under the guidance of two truly dirty dogs – Allen Dulles and Richard Helms – Peter Dale Scott wrote in *Deep Politics and the Death of JFK* that Angleton "managed a 'second CIA' within the CIA." Angleton operated so far beyond his legal parameters that he, along with William Harvey, formed the ZR/Rifle Team and hired the shooters who were to take out Cuban leader Fidel Castro. And although I won't delve into details at this point, Piper points out in *Final Judgment* that these were the same trigger men used for the Kennedy assassination.

More importantly, Angleton formed an extremely close relationship with the Mossad and David Ben-Gurion, and was fully aware of the Israeli Prime Minister's hatred for JFK. Angleton became so intimate with the Israeli's that he even helped them develop their secret nuclear program, while the CIA and Mossad became as one in the Middle East – a virtually indistinguishable entity working in unison to carry out their mutual goals.

The Mossad, you must know, has been called by Michael Collins Piper "the driving force behind the conspiracy" to kill JFK. Andrew Cockburn, appearing on C-Span's *Booknotes* on September 1, 1991, described their relationship with American intelligence. "There has been since almost the earliest days of the Israeli state and the earliest days of the CIA a secret bond, basically by which Israeli intelligence did jobs for the CIA and the rest of American intelligence. You can't understand what's going on with American covert operations and the Israeli covert operations until you understand this secret arrangement."

Another extremely important point that Michael Collins Piper brings up in *Final Judgment* is that during the time of Kennedy's assassination, Yitzhak Shamir (later Israeli Prime Minister) was the head of a Mossad hit squad that hired a trigger man from the SDECE (French intelligence) to kill President Kennedy. This information is confirmed by the Israeli newspaper *Ha'aretz* on July 3, 1992 when they reported that Yitzhak Shamir was once an underworld terrorist that became a Mossad agent, then later led an assassination team from 1955-1964. *The Washington Times* lends further credibility to this stance by reporting on

July 4, 1992 that not only did this secret assassination team exist, but that they "carried out attacks on perceived enemies and suspected Nazi war criminals." If you remember, David Ben-Gurion called JFK an "enemy of the state of Israel." From my perspective, that would make him a PERCEIVED ENEMY!

Now, if we consider for a moment that Yitzhak Shamir hired one of the hit men from France's secret service – the SDECE – what makes this situation even more bizarre is who James Jesus Angleton – the primary CIA force behind Kennedy's assassination – was with on the afternoon of November 22, 1963. It was Colonel Georges de Lannurien, Deputy Chief of the SDECE! They were both at CIA headquarters in Langley to get ready for hands-on damage control in case something went awry. In effect, then, we have the triangulation of three intelligence agencies – the CIA, Mossad, and SDECE – all converging around the murder of President Kennedy, while they made certain that Lee Harvey Oswald had already established links with Cuba and the Soviet Union so that a Communist "Cold War" cover story could be forwarded in the American press!

How did these intelligence agencies pull it off? Well, let me leave you with a quote from retired Air Force pilot Fletcher Prouty that Michael Collins Piper used to shine some light on this situation. Prouty tells us, "One of the primary necessary measures in an assassination plot is the process of removing or otherwise breaching the intended victim's blanket of security." He continues, "No one has to direct an assassination – it happens. The active role is played secretly by permitting it to happen … This is the single greatest clue - who has the power to call off or reduce the usual security precautions that are always in effect whenever a president travels?"

Now who do YOU think had the ways, means, and motive to erase President Kennedy's security that afternoon in Dallas? The Russians? No. The Cubans? No. The Mob? No. I'd place my bets on the CIA! Now are things starting to become clearer?

(As a side-note, who do you think had the ways, means and motivation to cover-up the truth about the 9-11 terrorist attacks in the media - a group of rag-tag terrorists, or the CIA? It's something to consider.)

THE CIA & ORGANIZED CRIME: TWO SIDES OF THE SAME COIN

Once a researcher strips away the veneer, wades through layers of illusion, disregards years of propaganda & misinformation, and finally sees history in its true perspective, they discover that the entire world-government corporate-controlled global power-structure is actually nothing more than a vast network of interrelated crime syndicates. Yes, CRIME SYNDICATES! In this article, we will briefly examine the Kennedy family's shadowy past and how certain alliances and betrayals with the Meyer Lansky-led Mob (in conjunction with elements of the U.S. government & CIA) ultimately resulted in JFK's assassination. As Michael Collins Piper so brilliantly points out, all of these groups – Intelligence, government, and organized crime – are intimately connected and operate outside the law (and public scrutiny) to preserve and promote their self-interests. Regrettably, they all joined forces in 1963 to eliminate the last American president who wasn't bought, sold, and controlled by the Globalist money interests.

To understand how JFK found himself in such a quandary on November 22, 1963, we must first look back in time at his father, Joseph Sr. As many people know, Old Man Kennedy built his fortune on illegal bootlegging, then by capitalizing on the stock market crash (i.e. inside information). But fewer people realize just how deeply Kennedy was linked with organized crime. To become so incredibly wealthy by running booze, Kennedy had to make agreements with some unseemly characters – agreements that would later come back to haunt him.

Another aspect of Joe Kennedy's personality that his family tries to sweep under the rug was his pro-Nazi sympathies. DeWest Hooker, a New York City executive in the show business field and mentor or George Lincoln Rockwell (founder of the American Nazi Party) said of Kennedy, "Joe admitted that when he was ambassador to England he had been pro-Hitler. However, in Kennedy's words, 'we' lost the war. By 'we' he didn't mean the United States. When Kennedy said 'we,' he meant the non-Jews. Joe Kennedy believed that it was the Jews who had won World War II." He continues, quoting Kennedy. "I've done everything I can to fight the Jewish power over this country. I tried to stop World War II, but I failed. I've made all the money I need and now I'm passing everything I've learned on to my sons."

But before Joe Kennedy got his foot in the political door via an ambassadorship to England, he was a highly successful criminal that made many powerful enemies. One of them was Meyer Lansky, whose associate, Michael Milan, relates the following story in *Final Judgment*. "Ask Meyer Lansky about Joe Kennedy and you'd see one of the few times that Mr. L. would actually get conniptions. What they said back during Prohibition was that you can't trust Kennedy to keep his word. He stole from his friends so much that he had no friends. And right before World War II, the sonofabitch turned around and said that we should all get on Hitler's side; that the Jews could go to hell."

This enmity between Kennedy and Lansky went all the way back to the 1920's and their bootlegging days. Michael Collins Piper tells us how Lucky Luciano and Lansky swiped an entire shipment of Kennedy's shine and killed off all of his guards, thus causing him to lose a boatload of money. Thus, due to Kennedy's dishonesty and Lansky's fierce loyalty to his Jewish heritage, Milan said that Lansky cursed the entire Kennedy family with revenge; then passed it down to his sons. Things got so bad that Joe Kennedy's life was actually on the line due to a Mob-ordered hit. Luckily for Kennedy, Sam Giancana intervened and cut a deal for Old Man Kennedy to make things right with the Mob again. To return his favor, Kennedy told Giancana that once one of his sons made it into the White House, he'd have an 'in'. To carry through on this promise, though, Old Man Kennedy would once again need Sam Giancana's help.

If this information is hard for you to accept, remember that one of the most famous women that JFK had an affair with (other than Marilyn Monroe) was Miss Judith Exner. And who was she? Sam Giancana's mistress! Also, according to David Heyman in *A Woman Named Jackie*, FBI papers and wiretaps prove that JFK had direct, person-to-person communications with Meyer Lansky during his 1960 presidential campaign. Plus, Sam Giancana himself is quoted as saying, "I help get Jack elected, and in return, he calls off the heat. It'll be business as usual."

As we all know by now, Sam Giancana was the key to JFK beating Richard Nixon in 1960 by giving him Chicago ("vote early, and vote often"). Problems arose, though, when, instead of turning their back on what the Mobsters were doing, JFK and his brother Bobby double-crossed them and brought out the heat full-strength.

Now, here's where things get sticky and we need to use some psychology. By all appearances, the Kennedy brothers going after the Mob was one of the stupidest moves of all-time. First, Old Man Kennedy was a bootlegger with intimate ties to organized crime. He knew how the Mob thought and operated. Plus, he wanted a Kennedy presidential dynasty starting with Jack, followed by Bobby and Teddy. And, with the likes of Sam Giancana behind them, they could rig other elections in the future.

So, with all this in mind, why would Jack and Bobby start trying to throw them all in prison? It seems ludicrous. But y'see, John Kennedy was no dummy – not by a long-shot. He knew that the longer his Presidency extended, the more demands the Mob would make of him. And, being that the Kennedy's had plenty of skeletons in their closet – Jack's philandering, plus Joe's Nazi sympathies and organized crime ties – JFK knew that he would eventually be bribed and held hostage by the gangsters. If he didn't bow to their wishes, they'd start 'leaking' this information to the press. And, considering how many people hated Kennedy, if the Mob felt like they weren't getting their fair share of the pie (i.e. government graft) they'd simply dangle Kennedy like a marionette on a string with continued threats of exposure. The entire scenario would have been a disaster for JFK, so Bobby and he decided to get rid of them.

Of course the Mob couldn't overlook Bobby's efforts as the Attorney General, especially since Joe and Giancana had made a pact. Now the Kennedy brothers were reneging, and such a stance could not be tolerated. Or, as Sam Giancana described the situation: "It's a brilliant move on Joe Kennedy's part. He'll have Bobby wipe us out to cover their own dirty tracks and it'll all be done in the Kennedy 'war on organized crime.' Brilliant."

Now, all of this subterfuge was bad enough for Kennedy, but when one adds the Mob's long affiliation with the CIA (who also despised Kennedy), you can see how the flames were getting higher. And although I can't begin to elaborate on the varied ties between these two entities, Michael Collins Piper relates how the United States government began cavorting with Lucky Luciano and the Mafia during WWII, then progressed to Fidel Castro's assassination attempts ("Operation Mongoose" and the ZR/Rifle Team), plus transporting and dealing drugs out of the Golden Triangle while the Vietnam War was being waged.

Sam Giancana described the CIA-Mob ties in very succinct terms. "That's what we are, the Outfit and the CIA – two sides of the same coin."

Now, some people may wonder why other prominent political figures didn't expose this horrendous situation. They quite possibly could have except for the fact that they were in as deeply as the Kennedy family was. In *Mafia Kingfish* published by McGraw-Hill, John Davis relates how Carlos Marcello filtered over $50,000/year in payoffs to Lyndon

Baines Johnson, while both James Jesus Angleton and Meyer Lansky had incriminating photographic evidence of J. Edgar Hoover (relating to his homosexuality). Thus, he too was bribed into silence. To make matters even more precarious, Michael Collins Piper points out the ADL's links to organized crime and to the highly secretive COINTELPRO, where they gathered intelligence reports on high-ranking officials. These Jewish mobsters that operated through the ADL were also the same ones who legitimized and controlled the liquor industry which was run by the Bronfman family.

Now that I've mentioned a Jewish link to organized crime, I might as well delve into one of Michael Collins Piper's biggest contentions in *Final Judgment* – that Meyer Lansky was the "capo di tuti capi" – the undeniable leader of the vast underworld of organized crime – and that the Jews were the ones who actually called the shots while using the Italians as a front to take the heat and divert attention away from them. In this sense, the Jews were the real brains behind the Mob, while all the other names – Giancana, Traficante, Marcello, etc – were subordinates of Meyer Lansky.

Hank Messick, in *Lansky*, published by Berkley Medallion Books in 1971, wrote, "The real leaders of crime have remained hidden while the nation's law enforcement agencies have chased minor punks." He adds, "Mafia leaders of crime have been hiding behind the vendetta-ridden society [the Italian Mafia] for decades."

This perception has been reinforced in the public consciousness for years by Hollywood movies and TV shows. It is well-known that the Jews founded Hollywood and still have a huge influence today, perpetrating the Italian mobster stereotype to this day with programs like *the Godfather* and *the Sopranos*. For those who don't believe that Hollywood was founded by those of Jewish descent, look at the names of its founders:

Universal Studios – Carl Laemmle – Jewish
20th Century Fox – William Fox – Jewish
Warner Brothers – HM Warner – Jewish
Paramount Pictures – Adolph Zukor – Jewish
MGM – Samuel Goldwyn – Jewish
MGM – Louis B. Mayer – Jewish

Neil Gabler says in *An Empire of their Own, How the Jews Invented Hollywood* published by Crown in 1988, "The Hollywood Jews created a powerful cluster of images and ideas ... so powerful that, in a sense, they colonized the American imagination. Ultimately, American values came to be defined by the movies the Jews made." Thus, similar to the tactics used by the Controllers where certain groups or individuals are in the forefront, here too, the Italians became the fall guy while Lansky and his cohorts hid behind the scenes.

As Michael Collins Piper shows, Meyer Lansky came to prominence via his drug running operations, which subsequently brought him into contact with the OSS and Naval Intelligence through an endeavor called "Operation Underworld." The headquarters for this operation were located at Rockefeller Center in New York City and were run by William Stephenson, who Ian Fleming patterned his James Bond character after.

Now, what follows is merely a thumbnail sketch of the interrelatedness between certain Jewish forces, the underworld, and secretive intelligence programs, and I certainly don't do it the justice that Michael Collins Piper does. Anyway, here goes. William Stephenson came to run anti-Nazi operations with the ADL and FBI, and later helped found the Mossad. (The ADL eventually became an intelligence-gathering and propaganda arm for the State of Israel.) Anyway, Stephenson's top man was Louis Bloomfield, who was a lawyer for the Bronfman's (illegal bootlegging and liquor magnates).

Here is where things get wild! Stephenson and Bloomfield were also gun runners for the Jewish underground (in today's vernacular they would be called terrorists), and they were the same people who BECAME the government of Israel! So, once again this reiterates my point that the governments of the world are nothing more than a vast organized crime syndicate. They're all criminals!

Anyway, it was Louis Bloomfield who coordinated the gun-running enterprises at the Jewish Sonneborn Institute. And who helped him? The Bronfman's and Meyer Lansky! Lansky fits specifically into the picture because he set-up the banks that were used to launder money for the Mossad.

As a side-note, if you don't think that these types of illegal government operations exist today, check out Mike Ruppert's *The Truth and Lies of 9-11*. Our government and many others still engage in money laundering, gun running, and drug trafficking on a large-scale. Plus, if you look into the backgrounds of those people who run the world – the Bronfman's, Kennedy's, Rockefellers, Bush's, those who founded Skull & Bones, and many others – you'll discover that they are ALL criminals. And I don't mean the laughable Richard Nixon-type criminal, but hard-core real-life illegal-type activities.

Anyway, Meyer Lansky became so powerful that Anthony Summers relates in *Conspiracy* (McGraw-Hill) how, to protect his gambling, prostitution, and drug interests, he convinced the Cuban dictator Fulgencio Batista to temporarily resign in the 1940s.

Apart from his criminal enterprises (and considering his Jewish heritage), Lansky's other undying allegiance was to the state of Israel, to which he made enormous contributions. When he saw how incensed David Ben-Gurion was becoming because of JFK's refusal to assist (or even permit) Israel's nuclear aspirations, his long-standing grudge against the Kennedy family became deadly. And, considering how Old Man Kennedy was a crook, the Controllers felt a huge sense of betrayal when they went to such lengths to get John Kennedy into office, then he turned and tried to destroy their two strongest enforcement and implementation arms – the CIA and the Mob. Someone like Sam Giancana could never forgive Kennedy for pulling a switch on them, especially when Old Man Kennedy sold his soul to spare his life. By reneging on a long-standing deal, then retaliating with destructive force, JFK literally signed his own death warrant. The Controllers were so irate after being double-crossed that they HAD to kill him. And, since Michael Collins Piper asserts that Meyer Lansky was at the head of the organized crime power structure, he, along with the Mossad and James Jesus Angleton of the CIA, were the driving "operational" forces behind Kennedy's assassination.

In the end, Sam Giancana best sums up the hit with these chilling words. "The politicians and the CIA made it real simple. We'd each provide men for the hit. I'd oversee the Outfit [Mafia] side of things and throw in Jack Ruby and some extra backup and the CIA would put their own guys on to take care of the rest."

VIETNAM AND THE CIA'S ILLEGAL DRUG TRAFFICKING

Perhaps the biggest secret of the Vietnam War is that our Central Intelligence Agency seized control of the infamous Golden Triangle during that time period, then, along with assistance from various elements of Organized Crime, shipped huge amounts of heroin out of that area into our country. Because piles of money were being made from this practice and many others, those who stood to profit from this horrendous war – the armament manufacturers, bankers, military men, and drug dealers – met any suggestion to withdraw from Vietnam with immediate consternation. But that's exactly what John F. Kennedy intended to do upon re-election. In fact, he had already planned on telling the American people that their troops would be back home by 1965. Think about this momentous decision for a moment. If we had exited Vietnam by 1965, EIGHT years of bloodshed in the jungles and civil unrest on America's streets and campuses could have been alleviated.

Michael Collins Piper writes in *Final Judgment*: "Kennedy's intended change in Vietnam policy – his plan to unilaterally withdraw from the imbroglio – infuriated not only the CIA but elements in the Pentagon and their allies in the military-industrial-complex. By this time, of course, the Lansky Syndicate had already set-up international heroin running from Southeast Asia through the CIA-linked Corsican Mafia in the Mediterranean. The joint Lansky-CIA operations in the international drug racket were a lucrative venture that thrived as a consequence of deep U.S. involvement in Southeast Asia as a cover for drug smuggling activities."

Piper's simple one-paragraph explanation may be the most concise overview of the Vietnam War ever written. The military men and defense contractors were making out like bandits from the War Machine, while the CIA crooks and Lansky-led Mobsters (via Santo Traficante as the major wheeler-dealer) were likewise padding their pockets. Author Peter Dale Scott, in *Deep Politics and the Death of JFK*, said of this phenomenon, "The flood of drugs into this country since WWII was one of the major 'unspeakable' secrets leading to the ongoing cover-up of the Kennedy assassination."

To provide a broader perspective on this situation, Professor Alfred McCoy stated in *The Politics of Heroin*, "Since the prohibition of narcotics in 1920, alliances between drug brokers and intelligence agencies have protected the global narcotics traffic. Given the frequency of such alliances, there seems a natural attraction between intelligence agencies and criminal syndicates. Both are practitioners of what one retired CIA operative has called the 'clandestine arts' – the basic skill of operating outside the normal channels of civil society. Among all the institutions of modern society, intelligence agencies and crime syndicates alone maintain large organizations capable of carrying out covert operations without fear of detection."

On the government side, the two main Golden Triangle runners were Ted Schackley and Thomas Clines – the same two men who ran *Operation Mongoose* (the plot to take out Fidel Castro). Thus, from 1960-1975, the CIA deployed a secret force of 30,000 Hmong tribesmen to fight the Laotian Communists. They also created heroin labs in this area; then brought it out via their own private airline – Air America.

Alfred McCoy, in *The Politics of Heroin: CIA Complicity in the Global Drug Trade*, describes how the CIA first gave smack to our own American soldiers in Vietnam before shipping it into the United States, where Lansky mobsters dealt it on the streets.

Sam Giancana's biographers reinforced this point by stating that while organized crime did its thing, "The CIA looked the other way – allowing over $100 million a year in illicit drugs to flow through Havana into the U.S. It was an arrangement similar to all the rest they'd made. The CIA received 10% of the take on the side of narcotics, which they utilized for their undercover slush fund."

After the Mob and the CIA generated this dirty money, they laundered it into secret bank accounts controlled by the international bankers. That way, the government couldn't get their hands on it and the funds could be invested in the stock market, loaned out to other businesses on the take, or channeled into Secret Service black budgets.

So, even though the above information is only the tip of the iceberg, now do you see why it was so important to the CIA/Mobster/international banker cabal that JFK didn't pull America out of Vietnam? The money (via illegal drug trafficking and for the War Machine) was incredible, while CONTROL of another area of the globe (the Golden Triangle) was secured.

As a final note, only FOUR DAYS after John Kennedy was assassinated, Lyndon Baines Johnson, his successor, put his name on NSAM 273, which secured our increased involvement in Southeast Asia. These guys weren't wasting any time! Within a few short months, our involvement in Vietnam went from 20,000 troops to a quarter of a million! The CIA had won, and ten years later 57,000 American soldiers were dead - truly shocking and abysmal behavior – an embarrassment and blight on the American consciousness.

MEDIA COMPLICITY IN THE KENNEDY ASSASSINATION

As I conclude this series on Michael Collins Piper's *Final Judgment*, the last piece of the puzzle that we need to examine is the media's role in covering up JFK's execution on November 22, 1963. As we've seen in earlier pieces, the organization with the greatest ways, means, and motive to pull-off this heinous act was the CIA, with direct assistance from the Mossad and Meyer Lansky's international crime syndicate. To further indict the spooks at Langley, all one has to do is investigate how extensively they have infiltrated the American media during the latter half of the 20th century. And if anyone hollers 'conspiracy theory' over these accusations, please remember this adage: something is no longer a theory once it has been proven to be true. Pulitzer Prize-winning journalist Carl Bernstein supports this point in his famous October 20, 1977 article for *Rolling Stone* when he wrote about how 400 CIA-funded journalists had infiltrated the American media under "Operation Mockingbird." He wrote: "[Joseph] Alsop is one of more than 400 American journalists who in the past 25 years have secretly carried out assignments for the CIA - ACCORDING TO DOCUMENTS ON FILE AT CIA HEADQUARTERS!" Also, in the 1950's and 60's, CBS News was nicknamed the "CIA Broadcasting System."

So, we need to ask ourselves, who had the resources and ability to implement the final step of this carefully-crafted assassination? The answer is provided by Jerry Pollicoff in *Government by Gunplay* (Signet Books). "The Kennedy assassination cover-up has survived so long only because the press, confronted with the choice of believing what it was told or examining the facts independently, chose the former."

To keep the people of this country confused, the media pushed every theory imaginable – except that of Israeli involvement. As filmmaker Oliver Stone told *The New York Times* on December 20, 1991, "When a leader of any country is assassinated, the media normally ask: what political forces were opposed to this leader and would benefit from his assassination?"

But as Michael Collins Piper points out in *Final Judgment*, Oliver Stone failed to pursue the Israeli angle, possibly because the executive producer of his *JFK* movie was a man named Arnon Milchan, who Alexander Cockburn said in *The Nation* magazine on May 18, 1992 was "probably Israel's largest arms dealer." In addition, Benjamin Beit-Hallahmi called Milchan a "Mossad Man."

What our media was essentially called upon to do was:

1)   Forward and support the Warren Commission's findings
2)   Perpetuate the "lone nut" theory
3)   Attack dissenters
4)   Prevent any discussion of Israeli involvement

As Michael Collins Piper shows, at the center of this cover-up was WDSU media, which was operated by the Stern family who were major league contributors to the ADL. Working in conjunction with this news outlet and the major networks was CIA mastermind James Jesus Angleton.

These forces were at the center of a conspiracy to feed the media false leads (misinformation), and to steer any investigation away from the true impetus of the Kennedy assassination.

Quite possibly the most important factor that was ignored by the media was an entity named Permindex that acted as the point of convergence for the CIA, Mossad, and the Lansky Mob. Who, you may ask, was Permindex? Well, Permindex was a weapons supplier located in Rome that also laundered money and had ties to the CIA, Meyer Lansky, and the state of Israel.

Although I won't be able to delve into this topic as thoroughly as Michael Collins Piper did in *Final Judgment*, below is a brief overview of this entity's role in the Kennedy Assassination. The Chairman of the Board of Permindex was Major Louis M. Bloomfield (previously mentioned in this series) who was one of the two primary figures in establishing both the Mossad and the state of Israel. Bloomfield also held half the shares in Permindex, was employed by J. Edgar Hoover in the FBI's infamous "Division Five," and became a front man for the powerful Bronfman family. The Bronfman's, you must remember, were bootleggers (like Joe Kennedy), who built their empire via the Lansky crime syndicate.

One of the other chief shareholders in Permindex was Tibor Rosenbaum, who established in Geneva an entity called BCI (Banque de Credit International). Rosenbaum was also the Director of Finance & Supply for the Mossad, while his BCI was the main money laundering arm for Meyer Lansky. Finally, BCI was intimately connected with the Mossad, while its founder, Tibor Rosenbaum, was called the "Godfather" of the Israeli nation.

Now, when we consider how crucial the state of Israel was to people like David Ben-Gurion and the above listed men and how threatened they felt in regard to its very survival, it becomes more than coincidental that all these forces (the Mossad, CIA, and Lansky's Mob) converged around Permindex. Each had direct ties to this entity, and each had their own reasons as to why they wanted Kennedy dead. Yet what angle did the American media pursue? The lone-nut theory where a stumblebum like Lee Harvey Oswald pulled off the biggest coup of the 20th century! It's beyond incredible.

Then, to cover their tracks and eliminate their "patsy" (who was obviously going to start singing), the conspirators brought in Jack Ruby to kill Oswald. But again the media failed in their duties to tell the truth. Rather than simply being a "grieving American" that felt compelled to kill

Oswald to spare Jackie Kennedy any further heartache, Jack Ruby (real last name: Rubinstein) was a member of Meyer Lansky's Jewish Mob! Why didn't *Time Magazine* let us in on this little tidbit of information?

Or, why hasn't journalist John Henshaw's "lost" film footage been released where Jack Ruby is led by Justice Department official through Dallas police headquarters past the screeners, FBI agents, and detectives that were supposed to secure the premises? This is PRIME EVIDENCE! Why hasn't it ever been brought to the public's attention?

Even more peculiar is Judge Earl Warren's decision to NOT let Jack Ruby testify before his Commission. Why? Maybe it had something to do with the fact that the Warren Commission was stacked with members of the Council on Foreign Relations, a Bilderberg attendee (Gerald Ford, who was later rewarded with the Presidency after Nixon was taken down), and Allen Dulles, who was FIRED by JFK! Think about how absurd this situation is. John Kennedy fired CIA Director Allen Dulles and threatened to shatter his organization into a thousand pieces and scatter it to the wind. Yet what happened? Allen Dulles was appointed to the Warren Commission to 'investigate' the murder of the man who fired him, and whose organization was integral in his assassination.

Researcher Dorothy Kilgallen told the *Philadelphia News* on February 22, 1964, "One of the best kept secrets of the Ruby Trial is the extent to which the Federal government is cooperating with the defense. The unprecedented alliance between Ruby's lawyers and the Department of Justice in Washington may provide the case with the one dramatic element it has lacked: Mystery."

There are countless other peculiarities that the media could have exposed, such as how the Kennedy's had future, large-scale plans to undermine the Rothschild-controlled Federal Reserve and how it had a stranglehold on the American economy and money system, but instead they were content to sell their souls and say that the ENTIRE debacle was carried out by a lone-nut assassin – Lee Harvey Oswald. And, to this day, even though the Church Committee found in the 1970's that a conspiracy to kill President Kennedy existed and that our government was involved, the media and our public schools continue to advance the lone-nut theory. Amazing.

But Michael Collins Piper goes further … much further … listing the ACTUAL names of those who were responsible for John F. Kennedy's assassination – the primary planners who had first-hand knowledge of the murder, plus the secondary players and those on the periphery. I strongly urge all of you to purchase this book and find out for yourselves who was behind this grisly act. Once you dive inside *Final Judgment* you'll see the roles each of the below entities played:

The Mossad – the blackened heart
The CIA – the demented mind
The Lansky Mob – the muscle
The American media – the blind eyes and muted mouth

Herve Lamarr, in *Farewell America*, sums up the situation as such: "President Kennedy's assassination was the work of magicians. It was a stage trick, complete with accessories and false mirrors, and when the curtain fell the actors, and even the scenery, disappeared. But the magicians were not illusionists, but professionals, artists in their way."

That's an incredible difference from a disillusioned "lone nut" assassin who pulled off this grandiose act all by himself. And if you think this horrendous situation has changed even one iota in the last forty years, you're sadly mistaken. To prove this point, I'll close with this excerpt from an interview with Greg Palast in the March edition of *Hustler* magazine. It concerns the premier cover-up artist Dan Rather, whose ENTIRE career was made off the Kennedy assassination.

<u>Palast</u>: I feel sick at heart when I see Rather because he's actually a journalist. He came on my program, *Newsnight*, in England and said, 'I can't report the news. I'm not allowed to ask questions. We're gonna send our children and our husbands into the desert now and I can't ask a question because I will be lynched.' He looked defeated and awful, and I was thinking, why am I feeling sorry for this guy who is worth millions? He should turn to the camera and say, 'Well, now for the truth. Over to you, Greg, in London.' The problem is that he can't report the story of the intelligence agents who are told not to look at the bin Laden family, not to look at Saudi funding of terror.

<u>Hustler</u>: What makes Rather afraid to do his job?

<u>Palast</u>: It's not just that there are brutal shepherds like Rupert Murdoch out there to beat the dickens out of any reporter that asks the wrong questions; its all about making news on the cheap … to some extent they know that there are certain things you cannot say. Rather says he would be necklaced for telling the truth.

Regrettably, the cover-up that took place with the Kennedy assassination forty years ago is exactly the same as it is today with the 9-11 cover-up. As yesterday, as today.

CHAPTER FIFTY-ONE

THE ROTHSCHILD-CFR CONNECTION

On the surface, the JFK assassination seems fairly cut-and-dried. On November 22, 1963 in Dallas, Texas, our 35th president was gunned-down in broad daylight while riding in his limousine through Dealey Plaza. But once we start digging a little deeper we realize that this "killing of the king" nearly forty years ago was one of the most complex events ever facing this nation. To show how complicated this matter has truly become, one needs to only look at how many pages have been devoted to this subject. Other than Jesus Christ and Adolph Hitler, there are probably more books about John F. Kennedy than any other figure in recent history. I have even dedicated a few sections of this book to that fateful day in Dallas.

Thus, in a sea of so multiple theories and explanations, one needs to find a steady harbor to lay their anchor. Over the years I've found one of the most reliable sources of information was journalist Jim Marrs, author of the highly-touted book, *Crossfire*. Lisa Guliani and I had the privilege of interviewing Mr. Marrs on April 7, 2002, and we asked him point-blank about the Kennedy assassination. Jim replied, "The shortest answer as to who killed JFK is that, as president, he was shaking up the status quo, and the status quo struck back. This resulted in elements belonging to "Operation Mongoose," the secret war against Castro, sending their Mafia/CIA/military operatives to Dallas in November, 1963. The cover-up, if not the assassination itself, carried the approval of the Council on Foreign Relations, as many of the CFR members participated in suppressing the truth."

One of the most crucial decisions Kennedy made during his short-lived presidency was to pull out of Vietnam. In his seminal work, *Rule by Secrecy*, Jim Marrs shows how the United States became interested in Southeast Asia in 1951 when the Rockefeller Foundation created a study group comprised of members from the Council on Foreign Relations and England's Royal Institute on International Affairs. This panel concluded that there should be a British-American takeover of this area. Soon, these goals were being forwarded by John Foster Dulles (one of the CFR

413

founders and Eisenhower's Secretary of State), and his brother, CIA Director Allen Dulles.

To understand how our global power structure operates, we need to know that the people who funded David Rockefeller and J.P. Morgan were members of Britain's "Roundtable" founded by Cecil Rhodes, and later headed by Lord Alfred Milner. And who directed the Roundtable? Answer: the notorious Rothschild family. In addition, the CFR is a direct American descendent of the Roundtable, which posed some serious problems for President Kennedy. Aware of how prevalent this organization was in every administration prior to his own, he stated at one point, "I'd like to have some new faces here, but all I get is the same old ones." Notice how President Kennedy crafted his words – he didn't say that HE selected them, but who he GETS ... in other words, those who were already CHOSEN for him!

Who, you may wonder, comprised the CFR in the early 1960's? Answer: the New York banking establishment, which wasn't particularly pleased with the way Kennedy was pushing to break the Federal Reserve's power base. He did this by urging businesses to deposit, invest, and borrow from *non*-Federal Reserve banks! He also encouraged these non-Fed banks to deal directly with and underwrite state and local financial matters. By taking this leverage away from the Federal Reserve, Kennedy could ultimately return the power to coin money to Congress, which was how our Founding Fathers originally established it in our Constitution. If this happened, we could become fiscally sound once again by not being forced to pay inordinate amounts of interest to the international bankers. The President's plan was quite ingenious, and he knew what he was talking about, for economist Seymour Harris said that Kennedy was "by far the most knowledgeable president of all time in the general area of economics."

So, what we had at that time in regard to the CFR/banking establishment was a slew of individuals very upset by what JFK was trying to do. And who specifically were these people and institutions? Well, take a look at this list of heavy-hitters that had aligned themselves against President Kennedy:

- Nelson Rockefeller – New York Governor
- David Rockefeller – Chase Manhattan Bank president, co-founder of the Trilateral Commission
- Douglas Dillon – Kennedy's Treasury Secretary & CFR member
- *The Wall Street Journal*

- *Fortune* Magazine editor Charles J. V. Murphy
- Dean Rusk – Secretary of State – Iron Mountain panel member
- Robert McNamara – Secretary of Defense until 1968, later President of the World Bank (an adjunct of the United Nations and CFR)
- McGeorge Bundy – National Security Advisor – Iron Mountain panel member
- William Bundy – editor of the CFR's *Foreign Affairs*
- Averill Harriman – instrumental in promoting Communism in the Soviet Union
- Henry Cabot Lodge – U.S. Ambassador to Saigon
- Joint Chiefs of Staff
- John J. McCloy – Assistant Secretary of War (WWII), Kennedy advisor
- Cyrus Vance – Secretary of the Army
- Walt Rostow – State Department's Policy Planning Council, LBJ's National Security Advisor
- Dean Acheson – Truman Secretary of State, Democratic foreign policy advisor

As you can see, this was quite a formidable list of opponents, and not one to be taken lightly. Donald Gibson, a professor at the University of Pittsburgh, wrote in 1994's *Battling Wall Street: the Kennedy Presidency*, "The Establishment's rejection of Kennedy became increasingly intense during his time in office." He continued, "Many of the most important advocates of U.S. involvement in Vietnam, both within and OUTSIDE the government, were members of the Board of Directors of the CFR." Gibson concludes this thought by adding, "By the early 1960's, the Council on Foreign Relations, Morgan and Rockefeller interests and the intelligence community were so extensively inbred as to be virtually a single entity.

The above words are important to understand for we are now clearly able to see that there were extremely powerful forces at work in the American financial, military, and intelligence communities (among others) who had a vested interest in promoting their business, banking, and Vietnam policies.

And what were the motives of those who wanted us to remain in Vietnam? Well, beyond the obvious profits to be made from war, the interest to be derived by bankers off of huge loans made to the U.S., and the opium market that would be cornered in the Golden Triangle, Vietnam came to epitomize a sinister Hegelian Dialectic at work. Here is the way it operated. First of all a PROBLEM was created where the Communist faction of the global elite's power structure took control of North Vietnam, thus "creating" a 'domino theory' scenario that could be used as an excuse for the anti-communists. A supposed SOLUTION offered to the American people as a reason to draw them into a war was to provide financial and military aid to South Vietnam. The resulting SYNTHESIS came about when the Controllers expanded their influence into Southeast Asia and exploited the area economically while at the same time transporting heroin into the United States and around the world.

So, on one side we have the CIA backing South Vietnam, while the Communists supported the North Vietnamese. And everyone (see the above list of names) was telling President Kennedy to send more troops into the area to carry out the Controllers goals. But Kennedy, unlike Harry Truman and Dwight David Eisenhower before him, wanted no part of this fiasco. In fact, on October 11, 1963, a little over a month before being assassinated, Kennedy approved of National Security Action Memorandum 263 which stated that the U.S. would pull-out of Vietnam by 1965. To prevent this from happening, the powers-that-be orchestrated a scenario where bullets rang out in Dallas on November 22, 1963, and less than two years later we had over 100,000 combat troops in Vietnam under code name "Rolling Thunder."

To show how prevalent the elitists were in this decision, President Kennedy's successor, LBJ, met on an almost daily basis with 14 of his Vietnam advisors, (nicknamed the "Wise Men"). Of these 14 men, 12 were members of the CFR, and all were either bankers or lawyers! Yes, you read correctly – bankers and lawyers were making President Johnson's decisions in regard to Vietnam!

Worse, as Jim Marrs points out in *Rule by Secrecy*, in 1985, a 26 page declassified *Congressional Record* report outlined the "rules of engagement" that were placed on our troops in Vietnam. As you read these restrictions, please hearken back to the military men who've said for years that they couldn't put their finger on it, but somehow felt as if they were being deliberately set-up to lose the war. Now you know which forces were calling the shots and implementing this defeatist policy. It was the CFR-led bankers and lawyers working through LBJ, who knew virtually nothing about foreign policy or war.

1) The Air Force could not attack prime targets that were determined by the military brass.
2) We could not fire upon the Viet Con unless we were shot at first.
3) If a tank or truck was more than 200 yards off of the Ho Chi Minh Trail, they could not be attacked.
4) A North Vietnamese plane could not be shot at unless it was in the air and overtly offensive in nature.
5) Enemy missile sites being built could not be bombed.
6) Vietnamese troops could not be tracked if they went into Laos or Cambodia.
7) The North Vietnamese were told that we could not attack certain installations, so guess what. That's where they put their anti-aircraft artillery to keep it safe!
8) Finally, arms and supplies that were necessary to perpetuate the war were permitted to go through the Port of Haiphone – 80% of which came from the USSR and China.

While the Vietnam War was still being waged, Louisiana Congressman John R. Rarick asked in no uncertain terms why the mainstream media was not telling us the truth about what was going on. "Why doesn't CBS tell the American people about the CFR and let the people decide whom to blame for the Vietnam fiasco – the planners and top decision makers of a closely knit financial-industrial-intellectual aristocracy or the military leaders under CIVILIAN CONTROL ..." Did you read the final two words – CIVILIAN CONTROL – not governmental control. Congressman Rarick was telling the American people that forces OUTSIDE the government were pursuing an agenda contrary to what was in the best interests of the United States. He continued, "Who will tell the people the truth of those who control 'the right to know machinery' also control the government?"

Folks, this isn't a conspiracy theory; these are the FACTS from a U.S. Congressman in the know. People always ask: why doesn't anyone ever come forward with information that exposes the truth? Well, they do all the time, as I've repeatedly shown throughout this book. The only problem is; those who call the shots from behind-the-scenes are also the same ones who own the mainstream media outlets and conceal this same information.

Someone could then ask: what about all the various theories as to who killed John F. Kennedy? Some people say it was the Masons, the Jesuits, the Israeli's, the CIA, Mob, or Russians. Who was actually behind the assassination?

In an e-mail dated February 11, 2003, Jim Marrs covered quite a few topics surrounding this tragic event. First, he explained that, being a reporter and native of the Lone Star state who was "intimately acquainted with Texas politics at the time," none of the above-mentioned groups "could have had such control over the Dallas Police, Texas authorities, the Mob, the FBI, the CIA or the anti-Castro Cubans." According to Jim Marrs, someone well beyond any of these entities was calling the shots.

The real power, he says, lies with the Rothschild family who control the Bank of England. Everything else filters down through the Rothschilds – all the 'implementers' in politics, business, industry, media, intelligence, banking, and even the State of Israel. Jim Marrs has finally pieced all together, as he writes in his e-mail:

"Baron Edmond Rothschild built the first oil pipeline from the Red Sea to the Mediterranean and founded the Israeli General Bank. He is now known as 'The Father of Modern Israel.' So, The Rothschild banking empire created and controls Israel, and Israeli campaign contributions influence and dominate the U.S. Congress (not to mention the mass media) and U.S. Foreign Policy along with the Rothchild's American agents which include the Rockefellers. England's desire to control all the Iraqi oil resources is behind the Bush bid for war. In fact, the Bushes are blood relatives of the royal Windsor family. It is not that England is such a great ally to us, but the other way around --- we are dancing to England's tune, as is Israel. And all are being played off against each other. For far too many years assassination investigators were distracted by arguing over who killed him --- the military, the CIA, FBI, Mob, right-wingers, oilmen, anti-Castro Cubans. The correct answer was "all of the above," as they were all working together under Operation Mongoose. Here is where the operational orders came from. JFK was his own man after his father suffered a stroke. He was out of control and actually believed he was President and was looking out for the best interests of the American public. The New World Order had him killed and then instigated the ridiculous Warren Commission (dominated by CFRers Dulles and McCloy). There is some truth to Michael Collins Piper's theory, but it goes far beyond the borders of Israel. The same game is being played today. We must look up toward the real rulers, the ones who created

Communism, Nazism, and all the other isms which they employ to keep us off balance, fearful, and at each others throats."

CHAPTER FIFTY-TWO

NOTES AND QUOTES: "Regicide: The Official Assassination of John F. Kennedy" by Gregory Douglas

----

1) One of the bullets used to kill President Kennedy was filled with mercury, and upon penetrating his body, the shell exploded, guaranteeing instantaneous death. (I suppose the fact that his brain was splattered all over the limousine, his wife, and one of the secret service agents behind him also had something to do with his demise!) This type of ammunition was a trademark of European trigger men, and was the primary reason why Kennedy's brain 'disappeared'. Those behind the killing could not allow this mercury additive to be discovered by the doctors, thus lending less credibility to Lee Harvey Oswald's role in the assassination.

2) A Russian Intelligence Study translated and analyzed by Army Colonel Vedder B. Driscoll in the *Driscoll Report* confirmed a Defense Intelligence Agency (DIA) report prepared in 1978 purporting that an extensive homosexual underground existed in connection to the Kennedy assassination. These reports verify that Lee Harvey Oswald and CIA operative Georges De Mohrenschildt were homosexuals, while Jack Ruby was bisexual. When added to the fact that other key figures such as Clay Shaw and pilot David Ferrie (along with his roommate Raymond Roshears) were also flamboyant homosexuals, along with transvestite homosexuals J. Edgar Hoover and his long-time assistant Clyde Tolson (known as J. Edna and Mother Tolson), what we see emerging is another aspect of the Kennedy case kept concealed by the government, Warren Commission, and the media. In his book, *The Bureau: My Thirty Years in Hoover's FBI*, William Sullivan even goes so far as to say that Robert F. Kennedy commonly referred to Hoover as "an old faggot."

3) These same Russian Intelligence and DIA reports state that Lee Harvey Oswald was an agent for both the U.S. Office of Naval Intelligence (run by the CIA), and a paid FBI informant. In other words, he worked in varying capacities for the United States Government!

4) <u>U2 Spy Plane</u> – (DIA Report) – "Internal CIA documents show very clearly that as their very existence was dependent on a continuation of the Cold War, any diminution of East-West hostility could easily lead to their own downsizing over the office of the President and also of U.S. foreign policy. It was proposed, according to top level CIA reports, to somehow use their U2 flights to create an increase in tension that could lead to a frustration of any détente that might result from a lessening of international tensions."

5) <u>Jack Ruby's Murder</u> – (DIA Report) – "[Jack] Ruby was given an injection of air with a syringe which produced an embolism that killed him. The official cause of Ruby's death was a blood clot. Ruby's fatal blood clot was the result of OUTSIDE ASSISTANCE." Russia's intelligence study confirms this claim, stating, "information indicates he was given a fatal injection."

6) <u>The Warren Commission</u> (DIA Report) – "A written comment by Chief Justice Earl Warren to former CIA Director Allen Dulles was that "people like Lane [New York attorney Mark Lane, author of *Rush to Judgment*] should never be permitted to air their radical views ... at least not before the Commission."

7) <u>CIA Ties to Organized Crime</u> (Driscoll Report) – "American gangsters had very close relations with the Central Intelligence Agency. This relationship began during the war [WWII] when the American OSS made connections with Sicilian members of the American gangs in order to assist them against the fascists [Mussolini]. The man who performed this liason was James Jesus Angleton, later head of counter-intelligence." This is confirmed by the 1978 DIA Report. "The connections of Angleton, chief of counter-intelligence for the CIA with elements of the mob are WELL KNOWN in intelligence circles. Angleton worked closely with the Sicilian and Naples mobs in 1944 onwards as part of his duties for the OSS."

8) <u>The basis for President Bush's "You're either for us or against us" motto</u> – (Russian Intelligence Study) – "American foreign policy was, and still is, firmly in the hands of the CIA. No nation is permitted to be neutral; all have to be either in the U.S. camp or are its enemies. Most often, American businesses are paramount in the determination as to

which [country] will receive U.S. support and which will not only be denied this support, but attacked."

9) <u>The Cold War</u> – author Gregory Douglas claims that "the Cold War was an engineered affair, and its chief architect was former German Army General Reinhard Gehlen, a former head of the Soviet military intelligence section of the Wehrmacht." He did this in 1948 by fabricating a report for the CIA which claimed the Russians had amassed artillery divisions on the European border and were set to attack. The Controller's motivation was twofold: 1) it would be a legitimate excuse for both the U.S. and USSR military to increase in size (via loans from the international bankers), and 2) it would bolster the U.S. economy, which began to slump once again after WWII (i.e. war = profits). Gehlen was employed by the U.S. Army in 1948, and then became a paid CIA employee until 1956.

10) <u>Staged Government Attacks Upon the U.S.</u> – Operation NORTHWOODS was a U.S. Joint Chiefs of Staff ploy to invoke American hatred against Fidel Castro so that they would support an invasion of Cuba. What they wanted to do was sink ships in the Atlantic Ocean, hijack aircrafts, set-off bombs in U.S. cities, and destroy civilian airplanes. (Does this sound familiar to 9-11?)

11) <u>Other Possible Asassination Plots against President Kennedy</u>:

a) February, 1963 – blow-up the President's airplane
b) Have Kennedy's doctor put deadly substances into his amphetamine injections
c) Blow-up his boat off the Massachusetts coast

12) <u>Operation Zipper</u> – Official code name for the Assassination of President Kennedy.

13) <u>Hit Men</u> – The four assassins were recruited by famed mobster Sam Giancana from the Corsican Mafia (*Unione Corse*) in Marseilles, Italy. The government contact was Robert Trumbull Crowley, Deputy Director of Operations for the CIA. Crowley met twice with Giancana at the Drake Hotel in Chicago. Meanwhile, CIA Director John McCone reigned in the FBI, while James Jesus Angleton got the Army and Joints Chiefs of Staff on board. In April, 1963, the trigger men were selected

(each being promised $100,000 a piece), and were overseen by former FBI agent and CIA Berlin operative William King Harvey. Angleton also brought on Israeli counterintelligence agent Amos Manor, head of the Shin Beth, to also coordinate the operation. This Israeli unit's main task was to kill the assassins after they took out Kennedy. This took place in Maryland, where three were eliminated after being flown out of Dallas by David Ferrie, while a fourth returned to Marseilles.

14) CIA Drug Trafficking – Author Gregory Douglas – "With increasing American military involvement in Vietnam and Laos, the increase in opium smuggling was highly significant and has not stopped to this day. It is a PUBLISHED FACT that much of the movement of raw opium from the so-called Golden Triangle was affected by the CIA and its Air America private air force." He concludes this paragraph by stating unequivocally that the U.S. government is one of the primary drug traffickers in the world.

15) The CIA and the Media – Frank Gardiner Wisner, head of CIA clandestine operations, was one of the primary forces in infiltrating the American and foreign media. Quote from the author: "By a judicious mixture of bribery, special favors, and outright payments of cash, Wisner and his associates could powerfully influence American perceptions and completely silence any media opposition. Prominent academics, revered newspaper columnists, historical writers, newspaper and magazine editors, book publishers, and later television executives all gorged at the CIA pig trough."

SECTION EIGHT:

THE MEDIA

&

SOCIETY

CHAPTER FIFTY-THREE

WHY DOESN'T THE MEDIA TELL US ABOUT THE BILDERBERGS?

I love America, especially the freedom and unlimited potential it represents. I also despise with every ounce of venom in my body the sick evil Satan Controllers that are deliberately in the process of destroying this great nation. And if you don't think it's happening, take a look at what occurred on September 11, 2001, and realize what those bastards are capable of. The destruction in Washington, D.C. and New York City was no accident, and the powers-that-be who rule our world were behind it.

Sure, Islamic terrorists played a role in orchestrating the World Trade Center disaster, but they were only a symptom of the overall problem. The real cause of this tragedy is a psychotic cabal of monstrous Globalists who have symbolically stated via this act that the world must now undergo a dramatic change.

Listen to me, folks. Everything that we've come to love in this country -- all of the cherished freedoms and rights -- are about to be slowly taken away from us. This is the real thing, and it's happening right before our very eyes. The United States has declared war on terrorists, but there's a much more important war taking place that the media isn't telling you about. It's a war between the Globalists, those who want a slavish New World Order, and a group of patriotic Nationalists who love America and want to save it from being destroyed.

Let me ask you a question. After the atrocity of September 11, we witnessed an outpouring of love by hundreds of thousands of honest, dedicated Americans who would do anything to guard and protect our country. These people are everywhere, and it fills my heart with joy to know they still exist.

By the same token, take a look at things happening in this country and ask yourself, "Do the people running the show have the American people's best interests in mind?" If you've read any of my past articles in *Babel Magazine*, you'll realize that we're being lied to on a daily basis; duped, deceived, manipulated, and undermined by a hidden cadre of Globalists who control our government, media and universities.

If these people want to bolster America, why aren't we being told the truth about the Oklahoma City Bombing, the downing of Flight 93, Votescam, AIDS and scores of other issues?

Why are we allowing our country to be overrun with illegal aliens when we could stop this problem within a week? Why are we allowing trade agreements such as NAFTA to destroy our industrial-based economy? Why are we allowing our votes to be stolen by letting self-serving politicians sit in Washington, DC and watch us be weakened just so they can fatten their wallets?

I'd like to ask a question: Where do you get your information about the world around you? Most people would say television, radio, newspapers, magazines, and the Internet. Well, let me put this revelation in the starkest terms possible. The same people who are destroying our country are those who own every media source that you get your information from.

What does that mean to you? Here's the way I see it. What if I was a thief and wanted to rob your house? In addition to being a burglar I also published a newspaper. Knowing I wanted to do something that didn't benefit you, what would I do? Print articles that said I was a thief? Of course not. I wouldn't want you to get even the slightest inkling of my motives. In fact, I'd do anything in my power to keep you in the dark.

That's what is happening to us. The media and government are lying through their teeth to the American people on a daily basis. When you tune into the Dan Rather News, it's no different from watching professional wrestling - neither program is real, both have pre-determined results, and they use a variety of dramatic techniques to hook the viewer.

It's time for all of us to think for ourselves rather than be conditioned into obedient little automatons. Read the political articles that appear in this book, then compare them to the lies the corporate media keeps laying on us. There's no comparison.

If you don't buy into how much is being kept from us, I'd like to tell you about a group called the Bilderbergs (a revolving group of political leaders, bankers, industrialists, and businessmen) who meet once a year to plan the world's future. Of course, considering that these men and women are the most influential individuals on the planet, you'd think there'd be some media coverage of their conferences. But the mainstream media *never* says a word about them. It's a total blackout.

Or, as James Tucker said in the now defunct *Spotlight* newspaper: "If the world's most popular film stars or football players gathered for a closed-door meeting over the weekend, the press would go crazy, demanding to know what was discussed. But when the world's most powerful private citizens gather in the company of key political figures, there's not the slightest cry of outrage."

What we have is a handful of people who control virtually ALL the information we receive. This system is perpetuated by the FCC, which regulates how many television and radio stations operate in a given area. The lockdown is so complete, in 1990, only 21 groups controlled the entirety of the printed media; 12 groups controlled all the newspapers, 3 controlled the magazines, and another 6 controlled the mainstream publishing industry. I guarantee these numbers have become even more appalling over the past decade.

Turn on your television and flick through the channels. How many alternatives do you have in regard to news? There is:

- CBS: CONTROLLED
- NBC: CONTROLLED
- ABC: CONTROLLED
- FOX: CONTROLLED
- CNN: CONTROLLED
- *Time* Magazine: CONTROLLED
- The *New York Times*: CONTROLLED
- The *Washington Post*: CONTROLLED
- *Newsweek*: CONTROLLED
- *U.S. News & World Report*: CONTROLLED

The people who dominate the media are part of "The Alibi Club," an elite group of 50 business executives and political officials who have joined together with the "Intelligence" community to influence what we see, hear, and read in the media. This idea is supported by a clandestine program called "Operation Mockingbird" in which the CIA recruited and used mainstream journalists to manipulate the media and directly affect the outcome of elections.

One of the biggest problems the Controllers suffer from is a propensity to reveal their motives every once in awhile. So, take a look at what these folks are saying about their own industry and practices:

<u>Richard Salent</u> (former president of CBS News): "Our job is to give people not what they want, but what we decide they ought to have."

Lyndon Johnson (former President of the United States): "Reporters are puppets. They simply respond to the pull of the most powerful strings."

Bill Moyers (television journalist): "Most of the news on television is, ultimately, whatever the government says is news."

Johnny Carson: "How much of the national news that you report to the public each night consists of information you've actually gone out and dug up on your own?"

Connie Chung (responding to Johnny's question): "In all honesty, we are often at the mercy of the White House for the news we report. Frequently, we simply report verbatim what the White House tells us."

The CIA and the Cult of Intelligence (Marchetti & Marks): "Only about 20% of the CIA's career employees work on intelligence analysis and information processing. About 2/3 of all CIA funds and manpower are spent on "covert operations," such as the manipulation of public opinion and elections and its mass media manipulation activity."

As a voice of reason, Noam Chomsky tells us, "If you're rational and honest, you're pretty much excluded from the educated classes, from the privileged classes. Those are properties (honesty and rationalism) that are very dangerous." In other words, Chomsky says if you're a liar, you can progress to the upper echelons of power. But if you're honest, you're seen as a threat to the established order.

On September 10, 2001, America was plunging into a recession; the Gary Condit sex scandal played on every station, crime was on an upswing; the Israeli/Palestinian peace talks were deteriorating; and NAFTA and illegal immigration had many people disgruntled.

One day later, on September 11, our nation was inspired by waves of patriotism, focused on a single act of brutality, and was willing to relinquish many of our civil rights. To fuel us, George W. Bush gave a speech that sent his approval ratings through the roof.

Do you think life has gotten better or worse since September 11? If you said worse, what are you going to do if things keep going downhill? Also, do you think Dan Rather, the *New York Times*, and *Newsweek* are going to be there to help you along the way, or will they continue to lie on a daily basis? I don't know about you, but I refuse to accept their deceptive practices any longer.

CHAPTER FIFTY-FOUR

THE AMERICAN MEDIA SHOULD BE ASHAMED OF

ITSELF

In mid-April, 2002, the Trilateral Commission met for four days at the Ritz Carlton Hotel in Washington, D.C. As is their custom, this highly influential group of world leaders from North America, Japan and Europe plotted ways to promote their Globalist agenda. Some of the items on their nefarious list this year were:

- America's upcoming invasion of Iraq, and how to lure Europe and other Asian nations into supporting our War Machine.
- The need to further create a multinational financial octopus, with the United Nations as the head of a one-world government.
- A decision to keep pumping money, technology, and computers into China, bolstering them as the next premier global superpower.
- A decision to funnel more American aid to "under-exploited" foreign countries, leading the way for the implementation of a World Tax.
- Prevention of the Israeli/Palestinian war from turning into a complete powder keg, thus endangering our Middle Eastern oil supplies.

Each of these issues seems vitally important, even crucial, to the world. Others thought so too, for some of the attendees included:

- David Rockefeller - Overlord, Chase Manhattan Bank
- Paul Volcker - Former Chairman, Federal Reserve
- Charles Robb - Former Senator
- Robert McNamara - Former Secretary of Defense
- Kenneth Lay - Former CEO, Enron
- Henry Kissinger - Former Secretary of State
- Winston Lord - Former China Ambassador

- David Gergen - Editor, *U.S. News and World Report*
- Zbigniew Brzezinski - Former Head of National Security, Trilateral Commission co-founder
- Madeline Albright - Former Secretary of State
- John Deutch - Former Director, CIA
- Richard Holbrook - Former U.S. Ambassador to U.N.
- Harold Brown - Former Secretary of Defense
- Strobe Talbott - Former Under Secretary of State
- Tom Foley - Former Speaker of the House

In addition to those in attendance was also the head of Goldman-Sachs International, one of the ten firms that hold the most stock in our nation's Federal Reserve System. Also, there were other representatives from:

- Fuji Xerox
- Germany (the U.S. Ambassador)
- Georgetown (professor)
- *Washington Post* (columnist)
- Archer-Daniels Midland (chair)
- Club of Rome (president)
- International Monetary Fund (managing director)
- Canada – UK (former High Commissioner)
- British Parliament (member)
- AFL-CIO (NITE branch - president emeritus)
- Federal Reserve (president)
- Levi-Strauss (chair)
- Rothschild & Sons (director)
- Citicorp, which owns 22% of NYFR stock (vice chair)
- Institution of Global Economics, Seoul (CEO)
- Mexican government (Former President, and Minister of Trade)
- Irish contingency of government (former Senator)
- Xerox (former CEO)

Some of the speakers and panelists were:

- Dick Cheney, Vice President of the United States
- Alan Greenspan, Chairman, Federal Reserve

- Colin Powell, Secretary of State
- Donald Rumsfeld, Secretary of Defense

In all, 251 of the most influential businessmen, statesmen, politicians, financiers, and academics met in Washington, D.C. -- and how much did you hear about it in your local or national media? I'll bet nothing!

Think of it this way (as veteran reporter Jim Tucker of the *American Free Press* so eloquently puts it): Every year when the world's greatest actors get together at the Academy Awards, is the media present? Yes.

How about when America's two best football teams meet at the Super Bowl? Is the media there? Of course.

TV's Emmy awards -- the media is there. Grammy's -- the media is there en force. The media even reports on hog-calling contests at the State Fair in Arkansas.

But when some of the most powerful men and women congregate to determine the course of future history, did any of the following cover their meeting?

- ABC - NO
- NBC - NO
- CBS - NO
- *New York Times* - NO
- *Newsweek* - NO
- *Time* Magazine – NO

The *Washington Post* and *U.S. News and World Report* even had journalists present! They should have been running full-color blowout cover story articles on the Trilateral Commission's meeting. Regrettably, they did not.

Instead, we got the same old sanitized, censored pabulum that keeps the masses socially controlled and uninformed.

In Russia there used to be an old joke about their two primary newspapers -- *Pravda*, which means "truth," and *Isvestia*, which translates to "News." The punch line was: "There's no truth in *Pravda*, and no news in *Isvestia*!" All of us in America laugh at that joke because we enjoy freedom of the press and openness in the media -- right?

Wrong. What differentiates us from the old hard-core Soviets if we're not being told the truth and we don't get the news straight-up?

433

Sure, there are alternate sources for information such as the Internet and underground press, but the mainstream media in this country should be ashamed of themselves.

Again I'll ask: why do they refuse to give us the whole story? The answer lies in an all-pervasive concept: Control. Y'see, since five multinational corporations now own the entirety of the mainstream media in this country, they essentially determine what you see and cannot see (or read or hear).

With this stranglehold over the media, here's how they control their output. Let's pretend there's a hotshot journalist who graduates from college and lands his first job at a small-town newspaper. Young and idealistic, he writes articles about township council meetings and profiles on little old ladies growing petunias in their backyard. Everything is running smoothly, and life is good.

Within a year the young journalist moves on to a small city paper, keeps shining, and soon finds himself writing at a nationally known publication. He gets married, has two children and buys a big house in a nice neighborhood. He even wins a few awards along the way. His future is bright.

Then, when all seems settled and cool, this reporter gets tipped-off to an incredibly horrendous program that is secretly being implemented against the American people without their knowledge. The reporter, outraged, does some research and discovers what he didn't want to learn. So, with facts in hand and a belly full of bravado to back him up, he storms into his editor's office and lays it all out, telling the editor he wants to expose this obvious injustice.

Now here's where things get sticky. The editor obviously knows what's going on, so he sits the reporter down and tells him frankly that these types of stories "CANNOT" be covered because of the potential damage it could cause to the Controllers.

The reporter freaks out and says if his newspaper won't blow the lid off this story, he'll take his notes and sources to another outlet. The editor, who had been through this same routine twenty years earlier, explains to the man that he's a great reporter with tons of potential, but if he pursues this story, he'll be blackballed within the Industry. Sure, he might get an underground publication to run his story, but in the mainstream he'll be all but washed-up. That means no more cushy assignments, hobnobbing with influential personalities, no more top-notch salary, and no more promotions or vacations in Hawaii. In all likelihood, he'll probably even be canned in the near future if he causes any more trouble.

The reporter protests, but his editor tells him to consider the impact on his career. Without the big money rolling in, how can he pay his mortgage, keep his trophy wife in pretties, send their two children to private school, and dine at the finest restaurants? He'll go from prince to pauper, get divorced ... and all the rest is history.

So, the reporter goes home and discusses his options with his wife, then returns to work the next day to tell his editor that, yes, he'll can the exposé and bury it. Pleased, the editor lets his superiors know his employee is a "team player," and soon he gets another promotion.

Then, a couple of years down the line the advancing reporter gets an assignment as the Executive Editor at a mid-sized newspaper. That's when some hotshot citizens come to him with a story that'll blow the lid off a government scam. They have tons of information, sources, and data -- and want the new editor to run their story.

By this time, though, the editor knows how the game is played. He wasn't assigned to this job to report on news that benefits the community. He was put there to "keep a lid" on everything -- to not blow any covers. So the editor tells his "higher-ups" what's going on and asks how he should handle it.

They instruct him to keep cool and cover it up, so the editor puts a dagger through the story and kills it. It's dead, done, and over, and no one's the wiser. The "higher-ups" are again pleased with Our Hero for being a "team player" and soon he's promoted to editor at a big-city paper.

The game goes on and the System stays intact.

That's the way it works, but not only in the newspaper business. It's the same in the television industry. Ask Dan Rather. As the "chosen" reporter for the JFK Assassination, he made his entire career by scamming us at that infamous event, and soon replaced Walter Cronkite as the anchor for the CBS Evening News.

In politics, if a candidate doesn't toe the line and instead decides to become a whistle-blower, all of a sudden the big Party Machine money from the Republicans and Democrats that had gone to their re-election campaigns suddenly dries up and is funneled to another candidate who is better "trained" in following the rules.

If this candidate insists on trying to expose the inner workings of the Machine, the media conveniently uncovers a "scandal" and the politician is publicly humiliated, insuring they'll never be re-elected again.

Almost all "falls from grace" are not because a certain politician is any dirtier than the rest; it's because they're bucking the System and trying to disclose graft and underhanded schemes.

In academia, if an instructor or professor adheres to the accepted curriculum and doesn't stray or tell the truth (especially in history, political science, economics, archaeology, and the science fields), they're in the running for all the benefits of academic life. But if they venture into forbidden territory, the promotions, cushy conference trips to Florida in January, research money and tenure fade away into oblivion.

In other words, teach what is included within the narrow confines established by the Controllers, or else you'll be passed over time and again for someone who a 'team player'.

The same rationale applies to the business world, medical profession and dog-eat-dog trenches of the legal profession. Either conform, or get bounced and rejected.

CHAPTER FIFTY-FIVE

TAKE BACK YOUR STOLEN VOTE: VOTESCAM

REVISITED

"Whenever a man has cast his eye on office, a rottenness begins in his character."

-- Thomas Jefferson

"Those who cast the vote decide nothing. Those who count the votes decide everything."

-- Joseph Stalin

QUIZ

During every Federal election, do the networks and major newspapers actually send their own reporters and researchers into polling places, scrambling to discern who the potential winners will be so they can be the first to "scoop" their competitors with the election results?

ANSWER

NO! The networks don't compete for vote totals. CBS, NBC, ABC, CNN and FOX all belong to VNS – the "Voter News Service," which is a consortium of mass media conglomerates that have pooled their resources and have the exclusive right (bestowed by Congress) to count the votes in every state. *None of them compete for these votes!* They all come from the same source – VNS – located at 225 W. 34th Street in New York City. In other words, when you watch the "drama" on each of the network broadcasts where they're frantically scrambling to be the first to announce a winner, it's nothing but an illusion. A lie!

VNS compiles ALL the data from every election; then posts it simultaneously for each network, plus the major daily newspapers.

In fact, both *Time* Magazine (March 2, 1992, page 22) and Margaret Sims of the "Federal Elections Commission Report" (1994) reported that the six primary members of this group (ABC, NBC, CBS, CNN, FOX, and AP) received the EXACT same "exit poll" information at the same time from the same company. That's why these networks can declare a winner in a multitude of races only one minute after the polls close. The *Associated Press* (June 1, 2001, page A04) even reported that the above six media organizations renewed their contract with VNS despite the overwhelming corruption and horror of the 2000 presidential election.

Do you see what's happening here? It's all professional wrestling. Why don't Dan Rather, Tom Brokaw, and Peter Jennings admit to the American public on election night that there is no drama, no scrambling for data, and no heated competition among them for election results? It all comes from the same source. The answer, regrettably, is that this frantic "professional wrestling scenario" is a technique or excuse that is needed to steal your vote.

If this is the case, some may ask, why haven't we heard about it before? The answer, quite simply, is that you should have because there are plenty of influential people in the media who know about it, but are simply covering for the Controllers. Mike Wallace of *60 Minutes* is aware of "Votescam," as are Geraldo Rivera, Ross Perot, Janet Reno, Pat Robertson, Ted Turner, Ted Koppel, Larry King, Helen Thomas, Mario Cuomo, Jerry Brown, and the recently deceased Katherine Graham. All of them know our votes are being stolen. Their silence is unforgivable.

Before delving into my overview of "Votescam," I'd like to provide a few example of how pervasive and appalling the electoral process is in this country. Following these case histories, we'll take a very hard look at not only the problems confronting us, but also a way to correct this situation.

STOLEN VOTES

Example Number 1 - In the 1970 Dade County, Florida election, Jim and Ken Collier, authors of *Votescam*, found that three minutes after the polls had closed, all of the major networks had already projected the winners in over 250 races! Only one minute after the polls had closed, Channel 7 projected that a certain candidate would not only win, but would receive 96,499 total votes. Well, when the official results were returned, guess how many votes this candidate received? -- 96,499. Channel 7 was 100% accurate only one minute after the voting had ended!

The Collier brothers went one step further and tracked down all the projections versus the actual results for all the major Florida races in 1970. Here is what they found:

RACE	PROJECTED	ACTUAL
Governor	141,387	141,866
Senate 43	45,696	45,881
House 98	97,031	96,499
House 10	67,940	68,491
House 107	81,802	81,539

The question we have to ask is: How can the networks not only be so accurate, but arrive at these startling projections one to three minutes after the polls close? Think about it. After the voting stations close at 9:00 PM, what needs to be done? Tens of thousands of punch card ballots need to be collected; then they must be fed into a punch card reader. Now, I know what this process entails because I operated an entire room full of IBM Mainframe computers during the mid-1980s (back when punch cards were still in use).

To read even a few drawers of cards was quite an ordeal, considering all the misfeeds, jams, etc. Anyway, after all the cards are read, the data needs to be compiled, organized, printed out, then transmitted to the television station where it'll be prepped for broadcast. Do you think all of these steps can be completed in one-to-three minutes?

The Collier Brothers found it very implausible, so they went to Channel 7 and tried to track down the "super computer" that made these projections only one-to-three minutes after the polls closed, all with 99-100% accuracy. The first thing they wanted to know was which reporter called in the raw totals to the television studio. They were told that it wasn't a reporter, after all, but a member of the League of Women Voters.

Since only a handful of reporters could be out in the field (considering that this was only an affiliate station), it would seem logical that only a few precincts could be sampled. But how, they wondered, could 99% of the precincts be reporting by 11:00 – only two hours after the polls closed? The League of Women Voters must be incredibly efficient.

So, the Colliers visited Joyce Deiffenderfer, head of the local League of Women Voters, and asked for a list of all the people who had counted votes on election night (since Channel 7 said that's where they got their results). Realizing the cat was out of the bag, Ms. Deiffenderfer, in tears, admitted that there weren't *any* LWV members in *any* of the precincts that night. They hadn't counted a single vote, and she didn't "want to get caught up in this thing."

Hmmm. Within three minutes of the poll's closing, the TV station had projections that were 99-100% accurate, and within two hours, 99% of all the precincts had supposedly reported their results. But it's funny because no one was able to locate the super computer that made these fabulous projections. Nor could anyone be found that even counted or reported the vote counts! I wonder where all the numbers came from?

Example Number 2 – In a 1973 Florida election, Printomatic Voting Machines had been installed to make the entire process run smoother. All of the Printomatic devices have a locked area in back that every election supervisor is supposed to check before the election to insure that all the wheels were set at zero. But all of the keys had been taken away from the supervisors, so none of the totals could be verified. Shortly after the polls opened, the paper rolls began to jam in all the machines, making them inoperable.

Since no one could vote, the backs of each device were eventually opened, and when the paper rollers were pulled out, they all had the final vote totals already printed on them at seven o'clock in the morning! Needless to say, every election volunteer walked off the job.

Example Number 3 - If you think voter fraud only happened during Al Capone's Chicago days (do you recall their helpful hint – "vote early, and vote often"), you're seriously mistaken. Here are a few other "tricks of the trade":

- Shave the wheels in the back of a voting machine so they skip ahead.
- Before the polls open, unlock the back of a voting device and set the total counters ahead for a certain candidate.
- If a clear ballot box isn't used, stuff it with pre-punched vote cards before the polls open.
- If a computerized machine is used, unplug it or turn it off so all the previous totals are erased.
- Finally, the League of Women Voters has been captured *on videotape* in Florida with pencils and tweezers punching out cards for certain candidates; then shoving them into ballot boxes.

The list could go on forever.

Example Number 4 - Finally, during the 1996 Republican Party Primary, Pat Robertson was beating every other candidate in the early stages of the race, especially Bob Dole and Steve Forbes. Then when he rolled into Arizona with high hopes of another victory that would catapult him toward getting his party's nomination, something strange happened. The computers broke down!

Yes, VNS had actually declared Buchanan the winner. Karen Johnson, Buchanan's Arizona State Coordinator, got a call from Governor Fife Symington congratulating her on what he called a "decisive" victory. Senator John McCain also drafted a congratulatory letter, while all three networks and CNN said that Dole would definitely finish third, while Forbes took second and Buchanan won.

Then the computers mysteriously went down. When they came back up, guess what happened. Pat Buchanan ended up a distant third, while Bob Dole won! When asked about this phenomenon, Buchanan joked about the computers (referring to the "fix" being in), "They seemed to work better after they brought 'em back!"

<u>VOTER NEWS SERVICE</u> (VNS)

As mentioned, VNS is the only American company that counts votes in every Federal election. Ponder this point for a moment. A faceless corporation that 99% of the people in this country have never heard of is responsible for tabulating our votes. This Service was created by the Big Six in 1964 - one year after JFK was assassinated, and is currently run by ABC, NBC, CBS, CNN, FOX, and AP. Over the years, VNS has gone through a variety of name changes and was originally called NES (News Election Services).

When you consider the ramifications of every Presidential, Congressional, and Gubernatorial race, you'll see that VNS is one of the most influential corporations in America. Yet, no one has ever heard of them. How can such a fantastic responsibility be placed in the hands of a company that was developed by a consortium of corporate media conglomerates? The most glaring observation one could make from this situation is: if a faceless, unknown agency (VNS) is the sole vote counter rather than accountable local volunteers in each precinct, is it conceivable that a wealthy politician or political party could clandestinely pay them off to rig an election?

The answer is obvious, especially when 99% of the American people don't even know about the existence of VNS.

Robert H. Lande, Professor of Law at the University of Baltimore in a letter (dated October 22, 2000) to the United States Justice Department and the Federal Trade Commission on behalf of the American Antitrust Institute, said, "The Government should file suit to break up the

VNS." He continued (shortly after the 2000 fall election): "Why the uniformity of wrong results? This can be explained by a lack of competition. All of the "competing" major networks are actually colluding with one another, and they call their collusion the VNS." Finally, Mr. Lande concludes, "If the six largest manufacturers of automobiles, canned food, or aluminum decided to close existing operations and pool resources to save money, the antitrust enforcement agencies would be after them immediately."

NETWORK NEWS REPORTING

"When you're dealing with the networks, you're dealing with a shadowgovernment."

--Tim O'Brien, ABC's Supreme Court Correspondent

On Monday, November 2, 1988, the night *before* the off-year elections, ABC News posted hundreds of election results – one whole day before a single person ever placed a vote!!!!!!

Now that we know the networks, CNN, FOX, and AP all get their election results from the same source – VNS – we need to ask ourselves, why is there such an emphasis on speed? Speed is the key, at least where the networks are concerned. Why? Because the illusion of reporting "speedy" results is the second piece of the puzzle needed to steal an election (I'll give you the first piece a little later). Here's a typical scenario:

Dan Rather appears on your TV screen at one minute after the hour ... one minute after the polls have closed in a certain part of the country. Naturally, he'll already have some "projections," and he'll even announce some winners – one minute after the polls close.

So, they'll rack up their totals, show who is ahead; and focus their attention on the last intangible ... those races that are "too close to call." Once you hear those words, you know you're in trouble. That's when there's a huge gap in reporting – the lag time – when Dan Rather talks to all his "boys" to get their expert opinion. Of course, not once is he mentioning that all their results are coming from VNS. That information isn't important enough for the American people to know.

Then, all of a sudden, one of two things happens. First, there are either some technical difficulties or else the computers break down. If you don't believe me, hearken back to the Florida debacle in 2000. After awhile the network head will report either a huge landslide of results with one candidate pulling way ahead, or else the "difficulty" was corrected and there was a drastic turnaround in votes, with the candidate in front falling far behind, or vice versa.

But speed is the key ingredient. While the polling place is closing down one minute after the hour and punch cards or computer data is being transferred to county headquarters, then onward to VNS, none of it can be verified or made official. A perfect example would be the 2000 Iowa caucus. With over 2,000 polling places, the AP announced a winner one minute after the caucus had *opened* (not closed) and not one vote had been cast.

Think about how absurd these examples are. ABC News is reporting election results a day *before* an election, and the AP is announcing winners before any votes are not only analyzed, but even cast!

POLLING

The first ingredient needed to assure the "desired results" from a particular election is the use of polls and exit polls. Before I continue, I'd like to make one thing perfectly clear:

THE POLL RESULTS THAT YOU SEE ON THE NIGHTLY NEWS AND IN YOUR LOCAL PAPER ON A DAILY BASIS ARE NOTHING BUT A CONDITIONING TOOL USED TO MAKE THE GENERAL PUBLIC THINK THE '*PROPER*' WAY.

In other words, the supposed polls you see every night on the World News do nothing but mold opinion, not mirror it. The concept is similar to the psychological test in which 20 "plants" are told to say that a certain flashcard is colored red, when in reality it is purple. When the 21st person is finally asked what color the card is, they've been so conditioned to think its purple (because everyone else said so), they go against their own natural inclinations and answer incorrectly.

Actually, a more appropriate psychological term for this process is called "psychic driving." To acclimate the voting public on how they're supposed to react, a specific message is repeatedly hammered into their heads on a daily basis.

Are you starting to see how this little game is played? First we're set-up with "public opinion" polls, which are nothing but an outright farce, and do not in any way indicate how we truly feel. All the numbers are cooked! But this con job plays a very important role by getting us "ready" for who the Controllers have decided will win in a particular election.

After the stage has been set by repeatedly saying that candidate X is ahead in the polls by 10 points (even though they may only have a 20% favorable rating by the voting public), we are now ready for stage two – the lightning fast projections and "exit poll" results. Exit polls, I hope you know by now, are even shadier than the pre-election surveys. Why? Because it's one last chance to condition the public and prepare them for who the "winner" will be. (As a side note, exit polls also play a large part in lessening the impact that voters in western states play in determining who will ultimately emerge as the victor.)

As we have already discovered, none of the networks "scramble" to get election results. All of their information comes from the exact source at the exact same time – VNS. They have already admitted this fact, although they do so as quietly as possible. Then, within one minute of the polls closing, the networks project a winner based on exit polls that are startling in their accuracy (with only 1 % of the vote actually in).

The next logical question to ask at this point is – if the networks aren't running around frantically doing election-day exit polling, then who is? The answer – an outfit called VRS – Voter Research Surveys. Now, try to guess who operates VRS. You're right – the same Big Six media conglomerates that run VNS!

Before we go any further, the networks would say, "Wait a minute. There is an organization that overlooks VNS called the NCCP – National Council of Public Polls. These folks guarantee that everything is on the up and up."

I must admit, there is indeed an organization called the NCCP that is made up of a consortium of pollsters and news outlets. But guess what? The same media members who founded VNS also belong to the NCCP. Pretty convenient, huh! So, between the networks, VNS, VRS, and NCCP, we have polls, exit polls, then finally those remarkable projections that are almost always right on the mark. But how can their estimates always be so close to what the final "tabulated" results are? That's easy. All the election supervisors have to do is doctor the computer numbers to match the exit polls; then they come up with what was already a pre-determined result in the first place. How do you think we keep getting all these asinine politicians in office (the same ones who stay there forever), especially when everyone hates them? We sure as hell aren't voting for them (at least if there's another choice). The picture is becoming a little clearer, isn't it?

COMPUTERIZED VOTING

In an election totally free of fraud, citizens would hand-write their votes on paper ballots, place them in a clear box; then watch as an impartial group of volunteers counted their votes in full view. The results would then be posted at the polling place before being shipped to the county courthouse.

With computerized voting, we simply send a "blip" through cyberspace. There is no paper trail (a physical ballot), nor are there any checks and balances. We're simply told to trust those in charge of the election and everything will be okay. Considering the evidence I've provided thus far, how much faith does that inspire in you?

What if we found that it's possible to manipulate these computerized unseen results to "correspond" to the projections (also doctored) that were given one minute after the polls closed so that everything would be *official*? What if someone told you – "Hey, it'd be very easy to find a computer programmer who could write some software that would already determine the winner regardless of the vote totals"? The procedure wouldn't be much more difficult to pull off than placing a paper roller into the back of a Printomatic voting machine that already had the totals pre-printed on them.

Now I'm sure someone will say that this notion is preposterous! To prove the process isn't corrupt, all the software designers have to do is show you the "source code" from their program. How complicated could it be to write a program that simply counts votes? Any tenth grade kid who has taken an introductory course in computer science could write it.

But guess what? Numerous researchers have tried to inspect the computer software at VNS. But instead of gladly allowing them to do so (these are fair and open elections, aren't they?) VNS flatly denied their requests, saying their programs were "trade secrets." In other words, their software is afforded the same protection as any other corporate trade secret. To me, though, the same rationale doesn't apply for two reasons.

First, a privately owned for-profit company is much different from one that is very influential in determining who will assume the Presidency and a large number of Congressional seats. My second argument is just as straightforward: What do these software designers have to hide?

445

They haven't created programs that prevent America from being bombed by incoming ballistic missiles like those used at NORAD. The only thing (supposedly) their software does is count votes. Why all the secrecy? Why don't they want anyone inspecting their source codes?

On the night before the 1988 Presidential election, the following conversation took place on the CBS Evening News:

Dan Rather: Realistically, could the fix be put on in a national election?

Howard J. Strauss (computer expert – Princeton University): Get me a job with a company that writes the software for this program. Then I'd have access to one-third of the votes. Is that enough to fix a general election?

Mr. Strauss has also said, "When it comes to computerized elections, there are no safeguards. It's not a door without locks; it's a house without doors."

Judge Richard Niehouse, in a 1985 ruling against the Cincinnati Board of Elections: "There is no adequate and proper safeguard against the computers being programmed to distort the election results."

Eva Waskell, an election researcher for over ten years, weighed in with this observation: "One major problem is that computer codes that run the machines are protected as trade secrets, which makes it very hard to have an election independently audited." She also added, "The election industry is virtually unregulated. There are no mandatory regulations or standards for accurately recording and counting votes."

Craig C. Donsanto, Deputy Attorney in the Justice Department, warned us in a July 4, 1989 edition of the *Los Angeles Times*: "You have to have access and some degree of technical knowledge to penetrate an electronic tabulating system. Most of them have been or will be … simply because voting is the way we determine who gets power in this country."

The following is a quote from the same *Los Angeles Times* article on voter fraud (7-4-89): "Some critics of computerized vote counting worry about the potential for 'trapdoors,' 'time bombs' and 'Trojan Horses.' A computer operator with the correct password could place a trapdoor, or a series of hidden vote counting instructions inside the system, according to *Election Watch Report*. Once into the system, the operator could program the computer to count votes for one candidate as votes for another. After the votes have been changed to swing the election, the trapdoor could be closed."

In a letter, Attorney Ellis Rubin (3-24-92) described to Attorney General William Barr how to rig computerized voting: "Anyone with access codes could punch into elections and change the results ... and nobody would be the wiser. That also goes for the software involved."

As you can readily see, many people from different walks of life are worried about the real dangers associated with computerized voting. It's clear that we've opened a Pandora's Box. The only question now – is it too late to close the lid, or have all the evils already escaped?

JFK AND WATERGATE

Since we've come this far, many people might be wondering, "How could we have allowed what was once the world's greatest democratic process to be tainted by the likes of VNS, computers, and the corporate media?"

According to famed researcher Mae Brussel, whom the Collier Brothers quote in *Votescam*, the roots of this atrocity can be traced directly to the assassination of John F. Kennedy.

After Kennedy was killed in 1963 and the Warren Report came out shortly thereafter, everybody (the media included) knew its claims were so preposterous that they bordered on the ridiculous. Any mainstream journalist worth their weight in salt could have blown the lid off that story in five minutes, so those in control knew they needed to scramble fast to keep the genie in the bottle. So the CIA, who was very instrumental in orchestrating JFK's demise, made a deal with the press. If they kept the lid on this ruse, they would get control of the vote count in every upcoming election.

"Votescam" is nothing more than a tradeoff between the media and the power brokers. The Warren Report was a complete load of bull. Lee Harvey Oswald never fired a shot! As reported by the Air Force Staff College and American University, the FBI, CIA and various media heads met in 1964 and came to an agreement. If the media bigwigs didn't expose the obvious lies about JFK's assassination, they could become the nation's official vote counters and source for election results.

In 1963, JFK was killed. In 1964, NES (News Election Services) was founded by the networks, AP, and UPI.

If anyone doesn't believe the Controllers placed a tremendous amount of heat on the media to cover the Warren Report lies, then check out CIA Document # 1035-960:

"We do not recommend discussion of the assassination question where it is already not taking place. Where discussion is active, however, addresses are requested:

To discuss the publicity problem with liaison and friendly elite contacts (especially politicians and editors), pointing out that the Warren Commission made as thorough an investigation as humanly possible, and that further speculative discussion only plays into the hands of the opposition. Point out that parts of the conspiracy talk appear to be deliberately generated by Communist propagandists. Urge them to use their influence to discourage unfounded and irresponsible speculation.

To employ propaganda assets to answer and refute the attacks of the critics. Book reviews and feature articles are particularly appropriate for this purpose."

It's fairly evident why the Controllers would want to conceal the truth about the Warren Report, but why were the spooks so enraged by JFK in the first place? The answer can be found in a statement that Kennedy uttered shortly before his death. It appears that he was so disgusted by the Secret Service and its nefarious practices, he vowed to "shatter it into a million pieces and scatter it to the wind!"

When threatened, the CIA reacts. JFK went for their throat, so he ended up with a bullet in his head a couple of months later. The assassination was messy, and a number of mistakes were made. To compensate for their obvious errors, ex-CIA founder and director Allen Dulles met secretly with Chief Justice Earl Warren and told him if their committee didn't bamboozle the American public, world peace would be in grave danger.

So, what happened? In November 1963, control of this country was ultimately handed over to the shadow powers – to the CIA, CFR, and the secret societies that lurk behind the curtain. Earl Warren put out a "fluff" report packed with lies that is still maintained by CIA disinformation to this day. Earl Warren buckled to Allen Dulles, thus tainting his image for all time, and subsequently selling a large part of his soul for eternity.

It seems that vote fraud not only took on greater importance with the Kennedy assassination, but also extended all the way to Watergate. Katherine Graham, a media powerhouse and ruling queen tyrant of the *Washington Post*, also owned a television station in Florida that was well aware of the "Votescam" allegations made by Jim and Ken Collier. After the brothers shouted their news to whomever would listen, Richard Nixon and his cronies found out about their evidence.

Since Nixon was never a fan of the media, especially the *Washington Post*, he laid the hammer down on Katherine Graham by threatening to revoke her FCC license at the TV station because she ignored such an abundance of "Votescam" evidence. Backed into a corner, Ms. Graham stumbled onto an insignificant break-in at the Watergate Hotel and turned it into a huge scandal that eventually destroyed Tricky Dick.

The story is much more complex, but what essentially happened was that the media, when threatened and forced to cover their tracks, asserted their power by railroading a sitting president out of office.

The octopus-like arms of "Votescam" keep extending outward!!!!

<u>SOLUTIONS</u>

DO YOU TRUST THE CORPORATE MEDIA IN THIS COUNTRY TO BE COMPLETELY HONEST AND FORTHRIGHT WITH YOU?

If you answered yes to this question, then you don't need to read any further because you obviously don't think we have a problem with the type of information the citizens of this country are receiving.

But if you answered in the negative, all I can say is this, if the media isn't being 100% honest with you in regard to the information it disseminates, how can we trust them with something as important as counting the votes in all of our major elections?

Think for a moment to whom we've given this responsibility. Believe me; the people who run the show aren't stupid. In fact, they're brilliant in their ingenious deceitfulness. And until we call them on it, they're going to keep snowing us like they've always done.

In the 1988 presidential election, CBS was the first to call George Bush the winner at 9:17 PM – only 17 minutes after the polls closed, with voting stations still open in the western states. What I'd like to know is –

why the rush? We elect the president in early November, and he's not inaugurated until mid-January – over two months later. Why do we need to prematurely announce a winner after only 17 minutes!??? It takes county officials at least a month to verify all the vote totals. Are we SO greedy for results that we're willing to sacrifice the very sanctity of our democratic process for the "ruse" of speed that the networks are leading us to believe?

Look at what we've done. The United States Government doesn't tabulate a single vote (thank God) in any of the gubernatorial, congressional, or presidential elections. But since this snake isn't involved in the process, we hand over the responsibility to a demon-beast that's equally as hideous. Plus, to add insult to injury, 60% of all the votes in this country are now classified as "computerized votes." That means we can't see them or physically count them ... we have to simply TRUST that VNS does everything properly in their "invisible" little clandestine world.

With the above premise in mind, I'm going to let you in on the most crucial secrets of our current age. Here it is:

DO YOU KNOW WHAT SCARES THE HELL OUT OF THE CONTROLLERS MORE THAN ANYTHING?

ANSWER: That a "renegade" candidate will emerge on the scene who rallies and inspires the people to such an extent that he or she steamrolls into the Presidency and EXPOSES the Big Lie! The Controllers spend practically every waking moment trying to prevent this scenario. Y'see, if this maverick candidate gets into office, the whole house of cards will tumble.

It'll be EXACTLY like the Wizard of Oz. Do you remember how feeble, horrified and in awe Dorothy and her cohorts were when they first entered Oz? The entirety of this huge, cumbersome, all-encompassing kingdom literally reduced them to trembling little saps.

But then the veil was removed. After that, the Wizard would never be able to rule over them with such terrifying brilliance as before.

The Controllers will do anything in their power to keep from being exposed. And I'll tell ya; it wouldn't take much to do the job. Think about it – a candidate who is truly "of, for, and by the People" would go on TV and say, "Guess what. These guys have been deceiving you for years; here's how."

Then this renegade would go down the line and say, "This is a lie, this is a lie, this is a lie, this is a lie ... and here is how we're going to change things." From that point forward, heads would start rolling and the Controllers, who have been plotting and deceiving us for at least a century or more, would stand like horrified deer in the headlights of a locomotive as their con job was brought out into the open.

The above scenario is the key to what's happening in the world right now. The Controllers obsess over every aspect of keeping the lid on their scam – from newscasts to mind control to elections. The thought of a renegade candidate who cares about the people and tells them the truth makes them wake up in the middle of the night in a cold sweat, shivering with fear. All it would take is ONE stinking revelation of truth and the whole game is over. Do you get it?!!!! If given the opportunity, one person CAN change the world. If this candidate did speak to us, the Controller's vision of a One World hellish government would go down the drain in a heartbeat.

To combat this scenario from ever coming to fruition, the Controllers need to do one thing – NEVER allow one of those renegade candidates to get into office. So what do they do? They know how sick everyone is of their corrupt "two-party" system. (Actually, it's nothing more than one snake with two-heads.) So, they rig the election process. Here is how the system currently operates. If punch card ballots are used, after everyone votes and the polls close, the "results" are either taken to county headquarters or shipped directly to VNS ... without verification. If voting is done by computer, the machines are linked directly to the VNS super-computers via phone lines so they can "interact." Then, minutes after the polls close, the networks project a winner based on supposed exit polls.

Within a day or so everything's swept under the rug, and then they have a month or two to make the actual results jive with the "projections." This, my friends, is called a "fix."

Now, get this. The Florida "hanging chad" debacle in the 2000 presidential election was vitally important for one very calculated reason. It made the voters so sick of punch card ballots that sometime soon a politician in Washington D.C. will come out and "save" us by sponsoring a bill that will put computers in *every* polling place across America. By touting how easy, fast, and reliable these computers are, they'll get the propaganda machine rolling and convince us that this idea will be our salvation.

But when you look past their veil of lies, here's what will happen to put the "fix" in. As things stand now (especially with punch cards or hand ballots), it still takes an enormous amount of people to be corrupted –

election supervisors, volunteers, etc. But if we switch to 100% computerized voting, think how easy it'll be to "throw" an election. You'd only need to bribe or pay off one or two programmers in the whole country instead of countless county and party officials. With one centralized computer existing in an invisible realm with programs that can't be checked due to "trade secrets," we'll never actually have a chance to see our ballots first-hand. We'll simply push a button, send our vote through cyberspace, then place our TRUST in VNS, sleazy programmers, and the corporate media.

Here is the solution:

- Instantly abolish VNS and exit polling.
- If the networks insist on perpetrating the status quo in light of the potential (and outright evidence of) voter fraud, bring charges of criminal negligence, fraud, and abuse of trust against them; also, revoke their broadcast license.
- If this course of action doesn't work, convict them on the RICO Act for racketeering and conspiracy. The American people could bring a class-action lawsuit against them (similar to the tobacco company cases) for unduly influencing the outcome of an election. If we don't inherently trust the information being fed to us by the networks and corporate media due to their constant lies and manipulation, how can we place our faith in them to be honest with something as important as the election process?
- Require positive picture I.D. when voting
- Allow ONLY American citizens to vote.
- Change the voting day to Saturday.
- Institute Vote Trakker. *Vote Trakker* is a computerized touch screen voting system that is accessed by a personalized voter I.D. card that allows every person to CONFIRM their vote. Here is how it works: Vote Trakker is a stand-alone machine that is not connected to any external communications networks – thus it can't be hacked. Since there are no modems or phone lines, outside forces can't clandestinely intrude and tamper with the results. Then, once a person votes, they will receive a numbered, printed receipt. At the polling place, each voter can then check their numbered receipts against a print-out that is posted at each voting station. By doing this, they'll be able to insure that their votes weren't switched somewhere along the line. Also, Vote Trakker will make it much easier to vote for a write-in candidate (as opposed to the extremely difficult current system). To make it more conducive to vote for write-in

candidates, we can more readily lessen the stranglehold of the two-party system.

- ALL results would be tabulated, verified, and confirmed at EACH POLLING PLACE before they are sent to the county courthouse (or onto a VNS-type institution).

That's it! No rigging, no hanging chads, no telephone lines or unverifiable hidden computer programs. This is all we need to do to put the election of public officials back into the people's hands.

The big question now is – do we want to take these rather simple steps, or do we want to allow the networks and VNS to keep operating as usual? If we do nothing, I GUARANTEE that the long-awaited candidate who tells us the truth will never be given an opportunity to speak. Instead, we'll be stuck with the same crooked politicians that have already sickened us to no end.

Here's the bottom line: The corporate media has to tow a fine line between perpetuating the Controller's lies and trying to maintain their credibility. If we quit believing them, guess what? The show is over! They've lost their ability to influence us any longer.

The media has already lost their credibility. Look at the JFK assassination. Almost 40 years later, they're still perpetrating the same bogus story that Lee Harvey Oswald was a lone-nut assassin. Now they've stolen our vote, too!

But we can finally see through their lies. The Wizard of Oz has been exposed!

Are we going to keep letting them snow us, or will we take steps to elect that candidate who will level with us and get rid of all the corruption? Time is running out. The New World Order isn't something that's going to happen in the "future." It's already here! It's now or never. Taking back our vote is the first step toward taking back our country.

CHAPTER FIFTY-SIX

MAINSTREAM MEDIA COWARDICE: AN OVERVIEW OF "INTO THE BUZZSAW"

Fact: Excluding home ownership, the wealthiest 10% of Americans own 76% of this nation's net worth. More than half of that is accounted for by the top 1%. These rich elitists also own television stations, newspapers, magazines, Internet news sites, and radio stations.

Whenever I see a preponderance of lies, half-truths, censorship, and steady streams of disinformation in the various media outlets each day, I ask myself, how can these people continue to sell their souls? How do they possibly look in the mirror after knowingly enabling drug traffickers, murderers and sexual deviants to get away with their crimes? And I'm not even referring to true-life criminals; I'm talking about politicians, government officials, intelligence operatives and the Controllers themselves. How can any member of the mainstream media sleep at night, pat their children on the head, or not cringe with shame when they pass an American flag knowing that a plethora of blatant crimes go unreported each day?

Into the Buzzsaw, an excellent book recently released in 2002 by Prometheus Books and edited by Kristina Borjesson, answers some of these questions. By giving eighteen different journalists a chance to speak freely on a number of issues (as opposed to being muted by the corporate media), this collection shows how the field of professional journalism has lost its fire and why its members continue to wallow like yellow-spined lemmings in pools of aloofness and deceit.

If you think I'm being too harsh, start reading this book. You'll find an overwhelming amount of evidence that proves not only that our military shot-down TWA Flight 800 off the coast of Long Island and commanded ships in the area to speed away (thus avoiding blame), but also that the mainstream media continues to cover for these MURDERERS to this day.

Then check out how the CIA has admitted to blatant cases of cocaine trafficking, yet our fine lily-livered journalists don't have the guts to expose these DRUG DEALERS in a meaningful way. Read about the Franklin pedophilia case, AIDS as a man-made genocidal disease,

Bilderberg secrecy, *Votescam*, Federal Reserve deception and theft, and the mysterious death count surrounding the Clintons.

What it boils down to is this – many of the devils in positions of power have intimidated the American mass media journalists to such an extent that they now tremble and cover for these killers, drug dealers, and deviants.

Why? Why are they enabling them to get away with this deception? Isn't it time to stand-up and expose these traitors?

Into the Buzzsaw brings to light what those in power want to conceal. When a reporter dares to trespass into forbidden territory – the truth -- they enter the "buzzsaw," which Kristina Borjesson defines as "a powerful system of censorship in this country that is revealed to those reporting on extremely sensitive stories usually having to do with high-level government and/or corporate malfeasance."

Bjorjesson continues to describe the 'buzzsaw' as "what can rip through you when you try to investigate or expose anything this country's large institutions -- be they corporate or government -- want kept under wraps. The system finally fights back with official lies, disinformation and stonewalling."

If the reporter or writer in question cannot be silenced, then the media big-wig moguls, who are merely pawns of the multinational corporations and international bankers, use a technique called "marginalization." In other words, when someone gets too close to the truth they are labeled a "conspiracy nut," then subjected to a propaganda juggernaut, which Borjesson says happens to "anyone who didn't believe the government officials or the journalists who unquestionably reported what the official said."

She further explains, "If you don't go along with the party line, you're shoved into the margins and eventually out of the picture."

What does this mean? Simply that the media is towing the party line. If you as a reporter walk outside the accepted parameters, they will turn on you like bloodthirsty sharks!

Rather than going after the guilty party, they attack the reporter who upset the apple cart. (See Gary Webb and his exposé on how the CIA imported drugs into L.A. during the mid-1980s to start the gang war crack craze.)

Philip Weiss reinforces this point by saying that we DO have freedom of speech and freedom of the press in this country, but to combat the dangers inherent to the elite class, it is marginalized by the Enforcers to the "fringe." Weiss goes on to tell us: "Corporate media outlets cannot entertain serious questions about the legitimacy of the powers-that-be, even when spokesmen are shown to lie."

Stated differently, the American media is extremely conservative in nature because stability is much desired, and the status quo reigns supreme above all. To validate this statement, Weiss observes, "Most well-paid reporters are urban liberals, firmly ensconced in the blue zone, physically and culturally."

By being comfortable and removed from the streets, isn't it interesting how an entire industry of left-leaning journalists is enveloped by a conservative corporate framework? The worst part is that most don't even realize the irony of how shackled and enslaved they are.

This strategy doesn't only apply to newspapers or TV. The publishing industry also censors itself, as Gerald Colby points out with the concept of "privishing." This phenomenon occurs, "when a publisher kills off an author's book without the author's awareness or consent." Basically, they "cut off the book's life-support system." Publishers can plunge a dagger through the heart of a book in a number of different ways, such as:

1) reducing the print run
2) refusing additional print runs
3) gouging the promotional budget
4) failing to support a book-signing tour
5) or by simply saying that a book is not available

One may wonder at this time how the corporate media is allowed to get away with such nonsense. The key word here is "corporate." As Ben Bagdikian notes in *The Media Monopoly*, in 1993 there were 50 major media corporations in America. Less than ten years later, there are six! Six multinational companies now control all the network, newspaper, radio, and magazine news departments in this country.

The corporations, of course, are owned and beholden to the international bankers, whose primary goal is globalization, which is reflected in their foreign policy decisions. In all, the media becomes a conditioning tool used to maintain the status quo while maximizing profits.

Greg Palast reflects on the result of this monopolized media: "If the Rupert Murdochs of the globe are shepherds of the New World Order, they owe their success to breeding a flock of docile sheep; snoozy editors and reporters who are content to munch on, digest, and then reprint a diet

457

of press releases and canned stories provided by officials and corporate P. R. operators."

Maurice Murad adds, "The manipulation of perceptions is replacing reality as the governing principle in human affairs."

When President Dwight D. Eisenhower delivered his farewell speech in 1961 before leaving office, he warned Americans about the dangers of a growing military-industrial complex. The media should act as a watch dog against these forces, but instead, the press has actually been meshed together with them under the same corporate umbrella.

Look at how many of these cowering dogs still refer to Lee Harvey Oswald as JFK's "lone-nut assassin," and rarely acknowledge how horribly their ranks have been corrupted and poisoned by the perpetuation of outright lies.

What do I mean? The New York Times came clean once in 1977 and verified to what extent the CIA had infiltrated the media and publishing industry. Author Michael Levine weighs in by saying: "If the CIA is good at anything, it is complete control of the American media. So secure are they in their ability to manipulate the media that they even brag about it in their own in-house memos."

Gary Webb adds further ammunition by writing: "The national news organizations have had a long, disappointing history of playing footsie with the CIA." Webb then asks, "Do we have a free press today? Sure we do. It's free to report all the sex scandals it wants, all the stock market news we can handle, every new health fad that comes down the pike and every celebrity marriage or divorce that happens. But when it comes to the real down and dirty stuff – that's where we begin to see the limits of our freedoms. In today's media environment, sadly, such stores are not even open for discussion."

George Seldes, author of *The Lords of the Press* (1983), lays it all on the line by sneering, "It is possible to fool all the people all the time – when government and the press cooperate." Unfortunately, we've reached that point in this country. Most everyone is being bamboozled!

In essence, then, the American media's cowardice is a direct reflection of their "don't rock the boat" mentality; starting with the editors, program directors, and network heads and filtering down to the reporters. By utilizing bias, omission, under-reporting and outright censorship, they remain beholden to corporate (and local) advertising, while preserving their incestuous relationship with governmental PR sources. These two forces make sick, twisted bed-partners.

The question I keep asking is this: how can these guilty parties live with themselves? Are the few dollars they get for keeping the lid on really worth it?

Carl Jensen reinforces this point quite nicely by writing, "The high salaries many of our leaders receive in newsrooms and business offices as well as corporate headquarters, have turned into golden handcuffs. And those handcuffs morphed into blindfolds and gags..."

Jensen goes on to describe how this failure to break free from their constraints leads to a journalistic conundrum. "The United States has a free press guaranteed by its Constitution, it has the world's most sophisticated communication system, and it has more independent media outlets disseminating more information 24 hours a day than anywhere else in the world. Considering our autonomous press and the quality of information that bombards us daily, we should be a very well-informed populace. Unfortunately, high-tech and a free press do not guarantee a well-informed society. The problem is not the quantity of information that we receive, but the quality."

With this in mind, we should look at the main function of journalism. Robert McChesney provides an excellent overview: "The media system must provide a rigorous accounting of PEOPLE IN POWER and people who want to be in power, in both public and private sectors. This is known as the watchdog role."

McChesney continues: "Contemporary journalism serves as a tepid and weak-kneed watchdog over those in power, especially in the corporate sector."

But these watchdogs have turned into simpering lap dogs that suckle at the tit of their corporate sponsors, while those who speak the truth are shoved to the fringe, or viewed as rabble-rousers and subversives.

But let's keep in mind the reality of the situation, of which Henry Adams reminds us: "The press is the hired agent of a moneyed system set up for no other reason than to *tell lies where their interests are concerned.*"

Robert McChesney explodes one of the prevailing myths of journalism: "Trained editors and reporters are granted autonomy by the owners to make editorial decisions, and these decisions are based on their professional judgment, not the politics of the owners and the advertisers, or their commercial interests to maximize profits." How laughable.

Closer to the truth, of course, is McChesney's summary of Public Relations in regard to the media: "By providing slick press releases, paid-for 'experts,' neutral-sounding but bogus citizens' groups, and canned news events, crafty PR agents have been able to shift the news to suit the interests of their mostly corporate clientele."

Alex Carey, who wrote, *Taking the Risk out of Democracy*" in 1997, adds weight to this argument by showing how these smarmy shysters add another level of confusion to America's social fabric: "The role of PR is to so muddle the public sphere as to take the risk out of democracy for the wealthy and corporations."

In other words, the media, when combined with public relations firms and their overlord Controllers, end up conditioning us with a game of misdirection – sort of like children when they played "hotter-colder" (you're getting hotter ... hotter ... now colder...). By using a variety of subtle techniques, the media directs us away from stories they deem too "hot" or "explosive." Robert McChesney describes professional journalism as being "biased toward the status quo. The general rule in professional journalism is this: if the elite, the upper two or three percent of society who control most of the capital and rule the largest institutions, agree on an issue, then it is off-limits to journalistic scrutiny."

McChesney continues: "To the United States elite, democracy tends to be defined by their ability to maximize profit." He also adds, "U. S. professional journalism, even at its best, serves as a propaganda function similar to the role of *Pravda* or *Izbestia* in the old USSR."

If we return to media ownership, we see that our faithful television broadcasters are essentially controlled by AOL Time-Warner, Disney, Viacom, GE, and Rupert Murdoch's News Corporation. Also, check out these disturbing facts:

- The ten largest media firms own ALL U.S. TV networks.
- They also own most every TV station in the major markets, all major film and music studios, nearly all the TV cable channels, and most all book and magazine publishers.
- In terms of news, Jim Squires, former editor of the *Chicago Tribune*, found this trend so disturbing, he said resentfully, "Our generation has witnessed the end of journalism."

As it stands now, the American media has relinquished its role as watchdogs of the high-and-mighty, therein surrendering their dignity and ability to help make the world a better place. And what a pitiful, disheartening surrender it has been – to not only themselves and their families, but also to the American public. This once proud, vital institution has allowed itself to be reduced to pathetic marionettes dangling from the Controller's strings. The profession has, by and large, lost its backbone and grit.

Hell, they'll even bend over for the international financiers and whip us into a frenzy so the death-mongers can ship our boys off to die in another one of their perpetual wars. McChesney sums up the media's role in fueling the greedy War Machine: "The government needs to lie in order to gain support for its war aims. The media system, in every case, proves to be a superior propaganda organ for militarism and empire."

McChesney continues (and *listen* to what he's saying --- this is important stuff): "The United States media conglomerates exist within an institutional context that makes support for the U.S. military seemingly natural. These giant firms are among the primary beneficiaries of both neo-liberal and globalization, and the U.S. role as the preeminent world power. Indeed, the United States government is the primary advocate for the global media firms."

Isn't it clear what's taking place? The mainstream corporate media and the power elite are no longer separate entities! There's no dividing line between them any longer. They're in bed together, with the multinational Globalists whipping the reporters, anchors and editors like obedient dogs. And I have to tell you, the scent they're following isn't one that benefits us, but only further promotes the Controllers' New World Order goals.

Here is my plea to reporters and journalists: Please, before it's too late, bury your cowardice and stand up to your bosses. Why are you selling your country, your family, and yourself out? Can't you see what's happening in America? We're being deliberately undermined by a group of power-hungry devils that allow 100,000 people to die of starvation EVERY DAY – that created a deadly sex virus and uses it to commit genocide on entire peoples – that advocates a perpetual, bloodthirsty War Machine that is now ready to start rolling in overdrive. These same people steal our money via an unjust tax system; then pilfer even more money through their privately-owned, for-profit Federal Reserve System. These same people run drugs, launder money, murder as if they lived outside the law, and are increasingly setting up a Big Brother type surveillance system that will alter the world in a way that'll bring us directly into George Orwell's "1984." They're also destroying the planet's environment with wild abandon, then building even more underground bases to protect themselves when shit starts hitting the fan (while we'll be locked out in the cold to suffer and gasp for breath). Hell, they've even trampled the very foundation of our democratic system via "Votescam," and do so with such arrogance, it's appalling.

So, I have to ask each and every journalist at CBS, the *New York Times*, *Newsweek*, CNN, local newspapers, and those of you talking on the radio: when are you going to expose these lying, murdering, traitorous devils for what they are? Why are you so afraid to stand up to them? If every journalist in this country decided to start telling the truth, we could run those bastards out of town in a week! That's all it would take – telling the TRUTH!

Be a MAN ... be a WOMAN ... be a TRUE PARENT and AMERICAN and do what's right. Quit telling lies and let the American people know what's REALLY going on in the world. That's your duty and responsibility. Forget about status, position and money. Just tell the truth, for in the end, what does it matter if you've gained the entire world, but lost your soul in the process? It's time for some dramatic changes in this country, and I challenge every member of the media to stand up and expose the Controllers and their loathsome goals. If we don't do it soon, we won't have another chance. Are you willing to have that on your conscience?

CHAPTER FIFTY-SEVEN

REVIEWED: "THE OCTOPUS – SECRET GOVERNMENT AND THE DEATH OF DANNY CASOLARO" BY KENN THOMAS AND JIM KEITH

The day before his "suicide," Danny Casolaro told his brother, "If anything happens to me, don't believe it's an accident."

The next day, August 10, 1991, Danny Casolaro was found dead in a hotel room, the slices in his wrists so deep, they couldn't possibly have been done by someone experiencing that type of trauma and losing that much blood.

If this were the only peculiarity surrounding Mr. Casolaro's death, it could be dismissed. But like other suspicious "suicides" surrounding those involved with governmental shenanigans, there's plenty of other evidence pointing to foul play. First of all, the suicide note found in Casolaro's hotel room was clearly bogus (considering the victim was a professional writer). Also, he was embalmed without his family's permission, while the autopsy was hastily performed and inconclusive.

In addition, Casolaro's room was cleared of all evidence before the authorities were notified, his briefcase and a voluminous amount of notes vanished, and the police investigation only started days after the death took place.

Now, the big question: what made certain individuals want to kill Danny Casolaro? The story begins with INSLAW, the Institute for Law and Social Research. This company developed a computer program for the United States Justice Department called PROMIS (Prosecutor's Management Information System). The software allowed government computers to communicate with other computers so they could follow certain people and monitor them over long periods of time.

Ari Ben-Menashe, author of *Profits of War*, describes the PROMIS software: "The program … would have the ability to track the movements of vast numbers of people around the world. Dissidents or citizens who needed to be kept under watch would be hard put to move freely without Big Brother keeping an eye on their activities."

Ben-Menashe then went on to describe how the program worked: "Using a modem, the spy network would tap into the computers of such services as the telephone company, the water board, other utility commissions, credit card companies, etc. PROMIS would then search for specific information."

The researcher concludes by saying, "PROMIS can suck in every other database on earth and correlate everything automatically."

The above information is troubling enough, but it gets worse. A covert sector of the government, specifically Edwin Meese's Justice Department, crafted a nefarious plot to steal the PROMIS program and modify it so that "back doors" could be opened to look into the databases of targeted individuals.

One of the companies involved in this scheme was Wackenhut, the world's largest private security firm. These are also the same cowboys who patrol the infamous Area 51, and were hired as security at the 2002 Winter Olympics in Salt Lake City. Former FBI Agent George Wackenhut formed this company in 1954. With connections to J. Edgar Hoover, by 1965, Wackenhut had files on over 2 1/2 million American citizens, which was less than one out of every 50 people!

William Hamilton, CEO of INSLAW, said that the ultimate purpose of stealing the PROMIS software was to forward information to the National Security Agency (NSA) satellites so they could more easily access it. "It will track anything once it's provided with the rules," he said.

In simplest terms, then, the PROMIS software could track a person anywhere -- on planes, trains, or automobiles. Even if an individual used fake IDs, they could still be fingered via their hairstyle, eye color, height, etc., then run through the system.

After the Justice Department stole this program, it was sold to various spy networks and military operations around the world, such as Iraq, Libya, South Korea, Israel, and Canada. The pirated software became so widespread that at one time it was used in nearly 1,000 locales in Canada and ultimately spread like the tentacles of an octopus. Worse, the users were involved in drug dealing, money laundering, arms sales, assassinations, and bio-warfare.

If it stopped here, things would be bad enough. But a computer program called "Brainstorm" took the surveillance abilities of PROMIS to the next level by tying it into artificial intelligence programs. After doing so, the Secret Service or Military could predict any person's behavior just by knowing their thought processes and personality traits.

Based on this overview, it's easy to see why Danny Casolaro was snuffed in 1991. If he had brought this information to light in a big way, the PROMIS software would not have been developed as it was, ultimately bringing us such nasty Big Brother tools as Echelon and

Carnivore. Things have gotten so out of control, recently the *Wall Street Journal* announced that authorities in Washington DC plan to install the nation's largest network of surveillance cameras in history. Thousands of cameras will be mounted on our national monuments, in malls, schools, public transportation facilities, and in open areas.

Once completed, this network will be a working model for other large and small cities in America. Do you know what the concept of BIG BROTHER means? I hope so, because it's rolling over us like a freight train under the guise of "Homeland Security".

Below are a few "Notes and Quotes" that I found interesting in the book by Kenn Thomas and Jim Keith.

• The Octopus was a secret group begun by CIA operative James Jesus Angleton. It wasn't the "government" per se, but it did influence every part of the government. They weren't highly ordered, but loosely based, like the Mob. Essentially they worked as a spy network, bringing about Richard Nixon's downfall at Watergate. They also ousted the Shah of Iran, ran drugs out of the Golden Triangle, orchestrated the Bay of Pigs fiasco, dirtied their fingers in the BCCI money scandal, brought about Ronald Reagan's October Surprise, ran drugs and guns into Latin America, worked on the peripheral of JFK's assassination, murdered Chile's Allende, and set events in motion to bring about America's war in Iraq.

• In essence, many of the same names kept popping up at each of the following events: Castro's failed assassination attempts, the Bay of Pigs, JFK's assassination, Watergate, and gun-running in Central America. These names were: Richard Helms, Ray Cline, E. Howard Hunt, Edwin Wilson, Thomas Clines, Ted Schackley, Frank Sturgis, and Felix Rodriguez.

• The CIA has enjoyed a long-term relationship with the Mafia that began in 1936 with "Operation Underworld." In the years that followed, they've supported their Black Budget Projects via money laundering, drug importing, casinos, and illegal arms running.

• George Bush took part in the Bay of Pigs fiasco, which utilized the code name "Operation Zapata." Zapata, coincidentally, was the name of his oil company at that time! Bush also had oil rigs 30 miles off the coast of Cuba that were a key CIA stronghold near Cay Sal. Here, he let the CIA use Zapata as a front company.

- Casolaro's notes: Zapata - 1953 Narcotics smuggling - shadow government. "The Bush Family fortune was secured in large part through the rise of Hitler, through his famous Union Banking Corporation, which acted as a front for the Nazis, specifically the major German financier Fritz Thyssen."

- Skull & Bones (Yale) - was founded by General George Russell, who controlled the United States opium market in the early 1800s. The authors contend that George Bush, while Ambassador to China, started the "Black Rose Organization" that ran drugs from the Golden Triangle to American through his offshore oil rigs.

- H. R. Haldemann, Nixon sidekick, admitted there was a halt to the Watergate investigation by the FBI because they were about to bring to light the "Bay of Pigs thing," which he admitted was a code word for the JFK assassination.

- In the May 7, 1977 edition of the *San Francisco Chronicle*, Frank Sturgis declared, "The reason we burglarized the Watergate was because Nixon was interested in stopping news leaks relating to the photos of our role (Helms, Hunt, Baker, Mosbacher) in the assassination of President Kennedy."

- Because President Nixon was trying to undermine the CIA's authority (as JFK also did, threatening to break them "into a thousand pieces and scatter them to the wind"), Watergate became a CIA plot to sabotage Nixon's administration.

- Casolaro on Oliver North and drugs: Diary entry -- July 9, 1984: "Wanted aircraft to go to Bolivia to pick up paste, want aircraft to pick up 1,500 kilos." July 12, 1985 entry: "$14 million to finance Supermarket came from drugs." (Supermarket is the code word for weapons storage area used in arms dealing.)

- The Octopus was a small band of CIA "outsiders" who joined forces to advance their agenda through international crime and political intrigue. Drug dealing goes hand-in-hand with international banking, for both reap huge profits, and also work with a world political crime syndicate.

CHAPTER FIFTY-EIGHT

THE AMERICAN CASTE SYSTEM

In an article entitled *The Outlaw Among the Other Classes* published in *Babel Magazine* # 59 - May 19, 2002, Professor X provides the best overview of the American "caste system" I have ever read. By clearly defining four separate groups that are, by and large, mutually exclusive (rulers, enforcers, slaves and untouchables), plus one other variable -- the outlaw -- the author exposes a phenomenon that that is an embarrassment to the rulers and media of this country.

Although it is possible to move from one class to another (as opposed to the Indian class system) as Professor X points out, generally built-in factors to this societal framework prohibit such movement. The outcome, regrettably, is a situation that contradicts everything we've ever been taught about American democracy since our earliest school days. (How about this first-grade lie: anyone can grow up to be the President. I'm sorry to tell you, but anyone *can't* grow up to be the Commander-in-Chief.)

First we'll examine the four primary classes; then in a later article we'll look at possibly the only hope we have to alter this system -- the outlaw class.

THE RULING CLASS

Also known as the "Controllers" and the "Princes of the Earth," these are the elite international bankers, heads of multinational corporations, and moneyed American families that largely determine the destiny of this planet. This group is undoubtedly the most exclusive and difficult to enter. Some would say it is virtually impossible to become a member of this class because of its obsession with bloodlines. The ruling class is far less than 1% of the total population (probably closer to .000000000001%). Its members belong to organizations such as the Bilderbergs, Trilateral Commission, Council on Foreign Relations, Club of Rome, Knights of Malta, etc., and rely heavily on secrecy to perpetuate their status.

Whenever we examine the evils of this world, such as the financing of war, usury, and divisiveness among the masses, the Controllers, or members of the ruling class are invariably behind it.

THE ENFORCEMENT CLASS

When pondering the seeming implausibility of a miniscule percentage of the population lording over the remainder of society, one has to ask, "How are these hidden figures able to maintain their position atop the Control Pyramid?" In all reality, when viewed in terms of "survival of the fittest," unlike Nimrod or Genghis Khan, none of these current Controllers gained their status because of their physical prowess. Rather, they utilize a more subtle technique.

Specifically, they create a network of "enforcers" to surround and protect their interests, then "reward" these individuals and entities with a few pieces of silver.

Who, you may ask, represents the enforcement class and acts in the employ of the Controllers?

The Media - Although it is generally perceived that the American media is, by and large, liberally oriented, it is, in reality, very conservative in nature. Now don't get me wrong. I'm not talking about the slant of its content, but its overall profile. To be conservative connotes an acceptance of and inherent desire to preserve the status quo (i.e., keeping things the way they are).

In this light, our media is extremely conservative because there isn't one element of the mainstream -- whether it's CBS, the *New York Times*, *Newsweek*, Rush Limbaugh, or *U.S. News and World Report*, that wants to shake things up. If they did, we'd see a flurry of reports on what's *really* going on in this country/world.

But then someone might ask, "Isn't it one of the journalistic credos to dig deep and convey the truth?"

Of course it is, but when every major media source is owned by only a handful of multinational corporations which are in turn owned by international bankers, then we see what's happening. The media, acting as a lapdog servant of the ruling class, enforces the status quo by only relaying half-truths, dis/misinformation, and a general atmosphere of conditioning that keeps the masses from rebelling against those who subjugate them.

The Police - Since there is strength in numbers and the Controllers are an extremely small percentage of the whole, some force is needed to keep the people in line. When they get a little "uppity" or want to rebel, these beings serve as the strong arm for the ruling class.

The Military - Likewise, since the Controllers don't have a particular allegiance to any nation or flag, their best interests are served by warring upon any country that seeks to buck their regimented framework of control. War is also used as a profit-making enterprise, and also to keep the "Machine" rolling along smoothly. They'd never want people sitting around too long without anything to do. That is why war is so vital to their interests. They have to keep the presses in the factories running -- making bombs and guns -- so the lowly people they're shipping off to war don't get enough time on their hands to start figuring out the Controllers' agenda.

By throwing in a dose of propaganda and patriotism and thinning out the herd, everything keeps rolling along smoothly. Regrettably, the only winners in war are the Controllers. They make money via interest off their loans and the rebuilding process, while all the rest of us are dead, maimed, or traumatized by the process.

Academia and the Educational System - Since the Controllers realize that truth and exposure would ruin the illusion they've so carefully created, they need another arm to prevent the masses from knowing too much. Thus, instead of truly educating them, they are "indoctrinated" with the proper mode of thinking so they fit into society like a good little cog in the wheel.

Similar to the media that could open our eyes (but opt not to), academia also suppresses the truth by feeding us the same old cultural myths -- and remember one important fact: he who wins the war writes the history book.

Since the Controllers are the only ones who win in war, guess who's spreading all the disinformation? Yup, you're right -- they are! If you don't believe me, sit in on any college history, political science, or economics class and I guarantee they won't be telling you any of this stuff.

The Court System - As an attached branch of the police (and sometimes the military), the courts penalize wrongdoers by removing their freedoms. Obviously, many members of society need restraint, but the threat of punishment also keeps the law-abiding citizen from becoming too "vocal" about the smokescreen.

Bureaucratic Institutions - Perfect examples would be the IRS, FBI, or CIA. Enough said.

Religion - Finally, by playing on notions which involve morality, the hereafter, salvation and punishment, the masses can be kept tranquilized by fears and blind faith, thus tempering their natural instincts and drives.

With the above information in mind, the next logical question should be, what purpose does the Enforcement Class serve? Professor X succinctly explains the situation by saying that these groups "maintain images of 'so-called normalcy' by perpetuating deception and manipulating the masses." He also adds that they are "designed to 'inoculate' any sign of free-thinking before it becomes 'contagious' to the slave class."

The most important question, though, is: why does the Enforcement Class carry out the Controller's plans when it's obvious that so many of their aims are not in this country's best interest?

The answer, I'm sorry to say, is two-fold: self-interest and cowardice. Even though the Enforcement Class will never in its wildest dreams attain the type of wealth enjoyed by the rulers, it is still, by and large, better off than the majority of society.

Stated differently; the System works for them. They're doing well. So, if they start exposing the truth and riling things up, a few consequences could occur. One would be economic uncertainty, which would result in a possible stock market crash, unemployment, or a drop in corporate profits (thus lower dividends). Or, if taken to the extreme, there could be such social turmoil that governments may collapse, anarchy could erupt in the streets, or a bloody civil war would result. To those who are lapping up the gravy and living easily, such options are not welcomed or desired. If trouble starts brewing among the masses, it doesn't bode well for a judge, reporter, police sergeant, professor, general, IRS agent, or a deacon in his plush rectory.

This rationale leads to our second point: cowardice. Why risk job security (when one doesn't have to stamp parts in a factory or bail hay on a farm, but instead sit in an air-conditioned office) when the result could threaten their house on the hill, a shiny Mitsubishi and SUV, manicured lawns and evenings at the country club?

The status quo, at least for the Enforcement Class, is much preferred to turmoil. Even if things aren't good or "right" in the world, at least these people are better off financially than most. Why rock the boat and jeopardize things? For someone to even mention subjects such as the Federal Reserve being a private, for-profit corporation, Votescam, or government black budget projects would encourage co-workers, fellow parishioners, neighbors or lodge members to label that person a "conspiracy nut" or "kook." Then, when it came time for advancement and raises, that "person with the off-balance ideas" would be passed over in favor of someone who's a "team player."

It's better to disregard the truth and stay away from such controversial topics, and safer to just cringe and accept things the way they are.

THE SLAVE CLASS

By far the largest segment of society, Professor X describes these folks as a "worker bee group that is cultured to support the ruling and enforcement class." In other words, these are the people who assemble parts for their microwaves in a factory, haul away the trash, unclog the sewers, serve food, pump gas, drive taxis, balance the books, clean hotels, and perform a thousand other jobs that "they" don't want to do.

But if the Slave Class comprises at least three-quarters of the societal whole, why doesn't it wise up to the system and try to overthrow it, or at least try to dramatically change it? Professor X provides three main reasons why the masses have been pacified:

- They're motivated by an illusion that they aren't, in fact, slaves, but rather free individuals.
- They feel blessed to live in the USA (the greatest nation in the world), and to be "overseen" by a caring government that immensely cares about them. This government is increasingly a type of "father-figure" that continues to exert more influence over each person's life, thus freeing them from any actual "responsibility."
- These individuals complain about taxes, inequality and the crooks in office, but are promised a reward at the end of the line (social security benefits, heaven if they've been good, etc.).

The Controllers maintain these programs with help from the Enforcers by making sure the slaves have, to quote Professor X, "full bellies, but never produce enough wealth to reach independence." He continues: "Wealth produced by the slave class must always be transferred to the ruling class. With our present system of taxation and mind control, this is extremely effective. In an efficient slave system, the slave must think he/she is in control, is 'free' in other words. But the slave must be left with only the bare minimum with which to provide for personal and family needs. The slave must work most of his/her life, giving over the bulk of his/her earnings to the ruling class. This is now being very efficiently accomplished in the United States, and for the most part, everyone is quite happy with the results."

To put the above words in perspective, allow me to use an illustration. Every once in awhile I eat at a Chinese restaurant that has an immense framed photograph of the Great Wall of China snaking through the mountains. Although this picture only captures a small percentage of the Wall's total 1450 miles, it is still mind-boggling in its enormity. While staring at this photograph, I thought about all the Chinese lackeys required to construct the Great Wall. Even in our current age, most Chinese citizens don't have many rights or freedoms. Just think how intolerable it was in those days when the Wall was being built (starting in 214 B.C.). These people were merely slaves.

I then started thinking about all the regal European castles and churches that were constructed during medieval times while the feudal system was in effect. Naturally, the Aristocracy (kings, queens, and princes) lorded over the serfs, who surrendered their sweat and muscle-power to erect these magnificent structures. Most people who would ponder this situation would think, "Man, what fools those people must have been. They were nothing but slaves!"

But has the overall class structure actually changed that much over the past millennium? Yes, certain "particulars" have improved, and today we have indoor plumbing, heat, automobiles, and modern medicine, to name just a few conveniences. But in terms of a hierarchal caste system, are things dramatically different?

Professor X estimates that 70% of America's population, and the number would be closer to 90% if we took the entire world into consideration, is still stuck in the slave class. The Controllers of today (bankers, CEO's, etc.) are merely the lords and emperors of times past.

Since this essay is called "The American Caste System," let's actually take a look at how things work in India. Hindu society is divided into five main groups:

- Brahmans: priests (those who lorded over society when this system arose). Do these figures remind you of today's ruling class Controllers?
- Kshatriyas: nobles and warriors (the Enforcement class)
- Vaisyas: Traders and farmers, plus Sudras (servants, the Slave class)
- Harijan: Untouchables

Hmmm, does this sound vaguely familiar to what we currently have in America today? Naturally, some upward and downward mobility exists in this country, but think about this. How many people do you personally know who have truly transcended their class? Certainly someone can go to college or work very hard and migrate from one class to the next. But what are the odds that a member of the slave class will join the elite class (or even someone from the Enforcement class, for that matter)? Or, how often does one of the untouchables ascend to become an enforcer?

Rarely. We're all pretty much stuck in our class, which in America is largely comprised of a middle class that is snowballed into thinking it has some say-so in how this country is being run. But, quite plainly, it doesn't. Look at the personal debt we're carrying – it's never been higher. What does that tell you? That the middle class is thriving? No. It's showing that most Americans are living from one paycheck to another, can't completely cover their expenses, and if they lost their jobs, would be in dire straits.

Actually, plenty of Americans *are* losing their jobs, especially in the industrial and manufacturing fields (due to NAFTA), and replacing them with lower-paying service jobs.

The slave class is so busy trying to make ends meet there isn't time to worry about much else. And guess what? That's *exactly* the way the Controllers have designed the System. Due to being heavily taxed, indebted, and with scores of bills to pay, plus lawns to mow, raking leaves, cooking dinner, taking care of the kids, fixing the car and so forth, there isn't much time left to "get involved." Or, as someone once said to me, "I do have a CAUSE -- putting food on the table and making sure I have enough money to keep the roof from leaking and paying the fuel bill this winter."

Do you still not think we have a caste system in this country? How much chance does this individual have of jumping up to the next level? But before you start screaming that I'm being pessimistic, let me clarify. I believe in hard work and industriousness as much as anyone -- that's why I write essays and make sure as many people as possible read them. I want to see this world become a better place.

But I'm also a realist who observes certain things. And what I see is a firmly established framework that was intentionally designed to keep people busy, enslaved, and too occupied to exert the effort to modify our caste system.

To keep the Machine running, the Controllers need people to *produce* goods and services for them. But if we make certain products, we also need to buy items such as CD players, $150 tennis shoes, boats, BMW's, and home entertainment systems. So, via a subtle form of conditioning called "advertising" coupled with the ingrained concept of our "American Dream," people are constantly striving to keep up with the Joneses and living beyond their means, all in the name of a larger "scheme" that most people don't even know exists.

By promoting concepts such as freedom, patriotism, and a materialistic American Dream, plus the utilization of various conditioning techniques, the masses remain "in their place," continually exploited and manipulated by the evil ruling class.

THE UNTOUCHABLES

Derided by members from nearly every walk of life, this class does not contribute to society in any meaningful way. Described by Professor X as, "inner city blacks, drug addicts, street people, and the criminal underclass," these individuals would not dramatically alter their lives regardless of who governed them. Simply surviving day-to-day, the Untouchables are corralled into pockets far removed from the rest of society, and are generally ignored unless they infringe upon the other classes; which then draws immediate punishment.

The bare essentials are given to them, and then they are forgotten -- out of sight, out of mind.

SECTION

NINE:

THE MAN WHO

RUNS

HAPPY VALLEY

CHAPTER FIFTY-NINE

THE MAN WHO RUNS HAPPY VALLEY

"Listen, Thorn. You better not get in our way. We've kept the people under our thumbs for this long. I'd hate to see you blow our cover," the man snarled while driving down Garner Street past the Carlton Apartments.

I'd like to tell you what this guy looked like, but he promised to have my legs broken if I revealed his identity. So, after gazing in the rear view mirror of his car (again, no descriptions allowed) as it idled at a red light on Beaver Avenue, he said in an even voice, "The most truthful statement ever made came from a man named Benjamin Disraeli. He said, 'The world is governed by very different personages from what is imagined by those who are not behind the scenes.' Believe me," he concluded with a sneer, "this is how the world works."

As I sat at the light with this monster ... this devil in disguise ... I actually thought he was going to drive me out into the middle of nowhere and have my kneecaps shattered. I knew the way these people did things. They didn't mess around. I was definitely skating on thin ice. As my heart beat like crazy, I kept asking myself, "Why would this guy let me take a peek inside their 'sanctum sanctorum' of power?" But before I tell you why, I should let you know how I got myself into this situation.

You may know I'm the founder of Sisyphus Press and *Babel Magazine*, and for the past two months I've been publishing some material that exposes the power mongers for what they are – a group of self-serving elitists who don't have our best interests in mind.

I figured somewhere along the line someone was going to start hassling me about the stuff I was printing. Face it: the people in power (whether it's on a local, state, national, or global scale) don't like having their dirty dealings exposed. It was only a matter of time until they figured out what I was up to and started pounding on my door in the middle of the night and threatening to kill me or burn my house down.

That day came last week when I answered the phone to hear a man ask (without a hint of humor or pleasantness), "Are you Thorn?"

Not wanting to let him have the upper hand, I said, "Who wants to know?"

Obviously frustrated by my answer, the man paused for a couple seconds; then growled, "That doesn't matter. Meet me at Sunset Park in College Heights tonight at eight o'clock."

As adrenaline shot through my veins, I snapped, "Why should I?"

The man sighed with noticeable irritation. "Listen, pal, don't bust my chops. You're the one who wants to know what's going on. I can fill you in on a few of the details."

Sensing from his tone that this guy wasn't someone to play around with, I asked, "How will I know you?"

"You just will," he snarled, and then hung up.

That's how it all started. And if you want to know the truth, that phone call scared the daylights out of me. Here I was – a small-time publisher with no money and bills galore. Then I get a call from some guy who says he has inside information. What was I supposed to do? Hell, he could have been setting me up. Maybe he was a knuckle-breaker from the County Commissioner's office, or a bigwig in College Heights who didn't like my Letter to the Editor in the *Centre Daily Times* about those horrendous traffic diverters.

I didn't know what to do. Should I blow him off? But this could be the biggest scoop in ages, at least for State College, Pennsylvania. The only problem was -- what if this guy *did* mean trouble? I don't have bodyguards or any of that stuff. And if I did decide to bring some muscle along, he'd see I wasn't alone and shine the whole deal. I knew I had to fly solo.

There wasn't any other way. But man, if this guy was for real, I might be lying six feet under somewhere in Stone Valley, never to be heard from again. Either that, or when I was away, they'd come and burn my house down. What was I getting myself into?

So, that night at 7:55 I left my house and drove to College Heights where I parked behind a stone marker that read: "In the memory of Donald W. Carruthers, Jr.," then sat in the darkness. I could feel the nervousness building inside me as the clock on my dashboard clicked away – 8:01... 8:02... 8:03... 8:04... As the minutes slipped away, I remembered the note I left for my son in the living room before I left:

"If you don't hear from me in a couple days, they got me."

Finally, at 8:11, a car (no descriptions allowed) pulled into the lot and flashed its high beams.

It was the man. This was serious! I was so nervous I felt like puking. Gulping deeply and not knowing what I was getting myself into, I grabbed my water bottle and stepped from my car to his. From that moment forward, I knew my life would never be the same.

"You're Thorn, huh?" the man asked without bothering to extend his hand.

What was I supposed to say? He knew who I was. So, rather than answering his question, I shot back sternly, "Who are you, and what do you want with me?"

Not taking my bravado seriously, my counterpart laughed, "I'm the man who runs Happy Valley!" (Note: Happy Valley is a long-standing nickname for State College, PA where I live.)

Not wanting to be made a fool of, I replied in a deadpan voice, "How do I know that?"

"You don't ... but you will."

"Is that so?"

"It is," he told me while shifting his car into drive.

Wondering where we were going, I asked calmly, "If you really do run Happy Valley, why did you call me?"

Warming to the subject, the man turned onto McKee Street; then replied, "Because you have guts. To me, that's a good trait. Oh sure, some of the folks in town write letters to the editor or sign petitions, but none of them do anything beyond that. They just lie down and let us roll over them. But you, Thorn ... you have fire! I like that."

Still feeling tense and unsure, I asked, "Why are you telling me this stuff? You know I publish *Babel Magazine*. I could blow your cover in a heartbeat..."

Slamming on his brakes while simultaneously grabbing my wrist and squeezing it in his hand, the man snarled, "Listen! I'm calling the shots, and you're listening. This is what you're allowed to tell your readers about me. First of all, no descriptions of any kind. That means you can't write about my face, my clothes, my car, or the tone of my voice. Do you have that straight?"

Pulling my wrist away from his hand, I gulped, "I got it. What *am* I allowed to tell them?"

"I'm glad you see things my way. I'm not messing around," the man said while curling his upper lip. "You're gutsy, but smart. I like that." After pausing a moment at Park Avenue, he turned left and started driving toward the stadium before answering my question. "You're allowed to tell your readers that I'm not an elected official, I'm not in the public eye, most of them wouldn't recognize me if they saw me on the street, and I'm not Joe Paterno! But I do have more impact on their lives than anyone in Centre County."

The man paused; then continued. "Now, let me ask you a question. How long have you lived in State College?"

"Actually, I've lived here four different times, the first time in 1982."

"So you've been around. Now, tell me, have you ever seen me before?"

I looked at the man's face as slivers of light shimmered through the windshield from a street lamp.

"Only once," I told him.

"Once! Where?" he demanded.

"Downtown."

"Are you sure it was me?"

"Don't worry, it was you. People have seen you before."

"That might be so, but they still don't know how I pull their strings from behind the scenes."

"Wait a second," I blurted as the man turned right onto University Drive. "I know enough about the world to ... if you really *are* such a high-roller ... why would you be spilling the beans to me? You guys usually hide in the shadows and do your work in the dark. There's something wrong with this picture."

"You *do* know what's going on!" the man sniffed while ... (I'd like to tell you more, but I am also prohibited from presenting any of my counterpart's habits or mannerisms) ... "Smart boy. And I'll tell you, you're absolutely right about the people who call the shots. Once we get control ... by whatever means necessary ... the best way to keep it is to lie to the people who are being controlled. Hell, we'll even deny that there *is* any form of control."

The man continued down University Drive, turned right on Prospect, then made a right on Garner, which is where this article began (with him threatening me if I blew his cover).

As he continued toward College Avenue, I asked, "How do I fit into the picture? I don't get it. Why am I even here with you? It doesn't make sense."

Perturbed by my inquiries, the man spoke without opening his mouth, instead opting to force his words between clenched teeth. "You're here because I'm using you."

"Using me?" I repeated nervously, wondering whether I'd ever make it home again. "For what?"

"I'm going to tell you things over the next few months that'll blow your mind," he began while driving through campus. "But here's the most important bit of advice that you can pass along to your readers." As I sat in rapt attention, he continued, "Tell them to look at the power structure surrounding them. Look at who controls their lives."

Becoming more animated, he snarled, "How can a person, or group of people, allow themselves to be so easily controlled by someone else? It amazes me. You people have rolled over and let us screw you. And we keep on doing it day in and day out!"

As the man took a right onto North Allen Street near the Business Administration Building, he approached a traffic diverter at Adams Street.

"Do you mean like these blockades?" I said sarcastically. "Those things drive me up a wall. I can't understand for a second how the Borough Council is allowed to get away with this."

"The diverters!" the man said gleefully. "I could have those things ripped out tomorrow if I wanted to."

"Then do it! Those blockades are the bane of my existence."

"Nah, I'm going to leave them where they are," my counterpart said coyly.

"Why?"

"Because I can!" he said triumphantly.

"Because you can?" I shouted, wondering if I was overstepping my bounds. "Thanks a lot. I got a ticket in January for driving through those diverters, and now you have a chance to make life better and you won't do it because of some lousy power trip. Y'know what I'm going to start calling you? Bane, because those diverters are the bane of my existence."

"Bane? Hmmm … I like that," he said without smiling. "My new name is Mr. Bane. I can accept that. But be careful. You're getting close to pushing me too far," he warned.

As he turned right at the diverter, Bane began, "Now that you know how we interfere with your life with those stupid traffic diverters, let's look at something really important."

"Like what?" I countered, feeling as tense as I had ever felt.

"How about taxes? Did you know that if you're a homeowner in Happy Valley, the total of all the taxes you pay is about 48% of your wages? That includes your federal income tax, state taxes, county taxes, local taxes, sales taxes, gasoline taxes, phone taxes, real estate taxes, school taxes, property taxes, occupational assessment taxes, occupational privilege taxes, inheritance taxes, and capital gains taxes."

"Holy cow! I never knew it was that much."

Bane continued. "Now, look at the situation in this context. Back in the days of slavery, a worker would spend ten or twelve hours a day in the field, and of the 100% of their income they *should* have gotten, how much did they actually get?"

"Zero."

"That's right. The plantation owner kept 100% of their income. Now, if you remember my example about the homeowner ... how much of their income is the plantation owner taking?"

"48%."

"That's right. And in Canada it's 60%, and in a few European countries it's up to 70%. That means that right here in Centre County we're already half way to slavery, and in the socialist countries with their health care programs and total government intrusion, they're almost three-quarters of the way to slavery. Pretty soon, if this trend continues, we'll all be working for the plantation owner again."

"You're right, Bane!" I exclaimed. But my excitement quickly dissipated as I realized I was entering dangerous territory. This was the real thing. The truth! "Why are you telling me this stuff?" I finally blurted with exasperation. "Why are you doing this?"

Bane remained silent for a few moments as we wheeled through College Heights and returned to the parking lot of Sunset Park. "I'm doing this," he said finally, "because I want the people out there to know they're being bamboozled ... they're being raked through the coals ... and it's only going to get worse. I want them to know what's happening."

"But you're one of The Controllers. Why do you want to help? You're supposed to be putting the screws to us."

"Yeah, that's the problem," Bane said with noticeable resentment. "I actually made a decision a few months ago that got me in trouble with the higher-ups. Y'see, I was on my way to the next level, and all I had to do was lay one last screwing on you people and I would have earned my stripes. But I couldn't do it any more. I saw what was happening, and ... man ... I never thought I had one of those things, but my conscience got the better of me. Well, those in the upper echelon didn't like my decision, so they told me I was done ... out ... at least temporarily. And to get back in, I'd have to do something even more atrocious. So I figured; I'll fight back another way."

"Why should I believe you?" I asked suspiciously. "What if this is all a set-up?"

"If I were you, I'd think the same thing," Bane told me matter-of-factly. "I wouldn't trust us as far as I could spit on us. But the fact remains

-- I'm playing it straight with you. If you want to roll the dice and hear me out, I'm sure you'll see that I'm on the up-and-up."

"Okay, then," I said cautiously. "Answer this question. What are you – a Republican or a Democrat?"

"Oh, a test!" Bane chuckled. "You know the answer to that. I'm neither. We don't fall into those petty little categories."

As the man continued to speak, I knew he was the real thing.

"Y'see, the Controllers only have one thing in mind – their own individual self interest. In the context of history, then, this means their chief goals are wealth and power. That, Mister Thorn, is the way the world works. Now do you believe me?"

"Yes," I nodded.

"Good. Now that we've put that hurdle behind us, let's get down to the nitty-gritty. Here's the first lesson everyone should learn. The supposed Republican and Democrat battle that we see on TV and read about in the newspapers is a fallacy. It's nothing but an illusion that we've created to keep people diverted from the truth.

"Anyone that falls for this trick has a very limited view of the world. They've been conditioned into believing the Big Lie! It's almost childish how these folks run around saying that the Republicans are to blame for everything, or the Democrats, or Bill Clinton, or George Bush are the problem. They have such foolish outlooks it becomes ridiculous to even watch them playing their little games – kind of like chickens running around with their heads cut off. Of course the Democrats and Republicans can be dangerous, but they're only puppets for the real power … the hidden power."

I could do nothing but sit silently in the darkness as he continued.

"Do you know what our greatest joy is? It's seeing all these talking heads on TV arguing about the Republicans being right and the Democrats being wrong, or vice versa. What a scam. All we need to do is keep a few 'plants' on each of the television and radio stations to perpetuate the ruse, and the meaningless debates will continue forever."

"That's all they are, aren't they?" I asked. "It's all a put-on. There's no difference between the Democrats and the Republicans. It's all a fallacy."

"Especially when they reach the upper echelon of power. Do you think it really mattered if Al Gore or George Bush won? We own both of them. They're both bought and paid for. Hell, by the next election, we'll probably even have the entire voting system rigged so it doesn't matter who you vote for – the outcome will already be predetermined."

"That's why there was such a big deal made about the chads and dimples and..."

"It's so we can make everyone so disgusted with the current system, they'll flock to online voting," Bane boasted. "This will completely eliminate the possibility of an outsider entering the Oval Office. You have to figure it's a helluva lot easier to control a few computer programmers than it is a countless number of volunteers working at the fire hall or county courthouse."

"I knew it!"

"Thorn, politics on a national level is nothing more than professional wrestling. Both of them have predetermined outcomes, and they suck people in with a bunch of phony dramatics," Bane explained. "That's why they can never learn about Votescam until it's too late. What we want to do is keep people divided ... to keep them fighting among themselves. That's why we keep polarizing the populace with superficial issues like social security, campaign finance reform, or whether to keep our borders open or closed. And y'know, it always works. We laugh like crazy at all you people battling against each other when in reality you should be focusing on the real enemy – US! If you really saw who was manipulating your lives, we'd never be able to keep pushing ahead with our agenda. If you really saw us for who we are, you'd run us out of town in a second. Then guess what would happen?"

"What?"

"You'd be able to increase your freedom, keep your money, govern yourself, and rise on the scale of understanding and truth. But, no, no, no, we don't want any of those things."

"So you keep creating new conflicts and phony issues that split people apart and..."

"... And divert their attention away from us. We get you people so enraged off that you actually hate each other. Look at the environmentalists versus the businessmen, or the abortionists versus the right-to-lifers. These people rip each other to shreds like dogs. It's sick. Then, if you really want to see how depraved we can be, take a look at war. We sit in our insulated offices in Washington, D.C. and send your kids into the jungles and deserts to kill each other ... all the while filling the folks back home with so much propaganda that they're standing on the sidelines cheering us on. Can you believe it? Can you believe what we're getting away with?

"We'll CREATE an emergency out of thin air to get rid of a troublemaker who threatens our power base, and manipulate YOU into doing our dirty work for us. And when it's all said and done, we'll use these wars to secure our stronghold and become even more powerful and dictatorial."

"And all the while our attention is being diverted from what's really going on?" I asked.

Bane smiled slyly without needing to say another word.

As I pondered these invaluable lessons, an urgent news report blared across the radio:

"Just in – a school shooting in San Diego has left an unknown number of students dead and wounded. More details as they come in."

I swore under my breath, shaking my head and thinking about the parents of the kids who were killed and what they must be going through right now. "Kids killing other kids. It's like cows deliberately walking into a slaughterhouse."

"Yes," Bane said softly. "The Controllers even have your teenagers killing each other."

"The Controllers?" I asked with disbelief.

"Of course," Bane snarled. "You don't think those kids are doing this of their own volition, do you?"

"They're not?"

"Of course not. Here's what's really going on with all those school shootings …"

CHAPTER SIXTY

THE STORY BEHIND THE HIGH SCHOOL

SHOOTINGS

As the news of another school shooting filled me with fury, I spat, "Do you know something about these kids that no one else knows? Because if you don't do something about it, they're going to keep killing forever..."

"That's the idea," Bane said after grabbing hold of my arm so tightly I actually thought the circulation was cut off to my entire body.

"That's the idea! What are you talking about?" I asked, pulling my arm away from his hand.

"Don't you get it?" he said resentfully. "These kids aren't killing of their own volition. The Controllers are making them do it."

"The Controllers? How? Why?" I asked with confusion.

"It all boils down to taking our guns away from us," Bane began as we continued to sit in the darkness at Sunset Park. "Can't you see the trend? Look at what happens after every shooting. The national news erupts with another segment on gun control telling us how terrible our weapons are. After people are repeatedly bombarded with this propaganda, the Controllers are going to unleash such an atrocious massacre on the people it'll make Australia's Port Arthur Massacre look like child's play."

"Wait a second," I shot back. "These school shootings are nothing but a ploy to get guns outlawed? How do they do it? How do they get the kids to kill each other? It doesn't make sense."

Turning the key in his ignition, Bane shifted his car into drive, then pulled from the parking lot.

"How do they do it? Simple. Y'see, the people who call the shots have nothing but *time* on their hands. They don't have real jobs, and they have more money ... way more money ... than they could ever spend. So, the only thing they do is control society by pulling our strings."

"I still don't get it."

"Listen, Thorn! To these guys, information is God. That's how they're able to keep running the show. So, when it comes to the school shootings, think about this. How many have they screwed up so far?"

"Screwed up?"

Once again, Bane rolled along McKee Street to Park Avenue, where he made a left, then a right, onto Shortlidge.

"Yeah, how many of the high school shootings have backfired on them? None so far. These guys have come a long way since they messed up with Oswald."

"How did Lee Harvey Oswald get into the picture?"

"Just listen. The Controllers fouled things up so badly with Oswald that they had to snuff him the next day before the whole thing blew up in their faces. Then, with Sirhan Sirhan, they blew it too. The only reason he isn't singing is because they turned his brain into Jello. But with these kids, none of them have gone off the deep end. All of them are doing exactly what they've been programmed to do."

"Man, you're starting to weird me out, Mister."

We took a right on Pollock and cruised past the Hub. "You still haven't told me how the Controllers actually do it."

"Okay, I'll give it to you in a nutshell. The Controllers are going into every school district in the country and finding kids that are already susceptible to hard-core conditioning."

"Kids that are beat up or on drugs or taking Xanax or something?"

"Exactly!"

"But how do they find them?"

"When you're an insider with access to every bit of information in existence, how hard is it to leaf through some school records or disciplinary files? It's a breeze. Then, when they find a few potential candidates, they start checking into their personal lives – y'know, where they hang out, who their parents are, what video games they play, and so forth. Then, when they find a few that'd be easy to crack, they really turn up the heat."

"But how ... how?" I asked as Bane wheeled onto Burrowes; then pulled beside Rec Hall near the Nittany Lion Shrine.

"It all boils down to Mind Control," he told me after shutting off his car and looking around suspiciously. "After the Controllers pinpoint a candidate – someone who's vulnerable, angry, insecure, picked on, using drugs or ready to drop off the edge – then they lay the final blow through the kid's computer or video games."

I tried to counter his claim, but I couldn't get any words to come out of my mouth.

"I know you don't believe me," Bane said with a fair amount of certainty, "so keep listening. I recently spoke with a retired Army officer, and guess what he told me. He said the extremely violent video games that are on the market today are *exactly* the same as the ones they use to indoctrinate their soldiers in the fine art of killing. Don't you get it, Thorn? At our core, humans aren't prone to killing other humans. They either need an intense amount of provocation, or they need an outside stimulus to urge them on. These kids aren't killing of their own volition. Look at them. They're like robots, or machines. All of them are so completely bent and absorbed by the messages that have been planted in their heads …"

"Do you mean that special messages are wired into the games …?"

"Yes … or onto their computers. It's all subliminal stuff like they used on Sirhan, or on Mark David Chapman, but much more advanced and full-proof. The military and the CIA have come a long way since then. Now listen to this. That same Army officer told me if we wanted to produce an entire generation of individuals that were completely indifferent to killing, we couldn't be doing a better job than what we're doing in this country right now. Plus, when you add in the Prozac and Ritalin and all the subliminal messages that are bombarding their already confused, feeble minds, what do you have? Kids who'll kill on command – many of them with a smile on their face. That's what's happening."

Feeling sickened by this information, I told Bane, "Take me back to my car. This is too much all at once. I knew I shouldn't have come here tonight."

"Okay, if that's what you want. But just remember, Thorn, you're the one who wanted to know. All I'm doing is laying it on the line for you."

As Bane started his car and drove past Pattee Library back to Park Avenue, I asked, "So, how do you fit into the picture?"

Sighing nervously, Bane began slowly. "That's why I'm here with you. Y'see, a few weeks ago, one of the Controllers phoned me and said that it was time to wire a potential shooter…"

"Right here, in State College?"

"You got it. They already have six kids picked out…"

"No way!"

"Six of 'em, Thorn, and they're already wiring them. They wanted me to pull the final strings and set one of them loose."

"Right here?"

"There's three of them in the State College Area High School, and three more in different schools that I won't mention. They're getting them ready, and I was supposed to be the point man to pull the trigger."

"Oh, man, now I get it. You would have been the one to set them off."

"Exactly," Bane said drearily, taking a left on McKee Street. "But I couldn't do it. I couldn't be a part of those kids killing each other. So that's when the Controllers blackballed me and said that most of my powers had been stripped." Bane paused for a moment; then concluded by saying as we pulled back into Sunset Park, "Now do you know why I'm here?"

"I do," I said, nodding my head. "But why me?"

"Because you're the only one who'll print my story!" he shouted, slamming his fists on the steering wheel. "Who else will? The *Centre Daily Times*? *Voices*? *State College Magazine*? *Town & Gown*? *The Collegian*? None of them will. It's too hot! But I could tell you were different. You react to the world very intimately. You have to run this story, Thorn. If you don't, those kids don't stand a chance."

As his words echoed through my ears, the ramifications became blindingly apparent. It was all-or-nothing, despite how much danger it put me in.

As these thoughts haunted me, I blurted, "Let me ask you one last question. Why do the Controllers want to keep having these kids kill each other? I know you explained it a little bit before, but I still don't get the big picture."

Focused intently, Bane told me, "Here's the way history has always worked. Conflict is what makes things happen."

"Conflict?"

"Listen! Quit interrupting me."

A momentary pause.

"The Controllers take one force and play it against its direct opposite. Now, when these conflicting forces come together and mesh, a third force, or synthesis, is created from them. This synthesis is then used as force number one, and the process begins all over again. So, when it comes to the school shootings, you have force number one, which is a high school bloodbath. Now what would be its opposite?"

I waited silently for his answer.

"Well, whenever there's a disaster, people expect some sort of solution. Now the government, fully aware of our Nature, perpetuates a situation until they can ride in on their white horses and save the day. So, here we have one force – the right to bear arms which represents FREEDOM. Its polar opposite is Mind Control, or wiring the kids through their computer and video games, which results in a synthesis – the school shootings. But this example doesn't stop there, for the synthesis becomes force number one to start the process all over again."

"So, force number one is now the school shootings …?"

"Yes. The shootings are CHAOS, and its polar opposite is ORDER, which will occur when, after a particularly horrendous shooting, the government will step in and pass legislation – or ORDER – that results in a new synthesis – laws making it illegal to own firearms."

"I finally see! There is a method to all this madness!" I yelled.

"Can't you see where it leads?" Bane asked. "Once we have no weapons, the government can raise our taxes and limit our freedoms because we won't have any way to defend ourselves against their tyranny. On top of that, they'll start using more and more Mind Control on us … like implants … until we reach the point of being…"

"…slaves who work all day for the plantation owner and don't get anything in return!" I exclaimed.

"You finally understand," Bane said, his eyes gleaming triumphantly. "The true villain in this scenario isn't the media, or the teenagers, or the school system, although they are complicit in the scheme; the real enemies are those who manipulate the opposing forces behind the scenes. These folks are the Controllers."

As I sat in Bane's car shaking my head, he wrapped up our session by saying, "Okay, that's enough for one night. In the future, once your articles start coming out, we won't be able to meet like this. I'm going to have a very high price on my head. So we have to start being careful. But for the time being, here's one last thing to think about. Did you ever notice how the people in control are always harping on the citizens to surrender their weapons, yet they never give up *their* weapons? Do you know what the people should say to their leaders? Since it's such a good idea to be without our guns, why don't *you* set an example for us and give *your* weapons away first? Then, when it's proven that *you* don't have any arms, then we'll follow suit. Can't you see the way things always work? Americans are practically the only people left in the *whole world* who still have the *right to bear arms*! Everywhere else in the world, the government has stripped the citizenry of their right to defend themselves, yet they always keep *their* weapons of destruction. When are people going to open their eyes to what's going on?"

With these parting words, Bane extended his hand and told me I was supposed to be at a certain phone … (location and date withheld for our own protection) where he would contact me again. Then he slipped me a folded piece of paper.

"What's this?" I asked.

"It's a website address. When you get home tonight, log on and start digging around. What you need to do is find the site's 'Easter egg.' Do you know what that is?"

"Yeah, that's a secret message hidden somewhere inside the program. We have one on my 3D novel, *Return to Eternity*."

"Precisely. Once you find the Easter egg, it'll blow your mind. Now get outta here. It's getting late."

And that was that. As I stepped from Bane's car, I caught a quick glimpse of his face one last time. It was incredible how much my impression of him had changed within the last hour. At first I saw the absolute worst side of humanity reflected in his face – the aspect that seeks to control and dominate another person. But as I left, I saw him staring straight ahead through his windshield into the darkness, his face marked by a distinct look of blankness and fear, as if he were saying, "What have I just done?"

It was then that I knew I had entered truly dangerous territory. Things would never be the same again.

Fearing I had made a drastic mistake, I started my car (sighing with relief that it didn't blow up), pulled from Sunset Park onto McKee Street; then cruised along Park Avenue toward the bypass. As I hit the on-ramp, I looked in my rear view mirror for the umpteenth time and realized that a black sedan had been following me the entire way.

CHAPTER SIXTY-ONE

AN ALIEN BASE BENEATH BEAVER STADIUM?

"Thorn?" a gravely voice growled through the telephone.

"Bane!" I exclaimed. "Is that you?"

"It's me..."

"Where have you been? I haven't heard from you in weeks. I thought..."

"Thorn, quit thinking and listen. I can't stay on the phone for too long or they'll find me."

"Do you mean my phone's tapped?"

"What do you think? Of course it is. Now let's drop this nonsense and get down to business."

Within less than sixty seconds, my heartbeat jumped from a normal rate to one that was off the chart. Why wouldn't he just leave me alone?

Bane continued, "I saw your piece on education in *Babel #11*, and on mind control in *#12*. You did very well. But now we have to start getting into some really heavy stuff. Are you ready?"

"Yeah. I have my pen and notebook right here. Let's do it," I said nervously.

"All right. Here's the headline I want you to run for your next story – *Alien Base Hidden Beneath Beaver Stadium*."

"An alien base!" I exploded. "Are you crazy? What is this, some kind of put on? What do you think I am – a fool? Do you want me to be the laughingstock of the whole town?"

As I finished with my dramatics, a long silence persisted until Bane finally spoke again.

"Are you finished? Huh??? Are you?"

"Yes."

"Okay then, let's get back to business."

"All right," I said with a noticeable touch of embarrassment.

"You don't believe there's an alien base beneath Beaver Stadium, do you?"

"No," I immediately said.

"Okay. Let me change your mind. I'll tell you the way things really are."

"I'm all ears." I clicked on my ballpoint pen, ready to start scribbling madly.

"Before Beaver Stadium was built, the football team played on a small field behind Rec Hall. In those days, the campus didn't stretch out to where it is now. There was nothing but cow pastures beyond University Drive. Now, I'm sure you know that Penn State does contract work for the military, especially the Navy."

"Yeah, they do it at ARL."

"Exactly. Well, back in the late 1940s, our government retrieved some bodies from a few downed alien crafts and transported them to Wright-Patterson Air Force Base in Dayton, Ohio."

"I know ... it's called Hangar 11."

"Correct. Well, word started to get out that the bodies were there, so the government had to find a place to put them, and also to do some experimentation. But it had to be somewhere out of the way that wouldn't attract a lot of attention. So, what did they do? They found a sleepy little college town in Central Pennsylvania and started building an underground base."

"Where Beaver Stadium now sits?"

"Exactly. Everything went smoothly, and they actually got the base built under the guise of laying some new water and sewerage lines. And I have to tell ya, Thorn, you should have seen what they built!"

"You've seen it?"

"Of course."

"How? Where did you get in?" I asked excitedly.

"If you wanna know the truth, you can still get in," Bane told me.

"You have to be kidding. How?"

"If you go to the northwest corner of the stadium, past where the press box is located, you'll find a manhole cover right beside a huge metal girder that's painted green – well, at least it was the last time I was there ... they keep changing it ... anyway, it's the only green one at the stadium. The cover is held down by some thick metal bolts, but if you unloosen them and remove the cover, you'll find an old set of steps that lead down to the laboratory."

"It's a laboratory?"

"Thorn, it'd blow your mind if you saw what they used to do down there."

"Like what?"

"It was hideous. There were all these human aberrations with six legs and four arms, and octopus-men with tentacles."

"No...!"

"Yes! It's time to wake up to what's going on, Thorn."

"But it can't be..."

"...There were aborted reptile fetuses, aliens with wings, humanoid-lizards, and even gargoyle children that were the result of some botched experiments."

"That's sick. I don't believe it." I was feeling ill. "Why hasn't anyone ever heard of this stuff before?"

"They have, Thorn, just not people like you. Hell, everyone knows how hush-hush Penn State is. They know how to keep a secret, especially after knocking off Roger Harkin."

"Who's he?"

"Harkin was a scientist in the Material Research Lab who started nosin' around out by the stadium. One day, he stumbled onto the laboratory and found out the secret. The administration and the military tried to keep him quiet, but Harkin wouldn't keep his mouth shut. So one day they put a bullet in the back of his head. Y'see, Thorn, when someone wants to kill a person, they don't mess around with death threats, publicity, or notifying the media. They just kill 'em."

"Then what happened? They got away with it, just like that?"

"Pretty much. When someone wondered what happened to Harkin, Penn State said he transferred to another school and they lost track of him."

"That's it?"

"Not exactly. It seems Harkin did a bit too much talkin', and people started nosin' around the base. So, in 1959, to allay suspicions, they started building Beaver Stadium to cover up their mess."

"I don't know ... it seems so ..."

"So what?" Bane asked.

"So far-fetched," I blurted out. "It seems ludicrous."

"What's so ludicrous?" Bane inquired disdainfully. "You don't think there are underground bases in this country?"

"Well..."

"Thorn, Socrates and Plato both wrote about men living in subterranean chambers. Hell, where do you think our race first lived when they came here from Atlantis and Lemuria? Look at the Egyptians and Incas and Mayans and Aztecs. They all hollowed out the earth and lived underground."

"Are you serious?" I asked incredulously, my brain overloading.

"Of course I am. Thorn, wake up! You have to start paying attention. This country has underground bases all over the place – tons of them."

"We do? Where?" I felt as if my mind was spinning.

"There's a famous one right here in Pennsylvania," said Bane. "It's called Raven Rock, or Site R."

"Where is it?"

"Down south between Gettysburg and Hagerstown. You oughta see this place. It's unbelievable. They call it the Underground Pentagon, and it's stocked with all these super-computers, a full-scale communications network, storage tanks with over two million liters of water, plus a hospital, huge banks of sophisticated telephone equipment, and it's even linked by an underground tunnel to Camp David. If a nuclear war ever breaks out, this is where all the shots are going to be called."

"Holy shit!"

"Yeah, then there's NORAD in Colorado, Camp David has an underground bunker, and the White House … get this … it goes down at least 17 stories underground."

"Are you sure?"

"Thorn, I've been down to level 4 myself, but that's as far as I could go. But I've been told by reliable sources that it goes down another 13 stories … maybe even more."

"This is too much."

"It doesn't end there, though. How about Mt. Pony in Virginia that's used as an underground Treasury Department. I hear they have billions of dollars in storage there. Or how about the Greenbriar Hotel in West Virginia. This underground palace can hold almost 1,000 people. That's where the U.S. Congress will go in case of a disaster. The National Security Agency in Maryland has thousands of the most complex supercomputers known to man underneath their headquarters, plus scores of surveillance equipment, telephones, and a radio and television station. This is where the CIA will be calling their shots from. And, oh, how could I forget about Manzano Air Force Base? This monstrosity is almost 300,000 square feet, with 95% of it underground. It's a pretty safe bet to say there's a lot of alien activity going on down there, too."

"Damn … does every government agency in existence have an underground complex?" I asked.

"I've heard there are at least 90 different government building projects going on underground right now, but it's not only them. Lockheed has underground facilities, and so do AT&T and Standard Oil. Plus, Northrop has an underground facility that's at least 40 levels deep, and McDonnell Douglas operates a place that has runways that lead to openings where planes can taxi into an underground hangar! You should see this joint – they have these diamond-shaped openings where huge pylons pop out of the ground, then go back down again. And man, at the Dulce underground base, you should see the doors. All of them have signs that are written in a weird alien language with all these strange symbols that no one can understand but them."

"It's like another whole world is being built underground that no one knows about."

"You're right."

"I wouldn't be surprised if tunnels are being built out there by the Penn Stater where they're putting up the new highway."

Bane laughed knowingly into the telephone, then kept rambling. "Some of the Oriental cities are building underground with a vengeance, while the Russians are spending billions on a huge complex in the Ural Mountains. So, y'see Thorn, it's going on everywhere."

"Okay, I believe you. But what does this have to do with the base beneath Beaver Stadium?" I asked, becoming wrapped up in the mystery.

"I'm glad you're starting to see the connection," said Bane, "because this is where it gets serious. See, the big daddy of all the underground bases is called Mount Weather in Bluemont, Virginia."

"Mount Weather?"

"Yeah, Mount Weather," he lowered his voice. "It's the underground headquarters for FEMA."

"You've been there?"

"Oh yeah. It's spooky. Once ya get to the entrance, you see this huge steel door that is so thick, 50 sticks of dynamite couldn't rip through it. Then inside, all the offices are reinforced with concrete and steel, while there are security personnel everywhere … all of them with hand guns or assault rifles."

"What's down there?"

"It's amazing, Thorn. There's a full-scale power plant, a hospital, a sewage treatment facility, plus an underground pond, and these quarter-million gallon tanks that are filled with drinking water."

"It sounds like a real city."

"It is! There are sidewalks, a cafeteria, paved streets, a diesel-powered generating plant, and closed circuit television cameras that monitor everything. Plus, everything is run by electromagnetic energy that's built into the walls. None of the elevators even have cables or electrical controls ... it's all electromagnetic. Do you know that when this place was being built in 1952, and finished in '58, it cost over a billion dollars ... and that was in 1950s dollars! Can you imagine how much it costs to maintain this joint, especially with close to 300 full-time federal employees working there, and the massive computer network they have to keep upgrading and maintaining? It's outrageous!"

"And you said there are other ones ...?"

"Hell yeah. The United States Government has at least 100 other facilities ... not as large, mind you ... but they're in Pennsylvania, Virginia, Maryland, North Carolina, and West Virginia. But Mount Weather's the king of the hill ... the big daddy."

"Why?"

"Because that's where they're housing the backup government that'll step in and take over if disaster strikes ... a disaster that's either real or created."

"A backup government?" I inquired as the situation began to take on an entirely new perspective. "Who are these people?"

"If you want to know the truth, I've learned almost every secret there is to know over the years, but no one talks about who these people are inside Mount Weather. No one knows who belongs to their shadow government. All I can tell you is that none of them are elected, and their terms aren't limited by the four-year presidential election cycle."

"In other words, they're a government unto themselves, completely unaccountable to anyone but the power elite."

"You got it."

"And when this supposed disaster strikes, let me guess. Only a select few will be allowed into Mount Weather, right?"

"Why do you think they have the steel doors and armed guards? They sure as hell don't want *us* there."

"But we keep paying to build these structures, and maintain them, right?"

"Just keep watching your paycheck and seeing how much they're taking out every week. Some of it is going to support our new underground capital."

"Why doesn't anyone know who these people are who're running the show down there? It's absurd."

"I agree," said Bane. "All I can tell you is that there is a cabal of men known as 'The 54/12 Group' that is an offshoot of the National

Security Council. These men are at the core of the Invisible Government … the hidden power center."

"And they're the ones who've built all these underground complexes?"

"Well, not them per se, but they work hand-in-hand with an organization named 'The Jason Group.'"

"Who are they?"

"They're a selective cadre of scientists who have capitalized on the dark side of technology."

"And they're the one's who built all those bases?"

"No. Y'see Thorn, whenever you deal with these shadow powers, you have to realize their tentacles extend in every direction, and they operate on a variety of different levels. So, first you have the Ultimate Controllers, then the 54/12 Group, then the Jason Group. Then, acting as the operational arm of this octopus is the Bechtel Corporation."

"Bechtel? Who are they?"

"They're a very shadowy international corporation that serves as an arm of the CIA."

"Now the CIA's in the picture?"

"Of course. Aren't they always?"

"So, what does Bechtel do?"

"They're the largest construction and engineering company on the planet … almost like a form of shadow government in and of themselves."

"So they're the ones who are building all these bases?"

"Thorn, nothing's ever so cut-and-dried as you'd like it to be, but yes, they're a part of what was called 'The Doomsday Project.'"

"What's that?"

"Well, almost twenty years ago, during the Reagan presidency, there were about 20 different programs that were started … in secret, of course … that revolved around how our government would perpetuate itself in times of nuclear war or global disaster."

"Now I'm starting to see. That's when these programs began in earnest."

"Not necessarily … they've been going on for decades, but yeah, that's when our technology developed to a point where Project Rand could be acted upon instead of just imagined."

"Project Rand? There's so much stuff going on that I can't keep it all straight," I complained as I scribbled madly on the pages of my notebook. "What is Project Rand?"

"Well, there's a very telling quote that came out of their symposium on Deep Underground Construction. It went like this: 'Just as airplanes, ships and automobiles have given man mastery of the surface of the Earth, tunnel-boring machines will give him access to the subterranean world.'"

"Wow. Then it is for real, huh?" I said vacantly, feeling overwhelmed by it all.

"Thorn, they have this machine called a Subterrene that'd blow your mind. It's nuclear-powered, and it snarls through the underground rocks by melting the stone into molten magma. It's amazing. Then, when the Subterrene burrows through a certain area, the rocks cool back down and the walls have a very fine, almost glass-like quality to them. You should see these tunnels. They're almost like..."

"They sound like the Glass Worms that were photographed on Mars!" I exclaimed.

"Yeah, you're right," Bane said approvingly, glad that I was keeping up with him. "But it goes beyond simple underground bases. See, there's a secret project called 'Noah's Ark' where all these complexes are connected by underground tunnels and people can shuttle back and forth between them without ever being detected by anyone up here on earth."

"You've got to be kidding!"

"But it gets even wilder," Bane continued enthusiastically, his voice animated by these revelations. "We now have the technology to lay tubes across the ocean floor that'll act as frictionless vacuum chambers where shuttles using electromagnetic power ... kind of like airplanes without wings ... can zip between the seas from one continent to another. Think of the advantages of this system."

"Yeah, if ya lay tubes on the ocean floor, ya don't even have to dig into the earth. It's perfect!" I paused for a moment until the ramifications settled in, then said, "Why don't any of us know about this stuff, or how we're setting up all these underground bases inside the earth?"

A lengthy silence persisted until Bane said softly "You want to know what we're doing there? Well, it's the same thing we're doing at all the underground bases – we're developing new technologies, housing aliens, and preparing for a catastrophic disaster that's going to hit the earth."

"Y'mean there's aliens living underground?"

"You got it."

"But why? What do they want with us? Are they performing some weird kinda experiments or something?"

"I'm sure they're doing those things, but that's not the reason they're here."

"Then what is?" I asked with anticipation, feeling as if I was about to be let in on the biggest secret of all time.

Bane replied, "They don't care about minerals or money or gasoline or zapping our cows with laser beams. The extra-terrestrials are here to harness the magnetic power that flows through the earth. It's free energy, Thorn! That's what they use to power their spaceships. Of everything we have on this planet, electromagnetic energy is without a doubt the most valuable. That's why it boggles my mind that Bill Clinton and George Bush and all the rest of The Controllers make us keep using oil-based products for fuel. It's disgusting how they're decimating our planet ... and for what? Do you know why they're doing it?"

"Money?"

"That's it – stinking filthy money. What a bunch of near-sighted egotists. They're going to keep depleting and destroying and poisoning this earth until..."

"...Until it's too late, huh?" I finished.

"Yes, until it's too late."

"Then what?"

"Well, when they think the end is near, they can do two things – either live in space, or move underground. And that's what they're preparing for, all off the sweat of our backs."

"What do you mean?"

"C'mon, get with it! Who do you think is paying for all these bases under the earth and in outer space? Do you think they are? Hell no! It's us, through taxation! This is what it all boils down to. You should see what kinda freaky stuff is going on down in Antarctica. Look on the Internet sometime and you'll find out. Can't you see, Thorn? We're the slaves that are allowing them to not only destroy our planet, but to also move onto greener pastures and SURVIVE! But do you think they're going to invite us along for the ride? Not a chance! We'll pay for the destruction, and we'll also pay for their escape. It's sickening."

Bane paused a moment, sighed deeply into the receiver; then continued. "Y'know, for years I've looked at structures like the Great Wall of China, or the Pyramids, or some of those fantastic castles and churches in Europe, and I thought, man, the people that built them ... that did the actual construction ... must have been real idiots. I mean, they were nothing more than slaves or serfs working for some Pharaoh or emperor or feudal lord, and they got paid chump-change, if anything at all. And I'd think, man, they must have really been stupid.

"But then it hit me one day! We're the same as them! We're the serfs and slaves that are allowing ourselves to be taxed to death while at the same time paying for their escape. And do you think they'll invite us along for the party? No way. The only thing they'll do for us is take a few blood samples for slave genes so we can build new palaces for them, dig their ditches, and shovel the crap out of their sewers."

"Why do we keep letting them get away with this?"

"That's what I've been asking you, Thorn. This is as close to the truth as you'll ever get. The Controllers are going to destroy our planet, escape the onslaught, create new secret societies and perpetuate the system all over again."

I stood frozen in my living room shaking my head with disgust before replying, "Then everything you told me is true, huh?"

"Everything," Bane laughed, "except for the alien base beneath Beaver Stadium!"

"It's not real? Why did you say it was? Why did you lie?"

"To prove a point. Thorn, if you want to figure out how these people operate, you have to develop a new way of thinking that matches theirs."

"What do you mean?" I asked, still somewhat peeved.

"Well, to put it as simply as possible, you're too honest, and you still harbor a sense of justice and fair-play. When someone tells you something, you essentially believe them. But the people who control the world are a different breed. These folks have spent generation after generation living a lie. Their entire make-up and existence is nothing but a lie. In fact, they're the Children of all Lies!

"So, if you want to know how they think, you have to realize that at the core of everything you find one concept – DECEPTION!"

At that point I heard a strange clicking noise buzzing through my phone, along with a strange voice saying, "We hear you… …"

Bane heard it too and instantly hung up while I stood alone in my living room freaking out.

CHAPTER SIXTY-TWO

AIDS: MAN-MADE VIRUS CREATED IN A

LABORATORY

As I wandered across the field next to my house for a nightly walk with my six cats, I heard a rustling in the bushes. My cats stopped in their tracks to take notice, then darted in the opposite direction.

I looked around and didn't see anything, so I kept walking toward a secluded rock pile. But ... after taking a few more steps I heard a strange noise coming from a thicket of trees.

All of a sudden a flock of blackbirds rose from a row of bushes and flew directly behind me. Reeling to see where they came from, I turned to notice a figure dressed in baggy bib-overalls sitting atop a rotted tree stump.

My heart nearly leaped from my chest until I noticed who it was. "Bane! What the hell are you doing back here in the woods? You almost scared the shit outta me! And look what you did to my cats. It's like they saw a ghost! Man, every time I talk to you, it gets weirder and weirder. Maybe we should just call this whole thing off ..."

Without batting an eye, Bane said smugly, "So, you got laid the other night, huh?"

Caught off guard, I said, "What?"

"You heard me, Thorn. You got laid the other night, huh?"

Smiling bashfully, I asked, "How did you know?"

"You still don't get it, do you? Information is our business. How else do you think we maintain control?"

"You even know about that?"

"Thorn, I'm not the only one who's watching you. Why do you think I met you back here in the woods?"

"How'd you get here anyway?"

"I came back through the swamp." Bane pointed into the distance.

"You gotta be kidding me," I laughed, looking at his pant legs, which were still wet.

"It might be funny to you, Thorn, but you don't know what'd happen if they found me. Do you realize what kind of information I've been giving you?"

"I do ... its remarkable..."

"Thorn, if they caught me here, they'd end up burying me in that marsh back there!"

"I know," I said vacantly. "The situation's seriousness is hitting me all at once." After standing in silence near the wood's edge for a moment, I asked, "So, why did you ask me about getting laid the other night?"

"Because you have to start being careful," Bane told me straight-faced. "The rules have all changed from what they were before."

"I don't get it." I said, looking around nervously.

"Thorn, there are people who aren't pleased with you in the least for what you've been running in *Babel Magazine*. Think about what you're doing!"

"I know..."

"You're exposing the biggest secrets of all time! This is the stuff that's been kept secret for years, even lifetimes."

"What does sex have to do with it?"

"Can't you see?" Bane demanded, raising his voice higher than he would have liked. After regaining his composure, he began, "I knew a man in Washington DC about ten years ago that did something similar to what you're doing now. He started spilling the beans and telling the secrets of the high-and-mighty. Plus, he did it in a fairly vocal way. So, the Controllers couldn't simply whack him because everyone would know that something fishy went down. But these guys ain't dummies. They did the next best thing."

"Which was?"

"This guy had a soft-spot for the ladies, so they found an AIDS whore ... "arranged" for a meeting – then WHAM – when they had sex, he got AIDS and died four years later."

"No way. You gotta be joshin' me," I sputtered, trying to convince myself that something like that couldn't happen to me.

"Now I'm not saying they pulled the same trick on you..."

"...No, I'm sure of it. I know this woman. She's clean."

"I hope you wore a rubber."

"Of course I did."

"...Not that they're full-proof ... but I'm tellin' ya, Thorn, ya gotta start being careful."

I stood silently for a moment as my gray Persian cat darted toward me. Bowing to pet her long, soft fur, I said absently, "They'd really do something like that – kill someone with AIDS?"

"Thorn, they invented the damn disease! They've killed millions of people already. Do you think they give a damn about yours?"

Well aware of all the AIDS rumors and theories, I asked sadly, "Did they really create it? I hate to think it's true."

"Thorn, I'm going to tell it to you straight. AIDS was created in 1974 at Fort Detrick, Maryland, which is now called NCI – the National Cancer Institute."

"At Fort Detrick … Maryland … I was in Baltimore last October at a publishing conference…"

"Officially, it was called the Fort Detrick Biological Warfare Center, which was an integral part of the National Cancer Institute."

"But why?" I asked shakily, my hands trembling as Tiger, my big cat, strolled toward me and meowed. "What purpose did it serve?"

"There are a few reasons," Bane began, as Sweety, my orange Tabby cat, circled his feet. "You have to understand that back in the mid-to-late '60s, the Controllers realized that ever since the end of World War II, the number of people on this planet was skyrocketing. They called it the 'Population Bomb.' To find a way to equal out increasing birth rates, these men came up with three ways to bolster the death rates.

"The first was proposed in the infamous *Report from Iron Mountain* that essentially said that world peace is not a desirable thing. So, instead of beginning another catastrophic war that would undoubtedly end in nuclear annihilation, they proposed a series of small, ongoing, isolated wars. Did you know that at the current time there are at least 39 different wars taking place in the world? And you have to ask yourself, who are the people fighting these wars? The answer – young, foreign men that are the most likely to reproduce.

"So, if you kill them off in a 'quiet' way with wars in remote regions of the world, you have successfully taken the first step towards lowering birth rates."

"Hmm, I never realized," I said as one of my other cats, Honey, strolled toward us. "What were the other two solutions?"

"Abortion, and the creation of an infectious disease," Bane told me matter-of-factly.

"War, abortion, and disease," I said vacantly. "Decrease the birth rate and increase the death rate, all managed by the Controllers like a

505

game of chess. It all seems so ... what are the words ... sterile and calculated and removed."

"You're starting to see the big picture, Thorn."

Unnerved by this information, I reached down and picked up my gray Persian, petting her more affectionately than usual. As her purring grew increasingly louder, I asked, "Who specifically are the people who created this disease? I know you call them the Controllers, but that doesn't tell me very much. I need something more definitive."

"I like how you're catching on and looking ahead to your next move. That's how you have to think with these people." Bane watched my cats chasing each other through the weeds. "If you want specifics, here goes. Like I said before, the AIDS virus was created at Fort Detrick, Maryland ... it was developed under the supervision of a CIA program called MK-NAOMI by the SOD – Special Operations Division -- of the Army."

"But who were they?" I asked urgently. "I still don't understand. Who are the people that created this virus?"

Our give-and-take became intense as Bane snapped, "They were cancer researchers working in biological warfare research."

"Biological warfare, Special Operations, cancer institutes ... I'm sorry, Bane, but I'm not following. It's all so confusing. I can't see the *core* of what you're trying to explain."

Frustrated, Bane snapped, "Okay! Listen! I'll try to put it in a timeline that you can better follow." Stopping to collect his thoughts, Bane furled his brow, then began, "The first study of this problem actually took place in 1957 in Huntsville, Alabama. A group of scientists met there and came up with a rudimentary plan called "Alternative 3." Eleven years later, in 1968, there was a Club of Rome study on how to limit population growth. They called this plan "Global 2000," and one of the prominent people in attendance was Doctor Aurelio Peccei, who founded the Club of Rome. He said a microbe should be developed that attacks the human immune system. Not only that, but he also suggested that a cure should be developed to counteract the disease. Around the same time, the Bilderbergs commissioned the Haig-Kissinger Depopulation Policy, which again focused on methods of keeping population growth to a minimum."

"You mentioned a..."

"Just hold on," Bane told me abruptly. "Let me run you through this time line. It's very important to see how all the pieces fall into place." Bane reached into a deep side-pocket of his overalls and pulled out a folded piece of paper.

"What's that?" I asked after setting Baby on the ground.

Handing me the sheet of paper, he said, "This is a copy of Congressional House Bill 15090 that relates to funding, or appropriations, for the Department of Defense in fiscal year 1970."

I unfolded the piece of paper and scanned its contents, reading words such as "91st Congress," "First Session," "June 9, 1969," "Hearings Before a Subcommittee of the Committee of Appropriations," "House of Representatives," and "Budget - $10 million."

After quickly absorbing as much as I could from the document, I asked, "What is this all about?"

"This," Bane said, shaking his head, "was what would eventually become MK-NAOMI where the DOD asked for and received 10 million dollars. Y'see, there was a man named Dr. Donald M. MacArthur who was the Deputy Director of DOD's Research and Technology Division. He's the one who provided the outline for this project that would be carried out by a small group of scientists. MacArthur testified before the House Committee in 1969 in hopes of producing a new virus or bacteria that would attack and destroy the body's immune system. They called this a refractory virus."

"Refractory?"

"Yeah, refractory is another way of saying 'resistant.' It means a germ that'll resist the body's own natural defense system. If you think about it, what better way is there to "acquire" an immune deficiency than to have it deliberately put there?"

"That's amazing." I bent to pet Tiger, who was meowing for more attention.

While I did so, Bane said, "Here, look at this statement that was written into the House Bill that you're holding."

"Where?" I asked.

"Right there," he pointed.

While I continued to stroke Tiger's black and brown fur, I began reading:

"Molecular biology is a field that is advancing very rapidly, and eminent biologists believe that within a period of five to ten years it would be possible to produce a synthetic biological agent, an agent that does not naturally exist and for which no natural immunity could have been acquired."

"Now, look down there, in the section entitled, 'Synthetic Biological Agents' and see what MacArthur reveals."

I began reading once again: "It is a highly controversial issue, and there are many who believe such research should not be undertaken lest it lead to yet another method of massive killing of large populations."

"Keep reading," Bane instructed me.

The report continued: "Within the next five to ten years, it would probably be possible to make a new infective micro-organism which would differ in certain important aspects from any known disease-causing organism. Most important of these is that it might be refractory to the immunological and therapeutic processes upon which we depend to maintain our relative freedom from infectious agents."

"This is amazing!" I gasped. "It sounds exactly like the AIDS virus."

"Well, how about this," Bane said confidently, pulling another piece of paper from his pocket and handing it to me.

I unfolded the tattered gray piece of paper and began reading: *World Health Bulletin 47:257-63*, dated 1972 – "An attempt should be made to see if viruses can in fact exert selective effects on immune functions. The possibility should be looked into that the immune response to the virus itself may be impaired of the infecting virus damages, more or less selectively on the cell responding to the virus."

"Now look down there," he grumbled, pointing to another section of Volume 47.

I did so, reading where members of the W.H.O. wanted to make a virus that would selectively destroy the T cell system. "An attempt should be made to ascertain whether viruses can in fact exert selective effects on immune function, e.g., by ... affecting T cell function as opposed to B cell function. The possibility should also be looked into that the immune response to the virus itself may be impaired if the infecting virus damages more or less selectively the cells responding to the viral antigens."

"Bane, what in God's name is this?" I yelled; the words I just read having a dramatic effect on me.

"In layman's language," Bane said in all seriousness, "the World Health Organization was looking into the possibility of creating a virus that *selectively* ... that's the key word ... selectively destroys the T-cell system of human beings. Can't you see – an acquired immune deficiency! Thorn, the AIDS virus wasn't an accident. It was deliberately created, and the World Health Organization was one of the agencies that asked for the production of this virus."

"And this happened in 1972?"

"Yes, the same year the DOD made another request of Congress by coming right out and asking for funding to produce … in their own words … 'a virus that selectively destroys the cells responsible for processing the virus.' Did you notice the use of the word 'select' again?"

"I did."

"This is an important point because in 1972, the World Health Organization chose a few geographical sites that they wanted to target with a smallpox vaccine."

"Some sites? Where?" I asked, watching Honey chase Sweety up an oak tree.

"Uganda and Central Africa, plus Haiti and Brazil."

"All those places had huge outbreaks of AIDS, didn't they?"

"Africa was practically decimated by AIDS. But before I start talking about that, let me continue with the timeline."

"Okay"

"Since the Controllers wanted both the death rate to increase and the birth rate to decrease, guess what happened in 1973? Abortion was legalized in this country. Y'see, the big Club of Rome meeting that I mentioned earlier took place in '68 where an overall plan was set in motion to achieve their objectives. Two years later, in 1970, Gloria Steinem co-founded the Women's Action Alliance, which was the beginning of the modern-day Women's Liberation Movement. Then, lo and behold, in 1973, the green light was given to abortion. It all fits into place quite nicely, don't you think?"

"Yes, very conveniently," I replied, shaking my head, "I still can't believe how easily women have been duped by the Controllers…"

"Without knowing any of the background manipulations of the Bilderbergs, the CIA, and so forth," Bane answered quickly. "So, in 1974, an alarming warning was given by the National Academy of Sciences. They recommended that 'scientists throughout the world join with members of their committee in voluntarily deferring experiments linking animal viruses.'"

"What does that mean?" I asked, confused.

"Just keep this little tidbit of information in mind for awhile. It's important. In the meantime, the actual AIDS virus was created in 1974 at Fort Detrick, and by 1977, the World Health Organization staged the first catastrophic act of disseminating this virus into the population."

"How'd they do it?"

"The W.H.O. went into Africa and spread the virus through a series of smallpox vaccinations."

"Smallpox vaccinations!" I shot back. "Whatever happened to the green monkey theory? I heard one of those monkeys bit an African man on the ass, and that's how the disease was started."

"You don't seriously believe that, do you?"

"No…"

"That's good, because it's the biggest hoax and the biggest LIE of all-time. Yeah, according to their story, a green monkey bit an African man on the ass; then this man had sex with someone and passed on the disease. Then that person had sex with someone else and spread the disease. But simultaneous to this "event," AIDS is also breaking out in Brazil, Haiti, other parts of Africa, and the United States. What were those green monkeys doing, flying around the globe with jet packs on their back?

"How many people even know what a green monkey is? If this monkey DID bite a man on the ass, it's still statistically impossible for the disease to spread so exponentially and to reach such epidemic proportions in so many places around the globe … all from a simple monkey bite. If you'd ever look at the numbers, you'd see the way it was disseminated around the world, proving that the disease was deliberately spread rather than just happening 'by accident' as the result of a monkey bite. Another interesting note is that if you ever looked at the gene structure of a green monkey, you'd discover that it is genetically impossible to transfer AIDS from a monkey to a man by natural means."

"Are you serious?"

"Completely. Plus, in Africa, as opposed to this country, AIDS is largely a heterosexual disease."

"What does that mean?"

"That the virus can be pinpointed … or at least its dissemination … to very SELECT audiences. In the early days of this catastrophe, certain groups of people were targeted to be the recipients of this virus."

"And the whole thing was run by the World Health Organization?"

"In Africa it was, but here in the United States there was something called 'Operation Firm Hand' that was administered by the National Institute of Health and the Centers for Disease Control."

"Operation Firm Hand? What was that?"

"Before 1978, there was no such thing as AIDS in the United States. Then, in November of 1978, an experimental Hepatitis B vaccine was introduced to New York City. The word was put out that this free vaccine was available at a local blood bank headed by Dr. W. Szmuness."

"Who was he?"

"He was a Polish doctor that immigrated to this country in 1969, and later became head of the New York City blood bank where the vaccine was administered."

"But what does a blood bank have to do with AIDS?" I asked as the sun began to set behind a row of trees.

"That's where the Hepatitis B vaccine was administered, but it wasn't given to just anyone. Y'see, the participants had to fill-out a detailed questionnaire."

"Oh, I get it..."

"Yeah, they wanted gay, non-monogamous men between the ages of 20 and 40. Now do you see? In all, between 1,040 and 1,083 gay men were inoculated with this vaccine. You also have to remember the times back then. It was the late '70s, and the concept of a lethal sex disease wasn't even heard of. Plus, you had clubs like Studio 54, cocaine, and gay bathhouses.

"Thorn, people screwed like crazy back in those days. Then, between 1979 and 1980, these same 'vaccination programs' were repeated in Chicago, San Francisco, Los Angeles, St. Louis, and Denver. Now, if you take only the New York City men who participated in this program – approximately 1,000 of them – and figure they had 50 different sex partners over the next few years – what do you come up with?"

"50,000."

"That's right. And say these 50,000 men had 50 different sex partners. What do you come up with?"

"A quarter of a million."

"Exactly. Now, multiply 250,000 by all the other cities that I just mentioned, plus throw in all the junky intravenous drug users, and what do you get?"

"An AIDS epidemic!" I snapped, filled with disgust.

"Did you know that by 1984, the CDC did a report on the New York City men that received this inoculation, and they found that 64% of them had either contracted AIDS or already died from it?"

"Oh my God!"

"After that, all of a sudden any further statistics mysteriously became "unavailable." I'll bet if they were found, though, the number would be 100% a few years later. So, think about this. If you drove up to the Centre Community Hospital and asked them, "If you had a vaccination program, say for the flu, and six years after it was administered 64% of the people that received it were infected with a lethal, incurable disease, what would you think?" They'd flip out.

"Now, take a second and think of the green monkey cover story. What seems more plausible when it's viewed in terms of an exponential explosion?"

"It's a downright crime!"

Bane then told me, "There is a researcher named Waves Forest who wrote an article called 'Designer Diseases: AIDS as Biological and Psychological Warfare.' At one point in this column he said, 'Another indication that AIDS has multiple origin points is that the 14-month doubling time of the disease cannot nearly account for the current number of cases if we assume only a small number of initial infections starting in the late 1970's.' Isn't it clear? This whole cover story about AIDS starting at one specific point is..."

"...Bullshit!"

"That's right. A very organized effort was behind it. By 1981, Thorn, AIDS became part of the popular consciousness. At first, due to the nature of who it infected in this country, the disease was originally called 'Gay Cancer.' From 1979 to 1981, the scientific community labeled it GRID – Gay Related Immune Deficiency. That was actually the first official name for AIDS. But let me keep this timeline going. In 1983, New York Congressman Theodore Weiss said, 'As far-fetched as it may seem, given the attitudes toward homosexuals and homosexuality by some segments of society, the possible utilization of biological weapons must be seriously considered.' Now that's a United States Congressman saying this! In 1984, then, the AIDS virus was officially 'discovered' by Dr. Robert Gallo. Finally, look at this." Bane pulled a faded newspaper article from his pocket. "The rest, as they say, is history."

I grabbed the article from him and read this front page headline:

London Times, May 11, 1987...
Smallpox Vaccine Triggered AIDS

After I scanned the article, Bane interjected, "Not surprisingly, this information didn't filter into the mainstream American media."

Exasperated, I asked, "Why, Bane, why? What was the purpose of it all?"

"Thorn, the creation of AIDS was a Bilderberg-inspired project that utilized the Department of Defense in conjunction with the CIA's 'Project MK-NAOMI' under the auspices of the World Health Organization. What these folks did was come up with a list of 'undesirables' that needed to be eliminated."

512

"Let me guess – blacks, junkies, and homosexuals."

"Yeah, and throw in a few Hispanics and Orientals, and you've got a pretty good idea of who they found to be undesirable."

"Wasn't there any other way?" I inquired as Honey took off wildly into the bushes.

"Do you think they care? Come on. The beauty of AIDS was that it accomplished their goal of population reduction by targeting specific racial and ethnic groups through bio-weaponry. Before AIDS, bio-weaponry was indiscriminate, killing at random. But once they came up with a more intelligent 'Agent,' it became much easier to target specific groups for elimination."

"They could infect whoever they wanted to."

"Pretty much so."

I stood for a second, overcome by sadness. "It really is man-made, huh?"

"Look at it this way, Thorn. You don't have a garage, do you?"

"No, I have to park out in the open."

"Well, imagine you did have a garage. What if you went out there one day and it was empty, then the next day you went out again, opened the door, and a car was sitting there. What would you think? Did the car materialize out of thin air or did someone drive it in there?"

"Damn!" I cursed, my sadness quickly turning to anger. "What the hell is AIDS?" I demanded; my mind filled with confusion. "I don't even understand what it is!"

Bane told me evenly, "AIDS is a form of viral cancer that resulted from the combination of two retroviruses – a bovine leukemia virus and a sheep visna virus. If these two viruses are combined, then injected into a human culture, what you get is the first retrovirus known to mankind."

I scratched my head with obvious confusion. "Tell me more."

"There were two doctors – Robert Strecker, famous for his 'Strecker Memorandum,' and Allan Cantwell – who were curious about this virus, so they punched the following words into a computer – bovine visna – and guess what they got."

"What?"

"The computer spit out reams of information that described a virus that was identical to the AIDS virus! Here, read this article," he told me, retrieving yet another piece of paper.

I grabbed the article and read about AIDS and the bovine visna virus: "It has the same morphology (shape), the same molecular weight, the same magnesium dependency; it has the same ability to kill cells; it

513

has the same T cell tropism (it attacks T cells); it has the same exact characteristics in cattle that AIDS does in humans. It produced a disease in cows, characterized by initial lymphomamphy within a few weeks of initial infection, followed by the production of antibodies against that virus, and subsequently, 5-7 years later, the cow died of a wasting disease – an immune deficiency."

"Unreal," I spat, crumbling the paper into a ball. "And it's so easy to pass along, isn't it?"

"You better believe it. To transfer the disease, all you need is a highly concentrated exchange of bodily fluids between two people. In other words, it you have sex without a rubber, or ram a dirty needle in your arm, you're going to eventually get AIDS."

"It's sickening, isn't it?" I whispered in a defeated tone.

"It is. But here's one last bit of information to pass along to your readers," Bane concluded. "Think of all the millions of people who have contracted AIDS over the years, and also how many died from it. Then, think of all the famous people who have lost their lives due to AIDS. They come from every walk of life – there are sports figures – Magic Johnson – musicians – Freddie Mercury, Liberace – movie stars – Rock Hudson – artists – Robert Mapplethorpe – plus dancers, theater stars, and countless others. AIDS has hit every group imaginable ... every one except high-ranking politicians and world leaders. Think about it, Thorn. Name one top-level politician that has died from AIDS. You can't do it, can you?"

"Not off-hand," I said quietly.

"And why do you think that is - because they're so much more virtuous, monogamous, and faithful than everyone else in the world?" Bane roared; his voice strong and demanding. "Think about it; then ask yourself, what are these monsters doing to us?"

At that precise moment, Honey, my black-and-brown tiger-striped cat, raced from the weeds with a ground mole in her mouth. Proud of what she had caught, Honey dropped the rodent at my feet. At first I thought it was dead, but the mole suddenly darted towards the woods. Intent on not letting it escape, Honey dashed toward it, pounced, then grabbed the mole in her mouth. After shaking her head a few times, she flung the creature in the air and pounced on it once again. Rather than laying a death blow on it, though, she batted it with her paw; playing, in effect, the ultimate game of cat-and-mouse.

Bane viewed this scene with interest, then laughed sarcastically, "There ya have it, Thorn -- the Controller and the victim. I can't think of a better way to end this conversation."

Saddened by the thought of his departure, I said softly, "When are you going to contact me again?"

"I don't know. I need to be careful. You better do the same."

And with those parting words, Bane strode toward the marsh as a setting sun cast eerie, extended shadows across the field.

CHAPTER SIXTY-THREE

TAXATION OR SLAVERY?

I would like to quote a paragraph from an editorial written by the folks at State College, Pa.'s *Centre Daily Times* on April 17, 2001:

"For the average Pennsylvania resident, every dollar earned between January 1 through early May is consumed by the direct costs of various levels of government, according to the Commonwealth Foundation, a conservative think tank based in Harrisburg. Another five weeks is consumed covering the costs of government regulation, according to figures used by the organization. Last year, the foundation said that when all those costs were added, average Pennsylvanians didn't begin to actually work for themselves until June 16."

Now, think about these startling figures.

- January – 31 days – all money earned given to the government – SLAVERY!

- February – 28 days – all money earned given to the government – SLAVERY!

- March – 31 days – all money earned given to the government – SLAVERY!

- April – 30 days – all money earned given to the government – SLAVERY!

- May – 31 days – all money earned given to the government – SLAVERY!

- June – first 16 days – all money earned given to the government – SLAVERY!

What is going on in this country? When Bane (in *The Man Who Runs Happy Valley*) said that we're halfway to slavery, he wasn't lying! Almost half of the money that we earn is surrendered to the government through some form of taxation or regulation.

Think about that!!!!! Since tax time has just passed, sit down and figure how much money you paid in total taxes last year. When you arrive at that figure, get a piece of paper and list all of the benefits you derived from those tax dollars, and put some type of value on it (if you were to get these benefits in the open market).

When you're all done, compare the list and see if you came out ahead, behind, or even from the money you paid in. If you think you came out behind, start presenting this scenario to other people and ask them the same question: Did you come out ahead, behind, or even?

I'll bet out of 100 people, 90 of them will say they came out behind. So, if everyone's losing, the logical question to ask is: WHO IS COMING OUT AHEAD?

I'll tell you who – all the people we've elected to the offices who are taxing us, and the one's who are getting paid off via graft.

Here's another way of looking at this situation. Say you made $40,000 dollars last year and you wanted to invest half of it ($20,000) in a stock. You do some research and you arrive at a company called ABC. You invest the money and then at the end of that year you receive a statement that tells you how you've benefited from your investment. Regrettably, though, it appears that you lost about $14,000.

What would any sensible person do? They'd pull their money out of ABC and find an alternate use for it. But what if XYZ Company is actually taking our tax dollars, and we're FORCED to keep investing in them every year despite the fact that we keep losing money hand over fist? So the next year you lose $14,000, and the next year $14,000, and the next year $14,000. Within ten years, guess how much money you've lost -- $140,000!!! And guess what you could buy with $140,000 – an entire house without even taking out a loan.

Is the picture becoming a little clearer now? Multiply that figure by every taxpayer in this country, and one thing becomes evident – SOMETHING IS WRONG WITH THIS PICTURE!

The only problem is – what are we going to do about it? We've already accepted a 48% taxation rate, so how high will it have to go before we do something about it? Will it be 50% ... 55% ... how about 60%?

I guarantee you it won't get any lower, so how about 65% of our wages STOLEN through taxation?

Maybe we'll even accept that amount ... but 70%? It's all up to us. How much longer are we going to tolerate this atrocity?

SECTION

TEN:

FINALE

CHAPTER SIXTY-FOUR

FROGS BEING BOILED TO DEATH IN A POT

Here's an analogy that my neighbor laid on me many years ago. He's a scientist, and although he never actually performed this experiment, he says it's true.

You have two pots of water on a stove – one holds *boiling water* and the other has water that is sitting above a low flame ... so it's lukewarm at best.

The next step involves a frog, which is a cold-blooded animal.

What happens if you drop the frog into the first pot of boiling water? The frog becomes immersed, then IMMEDIATELY jumps out – scalded and scarred – but still alive.

Now, if you drop a frog into the second kettle, which is just a *little* warm, the frog will adjust to the temperature and stay there.

The "hook" to the story is this – the experimenter, with his frog settled in the pot, can slowly turn up the heat by *small* increments, ever so slightly increasing the temperature ... but not by noticeable amounts ... until the water begins to boil and the frog eventually dies.

My neighbor said it's true. The frogs will stay in this environment until they eventually burn to death.

Isn't this an appropriate analogy for what's going on in our lives in regard to the government? We're the frogs being boiled to death by those in control.

Isn't it clear to everybody? Those in power rarely do things in a dramatic fashion or with wide-sweeping, drastic strokes. All they do is keep turning up the heat ever so slightly ... look at taxes, our losses of freedom, bureaucratic impositions, etc.

I hate to say it, but we're the frogs!

CHAPTER SIXTY-FIVE

DAVID ROCKEFELLER SPEAKS

Breaking News: Late last night, President George Bush admitted to *The Economist* Magazine that not only did he and other members of his Cabinet know about the 9-11 terrorist attacks on the World Trade Center in New York City, but that they also allowed them to happen so that American oil companies could further maximize their profits in the Middle East and Caspian Region of Turkmenistan.

Paul Wolfowitz, Deputy Secretary of Defense, confirmed this startling revelation to the *Washington Post* by saying that the airplanes in question were never actually hijacked, but were flown via remote-control into each skyscraper and the Pentagon while military jets were ordered to "stand-down" until this atrocity took place.

In another part of the world, Kofi Annan, Secretary General of the United Nations, held a press conference in Harare, Zimbabwe where he confessed that the AIDS virus did not happen 'randomly,' but was rather created by the World Health Organization in unison with rogue elements of the United States military in order to deliberately kill tens of millions of innocent people (or 'useless eaters' as they are called behind closed-doors). Annan further elaborated by saying that this genocidal program will continue indefinitely until "enough of the herd has been thinned."

While this startling news unfolded, *CBS Evening News* anchor Dan Rather broke into regularly scheduled prime-time programming to announce that the very foundation of American society – our right to a democratic vote – has been declared null-and-void, and that the American people have been bamboozled for the past twenty years via "Votescam." In other words, Rather said matter-of-factly, every President in recent memory has been 'selected' beforehand by a group of hidden Controllers, while the process of voting at the ballot boxes has been nothing but a ruse.

While all of these events took place, Alan Greenspan, Chairman of the Federal Reserve, sat before Congress under the glare of television cameras and laid it all on the line. He said in no uncertain terms that the Federal Reserve is a privately-owned, for-profit corporation, and that his international banker bosses laugh until their stomachs hurt over the tax system they've created to pad their already overflowing pockets.

Greenspan even went so far as to quote a Rothschild family member as saying, "The people of America, and indeed the world, are dumkopfs (idiots). They slave away at OUR companies and make US rich; then before we throw them a few scraps via their paychecks, we take our money first. Hell, we don't even take it … we STEAL it … anywhere from ¼ to 1/3 right off the bat. They don't even see it. And every year we raise their taxes and take even more! And what do they do about it? Nothing. They don't even fight back." All of the congressmen laughed uproariously as they left this session and hopped into their limousines, which took them to fancy steak and lobster houses.

George Tenet, CIA Director, got into the act by telling syndicated radio talk-show host Mike Gallagher his agency will increase its black-budget drug-trafficking practices while the FBI at the same time bolsters it War on Drugs. In other words, he said that while the CIA keeps bringing drugs into the country, the Justice Department will keep throwing the users into jail. He even said that President Bush might bring back Nancy Reagan's "Just Say No" program for good measure.

As this news flashed across computer screens the world over, David Rockefeller sat in a plush European boardroom with members of the Rothschild, Morgan, Warburg, and Bronfman families. And even though the above-mentioned revelations were highly damaging to the ruse they had perpetuated for decades, none seemed worried.

Mr. Rockefeller began with an air of superiority. "Why should we be concerned? Do you know what everyone on the Internet is going to do?"

"What?" one of his shadowy cohorts replied.

"They're going to tap out a message on their keyboards, then rifle it off into cyberspace. Then someone else will read it, post it on a message board; and continue tapping away. Hell, we rammed two jets into the World Trade Center, and now they know the truth about what we've done! THEY KNOW THE TRUTH! It's the same as when we blew-up the Murrah Federal Building in Oklahoma City and made Timothy McVeigh our fall-guy. But what are they going to do? Send more messages on their silly computers! It's a riot. Plus, we've also admitted that we actually STEAL their money via taxation, that we CREATED the AIDS virus to kill them off, that their votes DON'T matter, and that we're going to start shipping their sons and daughters off to another Vietnam War in Iraq to DIE so that WE can make more profits for our energy and drug cartels. They all know the truth now … there's no more doubt about it – and what do they do? Sit in padded chairs in front of their computer screens and type out messages to each other. It's like: "Hey, George, guess what. The government really DID know about the World Trade Center attacks, and they let it happen anyway. Now I'm going to see if I can find any information about the UFO's at Area 51.""

"Doesn't it trouble you, though, that there are so many people on the Internet finding out the truth?" another man blurted.

"Why should it?" Rockefeller smiled. "None of them are doing anything about it. Hell, they can read fifty articles a day. What do we care as long as none of them do anything about it? I laugh my ass off at all of them as they're tap tap tapping away. Why do you think we pushed this whole Internet idea on them anyway? To keep them secured to their screens and physically isolated from each other. It's hard to revolt against us when they're all sitting in front of a monitor."

"But David," a senior Rothschild official interrupted. "What if they start getting organized?"

"Then," Mr. Rockefeller sighed, "we have problems. But the good thing is; we control some of the most well-known 'alternative' news sites on the Internet. They're nothing but front-groups that give the appearance of being legitimate, but in reality they're nothing but plants."

"There's so much information on those sites, though," another man objected.

"That's true," Rockefeller said wryly, "but information is useless unless it's followed by action. I don't give a damn if they know every secret in creation … a lot of them already do! But as long as they don't do anything, let 'em keep passing their little articles back and forth."

"I agree," a stern-faced woman chimed-in. "But there's recently been talk about an independent Internet news and action group called WING – World Independent News Group – that's bringing all of these news services and websites together en masse so that they can actually challenge the mainstream media that we control."

"In all reality," Rockefeller responded, "this is currently the biggest challenge to our authority that exists in the world today. And if you want to know the truth, it would be so easy for them to pull-off. All they have to do is get a growing movement of regular, everyday citizens to see through our smokescreen, and in no time the illusion would be over. Once Americans; and people of the world in general, have lost utter faith in the credibility of our mass-conditioned media, we've lost the game. At the time being, most everyone questions the media, but they still tune-into

CNN and read *Time* Magazine. What a bunch of dupes. But if a viable alternative presents itself that is above and beyond the lies that we tell ... in other words ... if they tell the truth and expose us on this WING site – it's all over. And here's the clincher. The other night we listened to a telephone conversation between Victor Thorn and a well-known reporter, and she said that she couldn't believe that ANY of the alternative sites wouldn't want to be a part of this movement. And guess what. The everyday people who read Thorn's ideas are adamantly in agreement with him. But it's a few of the crucial alternative websites that aren't lending their support by informing their readers. And do you know why? Because they're the ones we control. They'll keep churning out articles and posting them on their sites, but when it comes to taking action, all of a sudden these sites are strangely silent. Why? Because they work for us! The techniques we use with these 'alternative' sites are the same ones we use in the mainstream media! We marginalize, we refuse to act, we alter and distort, and we refuse to run material or cover stories by certain people. I mean, why don't more of these cyberspace people see through our ploys? It's so clear, and the tactics we use are older than dirt. We're blatantly screwing them in the guise of providing 'secret' knowledge. But all-in-all, these 'traitor' sites keep people inactive, and inaction is our greatest ally. It's only when people stand-up and ACT that our power is threatened. All they'd have to do is ask themselves, which sites aren't promoting WING, then they'd have a starting point to figure out who the 'plants' are."

"And what do you expect in the future?" an aged European man inquired.

"Nothing but more of the same!" Rockefeller beamed. "I mean, look at these people. I've been waiting for them to rise up and REVOLT for years now, but they just keep sitting around letting us crap on them. We raise their taxes and they do nothing. We allow their Trade Centers to get attacked; then lie about it afterward, and they still do nothing. Now we plan on sending their children into war, and they sit back and take it. If I were them, I'd be out in the streets in a heartbeat with torches and guns ready to string us up by our feet! We keep manipulating them over and over and over again ... but they don't react. Why? C'mon, put up a fight!" Rockefeller roared, swinging his fist in the air. "We're going to kill your damn kids again. That's all war is anyway – one slave class killing another slave class for us – the ELITE CLASS. Then we make more money, gain more control, and steal more money out of their paychecks. It really blows my mind how they can allow us to steal their money; especially when we don't pay any taxes at all. We've figured out years ago how to get around that nonsense." Rockefeller took a deep breath and concluded, "Anyway, that's where we currently stand. We're still firmly in control, and if the people keep tap tap tapping on their keyboards and sending articles around, then nothing will change and the status quo will prevail. But if they decide to truly organize and stop putting up with our lies, we'll be out of business before we know what hits us!"

CHAPTER SIXTY-SIX

DO WE CARE ENOUGH TO SAVE AMERICA?

I'm not going to address you by saying, "My fellow Americans" or any of that other phony nonsense. Nor will I speak to you in a calm soothing voice as if you're eighth graders like Hillary Clinton and Al Gore do. They don't have any respect for you. In fact, they view the "everyday man and woman" with disdain. But I still believe in you. Also, things are so grave in the world today I don't have time to mess around with such trivialities.

Instead, I plan to lay out the truth in stark terms without any of the silly games other politicians play. So here goes.

If we allow the Controlling faction of international bankers, multinational corporate heads and secret society members to continue their rule of America, the luxuries, rights, privileges, and benefits that we currently enjoy will soon be gone. Take a look at what's happening in the world today. We're on the brink of WWIII. We're already at war with Afghanistan. Then there's Saddam Hussein and the twisted butchers in Iran and Iraq, plus the Jews and Palestinians tearing each other's throats out. When America intervenes in these blood baths, North Korea will invade South Korea; then Inda will invade Pakistan. Do you remember the Allied/Axis division in World War II? George Bush has already thrown down the gauntlet, setting us against the "Axis of Evil." Does the terminology sound eerily familiar? It should, because the same forces that manipulated and financed every war of the 20th century are the same ones setting the stage for WWIII.

Please, listen! We need to either save this nation right NOW, or surrender it! The people of the United States don't control their government. Worse, neither do our elected officials.

Then who does? Answer: an evil oligarchy lurking in the shadows. These deceitful devils, representing a "New World Order," have their sights set on bringing the American reign to an end, then leading the monstrous nation of China to the forefront as the world's next exploited superpower.

Folks, this is what's happening. Don't listen to the lies on TV, or to the propagandists that are weaving a masterful illusion. America is going to be brought to its knees.

Think it can't happen? Neither did the Romans, the French, Genghis Khan or the British Empire. But guess what? As arrogant and mighty as they all were, each was defeated and replaced by another. The British, one of the greatest dynasties of all time, NEVER thought they'd be knocked from the top of the mountain. But they were -- by us!

Now we think the same way. America is the greatest -- economically, militarily, socially and morally. And do you know what? I believe all these things, too. But a sick, nefarious cabal of evil men is plotting our demise as we speak.

How so? Realistically, America is not equipped at this moment to fight a war on more than one front (thanks to those who manipulated Bill Clinton). But with Afghanistan, Iraq/Iran, and the Israeli/Palestinian debacle, we'll be spread too thin. Then if India, Pakistan and the Koreas flare up, all hell is going to break loose and we won't be strong enough to contain the situation. That's where China enters the picture.

Did you know that the Red Army has as many soldiers in their military as we have people in our ENTIRE country? Think about how scary that is. Once we spread ourselves too thin in war after war, the Chinese are going to come in and wipe us away on the battlefield. Once that happens, the stock markets will collapse, financial havoc will ensue, and America will be thrust into a nightmare like none they've ever seen before.

Take a look at the big picture. We are on the verge of disaster in this country, and no one is doing anything to stop it. The people who are aware of it -- and I highly commend them -- can only go so far. But let's be truthful. More books, magazines, articles and videotapes aren't going to stop the juggernaut of destruction. Have they so far? No! And here's the reason why:

The Controllers, those people running the world, are evil. Pure and simple. If you don't believe me, look at what's happening. One-hundred thousand people die every day from starvation on this planet. One-hundred thousand! And guess what? We currently have the money, resources, and technology to feed every one of them. But we don't. We let them go so long without food that they DIE!

Who's running this world? It seems to me that they're adults, but they sure don't behave like it. These people have wealth beyond comprehension, but they don't act to make our world better. We're still killing each other like crazy, with the United States now ready to invade Iraq.

Haven't we learned anything? Can't these ADULTS do any better than to let people starve, or supply them with weapons so they keep killing each other?

Yes, think about it. Where are these wars being waged? Along the castle-lined rivers of affluence in Europe, or the fancy mansion rows of Long Island or Washington, DC? Of course not. Poor people are waging the wars. Most of them don't have enough money to feed their families or build houses that we would even consider living in by American standards. Yet, mysteriously, they have guns and rocket launchers to kill each other with.

Where are these weapons and resources coming from? Do they suddenly appear out of thin air? Hardly. They come from the "foreign aid" that the Controllers give them.

How many years have we been giving them this supposed "foreign aid" to end starvation? At least four or five decades, yet 100,000 people die every day from hunger. How many billions of dollars have we spent around the world to create peace? But we still have over 30 wars going on, with WWIII possibly right around the corner.

Doesn't the entire situation seem preposterous? Something's not right, and it isn't right because certain factions are guaranteeing that it's NOT made right. These factions are what we call the Controllers -- the New World Order, the Trilateral Commission, the Council on Foreign Relations, the Bilderbergs and the Club of Rome (among others).

These people want to create a one-world political, economic, and religious framework that will once and for all put an end to the sovereign existence we currently enjoy in America.

The ONLY way to stop these destructive forces is to EXPOSE them, then takeover the system they currently monopolize. Their ultimate plan is to assume absolute control by turning chaos into order.

This cabal controls all the banks, and they control most governmental entities. Using these two vehicles, with a compliant media to pave the way, the shadow powers will launch the next Great War. The terrorist attacks on 9-11 were a symbolic beginning, and if you think that catastrophe was horrific, WWIII will truly sicken you. This is going to be the real thing -- obliteration on a grand scale that mankind has never seen before.

But to the Controllers, war is a necessary step in their overall plan. Why? Because once we get so sick of the bloodshed and violence ... when we can't tolerate even one more second of fighting ... we'll finally lie down and accept their New World Order. Can't you see? It's CONTROLLED CONFLICT, and they're the ones in charge. They'll kill millions of innocent people -- they already have -- in order to promote their agenda and seize more control. As I said, fear and chaos will be the main ingredients in the equation. Out of chaos ... order ... a New World Order.

Some will say there is no such thing as the "Illuminati" or "Controllers." To them, history is nothing more than a series of random events. But don't believe them. Franklin Roosevelt said it best: "In politics, nothing happens by accident. If it happens, you can bet it was planned that way."

Folks, I implore you to listen. The greatness of this country is about to be taken from us. We're not as invincible as we once thought. Our fallen World Trade Center towers prove that. We are very vulnerable and very replaceable. Why? Because, quite simply, China now holds more economic potential than we do. Think about it. China is a virtually undeveloped market with over a billion residents, many of them without simple modern luxuries that we ignore like telephones and televisions. To the Controllers who have seized world control primarily via financial means, China is the ultimate frontier ... the final payoff.

Look at the British Empire of old. They had the greatest military on earth, the greatest banks, and the most advanced political system ever known. They were literally "king of the hill." But did their dynasty endure forever? No. We became the next superpower because, in simplest terms, we held more potential.

America was bigger; it could hold more people, and it could be exploited economically a thousand times more than England. So we REPLACED them.

Now look at China. Unlimited land, a billion people, and 99% don't have a tenth of the appliances, gadgets, vehicles, and "toys" that we enjoy. They are very EXPLOITABLE. Also, the labor is extremely cheap; and even better, the Chinese have never known freedom -- ever! That means they won't be trouble makers like us pesky Americans with our Constitution, free speech, guns, and Bill of Rights.

They're already a slave culture, and always will be. Americans will soon be implanted with microchips to guarantee their docility. But the Chinese don't even need them. They're already genetically hard-wired for pacification.

With all this information in mind, what are the leaders of our country doing? Everything in their power to stop China's economic locomotive? Hell no! The Controllers behind-the-scenes are using America -- our great nation -- to facilitate China's ultimate rise.

We are the ones who are operating under trade agreements that benefit the Chinese while harming our domestic producers and manufacturers. Our trade imbalance with them is so insulting it's a crime. In addition, we have given them "most favored nation" status. We are also giving them their computer hardware, technology and know-how to build their technological infrastructure.

We make sure our President visits them regularly to pave the way for even further advances. It was our ex-President (Bill Clinton) who gave them nuclear technology so that they could further develop their atomic weapons.

We are cows being led to slaughter, and we don't even know it! How are you going to like it when the next world leaders speak to you in Chinese?

This is the bottom line: America is being deliberately destroyed by a hidden cabal of Controllers who are intent on furthering their own agendas at our expense. Don't you get it? They're using us as a means to an end.

What does it take to get you mad or enraged? We need to topple this regime! And that's what it is -- a political and economic monopoly that's sick in its depravity -- a thousand times worse than all the legions of organized crime.

Look at what they've done. They toppled the World Trade Center right before our eyes. They've assassinated presidents in broad daylight, created the atrocious AIDS virus, assumed total control of our media, stolen our vote via Votescam, and lie to us every step of the way.

Wake up! They're killing us without conscience, undermining our way of life, and setting us up for a brutal downfall. Worse, they're doing it while we wave flags and rally around their War Machine. Try to imagine life when we're no longer the world's ultimate super power. Instead of the U.S. calling the shots, we'll be listening to and looking up at the Chinese Communists as they parade around on center stage.

We won't have as many freedoms, we won't have as much money (a much lower standard-of-living), and we won't have nearly as much dignity. We will be reduced to followers instead of leaders, no longer masters of our own destiny.

How will you enjoy being dominated by the United Nations and the Red Chinese? How much will you enjoy paying a World Tax? How will you like no longer being able to speak freely? The Chinese people aren't blessed with freedom of speech at this moment. Do you think they'll let you embrace it once they assume control? Not a chance. And guns? Forget about it. They'll all be gone.

As it stands now, the United States of America, as a whole, is eating steak while many other parts of the world settle for Hamburger Helper (or worse). It's a great feeling to eat until we're filled. But how will you feel if you are the one eating slop while the United Nations and Chinese dish it out to you? The taste will be even more bitter if we knew we had a chance to alter this situation and didn't do anything to change it while we could.

Yes, we have things pretty good in this country for the time being. But if we refuse to act, if we settle into a state of complacency and if we're too afraid to stake everything we have on keeping what we have, I assure you, it will be gone.

I liken this situation to someone who owns a 50-room mansion. This person hires some servants and agrees to pay them a certain wage. He tells the workers what to do and they do it. But over time, the servants begin to take control of the mansion. When they see they can get away with it, they start giving themselves pay raises and hiring more and more workers to suck up an even greater portion of the homeowner's money.

If that's not bad enough, the servants start telling the homeowner what to do! In other words, the servants are giving the owner orders! But y'see, these servants aren't really calling their own shots. Rather, some hidden outside agitators infiltrated their ranks; then took over the show.

In the end, the homeowner loses complete control of his house while the servants run wild doing whatever they please as the outside infiltrators move on to take over a new property with an unwitting owner.

Can you see the parallels to our own situation? We're the homeowners and the 50-room mansion represents the United States of America. The servants are our elected officials, while the hidden agitators symbolize the Controllers. Regrettably, this metaphor has come true in our country, and the results are obvious. We've lost control of our own home -- our nation -- to a band of sinister manipulators who act in their own best interest, not ours. These servants have become so arrogant in their power, they're virtually unreachable.

You don't believe me? Try to get a face-to-face meeting with Congressman Hillary Clinton. It's virtually impossible to have her even respond to an e-mail.

Isn't it clear? The people on TV are lying to you, and they've been lying to you for eons. Dan Rather's job isn't to give you the nightly news. It's to give you a daily dose of conditioning. In fact, do you know what CNN stands for? Conditioning, Not News!

Likewise, our government leaders don't make any decisions (at least meaningful ones). They only implement those made by the ones who pull their strings. Why? Because the people who call the shots aren't located in Washington, DC.

The real power brokers sit in New York City skyscrapers and tell our "selected" officials in the nation's capital what to do. I'm sorry to say, that is the brutal reality of our situation.

At this point, we need to ask ourselves: Is America worth fighting for? And I don't mean against some cave-dwelling psychopaths in Afghanistan. I mean for the true, essential soul of our country -- the America we've come to know and love.

If you're not sure, then I need to ask another question. Do you want to be a citizen or a servant? What's the difference? A citizen takes responsibility for their rights and freedoms and fights to preserve them. A servant simply follows orders that are bestowed on them from above. The choice is clear. Citizens will fight to keep America first; servants will lie down and allow themselves to be trampled over by the New World Order.

If you are willing to fight to save this great nation, what must you do? First: EXPOSE the lying, sick, evil devil-dog New World Order. Once everyone sees what their true motives are, it will be much easier to overthrow them. And yes, I am talking about revolution! But don't get me wrong. I'm not referring to the overthrow of our American government -- only those secretive, hidden Controllers who have slithered their way into it.

Of course they're going to fight back, but don't allow yourself to be sucked into their deceit machine. Y'see, here's how they operate. It's all based upon the old notion of "divide & conquer." To implement this technique, nearly every bit of information given to us is based on five variables: race, gender, class, party and religion. Look at your local newspaper or watch the nightly news. Almost every story is intended to divide us. Whether it's man vs. woman, black vs. white, Muslim vs. Christian, gay vs. straight, old vs. young, rich vs. poor, or Democrat vs. Republican, the result is still the same.

The longer we keep fighting against each other, the less time we'll have to focus our attention on the REAL enemy -- the Controllers.

So don't fall for these obvious tricks any more. Instead, start calling your local newspaper or TV station. Don't just suggest to them ... DEMAND that they start running stories on how destructive the New World Order and its Controllers are.

Don't let them off the hook. Call every day and tell them you refuse to be inundated with spin doctoring and propaganda day-in and day-out. Then tell every one of your friends and relatives to do the same. It won't take long before they get the idea.

In the same vein, I need to address the media directly. Whether you admit it or not, or whether you even know it or not, you're playing an increasingly vital role in implementing this New World Order.

But I'm going to level with you -- you're being duped, either wittingly or unwittingly.

What's the solution? Don't take it any longer. Defy your editor, owners, and station heads. Run stories that tell the truth, not just a slew of sanitized lies. I implore you; don't let the Controllers bamboozle you. You are responsible for the truth. Start giving it to us.

The final step is to get someone into HIGH elected office that hasn't already been bought, sold and controlled by the Council on Foreign Relations, the Trilateral Commission, or the Bilderbergs. It's our only hope. Thomas Jefferson once said there should be a revolution every generation to keep those in power honest.

That revolution is long overdue. We need a true revolution ... not one to overthrow the framework of our government, but one that will finally rid our political system of the slimy, sickeningly evil Controllers.

If you think America is worth fighting for, this is what we have to do. I don't know about you, but I'm throwing my hat in the ring and coming out swinging.

CHAPTER SIXTY-SEVEN

THE OUTLAW CLASS: AMERICA'S LAST HOPE

I hear it all the time: somebody should do something to change the way things are in this country. But the big question is: who's going to be the one to step forward and change things? Well, let's see. Is it going to be the Controllers/ruling class? Hell, no. They're the ones responsible for putting the world in this predicament in the first place. They're the evil Princes of the Earth – the manipulators – the usurers – the death-mongers and the bloodsuckers. These are the Sons of Darkness, the ones who have the money, resources and technology to feed every person in the world, yet allow 100,000 people to die of starvation every day. These are the psychotic Nazi eugenicists who created a godawful AIDS virus to wipe out large segments of the population.

These are the same Controllers who steal our money through illegal taxation and interest-bearing loans to our government. They've devised a way to steal our voices at the ballot boxes via electronic "Votescam," and orchestrated a "terrorist attack" on our New York City skyscrapers to further fuel their sick/hungry War Machine and to further implement more pervasive Big Brother tactics. When one looks around the world and sees a multitude of horrors, often the Controllers' invisible hand is behind the scenes pulling the strings.

The ruling class are the manipulators, the provocateurs; a leisure-class of bloodline-obsessed power freaks who conceal their motives, identity, and sources of hidden occult knowledge to further propagate their elitist status at the expense of all else (including the future of this planet and humankind itself).

Why doesn't somebody do something about these sadistic control junkies? That's a good question, especially when those with the most ability to affect serious change in the world – the Enforcement Class – are so attached to "vested interests" that they refuse to do what's right because it might affect their vaunted "position in life."

What do I mean? Well, most every member of the Enforcement Class – the military, police, politicians, judges, lawyers, and media (among others) realize there are things seriously wrong with this country -- but they still have it better than most, so why upset the apple-cart?

The crucial concept to remember is that of "vested interests" – doing what most benefits oneself without considering the ramifications of a bigger picture. If viewed in these terms, you can understand why the CIA is the world's largest drug trafficker (it provides extra black-budget money outside of Congressional inspection), why police forces in general don't want to completely eradicate crime (it would put them out of business), why the military is pro-war (it's their livelihood), or why politicians promote inherently flawed social programs (it keeps certain voters dependent upon them and perpetuates a system of conflict in which people must "turn to them" to solve their problems).

The examination of vested interests is one of the most essential tools in understanding our world power system, for it goes hand-in-hand with CONTROL!

The War on Drugs is a perfect example of what a horrendous scam-job is being pulled on us. Why? First of all, every drug agency in the world has a vested interest in addiction. Without it, they'd be on the streets looking for a new job. By the same token, with this "scourge" or fear, people are conditioned to turn to their "selected" leaders for guidance in this matter. When coupled with crime, terrorism, and inner-city problems, we become as dependent upon government as a junkie is on heroin. Finally, to "solve" this problem, our statesmen and media keep drumming up the "fact" (which is actually a fallacy) that they need more money to win this battle.

And what does more funding imply? You guessed it – higher taxes!

In all, the epitome of vested interests is played out in this simple "war on drugs" scenario. The CIA traffics the drugs, law enforcement allows it to keep occurring on the streets at an "acceptable" level, the legal system prosecutes those who are unlucky enough to get busted (thus in the best interest of lawyers, judges, court officials, and prison employees), while the government Machine keeps sucking out more money to feed itself.

It isn't real hard to figure this stuff out. In fact, there is one entity that could very easily blow the lid off this entire shell game. And who would that be? The yellow-spined, pusillanimous, corporate-controlled American mass media. These folks aren't as sleazy as lawyers, as destructive as military men, as hypocritical as our religious leaders, or as corrupt as politicians; but they're still among the lowest and vilest of the lot because more than any other, they could take a stand to change our current situation.

But they don't because they've sold their souls for a paycheck, job security, and a certain amount of phony status.

These people are cowards who slavishly turn a blind eye to the deeds of drug traffickers, murderers, traitors and sexual predators. And by doing so, their silence becomes equated with complicity. By serving as one of the Controllers' enforcers, they enable the crimes taking place in this country to continue. I would like to ask every journalist, reporter, news anchor and writer one question: How can you look at yourself in the mirror when you keep doing the Elite Class' dirty work?

Some of you say you're committed. Committed to what: Money, prestige, and security -- or the TRUTH? Don't just stop at finding the truth or telling the truth ... EXPOSE IT!! Drop the smokescreen of propaganda and disinformation and give us the truth. It's your responsibility, so take it seriously.

If the Elite Class and the Enforcers won't step forward to make life better for the whole of mankind, then who will? The middle-class everyday worker? I'm sorry, but they've been overloaded with such a burden, they're simply not equipped for such an undertaking -- at least at this moment. But to their credit, if enlightened and enraged enough, these folks will be on our side. And once they start ripping and tearing, the Controllers had better look out.

There are a lot more of US than there are of them, and that scares the hell out of the ones at the top of the control pyramid.

If no one else is willing or able to take the initiative to change our world, who else is left? The Outlaws! Our last hope. The final vestige for change.

The Outlaws – those who stand outside the conditioning process – those who refuse to bow and conform – those who can see beyond the veils, lies and illusion. The Outlaws – those who are sick and tired of the status quo crimes and corruption – those who are truly committed to taking us to the next level rather than allowing these creeps to keep dragging us down.

In all honesty, take a look at the world the Controllers have created. Has anything dramatically changed in the last 2,000 years? We still have people starving to death, murderers, rapists, greedy politicians, and an overall system that is corrupt to the core which benefits the wealthy while enslaving those beneath them.

Are you content being a dirty-dog slave that the Controllers use, manipulate, spit upon and ultimately laugh at as fools? Do you like the sound of this scenario? Does it fill you with an overwhelming sense of life-affirming pride and joy? Do you prefer having a boot stomping on your face, or are you finally fed-up with their crap?

If you are fed up, then it's time to become an OUTLAW – a rebel against the status quo – one who's ready to tear down the current system and eliminate completely those Controllers who've turned our world into one on the brink of WWIII. It's either that, or we can shrug our shoulders and say, "Oh well, that's the way things have always been" -- as the elite Globalists steal more of your money and throw salt into your open wounds … and as you slave away another day.

Before continuing any further, I suppose we should define exactly who comprises the Outlaw Class. The best explanation I've discovered to date was laid out by Professor X in *Babel # 59*. He begins by saying that, "the Outlaws are given this pejorative term by the ruling, enforcement, and slave classes because they seriously threaten them." He continues, "They're rarely mentioned, but if so, are excoriated in the severest terms by the media. They're code-named "right wing extremists," "Constitutionalists," "gun-nuts," "white supremacists," "fanatics," and other terms designed to evoke instantaneous and knee-jerk rebuke."

One may wonder: why would all of the above classes be made to feel so uneasy by the Outlaws? Professor X explains, "The 'Outlaws' represent the most dangerous threat to the ruling class because if their ideas were allowed to proliferate, the slave class could possibly be awakened and there would be real danger that the system could turn against the ruling class."

Thus, Professor X tells us, "The Outlaw Class lives more or less in secrecy, and very little is known about this class and very little is ever written or published about this class other than the "illusions" created … once again … by the media that is limited to printing the party line."

But lo and behold, here it is – *Babel Magazine* – quite possibly one of the greatest ongoing documents that chronicles a wide-array of activities and personalities associated with the Outlaw Class. We're not hiding; we're not concealing what we're doing, and we're certainly not suppressing our intentions and ideas. We're the ones on the fringe – at the edge of the bell curve – those who aren't satisfied with being held down, stifled, silenced, or screwed over.

The Controllers would like nothing more than to eradicate our rebellious voices, but as Professor X once again explains, "Any attempt to stamp out members of the Outlaw Class calls attention to the fact that there even *is* an Outlaw Class, and this might distract some in the Slave

Class from their primary allegiance, which is dedication to the objects of their indoctrination ... the ruling class."

Isn't it obvious? Who are you aligning yourself with – the Big Brother Overlord who spits on you and enslaves you, or those who seek freedom and truth? At the end of George Orwell's *1984*, the people are so resigned, conditioned and accepting of their overbearing tyranny, they come to LOVE it.

America is in dire straits, and if we want to change our situation and save this great nation, we're going to have to do it ourselves. The media won't help because they are a conditioning tool used by the Controllers to keep us in line. The military is only interested in feeding their bloodthirsty War Machine, and the Democrats and Republicans are merely two heads of the same single-bodied serpent.

The legal system gets its kick from laws and steel bars and handcuffs (all of which are utilized to once again keep us in line), and secret societies conceal their knowledge to preserve; then expand, their power base. In other words, none of these forces are ultimately on OUR side.

So, is everything hopeless? Hardly. But how can we overcome so many entrenched institutions? Easy. For once in our lives we need to join together instead of letting the Controllers divide and conquer us. Rather than our usual battles – black vs. white, men vs. women, liberal vs. conservative, rich vs. poor, or Catholic vs. Protestant, we need to ally ourselves with our only hope – US.

If we don't, I GUARANTEE you that in one year, five years, or ten years, not only will things not be better for us; they'll be worse. And passing information from one computer to the next is not enough. It takes ACTION – a revolution of information, economics, and outlook. We need to change our way of thinking and then run the Controllers out of town – EVERY TOWN!

It's now up to you, and you, and you and you and you! Are you willing to settle for the status quo, or do you seek a better life for yourself, your family, and your nation? We need action, and we need a REVOLUTION!

CHAPTER SIXTY-EIGHT

AN INTERVIEW WITH VICTOR THORN BY J. CONTI OF BANKINDEX.COM

J.C.: Hello, Victor. It's a great pleasure to have you. Please tell us a little about yourself, about the books you have written, and the driving force behind such controversial topics.

V.T.: The driving force behind my political writing is fairly simple - I see this country being deliberately undermined by hidden forces that have seized control of our government by nefarious means, and thus use it to further promote their Globalist agenda. These shadowy figures, who I've labeled the Controllers, don't operate with our best interests in mind. Thus, the only hope we have left of saving this nation is to expose them in a dramatic way, then eradicate them as quickly as possible.

J.C.: Obviously you are passionate about your work and the message you're trying to convey to the public. Why is it so important for the public to hear what you have to say?

V.T.: In my opinion, the importance of what I write stems directly from survival and preservation. Do the American people enjoy being the world's premier superpower, and all that this privilege entails? Do we appreciate our financial status, and the freedoms we're essentially taking for granted? If we do, and this point is very serious - if we do cherish these ideals and rights, we better start acting like it because the die has been cast to alter the way of life we've become accustomed to.

It's time that we look beyond the veil and actually see what the Controllers are planning for us ... and believe me, these devils are consummate pianners. As of now, China is set to become the world's next superpower, while America will assume a subordinate position (a la Russia in relation to us right now). The reason that China will assume the reins of power isn't because they necessarily want to, but because they've been "selected" due to one elemental factor -- exploitation. If viewed from a historical perspective, you'll see what I mean. Three centuries ago, the British Empire stood proudly as the world's preeminent superpower. No one else compared in terms of military or economic might, and if you would have asked any Englishman if they'd ever get toppled from their throne, they would have thought the notion absurd.

But lo and behold, America entered the picture, and those with global, far-reaching aims realized the potential this land possessed. Following both the American and Industrial Revolutions, our vast potential became apparent in terms of land, resources, and promise. Or, as Alphonse Rothschild said in 1849 while visiting New York City, "Without the slightest doubt, this is the cradle of a new civilization."

So, America boomed, bailed out Europe in a couple of World Wars, and rose to become the greatest nation of modern times. But now China enters the picture with a population of one-billion people, most of whom don't have cellular phones, microwaves, DVD players, or automobiles. So what actions do the Controllers take? They "select" Globalist leaders to implement their plans by not only giving China "Most Favored Nation" status, but they also sell them all the computer software, hardware, and know-how to move them into our league. It's absurd, like cows deliberately walking into a slaughterhouse to be butchered. Thanks, Bill Clinton and George Bush (I & II) for selling us out. And that's only the tip of the iceberg. Don't even get me started on the atrocities of war, NAFTA, etc.

J.C.: Can you tell us about the American money system? That is, how it really works. I think an overview will benefit us all.

V.T.: For any country to truly prosper, it must have control over its money system. It's that simple. Financial independence (not being beholden to anybody) is the key. That's one of the main reasons why our Founding Fathers broke free from England. Not only did they seek religious freedom, but also financial freedom. Or, as historian Ralph Epperson noted, "The cause of the Revolution was the resistance of the colonies to the idea of borrowed money, resulting in debt and inflation, as well as interest payments, and not 'taxation without representation' as is commonly believed."

I'm afraid, though, that over two centuries later we're as enslaved as a nation can be by outside forces that control the entirety of our purse strings. The money system controls America; and those who call the shots

546

are not located in Washington, D.C., but in the financial centers of New York City and beyond (London, Paris, Germany, etc.). Right now our country pays approximately $360 billion a year in interest payments on the National Debt. That's $360 BILLION every year! Imagine how much we could accomplish with that money if it wasn't funneled into the pockets of men who are already wealthy beyond words. From my perspective, this is the least-common-denominator to how our money system works. Usury is one of the greatest evils on this planet.

J.C.: Now, about the Federal Reserve. It's no secret that you advocate the abolition of the Federal Reserve, but why? Tell us what makes this Corporation so dangerous in your opinion.

V.T.: The Federal Reserve CORPORATION (and remember, that's what it is -- a privately-owned, for-profit corporation) is dangerous because it has allowed outside influences to usurp our government. Thomas Jefferson once declared, "I believe banking institutions are more dangerous than standing armies." Antony Sutton, in *The Federal Reserve Conspiracy*," added, "Nothing is more dangerous to the power of the elite than the public discovery and understanding of the PRIVATE control of the money supply."

The dangers of this institution lie in the fact that it was created in 1913 on a premise of pure deception. Rather than being a part of the Federal Government, as its name implies, the Federal Reserve is actually closer to a "Central Bank" described by Karl Marx in *The Communist Manifesto*. Thus, the Federal Reserve System is an aggregate of private banks owned by international financiers who meet and make decisions behind closed doors. Since profits are an integral part of any business enterprise, what do you think the primary stockholders of the Federal Reserve (many of them foreign based) have as their highest priorities -- our welfare, or their own agenda? What's worse, money isn't even the predominant factor in their decision-making process. Hell, they already have fortunes beyond their wildest dreams. It was even estimated that in 1900, the Rothschild family owned half the world's total wealth! No, what's really frightening is that power and control are their main motivations, and in that sense we have to ask ourselves, does someone like David Rockefeller or his ilk sitting in skyscrapers overlooking New York City have the same priorities as we do? The answer is no, they don't. That's where the danger lies.

J.C.: Do you know who the actual owners of the Federal Reserve are? Can you tell us how the ownership of the Federal Reserve is split?

V.T.: In *Economic Solutions*, Peter Kershaw provided a list of the ten primary shareholders in the Federal Reserve banking system:

i)	The Rothschild Family - London
ii)	The Rothschild Family - Berlin
iii)	The Lazard Brothers - Paris
iv)	Israel Seiff - Italy
v)	Kuhn-Loeb - Germany
vi)	The Warburgs - Amsterdam
vii)	The Warburgs - Hamburg
viii)	Lehman Brothers - New York City
ix)	Goldman & Sachs - New York City
x)	The Rockefeller Family - New York City

What's truly appalling is that 7 of the top 10 stockholders in the Federal Reserve are located in foreign countries! Jim Marrs adds in his excellent book, *Rule by Secrecy*, that the Federal Reserve Bank of New York, which undeniably controls the 11 other Federal Reserve branches, is essentially controlled by two financial institutions:

a)   Chase Manhattan (a Rockefeller stronghold) - 6,389,445 shares - 32.3%

b)   Citibank - 4,051,851 shares - 20.5%

Thus, these two entities control nearly 53% of the New York Federal Reserve Bank. The power they have is mind-boggling.

J.C.: What about our National Debt? How does it work, and ultimately, who is all the money owed to?

V.T.: The National Debt at this time is approximately $5.9 trillion. Of that, $2.54 trillion is owed to international bankers, or 37%. The other $3.38 trillion is owed to the public. The interest we pay each year is approximately $360 billion. My solution to this colossal problem is as such:

a)   Default on that portion of the National Debt not owed to private American citizens. How can we do such a thing? Well, if a person defaults on their car loan or mortgage, what happens? The automobile or house gets repossessed. But what are the international bankers going to do -- repossess our country? Hardly. We simply tell them point-blank that we refuse to pay them any more interest, or the principal. It may mean going to war, but it's time to show the world that these bankers are the REAL terrorists.

b)   We make a one-time payment to all public holders of our National Debt.

c)   Finally, return the creation of money back to Congress as is written in the Constitution: Article 1, section 8, subsection 5. Only Congress has the right "to coin Money, and regulate the Value thereof."

As a side-note, our National Debt rose in just 30 years from $409 billion in 1971 to $5.9 TRILLION in 2002. That means when Nixon was President, we only owed 1/15th of what we owe today.

J.C.: How does the Federal Reserve operate? If at all, can you estimate their profit margin?

V.T.: This is the trickiest question of all, and I must admit that there are economic scholars who could discuss the nuts-and-bolts details better than I. But I'll give a brief overview to the best of my ability. The Treasury Department prints money for the Federal Reserve, then in turn lends it to our government, at interest.

Here's where the scam enters the picture. According to Davy Kidd in *Why a Bankrupt America*, it costs $23.00 to print 1,000 one-hundred ($100) bills. If you printed 10,000 of these bills, it would naturally cost $230.00 ($.023 x 10,000). But here's the catch. 10,000 $100 bills would equal $1,000,000! So, the cost of "creating" a million dollars is only $230.00.

Those in the financial industry call this practice "seignorage," but to me, it's closer to outright THEFT. In fact, I view the Federal Reserve in the same light as I do organized crime. This privately owned corporation "creates" money for practically nothing; then lends it to us with interest. Then, to cover its debt, the U.S. government imposes taxes on its citizens. The higher the debt, the more interest we owe, and thus the higher taxes become. It's a vicious cycle, and guess who ultimately wins - the Controllers.

J.C.: Do you think this is why as Americans we will never be able to finish paying what we owe?

V.T.: I'm not a fan of the Republicans, Democrats, Independents, Greens, or Libertarians, so please don't think I'm 'bashing.' I dislike all of them equally. Anyway, George Bush's 2002 Federal budget came to approximately $2.05 trillion. If you stacked this amount of money in one-dollar bills, it would reach all the way to the moon and half-way back again. The National Debt is three times larger, so these stacked dollar bills would stretch from the earth to the moon and back, then from the earth to the moon and back AGAIN, then halfway to the moon yet again. Hell, we have trouble even paying off the interest, let alone the principle, and with our War Machine set to roll at top speed again, the debt will only get worse.

J.C.: It has been said that the same people that own the Federal Reserve own the media, the big oil companies, and even have powerful ties to the government of the United States and those of other countries. If so, how does this affect the dynamics of a true democracy?

V.T.: You are correct in that there is a definite pyramid of control in the world, with the international bankers at the top of it, secret societies and European aristocracy/royalty below them, followed by the heads of international companies and old-money American families at the third level, with ... get this ... certain political leaders at the fourth tier. It is my assertion that these political leaders (George Bush, Bill Clinton, Ted Kennedy, etc.) aren't elected, but "selected" by groups such as the Council on Foreign Relations, Trilateral Commission, and the Bilderbergs. If Americans ever peered behind the veil and saw the Wizard of Oz illusion that controls their political system, they'd be shocked beyond belief.

In regard to the dynamics of a democracy, again, I would say it is nothing but illusion. Once we examine Votescam, black budget enterprises, membership to certain Globalist groups, and how the true political power base isn't located in Washington, DC but in New York City, we'd realize that our say-so in how this country is run is extremely limited.

J.C.: In your opinion, do we even live in a real democracy? The Internet is festering with material showing that we are living an illusion; that our leaders are fronting for the "elite," and reports of government misconduct can be found everywhere. What does it all mean?

V.T.: The best answer to this question can be found in the Bilderberg meeting that took place from May 30-June 2, 2002 at the Westfields Marriott in Chantilly, Virginia only 7 miles south of Washington, D.C. One hundred and twenty of the world's most powerful bankers, statesmen, politicians, military leaders, CEO's, royalty, and media members met on the outskirts of our nation's capital.

Now, when the world's greatest actors meet every year at the Academy Awards, does the media cover the event? Of course. When our two best football teams meet at the Super Bowl, is the media there? Naturally. The Grammy's -- the media is there. The Emmy's -- the media is there. Paul McCartney's wedding -- the media is there. The President's inauguration -- the media is there. Hell, the media even covers frog-jumping contests in rural Mississippi. But when the Bilderbergs or Trilateral Commission meet to discuss such topics as our impending war with Iraq, a UN sanctioned World Tax, terrorism, and America's dollar becoming the common currency of North, South, and Central America, NOT ONE media source except the *American Free Press* covered this vitally important event.

I contacted the National Editor at the Washington Bureau of the Knight-Ridder newspaper chain, the Executive Editor of our local newspaper, and a nationally syndicated radio talk show host (Mike Gallagher) urging them to cover this conference, while scores of other people notified the major TV networks, CNN, and high-profile newspapers and magazines such as *Time* and the *Washington Post* (who even had a representative present at the meeting). But none of them covered the event. Why? Because the same people who control the President, Congress, banks and major corporations also own the media. (Essentially, five major corporations own the entire mainstream media in this country.)

Of course government misconduct is rampant in America, such as illegal chemtrail spraying by the military and the U.N., but the biggest crime facing us is that our government has been usurped, and the media refuses to expose the power structure that exists behind the scenes. To them, the chain-of-command stops with George Bush or Bill Clinton. But nothing could be further from the truth. These individuals are nothing more than "implementers" of decisions made by the shadow government. If the media EVER let this cat out of the bag, our world would be dramatically different, so the "secret" is guarded with obsessive care.

J.C.: Do you see any relationship between the "elite" and 9-11? If so, can you explain?

V.T.: God, where to start on this one? I guess the best place to begin is with the preponderance of evidence pointing out in glaring detail that those in positions of power were aware that an attack was going to occur on the morning of September 11, 2001. And I'm not talking about vague generalities -- but precise times, dates, where's, when's, and how's. Obviously, due to space and time limitations I won't delve into specifics, but if anyone gets on the Internet and starts researching this subject, they'd be blown away by how much so many people knew.

The underground press, alternative news sources, and online websites have been writing about 9-11 foreknowledge since late 2001, and finally Congress has convened to look into this matter. The only problem is, I examined a list of members from both investigative committees, and guess who is manning them: almost every person is a member of the Trilateral Commission, the CFR, Bilderberg, or has received huge campaign contributions from the Carlyle Group or defense contractors. Similar to the Roberts Commission investigating FDR's foreknowledge of Pearl Harbor and the Warren Commission looking into JFK's assassination (both of which, naturally, were shams), these current sessions will be nothing more than window dressing.

Now, you may wonder, why would the Controllers allow hijacked jets to plummet into the World Trade Center and Pentagon? The answer is simple. Similar to the sinking of the Lusitania, Pearl Harbor, and the Gulf of Tonkin, Americans need a dramatic event to raise their ire and pull them into war. That's what 9-11 accomplished. We were rocked to our very core.

The result was also quite evident. (The Controllers' motives are SO easy to see once you know what to look for.) Anyway, by setting our sights on Afghanistan and getting the War Machine rolling, the elite are capitalizing on the three biggest "industries" or money-making ventures in the entire world: usury, energy, and drugs:

i)   Usury - The Controllers make vast amounts of money off of war because every country involved needs money to finance their efforts, so where do they get their capital? From the international bankers. And what results from loans? Interest -- lots and lots of interest. Once each nation gets their money for the War Machine, they need to buy bombs, guns, tanks, bullets, planes, etc. And where do they get these "necessities?" At the local Wal-Mart? Nope, they have to buy them from the major defense contractors that are owned by whom? Yup, the Controllers! In this country, if you investigate the Carlyle Group, you'll see how it fits part-and-parcel into our war efforts.

ii)   Energy - There are huge deposits of oil in the Caspian region of Russia, and we have a plethora of pipelines already in place in the Middle East. The energy companies find immeasurable benefits in getting this oil to the pipelines. The only problem is; there's a little country sitting between them -- Afghanistan.

iii)   Drugs - The CIA is the largest drug dealer in the world, and has been involved in drug trafficking since its inception 50 years ago (and even before then as the OSS). All of their black budget projects are financed by drug dealing, along with money laundering, illegal arms sales and gambling, etc. Afghanistan is the world's leading producer of opium (75% of the total), and a few years ago the Taliban stopped all production. Now, if the CIA is deriving huge amounts of money from heroin and opium and morphine, then this source suddenly dries up, there's a problem. Well, I've just read that since the Taliban have essentially been eradicated from Afghanistan, guess what's back in full production again -- you guessed it -- the poppy fields.

In all, we need to remember that by-and-large, wars don't start with the masses. They're incited by the Controllers to "create a condition" as Abraham Lincoln's Secretary of War, Edwin Stanton, said. And that's exactly what's happening right now. A New World Order is being created, and we're simply bit players in this Theater of War.

J.C.: What do you think the "elite" are after? Can they be stopped? If so, how?

V.T.: The Controllers' aim for centuries has been the establishment of an occult-based New World Order where national boundaries will all but be eliminated. There will still be certain "regions" such as the "Americas," but the world will more closely resemble modern-day Europe with a common currency and unified States. The United Nations, or a similar organization, will replace individual governments, and there will be global concepts introduced, such as a World Tax, World Court, World Anthem, and World Army.

Specifically in regard to America, there is a battle being waged between the Globalists and Nationalists (or Populists -- those who want America to retain its sovereignty and not fall under the rule of a global hierarchy). Regrettably, most of the national players you see on TV fall under the Globalist category.

Another concept that must be considered is the United States deliberately being undermined by its leaders who are in the employ of the Controllers. By ratifying treaties such as NAFTA and GATT and giving our technological and computer know-how to China, we're chopping ourselves off at the knees. The industrial base upon which we built the greatest nation of all time is being eliminated at a frightening pace. Also, when you see how our military is being dispatched (thinned-out) across the globe in preparation for WWIII, you'll understand how vulnerable our position is. Keep your eye on China -- they're the key.

J.C.: Let's say you had access to the floor of Congress for 10-15 minutes, and that all the members were present. What would you say to them?

V.T.: In all honesty, I don't think it would much matter what I had to say to Congress. Why? except for a few rebels, Congressional members are in a position where they're more than satisfied with the status quo.

Here's my rationale: First of all, years ago George Wallace said, "There's not a dime's worth of difference between the Republicans and the Democrats." And it's true. Oh sure, it "appears' as if there is, but in reality, the entire media-political scene is nothing more than professional wrestling. How can I make such a statement? Well, both have predetermined outcomes that are established out of public view, and both present the results in a dramatic fashion. It's all illusion, folks.

J.C.: Finally, what would you say to the American people?

V.T.: Pure and simple -- if you want to preserve the rights and freedoms that you've become accustomed to and if you'd like to see America remain "king of the hill," then immediate, decisive action must be taken. I'm talking about a revolution to overthrow the Controllers that have illegally taken possession of our government. Now don't jump to conclusions or get me wrong. I'm not saying that we should overthrow the government.

First of all, it's against the law to make such a statement, and secondly, there's nothing inherently wrong with our government in theory as it was envisioned by our Founding Fathers.

Problems arose when the international bankers, both foreign and domestic, seized control of our money supply. That's who we need to eliminate. If we don't, I promise you that our quality of life will dramatically decrease in the coming years. But how do we get rid of these devils? Here's a partial answer:

a)   Abolish the Federal Reserve System
b)   Default on that portion of our National Debt owed to international bankers
c)   Return the creation of money to Congress, as it was prior to 1913
d)   Abolish NAFTA, GATT, and all other Globalist treaties
e)   Impose tariffs on every product imported into this country

Do we have the guts and courage to save this nation, or are we going to rollover and play dead? The Controllers have committed so many crimes and atrocities against the American people, it's time to retaliate. There's an individual named Rick Stanley who's running for a Congressional seat in Colorado that's organizing a "Million Gun March" in Washington, D.C. next July 4th, 2003. Such an idea is precisely what we need -- to assemble in large numbers with guns in hand, or if you don't like guns, then take a shovel, broom, torch, or whatever else would have an impact and SHOW the Controllers that we're not going to allow them to hold us hostage any longer.

It's now or never. If we don't get organized and take back our country, it's all over. It's up to you to decide if America is worth saving, or if we're going to let the Controllers steamroll over us. I'm ready and willing to do my part!

CHAPTER SIXTY-NINE

AFTERWORD: HE WHO WOULD FACE THE WINDS
by LISA GULIANI

"Cautious, careful people, always casting about to preserve their reputation and social standing, never can bring about a reform. Those who are really in earnest must be willing to be anything or nothing in the world's estimation, and publicly and privately, in season and out, avow their sympathy with despised and persecuted ideas and their advocates, and bear the consequences."

~ Susan B. Anthony ~

"An individual who breaks a law that conscience tells him is unjust, and who willingly accepts the penalty of imprisonment in order to arouse the conscience of the community over its injustice, is in reality expressing the highest respect for the law."

~ Martin Luther King, Jr. ~

"The average man does not want to be free. He simply wants to be safe."

~H. L. Mencken ~

In my city, everyone's talking about college football these days. Soon, the hot topic will be our upcoming holiday season. Like so many Americans across the nation, the community of State College, Pa. appears to be sleepwalking right through the passage of both the Patriot Act and the newly enacted Homeland Security legislation. The people of this bustling community seem unaware of these events and continue about their lives with a "business as usual" mentality. Out on the street, in restaurants, and in the bars, no one is talking politics. Everyone seems completely insulated from what is taking place in their own country. The world directly in front of their eyes is the only one they see, and the only one in which they live. Citizens across the country suffer from a similar affliction. Maybe that is why the voices of the People of America are not being heard. Most of the "People" aren't talking about things that matter. As I walk along the streets of this city, snippets of conversation drift by, and it boggles my mind to know that I am but one of a small minority that even realizes just how fragile is the thread that connects us to our freedom. I want to characterize it as ignorance, but it's more than that. It's disinterest. I would be lying if I said that people seem to be worried about what's happening to their own country. So, I won't lie.

America, I'm trying to reach you. Can you hear me? I'm feeling for some faint pulse that tells me you're alive – and I'm having trouble finding it. Tell me, how can you remain oblivious to the destruction of your way of life ... of the erosion of your liberty? While you sit in your little worlds, wrapped up in your personal agendas, focused on college football and other "really important stuff," your "government" is insidiously erasing what's left of your sovereignty, your privacy, your right to self-govern - YOU – and they're doing it right before your eyes. What do you say, America?

While the majority of you lie sleeping at night, insulated from and blind to the reality that is all but smacking you in the face, there are others out there like me who lie in our beds at night restless with misgivings, wide awake and wondering as to what the dawn will bring. The 'disconnect' is more than perceptible; the chasm so wide I doubt it can ever be bridged. To initiate discussion among those who remain unaware or apathetic to the current state of the Union is to suffer the wrath of those who mock what they fail to understand. Let's just say that I raise more than a few eyebrows when I talk to people around here.

I know how our ancestors must have felt at the time of the American Revolution. I can feel their presence around me like a whisper of conscience. They stand at the shoulder of every Patriot – and I don't mean the ones with the flags and stickers all over their vehicles. I'm talking about the REAL patriots like those who drove to Washington, D.C. for Freedom Drive 2002. Their voices are the voices of justice. Their words ring with life, with passion, with principle. Like our predecessors, the real patriots are people of courage and conviction. If they know fear – and I believe they do – they don't let it defeat them or dictate their actions. The true patriot stands to face the winds rather than bowing to them. Our ancestors knew that in order to defeat the enemy, they would have to stand together and rise above their fear. This, they did – which is why the "concept" of America ever got off the ground in the first place. Open your eyes, people. There's more to life than football and Christmas

558

parties. I hate to bring this up, but those presents you're saving up for aren't the only things that will cost you. I am reminded of the Korean War Memorial, which summed it up perfectly: "Freedom Is Not Free". The bell is not merely ringing – the bell is TOLLING – if you can't hear it by now, maybe you're not just sleeping. Maybe you're dead.

If Paul Revere were to ride through the streets of my city on one of these very dark nights and sound the warning to every man, woman and child throughout, who would hear him? Would you, Joe Q. Citizen? Would you rise from your slumber and take up your arms? Would you even roll over in your bed? God, I hope so. Do you know that those liberties you possessed just yesterday may not apply to you today? Which of your "freedoms" will you kiss goodbye tomorrow? Can you hear me?

I am calling to you, America. Shake off the cobwebs that have gathered in your brain and sniff the Revolution in the air. It's not something you're familiar with because life has been easier for you than it was for those who came before you. But it is there, nonetheless. Regardless of how much your ranking in the world's estimation might matter to you, believe me when I tell you that it matters NOT. Besides, you will rank even lower if you sit back and let your country die without at least trying to save her. And if you do that, then all those that have come and gone before you – those brave souls who fought and gave their lives to save her – will have died for nothing. They died for YOU and me. Remember that.

The Patriots of the coming Revolution are standing in the midst of this madness. On the horizon looms more of the atrocity we've seen in recent times, only far worse and more all-encompassing. By virtue of its magnitude, it will dissolve any feelings of disconnection the majority of unsuspecting folks currently feel at the present time. We are in for another "jolt" by the powers-that-be. Will you arise when that "jolt" shakes you from your slumber, America? Will that far-reaching catastrophe get your heart pumping again?

Last night I spoke with Rick Stanley on *The Victor Thorn Show,* and he said "America is ruined". I'm not sure how many people listened to what this man had to say, but his words were full of fire and they deeply troubled me. You see, on the inside, I keep a flicker of hope burning for America to survive. There are others out there, scattered here and there, who also carry this flame. These people bear proudly the tattered vestiges of what's left of our heritage. They are the scorned and reviled, the dissidents and radicals. We also know them as Patriots. Seldom acknowledged for what they do, they still stand at the ready for the worst, which is inevitably yet to come. I don't know if America is ruined, but she sure is fading fast. Her light is dimmed and her breath shallow. How long will she last at this rate? We are but a blink away from losing her forever. And once she is gone, we will not be able to breathe the life back into her. Are you ready to face that day? I'm not.

My hope still lives. Regardless of how the rest of the world or my countrymen see me, I will hear the rallying cry of Revolution when it comes, and I will be on my feet and ready for the chips to fall where they may. What about you, America? When the winds shift, will you stand and face them with courage, or simply sit and let them blow you off the map? This generation – ours – has the chance to bend history. If we don't embrace this one opportunity we now have, then we willingly and recklessly forfeit those freedoms given to us so long ago by men of great courage and conscience. Does this generation possess that kind of strength of character? It makes me wonder. America, can you hear me? You really need to wake up now. Tomorrow may be too late.

BIBLIOGRAPHY

Allen, Gary. None Dare Call It Conspiracy. Concord Press, 1972

Allen, Gary. The Rockefeller File. Seal Beach, CA: '76 Press, 1976.

Alpine Enterprises. The Occult Technology of Power. Port Townsend, WA: 1974

Atlantis Rising Magazine. The Search for Lost Origins. Livingston, MT: Atlantis Rising Books: 1996

Baker, Jeffrey A. Cheque Mate: The Game of Princes. Springdale, PA: Whitaker House, 1993

Bamford, James. The Puzzle Palace: A Report on America's Most Secret Agency. New York: Penguin Books, 1983

Barranger, Jack. Past Shock: The Origin of Religion and its Impact on the Human Soul. Escondido, CA: The Prometheus Project, 1998

Bernard, Dr. Raymond. The Hollow Earth: The Greatest Discovery in History. New York: Carol Publishing Group, 1969

Borjesson, Kristina. Into the Buzzsaw: Leading Journalists Expose the Myth of a Free Press. Amherst, NY: Prometheus Books, 2002

Bramley, William. The Gods of Eden. New York: Avon Books, 1989

Carr, William Guy. Pawns in the Game. Palmdale, CA: Omni/Christian Book Club, 1958

Carr, William Guy. Satan, Prince of This World. Palmdale, CA: Omni Publications, 1997

Carrico, David. A Study of Freemasonry and its Relationship to the Occult and Satanism. Clackamas, OR: Emissary Publications, 1991

Carroll, Gerald A. Project Seek: Onassis, Kennedy and the Gemstone Thesis. Carson City, NV: Bridger House Publishers, 1994

Coleman, Dr. John. Conspirators' Hierarchy: The Story of the Committee of 300. Bozeman, MT: America West Publishers, 1992

Coleman, Dr. John. Socialism: The Road to Slavery. Carson City, NV: Joseph Publishing Company, 1994

Collier, James M. & Kenneth F. Votescam: The Stealing of America. New York: Victoria House Press, 1992

Constantine, Alex. Psychic Dictatorship in the U.S.A. Portland, OR: Feral House,1995

Cooper, William. Behold a Pale Horse. Sedona, AZ: Light Technology Publishing, 1991

Dawson, Lawrence. The Death of Reality. Boise, ID: The Paradigm Company, 1996

Douglas, Gregory. Regicide: The Official Assassination of John F. Kennedy. Huntsville,   AL: Monte Sano Media, 2002

Dunfield, Neil. Not So Self-Evident Truths: Discovering the Freemasons' Game. Courtenay, BC: Trilithon Publishing Ltd, 1992

Ettinger, Richard. The Ultimate Frontier. Quinlan, TX: The Adelphia Organization, 1963

Fox, Hugh. The Invisibles: A Dialectic. New York & London: Horizon Press,   1976

Garrison, Jim. On the Trail of the Assassins. New York: Warner Books, 1988

Gatto, John Taylor. Dumbing Us Down: The Hidden Curriculum of Compulsory Schooling. Philadelphia, PA: New Society Publishers, 1992

Girard, Robert L. The Revolt of the Free. Stone Mountain, GA: Arcturus Book Service, 1990

Griffin, Des. Descent into Slavery. Clackamas, OR: Emissary Publications, 1980

Griffin, Des. Fourth Reich of the Rich. Clackamas, OR: Emissary Publications, 1976

Gurudus. Treason: The New World Order. San Rafael, CA: Cassandra Press, 1996

Harris, Jack. Freemasonry. New Kensington, PA: Whitaker House, 1983

Haupt, Reginald C., Jr. The Gods of the Lodge. Savannah, GA: Victory Publishing Company, 1990

Hieronimus, Robert. America's Secret Destiny: Spiritual Vision & the Founding of a Nation. Rochester, VT: Destiny Books, 1989

Hoffman, Michael A. II. Secret Societies and Psychological Warfare. Dresden, NY: Wiswell Ruffin House, 1989

Home, Stewart: Conspiracies, Cover-ups & Diversions. London: Sabotage Editions, 1995

Howard, Michael. The Occult Conspiracy: Secret Societies – Their Influence and Power in World History. Rochester, VT: Destiny Books, 1989

Humphrey, George. Uncommon Sense. Austin, Tx, 2002

Huntington, Samuel P. The Clash of Civilizations and the Remaking of World Order. New York: Simon & Schuster, 1996

Jackson, Devon. Conspiranoia: The Mother of all Conspiracy Theories. New York: Penguin Books, 1999

Keith, Jim. Black Helicopters Over America & Strikeforce for the New World Order. Lilburn, GA: IllumiNet Press, 1994

Keith, Jim. Casebook for Alternative 3: UFOs, Secret Societies, and World Control. Lilburn, GA: IllumiNet Press, 1994

Keith, Jim. Mind Control World Control: The Encyclopedia of Mind Control. Kempton, IL: Adventures Unlimited, 1997

Keith, Jim. Secret and Suppressed: Banned Ideas & Hidden History. Portland, OR: Feral House, 1993

Keith, Jim & Thomas, Kenn. The Octopus: Secret Government and the Death of Danny Casolaro. Portland, OR: Feral House, 1996

Kershaw, Peter. Economic Solutions. Englewood, CO: Quality Press, 1994

Kick, Russ. September 11, 2001: No Surprise. Port Townsend, WA: Loompanics Unlimited, 2002

Kick, Russ. You Are Being Lied To: The Disinformation Guide to Media Distortion, Historical Whitewashes and Cultural Myths. New York: The Disinformation Company LTD, 2001

Kilduff, Marshall & Javers, Ron. The Suicide Cult: The Inside Story of the People's Temple Sect and the Massacre in Guyana. New York: Bantam Books, 1978

Kinman, Dwight L. The World's Last Dictator. Woodburn, OR: Solid Rock Books, Inc., 1994

Lammer, Helmut & Marion. MILABS: Military Mind Control & Alien Abduction. Lilburn, GA: IllumiNet Press, 1999

Lee, Martin A. & Soloman, Norman. Unreliable Sources: A Guide to Detecting Bias in News Media. New York: Carol Publishing Group, 1991

Manifold, Deirdre. Fatima and the Great Conspiracy. Constable, NY: The Fatima Crusade. 1982

Marrs, Jim. Rule by Secrecy. New York: Harper Collins, 2000

Marrs, Texe. Big Sister is Watching You. Austin, TX: Living Truth Publishers, 1993

Marrs, Texe. Circle of Intrigue: The Hidden Inner Core of the Global Illuminati Conspiracy. Austin, TX: Living Truth Publishers, 1995

Marrs, Texe. Dark Majesty: The Secret Brotherhood and the Magic of a Thousand Points of Light. Austin, TX: Living Truth Publishers, 1992

Marrs, Texe. Days of Hunger, Days of Chaos: The Coming Great Food Shortages in America. Austin, TX: Living Truth Publishers, 1999

Marrs, Texe. Project LUCID: The Beast 666 Universal Human Control Systems. Austin, TX: Living Truth Ministries, 1996

McManus, John F. The Insiders: Architects of the New World Order. Appleton, WI: The John Birch Society, 1992

Moon, Peter. The Black Sun: Montauk's Nazi-Tibetan Connection. New York: Sky Books, 1997

Moore, William L. & Berlitz, Charles. The Philadelphia Experiment: Project Invisibility. New York: Ballantine Books, 1979

Mullins, Eustace. The World Order: A Study in the Hegemony of Parasitism. Staunton, VA: Ezra Pound Institute of Civilization, 1985

Nichols, Preston B. The Montauk Project: Experiments in Time. Westbury, NY: Sky Books, 1996

Noone, Richard W. 5/5/2000: The Ultimate Disaster. New York: Three Rivers Press, 1982

O'Brien, Cathy & Phillips, Mark. Trance-Formation of America. Las Vegas, NV: Reality Marketing Company, 1995

Perloff, James. The Shadows of Power: The Council on Foreign Relations and the American Decline. Appleton, WI: Western Islands Publishers, 1988

Piper, Michael Collins. Final Judgment: The Missing Link in the JFK Assassination Conspiracy. Washington, DC: The Center for Historical Review, 1994

Ravenscroft, Trevor. The Spear of Destiny. York Beach, ME: Samuel Weiser, Inc., 1973

Ravenscroft, Trevor & Wallace-Murphy, Tim. The Mark of the Beast: The Continuing Saga of the Spear of Destiny. York Beach, ME: Samuel Weiser, Inc., 1990

Robertson, Pat. The New World Order. Dallas London Vancouver Melbourne: World Publishers, 1991

Sauder, Richard Ph. D. Underground Bases and Tunnels: What is the Government Trying to Hide. Abingdon, VA: Dracon Press, 1995

Sitchin, Zecharia. Divine Encounters. New York: Avon Books, 1995

Sitchin, Zecharia. Genesis Revisited. New York: Avon Books, 1990

Sklar, Holly. Trilateralism: The Trilateral Commission and Elite Planning for World Management. Cambridge, MA: South End Press, 1980

Spanncus, Nancy. Stop the New World Order: Hitler in Blue Helmets. Executive Intelligence Review, 1994

Still, William T. New World Order: The Ancient Plan of Secret Societies. Lafayette, LA: Huntingdon House Publishers, 1990

Sutton, Antony C. The Federal Reserve Conspiracy. Boring, OR: CPA Book Publishers, 1995

Sutton, Antony. How the Order Controls Education. Phoenix, AZ: Research Publications, Inc., 1983

Sutton, Antony & Wood, Patrick M. Trilaterals Over Washington. The August Corporation, 1981

Sutton, Antony C. Wall Street and the Rise of Hitler. Seal Beach, CA: '76 Press, 1976

Sutton, William Josiah. The Illuminati 666: The New Age Movement. The Institute of Religious Knowledge, 1983

Thomas, Gordon. Seeds of Fire: China and the Story Behind the Attack on America. Tempe, AZ: Dandelion Books, 2001

Thomas, Kenn & Lawrence, Lincoln. Mind Control, Oswald & JFK: Were We Controlled. Kempton, IL: Adventures Unlimited, 1997

Thomas, Kenn. Popular Alienation: A Steamshovel Press Reader. Lilburn, GA: IllumiNet Press, 1995

U. S. Government. Report from Iron Mountain on the Possibility and Desirability Of Peace

Valee, Jacques. Revelations: Alien Contact and Human Deception. New York: Ballantine Books, 1991

Valorian Society. Human History Viewed as Sovereign Individuals Versus Manipulated Masses. Rochester, VA: Sovereign Press, 1986

Vankin, Jonathan & Whalen, John. 50 Greatest Conspiracies of All Time: History's Biggest Mysteries, Coverups & Cabals. New York: Carol Publishing Group, 1995

Victorian, Dr. Armen. Mind Controllers. London: Vision Paperbacks, 1999

Watkins, Leslie & Ambrose, David. Alternative 3. London: Sphere Books Limited, 1978

Woodrow, Ralph Edward. Babylon Mystery Religion. Riverside, CA: Ralph Woodrow Evangelistic Association Inc., 1966

Zepezauer, Mark. The CIA's Greatest Hits. Tucson, AZ: Odonian Press, 1994